KU-258-386

c ł s Y
efficiency
concepts

The ECONOMIC APPROACH
to LAW, *Second Edition*

The ECONOMIC APPROACH *to* LAW, *Second Edition*

Thomas J. Miceli

Stanford Economics and Finance
An imprint of Stanford University Press
Stanford, California

Stanford University Press
Stanford, California

Printed in the United States of America on acid-free, archival-quality paper

Library of Congress Cataloging-in-Publication Data

Miceli, Thomas J.
   The economic approach to law / Thomas J. Miceli.—2nd ed.
      p. cm.
   Includes bibliographical references and index.
   ISBN 978-0-8047-5670-9 (cloth : alk. paper)
   1. Law and economics.   I. Title.
   K487.E3M528 2009
   340′.1—dc22   2008011548

Designed by Richard Kharibian
Typeset by Newgen in 11/13 Times New Roman

Special discounts for bulk quantities of Stanford Economics and Finance titles are available
to corporations, professional associations, and other organizations. For details and discount
information, contact the special sales department of Stanford University Press.
Tel: (650) 736-1783, Fax: (650) 736-1784

To Ana, Tommy, and Nick. I do it all for you.

CONTENTS

Chapter 9 The Economics of Crime   268

TABLES AND FIGURES

The field of law and economics, though relatively new, is a rapidly growing area of specialization, for both legal scholars and economists. Courses in law and economics are now offered in most law schools and economics departments, although a course directed at law students would be taught quite differently from one directed at undergraduate economics majors. This book is primarily aimed at the latter audience. As such, it presumes a basic familiarity with principles of microeconomics. The book does not, however, presume any knowledge of the law, nor is its objective to teach students about the law so they can decide whether or not to go to law school (though this may be a by-product). Rather, the objective is to show students how they can apply the tools of economic analysis to understand the basic structure and function of the law. This objective is reflected in my decision to title the book *The Economic Approach to Law*, rather than the customary *Law and Economics*, which might suggest more of a legal orientation.

Since the book is not, first and foremost, about the law, it does not attempt an exhaustive coverage of legal topics. Rather, it tries to tell a coherent "story" about the law. To this end, it focuses on the core common law areas of torts, contracts, and property, along with a discussion of the litigation process, the economics of crime, and antitrust law. I have chosen these areas because (1) they best convey the ability of economic theory to provide a unifying framework for understanding law, and (2) they have received the most attention from economists and therefore reflect the highest level of development of the field. Two areas of law not covered in this book (with some exceptions) are laws written by legislatures (statutory law) and constitutional law. Economists have devoted considerable attention to the analysis of legislative law, and an economic analysis of constitutional law is emerging. Although both of these areas fall broadly under the umbrella of law and economics, they raise a different set of conceptual issues that are best treated in separate courses.

The primary subject of this book is instead the common law, by which we mean that body of law arising from judicial decisions and the resulting legal precedents. Much of the economic analysis of law in recent decades has been spurred by the conjecture, due in large part to the work of Judge Richard Posner (Posner 2003), that the common law has an underlying economic logic (a claim that is *not* generally made about statutory law). An important goal of this book is to illustrate and evaluate this claim.

The methodological approach in this book is primarily neoclassical, reflecting the perspective of the so-called Chicago School of law and economics. In my view, this represents the predominant approach to the field as reflected by current scholarship, but it is by no means the only approach. Other perspectives, such as public choice and neo-institutionalism, have also provided important insights, as have the various schools of thought that are critical of law and economics. These competing fields receive scant mention in this book given the goal of providing an in-depth treatment of "mainstream" law and economics rather than a broad survey of the field. (For such a survey, see Mercuro and Medema 1997, who refer to the Chicago School as "mainstream law and economics" [51].)

Despite the predominantly neoclassical approach, this edition includes several references to the emerging field of behavioral law and economics. The objective of this area of research is, first, to recognize that people's actual behavior often departs from the traditional assumptions of rationality, and second, to apply the resulting insights to law. Since these insights touch on many areas of the law, this material is scattered throughout the book. Students and instructors interested in a fuller treatment should consult Sunstein (2000).

Organization

As noted, the focus of this book will be on the basic common law areas of torts, contracts, and property. In addition, it will examine the economics of legal disputes, criminal law, and antitrust law, all of which have received considerable attention from economists.

The specific outline of the book follows. Chapter 1 provides an introduction to law and economics and defines the specific concept of efficiency that will be used throughout the book. It also introduces the Coase Theorem, perhaps the most important result that has emerged from the economic analysis of law, and provides a brief overview of the court system in the United States.

Chapters 2 through 7 constitute the core of the book and present a coherent economic theory of the common law. There are two chapters each on torts, contracts, and property. Chapter 8 turns to the economic analysis of legal disputes and their resolution. This chapter illustrates the ability of economic theory to explain how the litigation process works and, more importantly, how it can be modified to save administrative costs. Chapter 9 examines the economics of criminal law. Many will be skeptical about the ability of economics to say much about crime, but some of the earliest work in law and economics was done in this area, and it continues to be a vigorous field of research that has produced many insights on optimal punishment strategies. In addition, much of the empirical work on law and economics has been done in this area. Finally, Chapter 10 (which is new to this edition) surveys the economics of antitrust law. Many scholars refer to antitrust as the "old" law and economics, as it was the first field to which economists made substantial contributions. Recent advances in the area of industrial organization, however, have produced fresh insights that reveal the continuing vitality of the field.

For reasons noted below, the order of the chapters (especially Chapters 2–7) reflects a conscious choice, but instructors can vary the sequence to suit their own preferences. Also, the topics within chapters were chosen and organized to reflect my view of what constitute the key issues in a given area. Sections that discuss more difficult or esoteric topics, however, are marked by an asterisk (*) and can be skipped for a more streamlined treatment.

Finally, a word about economic models. Economists rely on mathematical models to simplify the world and to highlight certain relationships while holding all other factors constant. In this sense, they serve the same function as controlled experiments in a laboratory. But students often question what can be learned by simple models that rely on a multiplicity of assumptions. This is especially true in fields like law where they may be suspicious of the value of economics to begin with. The test of models, however, is the reasonableness of their assumptions (are we ignoring only inessential aspects of the problem being examined?), and their ability to generate verifiable predictions. Students are challenged to evaluate the models in this book based on these criteria.

Distinguishing Features of the Book

This book incorporates several features that distinguish it from other law and economic texts. Most importantly, the book emphasizes the ability of economic analysis to provide a coherent theory of the law. To accomplish this, I have limited the number of areas covered to permit an in-depth treatment of each, and I have also organized them in a particular way. Traditionally, the core common law areas are covered in the following sequence: property, contracts, torts. I have reversed this order because the key organizing model—the model of precaution—is literally a model of accidents and hence is best developed in that context. In addition, examining property last allows me to bring together several recurrent themes by way of summarizing the analysis.

A second unique feature of the book is that it is primarily directed toward undergraduate economics students. Previous books, in seeking to address both law students and economics students, have not addressed either adequately (law students want more law and economics students more economics). This book does not attempt this difficult balancing act—it is chiefly an economics book. The decision to emphasize economics, in addition to allowing a more focused argument, has freed me to present the latest in law and economics scholarship, which in recent decades has become more mathematical. (Extensive references to the literature are provided in endnotes.) Nevertheless, the book should be accessible to quantitatively oriented law students with some minimal economics training.

A final feature of the book is the inclusion in each chapter of exercises designed to illustrate key points and to encourage students to "do" some law and economics. Answers to these "in-chapter" problems are offered in the back of the book. In addition, several discussion questions and further problems are provided at the end of each chapter.

Changes to This Edition

The major change to this edition is the addition of Chapter 10 on antitrust law. Antitrust has long been of interest to economists because the rationale for regulation of markets has a solid foundation in economic theory. Thus, unlike some of the other areas of law examined in this book, the application of economic analysis to antitrust was largely uncontroversial. I decided to include this chapter both to reflect the long tradition of antitrust as a cornerstone of law and economics, and to discuss recent advances in the field. Inclusion of this chapter also gives instructors an additional option when designing their courses. Beyond that, I have revised all other chapters in the book to reflect recent scholarship, update data and graphs where appropriate, clarify existing arguments, and correct errors.

As a supplement to the text, students and instructors may wish to visit the book's companion website at www.economiclaw.org. The site provides a rich suite of resources, including a review of microeconomics (formerly included as an Appendix to Chapter 1); text from some key cases cited in the book; links to additional cases that can be paired with the book; discussion points, which deepen or supplement the analysis in the book; notes for use in an advanced (graduate level) law and economics course; and key points to help students review the highlights of each chapter. The site also offers additional discussion questions that are meant to stimulate classroom discussion and/or provide topics for short papers or written assignments. Instructors may gain access to an instructor's manual that provides answers to all of the end-of-chapter discussion questions and problems.

Acknowledgments

This book is the product of an undergraduate course in law and economics that I have taught at the University of Connecticut for more than fifteen years. The material has evolved based on my understanding of the field but also to reflect the invaluable feedback from students.

I wish to thank Richard Adelstein, from whom I first learned law and economics as an undergraduate and who has since become a friend and coauthor. Words cannot express the impact that he has had on my professional career. My colleague and coauthor Kathy Segerson has also had a significant influence on my thinking about many of the issues examined in this book.

The following people generously provided comments on the first edition: Daniel Graham, Don Vandegrift, Mark White, Daniel Berkowitz, James Roumasset, Geoffrey Turnbull, and especially Roger Blair. Roger provided lengthy written comments that have substantially improved both the content and presentation of the material. I appreciate his efforts more than I can say. Several anonymous reviewers also provided valuable comments. Thanks also go to Margo Beth Crouppen, Sarah Ives, and Martha Cooley at Stanford University Press, who enthusiastically supported my plan to revise the text and facilitated the logistics of doing so. I would also like to thank the late Ken MacLeod, who was a strong supporter of my idea to write this book in the first place.

As always, my greatest thanks go to my wife, Ana, and my two sons, Tommy and Nick, who have contributed to this project in untold ways.

The ECONOMIC APPROACH
to LAW, *Second Edition*

CHAPTER 1

INTRODUCTORY CONCEPTS

1   What Is Law and Economics?

Law is an ideal subject for economists to study because it provides a wealth of material for evaluating theories of rational behavior. The most creative researcher could not dream up the variety of situations that even a casual examination of legal disputes reveals.

Another reason that economists study law is that both disciplines are concerned, to varying degrees, with incentives. Rational decision makers in economics act to further their self-interest subject to the constraints that they face. Ordinarily, we think of individuals making economic decisions in the context of markets, subject to market prices and incomes, but nonmarket decisions can also be analyzed from an economic perspective. Indeed, the explanatory power of economics is most clearly illustrated in these interdisciplinary contexts.

The economic approach to law assumes that rational individuals view legal sanctions (monetary damages, fines, prison) as implicit prices for certain kinds of behavior, and that these prices can be set to guide these behaviors in a socially desirable direction. More than one hundred years ago, the most famous American judge and legal scholar, Oliver Wendell Holmes, set forth a theory of law that well reflects (one might say, anticipates) the economic approach to law described in this book.[1] The theory is sometimes referred to as the *prediction theory* of law.

The key figure in Holmes's theory is the "bad man," whom we will see has much in common with the rational decision maker of economic theory. The bad man is not bad in the sense that he sets out to break the law; rather, he is a rational calculator who seeks to stretch its limits and will break it without compunction if the perceived gain exceeds the cost. Thus, the bad man has a strong interest in knowing what the law is and what the consequences of breaking it are: "If you want to know the law and nothing else, you must look at it as a bad man, who cares only for the material consequences which such knowledge enables him to predict" (Holmes 1897, 459). The economic model of law does not focus on the bad man because economists think people are basically amoral. Many, perhaps most, people obey the law out of a sense of rightness and therefore are not affected by legal rules at the margin. (Such a person will not commit a crime regardless of the chances of being caught or how long or short the prison term is.) Thus, to examine the incentive effects of law—that is, to examine how it affects behavior at the margin—we must focus on those to whom it is a binding constraint. Nevertheless, we will see that most people respond to the law in this way in at least some circumstances. For example, even people who would not consciously commit a crime regardless of the threat of punishment make decisions while engaging in risky activities (like driving a car) that potentially subject them to tort liability (or even to criminal fines for speeding).

1.1   Positive and Normative Analysis

Economic analysis of the law comes in two varieties: positive and normative analysis. *Positive analysis* explains the consequences of legal sanctions for behavior by posing questions such as: Will longer prison sentences deter more crime? and, How will changes in tort rules affect the accident rate? More controversially, Does the death penalty reduce the murder rate? and, What would be the likely extent of the black market if abortions were outlawed? Positive analysis thus relies on the assumption that people respond to the law in the manner described above.

Positive analysis goes further, however, to assert that legal rules tend to reflect economic reasoning; in other words, efficiency is a social goal that is reflected in the law.[2] This is not a claim that judges and juries consciously undertake economic calculations to determine the best ruling in individual cases. Rather, it is a conjecture about the overall tendency of judge-made law (referred to as the *common law*) to reflect economic efficiency as an important social value. This is a somewhat controversial assertion, especially among traditional legal theorists who view the law as being mainly concerned with justice (however that is defined). Hopefully, however, the analysis in this book will convince you that the efficiency hypothesis has some validity.

In contrast to positive analysis, *normative analysis* asks how the law can be improved to better achieve the goal of efficiency. It is like asking how the welfare system or the education system can be made more efficient. This type of analysis relies on the assumption that efficiency is a goal that the law *should* reflect, and that legal rules should be changed when they fail to achieve it. In some cases this is uncontroversial, as with proposals aimed at improving the efficiency of the litigation process, but the general assertion that efficiency is a social value that the law should promote is not so universally accepted.

The analysis in this book will combine positive and normative analysis. It will focus on positive analysis because that has been the thrust of most recent scholarship in the field. But in those cases where the law seems to fall short of efficiency, we will propose better alternatives.

1.2   Is Efficiency a Valid Norm for Evaluating Law?

As noted, critics argue that it is inappropriate to judge laws on the basis of economic efficiency. Instead, they urge that the law should pursue goals like fairness and justice. These are vague terms, but one meaning has to do with the distribution of wealth in society (distributive justice), and economics surely has something to say about how a just distribution can be achieved with the least sacrifice in resources. Still another meaning of justice may simply be efficiency. In a world of scarcity it is "immoral" to waste resources, and the law should therefore be structured to minimize such waste, at least to the extent that it does not conflict with other goals (Posner 1998a, 30).

Kaplow and Shavell (2002) and Shavell (2004, ch. 29) have argued that social welfare, defined as the aggregation of some index of the well-being of all individuals in society, should be the sole basis for evaluating legal policy. According to this argument, notions of fairness should not influence policy except to the extent that they enhance people's well-being (which would be true if people have a "taste" for fairness). At the same time, they allow that narrow concepts of efficiency (like wealth maximization) are also inappropriate because they exclude factors that may affect well-being (for instance, the distribution of wealth).

Nevertheless, they suggest that, as a practical matter, efficiency may often be the best proxy for welfare in evaluating specific legal rules. This will be especially true of legal questions that are explicitly economic in nature. For example, breach of contract remedies should be structured to maximize the gains from trade, and laws governing property disputes should promote bargaining and internalize externalities. However, readers will no doubt object to the use of efficiency in other contexts (for example, in criminal law), or will see it as too narrow (for example, in medical malpractice cases or environmental accidents). Even the staunchest adherents of the economic approach to law understand this. But it should not deter us from applying economic logic to these contexts to see what insights it might yield, while remaining mindful of competing goals.

2   Efficiency Concepts

The economic approach to law is based on the concept of efficiency. The basic definition of efficiency in economics is Pareto efficiency.

2.1   Pareto Efficiency

Consider a society consisting of two individuals and a fixed level of goods and services to be distributed between them.[3] Define an *allocation* to be any such distribution. The allocations that we call Pareto efficient (or Pareto optimal) are "best" among all possible allocations in the sense that they satisfy the following two definitions. First, an allocation A is said to be *Pareto superior* to allocation B if both individuals are at least as well off under A as compared to B, and at least one is strictly better off. Note that this is a criterion for making pairwise comparisons of different allocations. It merely requires that the two individuals be able to evaluate their welfare (or utility) under any two bundles and decide whether they are better off under A, better off under B, or are indifferent between them. Second, an allocation A is said to be *Pareto efficient* (or Pareto optimal) if there exists no other allocation that is Pareto superior to it.

Note that this definition of Pareto efficiency has the appealing feature that it achieves a kind of unanimity: reallocations are only allowed if neither party is made worse off. In this sense, any changes consistent with Pareto superiority should be *consensual*; that is, all individuals should agree to them (or at least not seek to block them).[4]

Pareto efficiency does, however, have two rather unappealing features. First, it does not lead to a unique allocation. In fact, an infinite number of allocations satisfy the definition, even in our two-person world. This can be seen by looking at Figure 1.1, which graphs the utility possibility frontier for the two individuals in the economy. The utility of an individual is simply an index of his or her satisfaction given any allocation of goods and services. It is this index that allows individuals to make comparisons for the purpose of applying the criterion of Pareto superiority.

The negatively sloped curve defines a region that contains all feasible levels of utility for the two individuals, given the fixed level of goods and services available. Points on or inside the frontier represent all feasible allocations. Consider an arbitrary initial allocation, labeled A. Starting at this allocation, we can use the criterion of Pareto superiority to define the area ABC, which contains all of the allocations that are Pareto superior to A. For example, if the utility of person two were fixed at $U_2(A)$, then the set of allocations that are Pareto superior to A would be those on the line segment AB since they

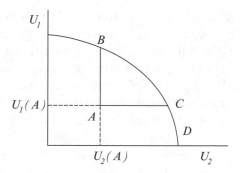

Figure 1.1

Utility Possibility
Frontier

yield person one at least as much utility as she gets at A while making person two no worse off. The same applies to person two if person one's utility were fixed at $U_1(A)$. Points inside area ABC obviously make both people better off than at A. Thus, point A cannot be Pareto efficient.

The Pareto efficient points in this example are those on the line segment BC since there is no feasible reallocation that can make both people better off. The only possible movement is along the segment, which makes one person better off but the other worse off. Such movements, however, cannot be evaluated according to the Pareto superiority criterion. We therefore say that Pareto efficient points are *noncomparable*; in other words, the criterion of Pareto efficiency has no way of ranking them.

The second unappealing feature of Pareto efficiency can be seen by comparing points A and D. Note that point D is Pareto efficient and point A is not, *yet they are also noncomparable*: moving from A to D makes person two better off and person one worse off, while movement from D to A has the reverse effect. The reason for this problem is that the definition of Pareto efficiency depends on the initial allocation, or starting point.

These weaknesses of Pareto efficiency, both of which have to do with noncomparability, are significant because most (if not all) interesting questions of legal policy concern changes that help one group of individuals and hurt others. For example, more restrictive gun laws hurt legal gun owners but help victims of gun accidents or violence, and more liberal liability rules for product-related accidents help consumers of dangerous products but hurt manufacturers and their workers. This suggests that Pareto efficiency is not a workable criterion when it comes to evaluating proposed changes to actual legal rules. (In addition, Pareto optimality permits very unequal distributions of income.)

2.2 Potential Pareto Efficiency, or Kaldor-Hicks Efficiency

Economists address this noncomparability problem by employing a relaxed notion of the Pareto criterion referred to as Potential Pareto efficiency, or

Kaldor-Hicks efficiency. Movements from B to C (or from A to D) in Figure 1.1 could satisfy the Pareto criterion if person two (the gainer) is sufficiently better off that he would be willing to fully compensate person one (the loser) and still realize a net gain. For example, suppose that the movement from A to D yielded person two an increase in wealth of $500 but cost person one $400. Person two would thus still enjoy a net gain of $100 after compensating person one, and the outcome would be Pareto superior to point A.

Of course, it is not practical to arrange such compensation in the case of actual changes (imagine how this would be done for welfare reform), but the fact that it could be done in theory suggests that point D is more efficient than point A. Movements for which full compensation is possible in the sense that gainers gain more than losers lose, but for which compensation is not actually paid, are said to be Kaldor-Hicks efficient. (If compensation were paid, the move would be truly Pareto efficient.)[5] Note that Kaldor-Hicks is therefore based on cost-benefit analysis—changes in policy or law are efficient if gains exceed losses.[6] It is also consistent with the goal of wealth maximization in that changes that satisfy Kaldor-Hicks must increase aggregate wealth by the difference between benefits and costs. Thus, if all changes dictated by Kaldor-Hicks were made, aggregate wealth would be maximized.

2.3   Consensual Versus Nonconsensual Exchange

Although Kaldor-Hicks gets around the problem of noncomparability under Pareto, it has the disadvantage that we cannot claim changes are consensual since there are actual losers. This reflects an important trade-off that will arise throughout this book. On one hand, consent guarantees mutual gains, which is the basis for the efficiency of competitive markets. On the other hand, when markets fail as the result of some sort of externality like pollution, not all gains from trade will be exploited. An important economic justification for government intervention in markets (including the creation of legal obligations) is therefore to correct market failures.

But such intervention will nearly always create winners and losers. The hope is that those who lose from one policy will benefit from others and that, on net, everyone will gain as aggregate wealth is increased. That is, as the overall size of the pie expands, the average slice increases. In this way, one can argue that *implied consent* for the use of the Kaldor-Hicks criterion replaces *actual consent* under Pareto.

The economic approach to law as examined in this book will focus primarily on judge-made law rather than statutory or constitutional law (though we touch on constitutional issues at various points). One reason is that the preceding argument is more compelling for common law because judges are, for the most part, insulated from the political process and hence less apt to be influenced by special interests. This minimizes the risk that there will be systematic losers in the legal process.

3 The Coase Theorem

The role of legal rules in restoring efficiency in the presence of market failure was critically examined in a seminal article by Ronald Coase.[7] Prior to Coase, the prevailing view among economists was that externalities like pollution could only be internalized by means of government intervention, for example, by imposing financial liability (a tax or fine) on the polluter. But Coase's analysis changed that by emphasizing the role of bargaining and transaction costs in determining the ultimate allocation of resources against the background of legal rules.

Coase's basic insight is best illustrated by means of one of his simple numerical examples. Consider two adjacent parcels of land, one owned by a farmer and one owned by a rancher. The problem is that the rancher's cattle sometimes stray onto the farmer's land, causing crop damage. Table 1.1 shows the farmer's total and marginal damages (in dollars) as a function of the rancher's herd size.

Suppose that the marginal benefit to the rancher (marginal revenue minus marginal cost) of each additional steer is $3.50. Thus, the joint value of ranching and farming is maximized at a herd size of three. This is true because, for each steer up to three, the increment in profit from ranching exceeds the additional cost in terms of crop damage. However, for the fourth steer, the incremental gain is less than the cost. A single individual who owned both the ranch and the farm would therefore choose a herd of three because he would internalize both the benefit of additional steers and the damage to crops. With separate owners, however, we would expect the rancher to ignore the crop damage and expand his herd to four (the maximum possible size). This provides the basis for government intervention to force the rancher to internalize the farmer's loss, for example, by means of a tax on ranching or by allowing the farmer to file a nuisance suit for damages.

But let us consider more carefully the case where the rancher is not legally responsible for the farmer's loss. In the absence of liability, the rancher can add the fourth steer for a profit of $3.50, while ignoring the additional $4 in damages that the farmer must bear. Suppose, however, that the farmer and the rancher can bargain, and the farmer offers to pay the rancher, say, $3.75 not to add the fourth steer. The rancher will accept the offer because it yields

TABLE **1.1**   **Farmer's Crop Damage as a Function of Rancher's Herd Size**

Herd size	Total damage ($)	Marginal damage ($)
1	1	1
2	3	2
3	6	3
4	10	4

SOURCE: *Coase (1960).*

a greater profit than he would have earned from the steer, and the farmer is better off because he saves the damage of $4 by spending $3.75. Further deals are not possible because the marginal damages from the first three steers are less than their value in ranching. The herd thus ends up at the efficient size of three, even though the rancher is not required to pay for the farmer's damage.

EXERCISE 1.1[8]

Suppose in the above example that crop damage from straying cattle can be entirely eliminated by fencing in the farmer's land at an annual cost of $9. Show that the optimal herd size is now four, and that this outcome will be achieved regardless of whether the rancher or the farmer is legally responsible for crop damage (assuming that the parties can bargain).

What the preceding analysis shows is that when bargaining is possible, the efficient outcome can always be achieved by private agreements between the parties to an externality, regardless of how the law assigns liability. In other words, whether or not the rancher is liable for crop damage, the herd size will be the same. This surprising conclusion turns out to be quite general and hence has come to be known as the Coase Theorem. The Coase Theorem, as we will see, has far-reaching implications for the economic analysis of law. We point out two of these implications here. (We examine the Coase Theorem in more detail in Chapter 6.)

First, the Coase Theorem implies that the social goals of efficiency and distributional justice are not necessarily incompatible, as is often assumed. To see this, note that in the above example, although the herd size was invariant to the assignment of liability, the distribution of income was not. Specifically, when the rancher was liable for crop damage, he had to make damage payments to the farmer. In contrast, when the rancher was not liable, the farmer had to pay the rancher to keep the herd size from expanding beyond the efficient level. Thus, variations in the assignment of liability can be used to alter the distribution of wealth without affecting the allocation of resources.[9] This suggests that when the conditions of the Coase Theorem are met, judges can pursue the goal of distributional justice without worrying about sacrificing efficiency.

But how likely is it that the conditions of the Coase Theorem will be met? It depends on the cost of bargaining between the parties to an externality. If these costs are high, as they often will be (especially when large numbers are involved), then private agreements are unlikely, and the rule for assigning liability will dictate the final allocation of resources. This leads to the second important implication of the Coase Theorem: When bargaining costs are high, the law matters for efficiency (Demsetz 1972).

Although this conclusion may seem obvious, it has important consequences for the nature of legal rule making. In particular, it bears on the fundamental question of whether to structure laws in the form of inflexible *rules* that dictate certain conduct or consequences irrespective of circumstances, or whether to leave some *discretion* so that judges can tailor outcomes to individual cases. In his classic treatise, Hart (1961, 127) framed the choice in this way:

> In fact all systems, in different ways, compromise between two social needs: the need for certain rules which can, over great areas of conduct, safely be applied by private individuals to themselves without fresh official guidance or weighing up of social issues; and the need to leave open, for later settlement by an informed, official choice, issues which can only be properly appreciated and settled when they arise in a concrete case.

An example of this in the area of tort law is the choice between strict liability, which holds injurers liable for any damages that they cause, and negligence, which only holds them liable if they failed to take "reasonable care," where reasonableness varies from case to case.

Economic theory, and the Coase Theorem in particular, provide some insight into the choice between rules and discretion (Ehrlich and Posner 1974). The advantage of rules is that they are predictable and hence allow individuals to plan for the consequences of their actions. This is highly desirable when markets function well and there are few impediments to private bargaining. In this low-transaction-cost world, the role of the law is minimal—it is limited to the delineation of rights and the enforcement of contracts. The fact that rules are inflexible to specific circumstances does not result in inefficiency because, as we have seen, the allocation of resources is invariant to legal rules.

But this world is of limited relevance for most problems confronting the law. More pervasive is the existence of situations involving high transaction costs, which prevent parties from bargaining around inefficient rules and from resolving disputes without legal intervention. In this more realistic setting, the law matters for efficiency, so rules must give way to standards that allow a balancing of costs and benefits in individual cases. This realm will receive most of our attention in this book.

4   The Law in "Law and Economics"

The system of law in the United States is largely inherited from England. In this so-called common law system, there are three primary sources of law. The first is the Constitution, which sets out the basic structure and duties of the government, as well as certain fundamental rights of citizens. The second is the legislature, which is made up of elected representatives who enact laws reflecting the "will of the people."[10] (The executive branch of government is primarily charged with carrying out the laws enacted by the legislature, but it also has some limited law-making ability.)

Finally, the judiciary enacts laws as a by-product of its role in resolving legal disputes. These laws take the form of legal "precedents," and the accumulation of precedents constitutes what is known as the common law. It is this body of judge-made law that economists typically study under the heading of "law and economics."[11]

4.1   The Nature of the Common Law

Common-law rules (precedents) arise out of decisions by appeals courts and are binding on lower (trial) courts in future, similar cases. (See the discussion of the court system below.) Precedents are valuable to society, as we have seen, because they provide information to people about the consequences of their actions. This information allows them to make rational decisions in settings that might entangle them in legal disputes, as when they engage in risky activities, enter into contracts, or plan to develop property.

At the same time, the law must be adaptable to changing circumstances. The common-law process permits this by allowing judges to alter or overturn precedents in the presence of new information. A central theme of the economic analysis of law (a component of positive analysis), and one that pervades this book, is that the common law tends to display an economic logic. It is important to emphasize that this assertion is not based on a claim that judges consciously act to promote efficiency (though they sometimes do, the most famous example being Judge Learned Hand's formula for a negligence standard in *United States v. Carroll Towing Co.*, discussed in Chapter 2).[12]

Nor is it a claim that all common-law rules are efficient at any point in time. Rather, the argument is that there are forces inherent in the common-law process that propel it in the direction of efficiency.[13] The idea is similar to the Invisible Hand Theorem of market efficiency first proposed by Adam Smith and later formally proved as the First Fundamental Theorem of Welfare Economics.

4.2 The Court System in the United States

As a preface to our analysis of specific areas of the common law, it will be useful to provide an overview of the institutional structure of the court system in the United States.[14] The structure of courts at both the state and federal level is hierarchical. At the lowest level are the trial courts, which have general jurisdiction. That is, they hear a wide range of cases on both civil and criminal matters. At the state level, these courts (commonly called district or circuit courts) are organized according to counties. At the federal level, they are organized into ninety-four judicial districts (so-called district courts), with at least one district court in each state, depending on the volume of business, and one in the District of Columbia.[15]

At the next level are intermediate appellate courts, whose responsibility is to hear appeals from the trial courts and to uphold, reverse, or modify those decisions. Not all states have these intermediate courts (in which case the single appeals court is the state's highest, or supreme, court), but all federal districts do. At the federal level, appeals courts are organized into twelve regional circuits, each covering several states. These courts hear appeals from district courts within their circuits, as well as appeals from federal administrative agencies. There is also a Court of Appeals for the Federal Circuit in Washington, D.C., which hears appeals from cases involving patent laws and cases decided by the Court of International Trade and the Court of Federal Claims. Unsuccessful litigants always have the right to have their appeals heard by these intermediate courts, provided that they are willing to pay the costs.

The highest court in the federal system is the Supreme Court of the United States. It is composed of nine justices, appointed for life by the president. Unlike intermediate appellate courts, the Supreme Court and the highest courts in states have discretion over the cases they will hear. If the highest court declines a case, it simply means that the ruling at the previous level stands. The Supreme Court usually agrees to hear only a small fraction of cases submitted for review. In addition to appeals from federal appellate courts, the U.S. Supreme Court will occasionally hear appeals from state supreme courts.

There are rules that dictate the jurisdiction of courts. The jurisdiction of state courts is typically limited to disputes between residents of that state, while the jurisdiction of federal courts is dictated by Congress based on powers granted to it by the Constitution. Most federal district court cases fall into one of three categories: cases that involve a "federal question" (cases arising under the Constitution, federal law, or treaties), cases involving citizens of different states ("diversity of citizenship" cases), or cases where the United States is a party (usually criminal cases). Federal courts generally apply the law of the state in which they are located.

As noted, Supreme Court judges are appointed for life by the president (with oversight by the Senate), as are federal appeals court judges. The manner of selecting state court judges varies by state, but most are elected for a limited term.

5 Conclusion

This chapter began with an introduction to the study of law and economics and discussed several key issues that will figure prominently in the following chapters. Chief among these was the question of whether efficiency is a valid norm for evaluating legal rules and institutions. The normative economic theory of law says that it is (possibly in conjunction with other norms), while the positive theory contends that the common law as it exists embodies an economic logic. This book will examine both of these branches of law and economics.

After discussing various efficiency concepts (and settling on Kaldor-Hicks, or wealth maximization, as the most workable), we introduced the Coase Theorem, perhaps the most important building block in the economic approach to law. We will make use of the insights embodied in this Theorem throughout the book. The chapter concluded with an overview of the nature of the common law and the legal system in the United States.

DISCUSSION QUESTIONS

1. Describe the sense in which Holmes's "bad man" corresponds to the rational decision maker of economic theory.

2. Under the law of negligence, individuals engaged in activities that may cause harm to others (external harm) are expected to take those precautions that a "reasonable person" would take in the same circumstances. How does the reasonable person of negligence law relate to the rational decision maker of economics?

3. It is often said that efficiency and fairness are incompatible objectives for an economic system. Explain why this is not true when the conditions of the Coase Theorem are met.

PROBLEMS

1. Suppose a law is passed that prohibits farmers from using certain chemical fertilizers because they contaminate ground water. The expected reduction in illness to water users is $10 million, but the loss to farmers is $8 million.

   (a) Is the law a Pareto improvement relative to the status quo? Is it a Kaldor-Hicks improvement? Explain.

   (b) Now suppose the government taxes water users and uses the revenue to fully compensate farmers for their losses. Is the law now a Pareto improvement? Is it a Kaldor-Hicks improvement? Explain.

2. Suppose there are three mutually exclusive groups in a particular state: timber company shareholders, environmentalists, and neutral parties. The numbers of each are as follows:

Shareholders	100
Environmentalists	500
Neutral parties	1,500

   The total profit from logging is $8,000, which is evenly divided among shareholders. Environmentalists wish to stop all logging and are willing to pay $25 each to do so. Neutral parties are uninterested in this debate.

   (a) Is a law banning logging Pareto optimal? Is it Kaldor-Hicks efficient?

   (b) Suppose that loggers would be fully compensated if logging were prohibited, but this would require raising tax revenue of $8,000 and paying it to shareholders. For each of the following scenarios, state whether a law banning logging, coupled with compensation, is Pareto optimal, and whether it is Kaldor-Hicks efficient:

   (i) The tax is assessed equally on both environmentalists and neutral parties;

   (ii) The tax is assessed only on environmentalists.

3. The case of *Sturges v. Bridgman* (11 Ch.D. 852, 1879) involved a confectioner who had operated heavy machinery at a certain location for several years as part of his candy-making business. When a doctor built a consulting room directly against the confectioner's premises, however, he found that the noise and vibration were a disturbance to his practice. He therefore sought an injunction to prevent the confectioner from using the machinery. Suppose it would cost the confectioner $150 to move his machinery to a location where it would not disturb the doctor, and it would cost the doctor $200 to relocate the consulting room.

   (a) Assume that the doctor and confectioner can bargain costlessly. What will be the outcome if the court grants the injunction? What if it does not grant it?

   (b) How would your answer to (a) change if the parties cannot bargain?

4. The owner of a particular house has an unobstructed view of the ocean from his front window. However, the owner of a vacant lot in front of the house announces plans to build a house of his own. Suppose that a one-story house will partially obstruct the view, but a two-story house will block it completely. The builder's profit and the value of the owner's view are shown below:

No. of stories	Profit	Value of view
0	0	$70,000
1	$100,000	$60,000
2	$150,000	0

(a) Is it efficient for the house to be built? If so, how many stories should it be? Suppose the original owner seeks an injunction halting construction.

(b) Describe the bargaining between the builder and the owner if the court refuses to grant the injunction.

(c) Suppose the court grants the injunction. Can the builder bribe the owner not to enforce it?

CHAPTER 2

AN ECONOMIC MODEL OF TORT LAW

This chapter and the next develop the economic model of accident, or tort, law. The model is based on the proposition that the rules of tort law are designed to give parties engaged in risky activities an incentive to undertake all reasonable means of minimizing the costs arising from those risks. For this reason, the economic model of accidents is usually referred to as the *model of precaution*. The purpose of this chapter is to develop this model in a general way so as to derive a set of basic principles that apply broadly to different areas of accident law. The next chapter then applies these results to specific areas.

The total costs of accidents consist of three components: the damages suffered by victims (in dollar terms); the cost of precautions against accidents by injurers and victims; and the administrative costs of the tort system. In this chapter, we focus on the first two of these costs as reflected in the model of precaution, while referring to administrative costs only in qualitative terms. In Chapter 8 we undertake a detailed analysis of administrative costs.

Although the model of precaution is outwardly a model of accidents, we will see in subsequent chapters that its usefulness extends beyond tort law to the areas of contracts and property. As such, it will be a useful tool for identifying connections across traditional legal boundaries.

1 What Is a Tort?

As noted, tort law is that area of the common law concerned with accidental injuries. Examples include personal injuries, products liability, workplace accidents, medical malpractice, and environmental accidents. As this list suggests, risk is a necessary by-product of many socially beneficial activities, including driving, use of vaccines, medical procedures, and so on. And although we cannot ordinarily eliminate the risk without cutting out the activity altogether, we should nevertheless take all cost-justified steps to minimize the resulting cost. That means that we should invest in risk reduction to the point where saving an additional dollar in accident losses can only be achieved by spending more than one dollar in precaution.

Society has many ways of controlling risks, including safety regulation, taxation, and even criminal penalties for risky activities (for example, fines for speeding). These are all examples of "public" controls imposed by the government. This chapter is concerned instead with a private remedy—the right of accident victims to sue injurers for damages under tort law. (We consider the use of the public remedies just mentioned in later chapters.)

1.1   The Social Function of Tort Law

The primary social functions of tort law are twofold: to compensate victims for their injuries and to deter "unreasonably" risky behavior. Although the economic approach to tort law is not unconcerned with the goal of compensation, its primary goal is optimal deterrence. To this end, tort rules are viewed, first and foremost, as providing monetary incentives for individuals engaged in risky activities to take all reasonable (cost-justified) steps to minimize overall accident costs.

1.2   Elements of a Tort Claim

Since tort law is a private remedy for accidental harms, enforcement is in the hands of victims. In order to recover damages, a victim (plaintiff) must file a lawsuit against the injurer (defendant). (The fact that suits are costly has implications to be discussed below.) In order to prevail in the suit, the plaintiff has the burden of proving that the defendant is *legally responsible* and therefore must pay compensation. This requires that the plaintiff establish the following: (1) she sustained some damages; and (2) the defendant was the "cause" of those damages. In some cases, proving these two things is sufficient for the plaintiff to recover for her losses; in others, she must also prove "fault" on the part of the injurer. We will assume that the plaintiff succeeds in demonstrating damages and turn immediately to the second element, causation. Later, we examine the issue of fault.

Proving causation in a legal sense requires the plaintiff to establish two things: first, that the defendant's action was "cause-in-fact" of the damages; and second, that it was also "proximate cause." We examine these two notions of causation in turn.

1.2.1   Cause-in-Fact

Cause-in-fact is established by using the "but-for" test. Specifically, the plaintiff must prove that "but-for the defendant's action, the plaintiff would not have sustained any harm." In many cases, this is a straightforward matter: for example, but for the explosion of the soda bottle, the plaintiff would not have been injured. In other cases, it is more problematic. One difficult case concerns two or more causes that simultaneously produce a harm that either would have caused acting separately. For example, suppose sparks from a train start a fire that combines with a fire set by a farmer clearing his land to burn another farmer's crops.[1] In that case, neither injurer's action will satisfy the but-for test because each can (correctly) claim that the damage would have occurred even if his fire had not gone out of control.

A second problematic situation arises when two or more injurers act to produce a harm that would *not* have occurred if each acted separately. For example, suppose that I push you backward while another person simultaneously pulls the chair out from under you, causing you to fall and injure yourself. In this case, *both* injurers satisfy the but-for test. The question then becomes how to apportion liability among the two injurers. These and other issues of causation can become extremely complicated. Thus, for most of this chapter, we ignore them by focusing on single-injurer accidents. (See Section 3.3 below and the discussion of multiple injurers in the context of environmental accidents in Chapter 3.)

A final problem with the but-for test, even in the single-injurer case, is that it will often implicate extremely remote causes. As an illustration, consider the famous case of *Palsgraf v. Long Island R.R.* (248 N.Y. 339, 162 N.E. 99, 1928). The facts of the case are as follows:

> Plaintiff was standing on a platform of defendant's railroad after buying a ticket to go to Rockaway Beach. A train stopped at the station, bound for another place. Two men ran forward to catch it. One of the men reached the platform of the car without mishap, though the train was already moving. The other man, carrying a package, jumped aboard the car, but seemed unsteady as if about to fall. A guard on the car, who held the door open, reached forward to help him in, and another guard on the platform pushed him from behind. In this act, the package was dislodged, and fell upon the rails. It was a package of small size, about fifteen inches long, and was covered with newspaper. In fact, it contained fireworks, but there was nothing in its appearance to give notice of its contents. The fireworks when they fell exploded. The shock of the explosion threw down some scales at the other end of the platform many feet away. The scales struck the plaintiff, causing injuries for which she sues.

Even though the railroad employee's action clearly satisfied the but-for test (that is, the accident would not have occurred but for the employee's actions), the law did not hold the railroad liable. Limiting causation in this way is the purpose of proximate cause.

1.2.2 Proximate Cause

In addition to proving cause-in-fact, the plaintiff must also prove proximate, or legal, cause. That is, the connection between the injurer's action and the harm cannot be too remote. The usual test for proximate cause is the *reasonable foresight* test. In the *Palsgraf* case, for example, Judge Cardozo denied liability based on the argument that a reasonable person would not have foreseen that the railroad employee's action would result in harm to the victim.[2]

The foregoing shows the sorts of complications that arise from consideration of causation. Fortunately, we will see that the economic approach to tort liability simplifies the analysis of accidents to the extent that explicit considerations of causation can be largely ignored. Causation nevertheless plays such an integral role in actual tort cases that a positive economic theory of tort law cannot ignore it. We therefore return to this topic below.

1.3 Liability Rules

Once harm and causation have been established, the assignment of liability is determined by the application of a *liability rule.* A liability rule is simply a rule for dividing the damages between the injurer and the victim. Suppose, for example, that the victim has suffered damages of $10,000. A rule of *no liability* says that the victim should bear all of these costs herself. For example, in the area of products liability, the old rule of caveat emptor, or "buyer beware," is a form of no liability. In contrast, a rule of *strict liability* imposes all of the damages on the injurer; that is, the injurer must pay $10,000 to the victim. Strict liability therefore shifts liability from the victim to the injurer once causation is established.

A third type of liability rule, referred to as a *negligence rule*, shifts liability from the victim to the injurer only if the injurer is found to be "at fault" or "negligent." A negligence rule is based on the idea that injurers owe potential victims a legal duty to take reasonable efforts to prevent accidents. If the injurer is judged by the court to have satisfied this duty, he is absolved from liability, even if he is the legal cause of the accident. However, if the injurer breached his duty, he is negligent and therefore liable for the victim's losses. In a sense we can think of negligence as a combination of no liability and strict liability, where the two are separated by a "threshold" based on the injurer's level of precaution. This way of thinking about negligence as a hybrid rule will prove useful in our discussion of other types of liability rules below.

2   An Economic Model of Accidents: The Model of Precaution

The economic analysis of tort law is based on the idea that legal rules for assigning liability are designed to minimize the total costs associated with risky activities. The basic model for doing this is referred to as the model of precaution.[3] In the simplest version (the unilateral care model), only the injurer can invest in costly precaution, or care, to reduce the likelihood and severity of the damages borne by the victim. In the more general model (bilateral care), both the injurer and victim can invest in precaution. In addition to the cost of precaution and damages, we need to take account of the administrative costs of using the legal system to resolve tort claims, including the costs of filing suit and conducting judicial proceedings. However, we initially ignore these costs and focus on precaution and damages.

We further simplify the analysis by assuming that injurers themselves suffer no damages. This could be relaxed, but doing so adds few additional insights.[4] We also ignore for now the question of whether it is beneficial for the injurer and victim to be engaged in the risky activity and at what level. Below we explicitly consider this decision. Finally, we assume that injurers and victims are risk neutral; that is, they make decisions based on expected costs and benefits. We relax this assumption in Section 3.7 below.

In analyzing the model, we first derive the socially efficient level of precaution, defined to be the level that would be chosen by a social planner. This outcome will then serve as a benchmark for examining the incentives created by actual legal rules.

2.1   The Unilateral Care Model

In developing the unilateral care model, we make use of the following notation:

x = dollar investment in precaution spent by the injurer;

$p(x)$ = probability of an accident;

$D(x)$ = dollar losses (damages) suffered by the victim.

We assume that both $p(x)$ and $D(x)$ are decreasing in x, reflecting the fact that greater precaution reduces both the probability and severity of an accident. Thus, expected damages, given by $p(x)D(x)$, are also decreasing in x. We further assume that they are decreasing at a decreasing rate. This means that precaution has a diminishing marginal benefit in terms of reducing accident risk. Intuitively, injurers invest first in the most effective precautions and only later turn to less effective measures.

Figure 2.1

Social Costs in the
Basic Accident Model

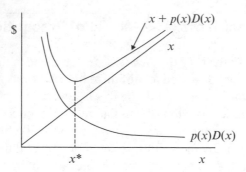

2.1.1   Social Optimum

The social problem, as noted above, is to choose x to minimize the costs of precaution plus expected damages. Formally, the problem is to

$$\text{minimize} \quad x + p(x)D(x). \tag{2.1}$$

The solution to this problem is best seen graphically in Figure 2.1, which graphs the cost of precaution (the positively sloped line), expected damages (the negatively sloped curve), and the summed costs (the U-shaped curve). The cost-minimizing level of care, labeled x^*, occurs at the minimum point of the total cost curve. At levels of care below x^*, an extra dollar of care reduces the victim's expected damages by more than one dollar, so total costs are reduced. However, beyond x^*, an extra dollar of care reduces expected damages by less than one dollar, so total costs rise.

Formally, x^* occurs at the point where the *slope* of the x curve equals the (negative) of the slope of the $p(x)D(x)$ curve. The slope of x reflects the *marginal cost of care* ($= \$1$), while the slope of $p(x)D(x)$ reflects the *marginal benefit of care* (the reduction in expected damages). (The optimal care level therefore does not necessarily occur at the intersection of these curves, which reflect total rather than marginal costs.)

2.1.2   Actual Care Choice by the Injurer

Consider now the actual choice of x by the injurer. To do this, we need to introduce the liability rule. First suppose the injurer faces no liability. In this case, the victim's damages are external to the injurer, so he simply minimizes his expenditure on precaution. Thus, he sets $x = 0$, and total costs are not minimized.[5] (The injurer's private costs in Figure 2.1 therefore correspond to the x-line, which is minimized at the origin.)

Now suppose the rule is strict liability, such that the injurer is liable for the victim's full costs. (We ignore here problems in assigning a monetary value to a personal injury; see the discussion of this issue in Section 3.12 below.) In this case, the injurer will choose the socially optimal care level, x^*, because the threat of liability forces him to fully internalize the victim's expected damages. The injurer's costs now coincide with the social costs. Note that liability in this case functions exactly like a tax in terms of its impact on injurer incentives, though it is different in that the victim rather than the government collects the revenue.

· Finally, consider a negligence rule. Above we saw that under negligence law, the injurer owes a duty of reasonable care to all potential victims. If, in the event of an accident, the injurer is judged by the court to have met this duty, he avoids all liability (though he still must pay his cost of precaution). In contrast, if he breached this duty, he is fully liable. As noted above, negligence is therefore a combination of no liability and strict liability, with the switch point at the due standard of care.

What is the due standard? The law talks about it in terms of the "reasonableness standard"—what level of care would a reasonable person undertake in the circumstances faced by the injurer? The economic theory of tort law equates the reasonableness standard with efficient care, or x^*. Below we discuss the justification for this equivalence. Here we focus on its impact on injurer incentives.

If x^* is the switch point between strict and no liability, then we can write the injurer's problem under negligence as follows:

$$\text{minimize} \quad \begin{matrix} x, & \text{if } x \leq x^* \\ x + p(x)D(x) & \text{if } x < x^*. \end{matrix} \quad\quad (2.2)$$

According to the first line of (2.2), the injurer can avoid liability for the victim's damages (and only pay his own cost of care) by just meeting the due standard. In contrast, the second line says that if he fails to meet the due standard, he must pay the victim's damages in addition to his own cost of care. To see that choosing x^* is the cost-minimizing strategy of the injurer, look at Figure 2.2, which is a version of Figure 2.1.

Figure 2.2

Injurer's Choice of Care Under a Negligence Rule

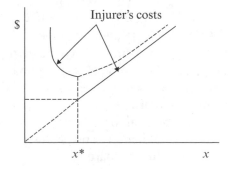

Note in particular that the injurer's costs coincide with social costs when he fails to take due care ($x < x^*$), but his costs are only the costs of precaution when he meets (or exceeds) the due care standard ($x \geq x^*$). Clearly, the lowest point on the injurer's cost curve (the discontinuous solid line) occurs exactly at x^*.

Intuitively, if the injurer is taking less than due care, he benefits by increasing his care to x^* because by doing so, he *avoids all liability.* This is shown by the discrete drop in costs at the due standard. Further, the injurer gains nothing by raising x above x^*, but he must incur the additional costs of care. Thus, he will choose exactly x^*.

2.1.3   Comparison of Strict Liability and Negligence

The preceding shows that, in the unilateral care model, both strict liability and negligence result in efficient injurer care. However, this includes only the injurer's costs of precaution and the victim's damages. We noted above that we also care about administrative costs. Can we choose between the two rules on this basis? First consider the cost per case. Strict liability will be cheaper to apply because plaintiffs need only prove causation, not fault. In contrast, in a negligence suit, the plaintiff will have to prove causation *and* fault. Thus, strict liability suits require less fact-finding and therefore involve less costly trials.

The cost per lawsuit is lower under strict liability, but there may be more suits. Remember that a tort claim must be initiated by the victim, who will only file a suit if the expected gain exceeds the cost. If a victim expects to lose, she will not file suit. Thus, under strict liability, the victim will file if (1) she can prove that the injurer caused her injuries, and (2) her losses exceed the cost of bringing suit.

Under negligence, the preceding conditions for filing must be met, but in addition, the victim must prove that the injurer is at fault (that is, that he failed to meet the due standard of care). And since we saw above that the injurer has a powerful incentive to meet the due standard, victims will often be deterred from filing suit under negligence. (Below we note some reasons why actual injurers may sometimes fail to meet the due standard.)

Thus, we expect fewer lawsuits under negligence as compared to strict liability. Taking this fact into account, we conclude that the calculation of overall litigation costs under the two rules is ambiguous: while strict liability likely leads to less costly suits, negligence leads to fewer overall suits. The comparison is therefore an empirical one.

Consider three other factors that, based on the analysis to this point, may affect the choice between strict liability and negligence. First, suppose there are errors in calculating the due standard of care (we examine this issue in more detail below). If the court systematically errs in setting the due standard,

Figure 2.3

Injurer's Choice
of Care When
Victim's Damages
Are Measured
with Error

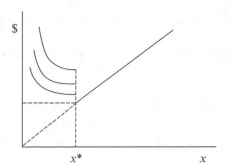

it may result in an inefficient care choice by the injurer. This is not a problem under strict liability because the court need not calculate a due standard.

Suppose instead that the court makes errors in calculating the amount of the victim's damages. This will result in an inefficient care choice under strict liability, but so long as the error is not large, it will not distort the injurer's care choice under negligence (assuming that the due standard is set correctly). This is true because of the discontinuity in the injurer's costs under negligence, as shown in Figure 2.2. In particular, as Figure 2.3 shows, if damages are set too high or too low, the segment of the injurer's costs to the left of x^* shifts up or down, but so long as it doesn't shift down too much (that is, so long as the victim's damages are not underestimated by too much), the discontinuity remains and the injurer's cost-minimizing choice of care is x^*.

A final basis for choosing between strict liability and negligence is the goal of compensating victims, which strict liability accomplishes but negligence does not. Indeed, the fact that strict liability simultaneously achieves the twin goals of deterrence and compensation would seem to be strong argument in its favor. The question, however, is whether this advantage carries over to the model where victims as well as injurers can take care.

2.2   Bilateral Care Model

We now make the above model more realistic by allowing victims as well as injurers to take care to reduce the likelihood and severity of an accident. For example, pedestrians decide which side of the street to walk on, and consumers of dangerous products decide whether to follow the manufacturer's safety instructions.

The above model only needs to be amended slightly to incorporate this change. Thus, we define:

y = dollar investment in care by the victim;

$p(x, y)$ = probability of an accident;

$D(x, y)$ = damages suffered by the victim in the event of an accident.

We now assume that expected damages, $p(x, y)D(x, y)$, are decreasing in both x and y.

The social problem in this case is to choose both x and y to

$$\text{minimize} \quad x + y + p(x, y)D(x, y). \tag{2.3}$$

Let x^* and y^* denote the resulting levels of care, both of which are assumed to be positive. (A graphical depiction of the optimum would require a three-dimensional analog to Figure 2.1.) Now consider the actual choices of x and y under the various liability rules.

2.2.1   No Liability and Strict Liability

We consider no liability and strict liability together because, in the context of the bilateral care model, they turn out to be mirror images of each other. (This symmetry demonstrates the sense in which "no liability" is in fact a liability rule.) First, under no liability, the injurer bears none of the victim's damages and therefore, as in the unilateral care model, invests in no care; that is, $x = 0$. The victim, in contrast, fully bears her own damages and therefore chooses the level of care that minimizes her costs. Since the victim knows that $x = 0$, she will probably choose more than y^* in order to "compensate" for the injurer's inaction.[6] (In this sense, the victim's behavior is efficient *given* the injurer's behavior.) Correspondingly, under strict liability the victim is fully compensated for her losses and hence chooses zero precaution, or $y = 0$. In contrast, the injurer faces full liability and therefore invests in care. As was the case under no liability, he will probably exceed x^* in order to compensate for the victim's failure to take care.

The preceding shows that in the bilateral care model, neither strict liability nor no liability leads to the efficient outcome. This illustrates a fundamental problem—namely, that both parties must face full responsibility for the damages at the margin in order to have the proper incentives. Otherwise, there is a *moral hazard problem* that results in too little precaution by one of the parties (or both if the damages are shared).

Note that one way to achieve bilateral responsibility is to assess the injurer the full amount of the victim's damages, but then *not award the injurer's payment to the victim*. This will lead to the efficient outcome because the injurer will act as if the rule were strict liability, and the victim will act as if the rule were no liability. This is in fact the case under a pollution tax (and criminal fines), where the revenue from the tax is not used to compensate victims. The problem is that actual liability rules are not structured in this way; instead, they require that the victim receive whatever the injurer pays.[7] Of course, this reflects the compensatory function of tort law, but the analysis of the bilateral care problem suggests that this constraint (namely, that the victim must receive what the injurer pays) conflicts with its deterrence, or incentive function. It turns out that this is not true under negligence law.

2.2.2   Negligence

As discussed above, under negligence law, the injurer can avoid liability by meeting the due standard of care, x^*. This does not change when the victim also has the opportunity to take care. If the injurer chooses $x \geq x^*$, he avoids liability *regardless of the victim's choice of care*. Thus, as in the unilateral care model, the cost-minimizing strategy by the injurer is to meet the due standard.

Now consider the choice by the victim. Because she rationally anticipates that the injurer will meet the due standard, she expects to bear her own losses. Thus, she chooses her own care level, y, to

$$\text{minimize} \quad y + p(x^*, y)D(x^*, y). \tag{2.4}$$

Since she internalizes the full damages, she also chooses efficient care, y^*.

This shows that in a Nash equilibrium, a negligence rule with the due standard set at x^* induces both the injurer and victim to choose efficient care. Negligence therefore succeeds in achieving bilateral responsibility at the margin. The reason it can do this is that it employs two methods for inducing efficient behavior: first, it sets a threshold that allows the injurer to *avoid liability by meeting the threshold*; and second, it simultaneously imposes *actual liability* on the victim. We will encounter this use of a *threshold rule* for achieving bilateral responsibility in other areas of the law, but it is most clearly exemplified by the negligence rule.

Note the following aspects of this equilibrium. First, the victim is not compensated for her damages. This suggests that, contrary to the case of strict liability in the unilateral care model, the compensatory and deterrence functions of tort law may be incompatible after all. (It turns out, however, that another threshold rule to be discussed below allows compensation of the victim while achieving bilateral efficiency.) Second, this equilibrium implies that no one is ever negligent—a result clearly at odds with reality. Below we discuss several reasons why parties may actually be negligent in equilibrium, including uncertainty over the due standard, differing costs of care across individuals, and limited injurer wealth.

2.3   The Hand Rule

Before extending the accident model in these and other directions, however, we first consider the extent to which actual negligence law corresponds to the economic ideal as just developed. In particular, we compare the legal definition of the due standard of care with the efficient standard, x^*. For purposes of this discussion, it is sufficient to restrict our attention to the unilateral care model.

The centerpiece of the positive economic theory of tort law—the argument that tort law embodies an economic logic—is the famous case of the *United States v. Carroll Towing Co.* (159 F.2d 169, 2d Cir. 1947). The facts of the case are simple. A barge owner was accused of being negligent when he failed to post an attendant on board to make sure that the barge would not break loose from its moorings and cause damage to other ships and their cargo. The decision of the court was written by Judge Learned Hand, who wrote, in part:

> Since there are occasions when every vessel will break away from her moorings, and since, if she does, she becomes a menace to those about her; the owner's duty, as in other situations, to provide against resulting injuries is a function of three variables: (1) The probability that she will break away; (2) the gravity of the resulting injury, if she does; (3) the burden of adequate precautions. Possibly it serves to bring this notion into relief to state it in algebraic terms: if the probability be called P; the injury, L; and the burden, B; liability depends upon whether B is less than L multiplied by P; i.e., whether $B < PL$.

The court ruled that in the circumstances at hand, the barge owner was in fact negligent for failing to post an attendant on board because the cost of doing so was less than the expected benefit, or $B < PL$. How does this simple inequality relate to the above model of accidents?

Recall that in the economic model, the due standard x^* was interpreted to be the level of injurer care that minimized the sum of the costs of precaution and expected damages. Thus, at x^*, the marginal cost of an additional unit of precaution equals the marginal benefit in terms of reduced damages. If we interpret B as the *marginal* cost of care and PL as the *marginal* reduction in accident costs from that last unit of care, then the injurer will be found negligent under the Hand rule if and only if $B < PL$, which is exactly the range over which $x < x^*$ in the economic model.[8] The resulting marginal Hand rule is illustrated in Figure 2.4.

One complication in applying marginal analysis to actual accident cases is that care usually does not vary continuously but comes in discrete bundles. The following exercise, based on the *Carroll Towing* case, illustrates the proper use of marginal analysis when applying the Hand rule to discrete care situations.

Figure 2.4

The Marginal
Hand Rule

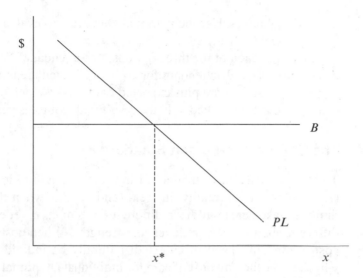

EXERCISE 2.1

Consider a barge owner who is deciding whether to post an attendant on
his barge to make sure that it remains properly moored to the pier. The
following table gives the total cost of hiring the attendant, the probability
of an accident, and the fixed cost of an accident:

	Cost of Care	Probability	Damages
No attendant posted	$ 0	.25	$400
Attendant posted for 24 hours	$94	0	$400

(a) Calculate the marginal cost, B, and marginal benefit, PL, of
    posting the attendant. According to the marginal Hand rule,
    would the barge owner be found negligent for failing to post an
    attendant?
    Now suppose that the barge owner had a third option: post the
    attendant only during the day. The data for this option are as fol-
    lows: Cost of care = $50, Probability of an accident = .10, and
    Damages = $400.

(b) Assume that the barge owner's only two options are "no atten-
    dant" and "post an attendant during the day." In this case, would
    the owner's failure to post an attendant be judged negligent by the
    marginal Hand rule?

(c) Assume that, prior to the accident, the owner had posted an
    attendant during the day. Suppose that the victim claims that
    the owner is negligent for not having posted the attendant for

24 hours. Use the marginal Hand rule to evaluate the merits of this claim.

(d) For each of the three options, "no attendant," "attendant during the day," and "attendant for 24 hours," calculate total expected costs (costs of care plus expected damages). Which option minimizes this total? Reconcile the result with your answers to (a)–(c).

2.4   The Reasonable-Person Standard

To this point we have treated all injurers as having identical costs of care (= $1 per unit). In reality, injurers (and victims when they have an opportunity to take care) will have different costs of care, reflecting, for example, different ability levels, reflexes, or strengths. When costs of care differ, the cost-minimizing level of care will naturally be individual-specific. To see why, let c_j be the unit cost of care for individual j. Optimal care for that person will therefore minimize

$$c_j x + p(x)D(x). \tag{2.5}$$

Since c_j is the marginal cost of care in this case, individuals with higher values of c will have *lower* optimal care levels (given equal marginal benefits of care across injurers). For example, if there are three types of injurers such that $c_1 < c_2 < c_3$, their cost-minimizing care levels will satisfy $x_1^* > x_2^* > x_3^*$. Intuitively, individuals with lower marginal costs of care should be held to higher due standards of care.

In general, however, the law does not individualize standards in this way. Rather, it sets a single standard applicable to all. This standard is based on a fictitious person referred to as the "reasonable person," who is defined to be "a personification of a community ideal of reasonable behavior, determined by the jury's social judgment. . . . Negligence is a failure to do what the reasonable person would do under the same or similar circumstances."[9]

The economic model implies that a single standard will not minimize overall accident costs when injurers differ in their marginal costs of care, so how can we explain the reasonable-person standard in the context of the economic model of tort law? The answer is that we have ignored administrative costs. Establishing what particular standard is appropriate in a given case would place a very high information burden on the court, a cost that is ordinarily too high compared to the savings in accident costs that would result from an individualized standard. (When the cost of individualizing the standard is low, however, the court will generally do so.)

What are the costs of setting a single standard, call it x^*, when injurers differ in their marginal costs of care? Two types of inefficiency result.[10]

1. For individuals with below-average marginal costs of care, the due standard is lower than what their individualized standard would be, or $x^* < x_j^*$. These individuals will have no incentive to increase their actual care above x^*, even though by doing so they would, by definition, lower social costs. (Remember that under a negligence rule, injurers avoid all liability by meeting the due standard, but they gain nothing privately by exceeding it.) All individuals with less than average costs of care therefore take too little care.

2. Individuals who have a cost of care that is slightly above average— and hence have an individualized standard less than the average (or $x^* > x_j^*$)—will actually increase their care level up to the due standard. This occurs because of the discontinuity in costs under the negligence rule, which creates a strong incentive for injurers to comply with the standard in order to avoid liability. Those injurers who find this privately beneficial, however, increase social costs by taking too much care (that is, the last dollar spent on care by these injurers reduces expected damages by less than one dollar).

There is a final group of injurers who actually choose the efficient level of care under the single standard. These are injurers whose cost of care is so high, and their individualized standard is so low relative to x^*, that they find it too costly to raise their care level up to x^*. Instead, they choose x_j^* and are judged negligent. For these injurers, the negligence rule is equivalent to strict liability.[11]

Figure 2.5 shows the actual care choices of injurers (the darkened segments) compared to the level of care that minimizes accident costs (the downward-sloping curve). As the cost of care increases from left to right in the figure, we first see the set of injurers who take too little care ($c < c_1$), then those who take too much care ($c_1 < c < c_2$), and finally those who take efficient care and are found negligent ($c > c_2$). The fact that some injurers overinvest in care while others underinvest implies that we cannot say whether there will

Figure 2.5

Comparison of Actual and Efficient Care Under a Single Due Care Standard

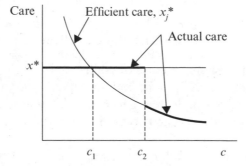

be more or fewer accidents compared to a rule with individualized standards (or under strict liability). However, total costs must be higher as a result of the inefficient care choices of the first two groups.

2.5 Contributory Negligence

Our discussion of the negligence rule has to this point focused on the legal duty of injurers to meet the standard of care. We have said nothing about a corresponding duty for victims, even though in our bilateral care model they can take care to avoid an accident as well. In fact, there is a form of negligence that is applied to victims; it is referred to as *contributory negligence.* Under a contributory negligence standard, victims are also required to meet a due standard of care as a condition of recovering for their injuries. For this reason, contributory negligence is a *defense* for injurers, which means that, even if an injurer admits to being negligent, he can still try to avoid liability by proving that the victim failed to meet the due standard (that is, was contributorily negligent).

Contributory negligence was first introduced in the old English case of *Butterfield v. Forrester* (11 East 60, K.B. 1809). The plaintiff in this case was injured while riding down a street when his horse collided with an obstruction that was negligently placed there by the defendant. The court held that, despite the defendant's negligence, the victim could not recover for his damages because of his own failure to act with due care. Specifically, the court said:

> A party is not to cast himself upon an obstruction which had been made by the fault of another, and avail himself of it, if he does not himself use common and ordinary caution to be in the right. . . . One person being in fault will not dispense with another's use of ordinary care for himself.

Contributory negligence can be paired with either a "simple" negligence rule or with strict liability. Let's examine it first when paired with simple negligence.

2.5.1 Negligence with Contributory Negligence

Under negligence with a defense of contributory negligence, the law establishes a due standard of care for both the injurer and the victim. Consistent with our analysis of simple negligence above, let these due standards be the efficient levels of care for the two parties—x^* for the injurer and y^* for the victim.

As noted above, contributory negligence bars recovery by the victim if she fails to meet her due standard of y^*, regardless of the injurer's choice of care. In contrast, if the victim chooses $y \geq y^*$, the injurer can still avoid liability by

Figure 2.6

Assignment of Liability Under Negligence with Contributory Negligence (a) and Strict Liability with Contributory Negligence (b)

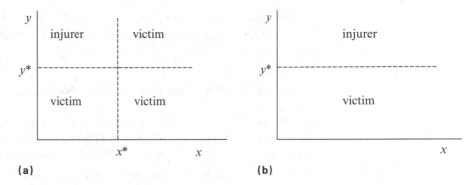

(a)   (b)

meeting his own due standard. Figure 2.6, panel (a), shows the assignment of liability for all choices of care by the injurer and victim under negligence with contributory negligence. Note that this differs from the assignment under simple negligence only in the lower left quadrant, the region where both parties are negligent. Under simple negligence (where the victim's choice of care is irrelevant), the injurer is liable in this case, while under negligence with contributory negligence, the victim is liable. In the other three quadrants, the rules are the same.

Does this change affect the efficiency of the negligence rule? The answer is no, provided that both due standards are set correctly. Consider first the choice of care by the injurer, and suppose that he expects the victim to satisfy the due care standard (the upper half of Figure 2.6[a]). In this case, the analysis is identical to that under simple negligence—the injurer chooses due care to avoid liability. (Note that the answer is different if the injurer expects the victim to be negligent, for in that case, the injurer faces no liability and will therefore choose *zero care*. We consider this case in Section 3.1 below.)

Now consider the victim's incentives. If she expects the injurer to meet his due standard, the outcome is again identical to simple negligence—the victim bears her own losses and chooses efficient care of y^*. Thus, in a Nash equilibrium, both parties choose efficient care. This establishes that adding a defense of contributory negligence to simple negligence does not distort incentives. It also turns out not to affect the allocation of liability in equilibrium. Under both negligence rules, the victim bears liability in an efficient equilibrium.

According to the previous analysis, contributory negligence adds nothing to simple negligence in terms of either efficiency or allocation of liability. Further, it is likely a costlier rule to administer than simple negligence because it requires courts to evaluate compliance with two standards of care rather than one. Why then, until recently, has negligence with contributory negligence been the predominant tort rule in the United States? One possible reason will be illustrated below when we examine torts in which injurers and victims choose their care levels *sequentially* rather than simultaneously. However, we first examine contributory negligence when paired with strict liability.

2.5.2   Strict Liability with Contributory Negligence

Figure 2.6, panel (b), shows the assignment of liability under strict liability with contributory negligence. Note that in this case, only the victim's standard of care matters. In this respect, strict liability with contributory negligence is essentially a "negligence rule for victims." Thus, the Nash equilibrium is derived exactly as in the case of simple negligence, with the injurer and victim reversed. Specifically, the victim chooses due care to avoid liability, and the injurer, who is therefore strictly liable, chooses efficient care to minimize his costs.

Like the previous negligence rules, strict liability with contributory negligence therefore achieves bilateral efficiency, but it differs from the two negligence rules regarding the assignment of liability. Specifically, in an efficient equilibrium, the *injurer* bears the damages. This difference provides a basis for choosing between strict liability with contributory negligence and the two negligence rules on distributional grounds. If, for example, we determine, for policy reasons, that we want to favor victims as a group over injurers, but we don't want to distort incentives for efficient care, then we can employ strict liability with contributory negligence rather than negligence. (We will see a different reason for choosing strict liability with contributory negligence in our discussion of products liability in the next chapter.)

3   Further Topics

3.1   Sequential Care Accidents*

The bilateral care model to this point has been based on the assumption that injurers and victims make their care choices simultaneously, or, equivalently, that they make them without first observing the actual care choice of the other party. In this case, the parties had to form expectations about what the other party was doing. This actually helped promote efficiency because each party could act *as if* the other were taking due care. There is a substantial class of accidents, however, in which the injurer and victim move in sequence, and, as a result, the second mover can observe the *actual* care choice of the first mover before making his or her own choice. These are referred to as *sequential care accidents*.

In this type of setting, suppose the party moving first is observed to be negligent, due to inadvertence, error, or strategic behavior. Although the efficient outcome in which both parties take efficient care is now foreclosed, it is still desirable for the second party to take efficient care to avoid the accident. The question is whether the liability rules we have examined create such an incentive *once the second mover has observed the first mover's negligence.*[12]

3.1.1 The Injurer Moves First

Consider first the case where the injurer moves first. An example is provided by the facts of *Butterfield v. Forrester.* Recall that the injurer had negligently placed an obstruction in the street, and a passing rider collided with it and was injured. Assuming that the rider observed the obstruction in time to react, the question is whether the standard negligence rules provided him an incentive to take efficient steps to avoid the accident. Consider first simple negligence. According to the above analysis of the negligence rule, if the victim knows that the injurer has violated his due standard, then the victim has no incentive to take precautions because she knows that the injurer will be held liable for any damages. Thus, a simple negligence rule does not create incentives for victim precaution in the presence of observed injurer negligence.[13]

Now suppose a contributory negligence defense is added. Recall that under contributory negligence, negligent victims are liable regardless of the injurer's actions. Thus, even though the victim knows the injurer has been negligent, the victim nevertheless must take care in order to avoid liability. The conclusion is similar under strict liability with contributory negligence—once the victim takes due care, the injurer is strictly liable. This argument illustrates one advantage of adding a contributory negligence defense to simple negligence (Landes and Posner 1987, 76).

3.1.2 The Victim Moves First

We next consider the case of *Davies v. Mann* (10 M&W 546, 152 Eng. Rep. 588, 1842), which involves a similar situation to that in *Butterfield v. Forrester* except that the victim moves first. The victim in this case was the owner of a donkey that he had tied up next to a highway. The injurer subsequently drove this wagon down the highway and collided with the donkey, killing it. The court found that the owner of the donkey was negligent in having left it unattended on the side of the road, but the driver of the wagon was also found negligent because he was traveling at an excessive rate of speed.

Note that under a contributory negligence rule, the victim in this case would have been barred from recovery, in spite of the injurer's negligence. Thus, the injurer, who had time to observe the prior negligence of the victim, would have had no incentive to take reasonable care to avoid hitting the donkey. The above benefit of contributory negligence when the injurer moves first is therefore absent when the victim moves first. In contrast, a simple negligence rule would do better in this case because the injurer would have had to meet the due standard to avoid liability, regardless of the prior negligence of the victim.

3.1.3   Last Clear Chance

The preceding cases suggest that neither simple negligence nor negligence with contributory negligence can in all cases create incentives for the second mover in sequential accidents to take care in the presence of observed negligence by the first mover. The efficient rule depends on which party moves first. In response to this perceived deficiency, the court in *Davies v. Mann* articulated a rule that has since become known as *last clear chance*. Simply stated, the rule says that in sequential care accidents, the party acting second, whether the injurer or the victim, has the ultimate duty to exercise precaution against an accident, regardless of any prior negligence by the other party.

Note that in cases where the injurer moves first, like *Butterfield v. Forrester*, last clear chance is essentially equivalent to contributory negligence. If the injurer has acted negligently, both rules require the victim to take due care in order to avoid liability. However, in cases where the victim moves first, like *Davies v. Mann*, last clear chance is a necessary supplement to contributory negligence because it compels the injurer to take care despite the prior negligence of the victim. We therefore say that last clear chance "defeats" the injurer's attempt to use contributory negligence as a defense for his own negligence. As the court in *Davies v. Mann* recognized, were last clear chance not required of injurers, "a man might justify the driving over goods left on a public highway, or even over a man lying asleep there, or purposely running against a carriage going on the wrong side of the road."

3.2   Comparative Negligence

All the liability rules that we have studied so far are what we call "all-or-nothing" rules. That is, one party, the injurer or the victim, bears all of the damages from an accident. In contrast, comparative negligence divides the damages between the injurer and victim in proportion to their relative fault. As of 1992, forty-four states had adopted some form of comparative negligence in place of standard negligence rules (Curran 1992). The principal reason for the conversion seems to have been a dissatisfaction with the perceived unfairness of all-or-nothing rules, especially in cases where, for example, slightly negligent victims are barred from recovering against grossly negligent injurers.

To illustrate the application of comparative negligence, consider a case in which a speeding motorist hits a pedestrian walking on the wrong side of the road. Suppose that the pedestrian incurs medical bills of $50,000. Under contributory negligence, she would be barred from recovering anything against the motorist, even if the court judged that 75 percent of the damage was due to his excessive speed. Under comparative negligence, in contrast, the injurer would be responsible for paying (.75) × ($50,000), or $37,500.

Although comparative negligence may be a fairer way of assigning liability for accidents, we need to ask whether this gain in fairness requires us to sacrifice the desirable efficiency properties of the all-or-nothing negligence rules. To answer this question, we examine the incentives for injurer and victim care under the most common form of comparative negligence, referred to as "pure" comparative negligence.[14]

As above, let x^* and y^* be the due standards of care for the injurer and victim, respectively. We can then define pure comparative negligence as follows: (1) if $x \geq x^*$ the injurer avoids all liability regardless of the victim's care choice; (2) if $x < x^*$ and $y \geq y^*$ the injurer is negligent and the victim is not, so the injurer bears full liability; and (3) if $x < x^*$ and $y < y^*$ both parties are negligent so they share liability in proportion to their fault. In the latter case, suppose that the injurer bears a fraction s of the damages, and the victim bears the remaining fraction $1 - s$, where s depends *positively* on the degree of injurer negligence and *negatively* on the degree of victim negligence.

Note that this rule and the two negligence rules (simple negligence and negligence with contributory negligence) differ from one another only in the assignment of liability when both parties are negligent (the lower-left quadrant in Figure 2.6 [a]). The injurer bears liability in this case under simple negligence, the victim bears it under negligence with contributory negligence, and the parties share it under comparative negligence. Thus, one can usefully think of simple negligence and negligence with contributory negligence as *special cases* of the more general comparative negligence rule. To see why, note that if we constrain $s = 1$, then the injurer bears full liability when both parties are negligent, as is true under simple negligence. In contrast, if we set $s = 0$, then the victim bears full liability when both parties are negligent, as under negligence with contributory negligence. Since both special cases provided efficient incentives for injurer and victim care, it is not surprising that the general rule can also be shown to provide efficient incentives. The proof is identical to that for the two negligence rules and is left as an exercise.

Exercise 2.2

Show that the comparative negligence rule as defined above results in an equilibrium in which both the injurer and victim take efficient care. To do this, first show that if the victim chooses due care of y^*, the best thing for the injurer to do is to choose x^*, and then show that if the injurer chooses x^*, the best thing for the victim to do is to choose y^*.

The fact that comparative negligence leads to an efficient equilibrium, and is fairer, suggests that it is superior to either of the all-or-nothing negligence rules. However, this is not necessarily true for two reasons. First, notice that in an efficient equilibrium, comparative negligence loses its desirable fairness properties because when both parties choose due care, the victim bears her own liability as under the other negligence rules. This is due to the threshold nature of the rule, which is the distinguishing feature of negligence rules, and the reason they are able to provide efficient bilateral incentives.

Second, comparative negligence has the drawback that it is probably cost-lier to administer than the other negligence rules because it requires the court to apportion damages based on relative fault. In many cases this will be a difficult task. Imagine, for example, trying to determine relative fault in a case where the customer at a drive-through restaurant spills hot coffee on herself while holding the cup between her legs. How much of the victim's damage was due to the coffee's having been too hot, and how much was due to the victim's mishandling of the cup?

Some economists have sought to demonstrate the superiority of comparative negligence over other forms of negligence by examining variations of the simple accident model. For example, they have shown that comparative negligence may be preferred when injurers and victims are risk averse (Landes and Posner 1987, 82), when there is uncertainty about the due standard of care (Cooter and Ulen 1986), when injurers differ in their costs of care (Rubinfeld 1987), or in the case of sequential care accidents (Rea 1987).[15]

Of course, only evidence from actual accidents can resolve the question of whether comparative negligence is more efficient than other negligence rules. White (1989) attempted to gather such evidence in the context of automobile accident cases in California from 1974 to 1976. (California switched from contributory negligence to comparative negligence in 1975.) Her results showed that contributory negligence created stronger incentives for accident avoidance, and further, that drivers took less than efficient care under comparative negligence. This suggests that the primary advantage of comparative negligence, in automobile accident cases at least, lies in its greater fairness.

3.3   Causation and Liability*

We return now to the issue of causation in relation to its impact on the assignment of liability. As noted above, issues of causation are often central to the actual assignment of liability in tort law, yet the economic model of accidents to this point has not explicitly raised the issue of causation. Cooter (1987a) has argued that this is because the economic model implicitly embodies a mathematical notion of causation through the functional relationship between precaution and expected damages. As a result, additional notions of causation are unnecessary to achieve efficient incentives for care. Nevertheless, a positive theory of tort law needs to address the court's use of causation principles in determining the scope of liability.

To keep the analysis simple, we focus on the unilateral care model and the simple negligence rule. Recall that in order to be held liable under negligence law, the injurer's failure to take due care must be both cause-in-fact and proximate cause of the victim's damages. We consider first the impact of the cause-in-fact requirement on the efficiency of the negligence rule.

3.3.1   Cause-in-Fact

To illustrate the impact of cause-in-fact on the negligence rule, consider the following example.[16] During a cricket game being played in a field enclosed by a 9-foot fence, a ball flies over the fence and injures a passerby. Suppose that the efficient height of the fence—the height that balances the cost of increasing its height against the savings in accident costs—is 10 feet. Based on the above characterization of the negligence rule, the owner's failure to build a 10-foot fence should therefore subject him to liability for *any* injuries suffered by a passerby.

Actual negligence law, however, does not operate in this way. According to the but-for test for causation, the owner would instead only be held liable for those accidents caused by his *negligence*, that is, for accidents caused by balls that went over the 9-foot fence *but would not have gone over a 10-foot fence*. In other words, any balls that would have cleared a hypothetical 10-foot fence would not result in a valid claim for liability against the owner.

Does this restriction on liability eliminate the injurer's incentive to take due care under negligence? The answer is that it does not, though it does eliminate the discontinuity in the injurer's costs at the due standard of care (refer to Figure 2.2 above). The following numerical example, based on the cricket case, shows why. Table 2.1 shows the costs facing the owner of the cricket field, and Table 2.2 shows the owner's liabililty under a negligence rule, with and without the causation requirement, assuming that the due standard is a fence of 10 feet.

Consider first the injurer's behavior under the standard negligence rule (column two in Table 2.2). If the owner builds a fence of less than 10 feet, he is negligent and therefore faces expected liability of $120, making his total expected costs $210. However, if he builds a fence of at least 10 feet, he is not negligent and hence faces only the cost of building the fence. His cost-minimizing choice is therefore to just meet the due standard of care by

TABLE **2.1**   **Data for Cricket Example**

Height of fence (ft.)	Cost of fence ($)	Accident costs ($)	Total costs ($)
9	90	120	210
10	100	100	200
11	110	95	205

SOURCE: *Kahan (1989).*

TABLE **2.2**   **Injurer's Costs Under Negligence Rule**

Height of fence (ft.)	Cost under std. negligence rule ($)	Cost under negligence rule with cause-in-fact ($)
9	210 = 90 + 120	110 = 90 + 20
10	100	100
11	110	110

SOURCE: *Adapted from Kahan (1989).*

building the 10-foot fence at a cost of $100. In doing so, he expects to save the $120 in liability costs.

Now consider negligence with a cause-in-fact requirement (column three in Table 2.2). The only difference from the standard negligence rule is in the first row, where the injurer negligently builds a 9-foot fence. Although the injurer is liable for damages in this case, he is only liable for those damages caused by balls flying over the 9-foot fence that would not have cleared the 10-foot fence. Thus, his expected liability is the difference in expected accident costs with a 9-foot fence compared to a 10-foot fence, or $120 − $100 = $20, making his total expected costs from a 9-foot fence $110. Note that this is still more than his cost from building a 10-foot fence, so the incentive for efficient care remains. The difference is that there is no longer a dramatic drop in the injurer's costs at the due standard of care.[17] This shows that, although the cause-in-fact requirement limits the injurer's liability under negligence, it does not distort his incentives to act efficiently. It is important to emphasize that the preceding analysis does not provide an economic theory for the existence of the cause-in-fact limitation. It only shows that cause-in-fact is not inconsistent with efficiency. At the same time, however, it may eliminate the benefits associated with the discontinuity of the injurer's costs under a negligence rule.

3.3.2   Proximate Cause

In addition to proving that an injurer's negligence was cause-in-fact of an accident, the victim must prove that it was the proximate cause. Recall that the usual test for proximate cause is to ask whether the connection between the injurer's negligent act and the resulting accident was sufficiently close that a reasonable person, standing in the position of the injurer before the accident occurred, could have foreseen it. Proximate cause is therefore based on a "forward-looking" view of the accident, starting from the point in time when the injurer made his care choice. Note that this is in contrast to the backward-looking nature of cause-in-fact, which examines the causes of an accident with the benefit of hindsight.

The important consequence of the forward-looking nature of proximate cause is that the economic model of accidents takes the same perspective. Thus, we can use the apparatus of that model to construct an analytical version of the reasonable foresight test. To see how, consider an injurer whose actual care level was x', which is less than the due standard, x^*. Call $x^* - x'$ the "untaken precaution."[18] Assume that it has already been determined that the injurer's negligence was cause-in-fact of the accident. To determine if it was also proximate cause, the reasonable foresight test asks whether a reasonable person would have foreseen that his failure to meet the due standard would cause the victim's injuries. From the injurer's perspective before the accident has occurred, this amounts to asking how much his failure to exercise due care would *increase the expected damages to the victim.*

In terms of the economic model, the injurer's choice of x' rather than x^* increases expected damages by $p(x')D(x') - p(x^*)D(x^*)$. Note that this coincides with our definition above of the marginal benefit of increased care under the marginal Hand test, which we labeled PL. Under the reasonable foresight test, a finding of proximate cause requires that the increase in expected damages due to the untaken precaution must exceed some threshold, call it T. That is, the injurer's negligence is proximate cause of the accident if $PL > T$, and it is not proximate cause if $PL < T$. Now, if we let $T = B$, the marginal cost of care, then *the test for proximate cause becomes identical to the marginal Hand test.*

It follows that the test for proximate cause and the test for negligence are in essence redundant tests. That is, both are forward-looking threshold tests for limiting the injurer's liability. On the one hand, this redundancy helps to explain why economic theories of negligence apparently have no need for causation principles (except for the notion of causation implicit in the functional relationship between care and expected damages). On the other hand, it again raises the question of why the law requires both inquiries before assigning liability. There are several possible reasons for including both tests.

First, proximate cause may serve to offset an inherent bias in the Hand test, which arises from the fact that in actual tort suits, the burden is on the plaintiff to propose the specific untaken precaution that constitutes negligence on the part of the injurer. To see the nature of this bias, consider an example based on

TABLE **2.3**   **Data for Lifeguard Example**

Action	Cost of care	Probability	Damages	Total costs
No sign or lifeguard	0	.10	$1,000	$100
Sign	$5	.075	$1,000	$80
Lifeguard	$70	.005	$1,000	$75

the case of *Haft v. Lone Palm Hotel* (3 Cal.3d 756, 478 P.2d 465, 1970). The plaintiff in this case sought to recover damages when her husband and son, who were inexperienced swimmers, drowned in a hotel pool. Suppose that at the time of the drowning, there was no lifeguard on duty, nor was there a sign warning guests of this fact. Table 2.3 provides the data for this example.

As the table shows, a sign is inexpensive and reduces the probability of an accident slightly (from .10 to .075) by deterring some inexperienced swimmers, while posting a lifeguard is costly but reduces the probability significantly (from .10 to .005). The example assumes that posting a lifeguard minimizes total costs, so it is the efficient precaution. However, the plaintiff might find it easier to prove that failure to post a sign constituted negligence according to the marginal Hand test. Specifically, applying the test to the hotel's failure to post the sign, we find that $B = \$5$ and $PL = (.10 - .075)(\$1,000) = \$25$. Thus, the marginal savings in accident costs exceeds the marginal cost of care by a factor of five, so the test is easily satisfied. Now suppose that the plaintiff proposed the failure to post a lifeguard as the untaken precaution. In this case, the marginal cost and benefit of posting a lifeguard are calculated relative to taking no action. Thus, $B = \$70$ and $PL = (.10 - .005)(\$1,000) = \$95$. The Hand test is again satisfied (as it must be since posting a lifeguard is efficient), but it is a much closer call as compared to the sign.

This example illustrates the incentive for plaintiffs to propose untaken precautions that are "too small" (that is, that fall short of the efficient precaution) in order to make it easier to satisfy the Hand test.[19] As a result, potential injurers looking at decisions in tort cases with this bias may perceive a due standard that is too low from a social perspective. A possible function of proximate cause in this setting, therefore, is to limit this *downward bias* in the Hand test by putting a lower bound on those untaken precautions that will pass the reasonable foresight test. In this case, for example, posting a sign reduces expected damages by $25, while posting a lifeguard reduces expected damages (relative to no action) by $95. Thus, by setting the threshold for the reasonable foresight test between these two values, the court can force the plaintiff to propose the efficient untaken precaution.

A second possible reason for requiring both the Hand test and causation may be to save on the administrative costs of using the legal system by limiting the scope of liability. That is, by requiring plaintiffs to prove both cause-in-fact and proximate cause, the law limits those circumstances in which a victim can recover against a negligent injurer (Shavell 1980a). This will deter some victims from filing suit, thereby saving on litigation costs. A third reason, also based on administrative costs, is that it may be intuitively easier for judges or juries to apply one or the other of the tests, depending on the facts of a particular case. That is, some cases may be easier to conceptualize in terms of cost-benefit principles, while others may be easier to see in terms of causation. Finally, it may simply be true that the causation requirement—both cause-in-fact and proximate cause—are designed to achieve goals other than efficiency such as fairness or distributive justice (Cooter 1987a).

3.3.3   *Res Ipsa Loquitur*

In some cases, the plaintiff may be unable to prove that the defendant's negligence was the cause of her harm, even though the circumstances of the accident make it exceedingly likely that it was. In these cases, the court may allow the plaintiff to recover, absent formal proof of causation, by invoking the doctrine of *res ipsa loquitur*, or "the thing speaks for itself." For example, in *Richenbacher v. California Packing Corporation* (250 Mass. 198, 145 N.E. 281, 1924), the plaintiff was allowed to recover against a food-packing company for damages suffered when she cut her mouth on glass found in a can of spinach. Although there was no evidence of negligence in the defendant's packing operation, the court ruled that the only way the glass could have gotten into the can was by improper care during packaging.

When is it appropriate from an economic perspective for courts to apply the doctrine of *res ipsa loquitur*? Suppose that the accident technology is such that when the defendant employs due care, the probability of an accident is virtually zero (that is, $p(x^*) = 0$). In that case, the occurrence of an accident is necessarily evidence of negligence and also of cause-in-fact. In practice, however, this will not often be the case since efficient care usually does not prevent an accident with certainty. Note that if the doctrine is invoked in cases where $p(x^*) > 0$, then the liability rule effectively becomes strict liability because the injurer does not necessarily avoid liability by meeting the due standard. We will see in the next chapter that this was one route by which strict liability became the rule in products liability cases.

3.3.4   Uncertainty over Causation

Another circumstance in which a plaintiff might have difficulty proving causation is when there are multiple possible causes of her injuries (Shavell

1985). An example is when exposure to a toxic substance increases the "background" risk of developing cancer. If the victim develops cancer, it is not known whether it is due to the exposure or to a "natural" cause. Another source of uncertainty over causation is when there are multiple injurers. For example, suppose that two hunters both fire in the direction of a third party, but only one bullet strikes the victim.[20] In these cases, how should liability be assigned to the injurer(s) in order to induce efficient precaution?

To answer this question, we consider the case of a single injurer coupled with a background risk. (We consider the case of multiple injurers in the next chapter in the context of environmental accidents.) Specifically, let the probability of an accident be $p(x) + q$, where q is the background risk. For simplicity, let the victim's damages in the event of an accident be fixed at D. Since the background risk is constant, the social problem is to choose x to minimize expected costs, or to

$$\text{minimize} \quad x + [p(x) + q]D. \tag{2.6}$$

The resulting efficient level of precaution is x^*. In terms of the injurer's incentives, note that either a strict liability rule or a simple negligence rule with the due standard set at x^* continues to yield the correct incentives. To see this, rewrite expected costs in (2.6) as $x + p(x)D + qD$. Since the term qD is additive, it does not affect the minimum point. Thus, the background risk has no effect on incentives, and the problem becomes identical to the unilateral care model. In this respect, uncertainty over causation does not present a problem regarding efficient care. However, it does potentially subject the injurer to liability for injuries that he did not "cause." In addition to being unfair, this increases administrative costs by expanding the scope of liability, and also may cause injurers to reduce their level of activity to an inefficiently low level (see the next section).

There are two ways to limit the scope of liability in the case of uncertainty over causation. The first is to employ a proximate cause limitation that holds the injurer liable only if the *conditional probability* that he caused the injuries exceeds some threshold. In the background risk model, this conditional probability is given by $p(x)/[p(x) + q]$. If the rule is strict liability, then the injurer's problem with the proximate cause limitation is

$$\text{minimize} \quad \begin{array}{ll} x, & \text{if } p(x)/[p(x) + q] \leq T \\ x + [p(x) + q]D, & \text{if } p(x)/[p(x) + q] > T \end{array} \tag{2.7}$$

for some threshold T. Now suppose that we set $T = p(x^*)/[p(x^*) + q]$. Since $p(x)/[p(x) + q]$ is decreasing in x (that is, the injurer's conditional probability of causation is decreasing in his care level), the condition for the injurer to avoid liability (the top line in [2.7]) is just $x \geq x^*$. The injurer's problem in

(2.7) therefore becomes identical to that under simple negligence, and the injurer chooses efficient care.[21]

The second way that the injurer's liability can be limited in this case is to hold him strictly liable in all cases, but for less than the full amount of the victim's damages. Specifically, suppose that in the event of an injury to the victim, the fraction of the damages that the injurer must pay is equal to the conditional probability that he caused the damages. The injurer's problem in this case is to

$$\text{minimize} \quad x + [p(x) + q] \times \left(\frac{p(x)}{p(x) + q} \right) D. \tag{2.8}$$

Note that this is equivalent to minimizing $x + p(x)D$, which has the solution x^*. Thus, this sort of proportional liability also induces the injurer to take efficient care.

A court actually employed a rule of this sort in a well-known case involving several manufacturers of a drug that was later found to be a cause of cancer.[22] Because of the time lapse between the purchase of the drug and the discovery of its carcinogenic nature, the plaintiff did not know which of several companies had sold the drug to her. The court therefore apportioned liability among the companies according to their market shares at the time of the sale, the latter serving as a proxy for the probability that each was responsible for the victim's damages.

3.4 Activity Levels

To this point, we have focused on injurer and victim *precaution* as the primary determinant of the probability and severity of accidents, but in many cases an equally important factor is their *activity levels*. That is, how intensively do the parties engage in the risky activity? For example, a motorist decides how fast to drive and how often to have his car inspected (both measures of care), but also how many miles to drive (his activity level). Similarly, the manufacturer of a dangerous product decides what safety features to include, as well as how many units to sell.[23] We illustrate the role of activity levels in the context of the unilateral care model and then generalize the results to the bilateral care model below.[24]

Let the injurer's activity level be denoted a, which yields him benefits of $B(a)$. Assume that $B(a)$ is a single-peaked curve that is maximized at a unique activity level a_0, as shown in Figure 2.7. Thus, in the absence of any accident risk, this is the level of activity that the injurer would choose, and it is also the efficient level.

We next need to specify the impact of the injurer's activity on accident costs. Assume that expected damages and costs of care are proportional to

Figure 2.7

Injurer Activity Levels
Under Different
Liability Rules

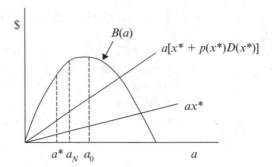

the injurer's level of activity. Thus, for example, if the motorist drives twice as many miles, his cost of precaution and the expected damages to victims both double.[25] Given this specification of the accident technology, we write total expected accident costs as $a[x + p(x)D(x)]$. The social problem is now to choose the injurer's level of activity and care to maximize net benefits, given by

$$B(a) - a[x + p(x)D(x)].\qquad(2.9)$$

Note that this problem can be broken into two parts. The first is to choose the level of care to minimize expected accident costs. Given the proportionality of accident costs to the activity level, it turns out that the optimal care level, x^*, is independent of a. Intuitively, the injurer should simply replicate his optimal care choice each time that he engages in the activity. For example, the motorist should drive carefully on each trip, and the manufacturer should make each unit of output equally safe.

The second part of the problem is to choose the optimal activity level, a^*, given optimal care. This choice is shown graphically in Figure 2.7, where the optimal activity level occurs at the point of greatest vertical distance between the $B(a)$ curve and the ray representing expected accident costs, $a[x^* + p(x^*)D(x^*)]$. Equivalently, it occurs where the slopes of the two curves are equal, or where the marginal benefit of engaging in the activity equals the marginal accident costs. Note that the socially optimal activity level is less than the level that maximizes gross benefits $B(a)$ ($a^* < a_0$) because the latter does not take account of accident costs.

Now consider the injurer's choice of care and activity level under different liability rules. First note that under a rule of no liability, the injurer will choose an excessive activity level of a_0 (and also zero care) since he ignores the victim's damages. Next, consider the rules of strict liability and negligence. Recall that in the unilateral care model, both rules induce the injurer to take efficient care of x^*. Under strict liability the injurer will also choose the efficient activity level, a^*, since he fully internalizes the victim's damages. That is, his private benefits coincide with social benefits.

Under a negligence rule, however, he will not choose the efficient activity level. To see why, recall that once he meets the due standard of care, he avoids all liability for the victim's damages, though he does bear his costs of care. Thus, the injurer will choose his activity level to maximize $B(a) - ax^*$. As shown in Figure 2.7, this results in an activity level of a_N, which is too high from a social perspective (though it is not as high as under a rule of no liability). This shows that when activity levels matter, *strict liability is preferred to negligence in the unilateral care model.*

How does this conclusion extend to the bilateral care model in which victims as well as injurers can choose care and activity levels? To answer this question we first need to understand more clearly why the negligence rule induces efficient care but too much activity by the injurer. The reason is that it sets a due standard of care that allows the injurer to *avoid liability* by meeting the standard. While we have seen that this provides a powerful incentive for the injurer to comply with the standard with respect to care, it results in excessive activity precisely because the injurer does not internalize the full cost of his activity. In contrast, the injurer chooses efficient activity under strict liability because he does face full liability for the victim's damages. The general principle is that a party will choose the efficient activity level *only if he faces the residual damages from the accident.*[26] And since the liability rules we have studied impose actual damages on only one of the parties, it follows that none of them can simultaneously induce efficient activity levels by both parties.

Consider, for example, simple negligence, negligence with contributory negligence, and strict liability with contributory negligence. As we have seen, all three rules induce efficient precaution by both the injurer and the victim. Under the first two rules, victims will also choose the efficient activity level since they bear the residual liability, while injurers will choose an excessive level of activity. The reverse is true under strict liability with contributory negligence because under this rule, the injurer bears the residual liability. Since none of the rules we have studied yields the efficient outcome along all four dimensions (the choice of care and activity by the injurer and victim), the best rule depends on a comparison of overall accident costs under each of the rules.

As a final point, note that an important example of an injurer's activity level is the number of units of a dangerous product sold by the manufacturer (as distinct from the safety of each unit of the product). We will see in the next chapter that when the victims of an accident are customers of the injurer, some of the conclusions reached in this section regarding activity levels need to be altered.

3.5   Punitive Damages

To this point, our discussion has focused exclusively on *compensatory damages*, which are aimed solely at compensating victims' losses. However, in cases where the injurer's actions are seen as intentional or reckless, the court may also award *punitive damages*. As the name suggests, punitive damages are intended to punish the injurer for some perceived wrongdoing, as well as to deter future injurers from engaging in similar actions.[27] In this sense, punitive damages are similar to fines in criminal law (see Chapter 9).

The economic theory of punitive damages is based solely on the deterrence motive, that is, the desire to provide injurers with the correct incentives for care.[28] Our analysis of the accident model to this point, however, has shown that compensatory damages alone are sufficient to achieve this goal. It follows that adding punitive damages will actually result in *excessive* deterrence (too much care by injurers). What this conclusion ignores is that injurers may sometimes be able to escape liability for damages that they caused. One reason is the problem of uncertainty over causation discussed above—in some cases victims may have difficulty in identifying or proving the specific cause of their injuries. A second reason is that the cost of litigation may prevent some victims from bringing suit to collect damages.[29] Finally, injurers may sometimes take conscious steps to conceal their identity, especially when the injury was inflicted intentionally.

For these reasons, injurers may not expect to face the full damages that they cause and will therefore take too little care. Punitive damages address this problem by increasing the amount of damages injurers expect to pay in those cases where victims succeed in recovering damages. By appropriately specifying the amount of these damages, courts can restore efficient incentives for injurer care.

We illustrate this in the context of the unilateral care model with a strict liability rule. Assume that an injurer expects to face liability for only a fraction α of the damages he causes, where $\alpha < 1$. In choosing his care, we will therefore minimize

$$x + p(x)\alpha D(x). \tag{2.10}$$

Since his expected liability is less than the full damages he causes, $p(x)D(x)$, the injurer will take less than efficient care. Further, the lower is α, the lower will be his care choice. Now suppose that courts are able to award victims compensatory damages of $D(x)$ plus punitive damages of R, making the injurer's overall expected liability equal to $p(x)\alpha[D(x) + R]$. Incentives for efficient care are achieved when the injurer's expected liability equals the full expected damages of the victim, or when $p(x)\alpha[D(x) + R] = p(x)D(x)$. Solving this equation for R yields

Figure 2.8

The Level of
Punitive Damages
that Achieves
Efficient Deterrence

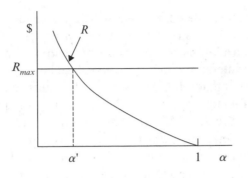

$$R = \frac{1-\alpha}{\alpha} D(x). \tag{2.11}$$

The efficient level of punitive damages is thus proportional to actual damages, where the factor of proportionality is given by $(1 - \alpha)/\alpha$. This factor is sometimes referred to as the punitive multiplier. It follows immediately from (2.11) that the amount of punitive damages is decreasing in α and equals zero when there is no risk of the injurer's escaping liability (that is, when $\alpha = 1$). Figure 2.8 graphs R as a function of α.

EXERCISE 2.3

Suppose that an injurer causes $500,000 in damages to a victim, but only faces a one-in-three chance of being found liable.

(a) Calculate the punitive multiplier.
(b) Calculate the amount of compensatory damages and the amount of punitive damages that a court should award if the victim brings suit. What is the injurer's overall liability?

How closely do courts follow the above theory in calculating actual punitive damage awards? Based on their analysis of punitive damages, Mitchell Polinsky and Steven Shavell (1998, 898–99) conclude that they do not follow it very closely. In particular, they conclude, "Courts . . . do not pay systematic attention to the probability of escaping liability, even though this is the central element in determining the appropriate damages multiplier for the purposes of achieving proper deterrence." In fact, Sunstein et al. (2000) note that punitive damage awards tend to be "erratic and arbitrary" (p. 255). They attribute this to the difficulty juries have in translating degrees of moral outrage at a defendant's behavior into a dollar scale.

Should Punitive Damages Be Capped?   Excessive punitive damage awards in high-profile tort cases often lead policymakers to propose caps on punitive damage awards. Indeed, many states have enacted such caps. The usual argument in favor of caps is that they limit incentives to file frivolous claims, thereby saving on administrative costs. Though this argument has some merit, there are two counterarguments, one theoretical and one empirical. The theoretical argument is that arbitrarily set caps on punitive damages may inhibit the deterrence function of punitive damages. For example, suppose a cap is set at R_{max} in Figure 2.8. This will have no effect on the ability of courts to achieve efficient deterrence when $R < R_{max}$, but in the range where $R > R_{max}$ (those cases where $\alpha < \alpha'$ in Figure 2.8), the cap will result in underdeterrence. Any benefits of a cap in terms of saved litigation costs must therefore be weighed against the cost of underdeterrence.

The empirical argument against caps is that punitive damages are not frequently awarded, and when they are, they are often overturned or reduced on appeal.[30] Thus, the popular perception of excessive awards, which is primarily based on a few high-profile cases, apparently is not reflective of the overall population of cases.

3.6   The Judgment Proof Problem

In some cases, defendants who are found liable have insufficient assets to pay the victim's damages. When an injurer has limited assets, we say that he is "judgment proof" (Shavell 1986). For example, a manufacturer of a dangerous product may go bankrupt before an accident occurs. The problem is that, if a potential injurer anticipates that he will be judgment proof in the future, he may take too little precaution in the present to avoid accidents. To illustrate, suppose that at the time he makes his care choice, an injurer expects to be solvent in the future with probability α and insolvent (or judgment proof) with probability $1 - \alpha$. (Equivalently, the injurer expects to have assets equal to a fraction α of the victim's expected damages.) Note that, under a rule of strict liability, the injurer's problem in this case is identical to that in (2.10); as a result, he takes too little care.

The outcome may be different under a negligence rule. In particular, if the probability of being judgment proof is not too large (that is, if α is not too small), the injurer will still find it optimal to meet the due standard and avoid *all* liability.[31] The discontinuity in injurer costs under negligence thus helps to counteract the judgment proof problem.

The fact that injurers may be able to avoid liability costs by being found judgment proof creates an incentive for firms to act strategically by, for example, divesting themselves of risky activities and locating them in small subsidiary firms, given the limited liability of assets within a corporation (Ringleb and Wiggins 1990). This may be privately profitable for the firm, but it distorts incentives for care as well as for the organizational structure of firms. As a result, if there is even a slight chance that the parent company will be held "vicariously liable" for the subsidiary's negligence, the expected costs of subcontracting may outweigh the benefits. In fact, Brooks (2002) found that oil companies actually decreased their use of independent shippers following the Exxon *Valdez* oil spill because subsequent legislation greatly increased the risk of vicarious liability.

The preceding analysis of the judgment proof problem has assumed that the injurer's asset level limited the amount he could pay in liability but not his expenditure on care. If care is also subject to this constraint (for example, if it involves a dollar investment in safety equipment), then the injurer may have an incentive to invest in *too much* care (Beard 1990). The reason for this paradoxical result is that greater spending on care before an accident reduces the injurer's asset level, which makes it more likely that he will be bankrupt (and hence shielded from liability) in the event of an accident. Thus, from the injurer's perspective, each additional dollar spent on care up front costs less than one dollar, which creates an incentive to spend more.

3.7 The Impact of Liability Insurance

Most individuals who engage in risky activities purchase liability insurance to cover, at least partially, any damages that they may cause to themselves or others. In fact, most states require drivers to purchase accident insurance before they will issue a vehicle registration. Most drivers would purchase insurance willingly, however, because they are risk averse; that is, they are willing to pay some amount of money to avoid random fluctuations in their wealth. (Recall that our analysis to this point has assumed that people are risk neutral.) The problem with insurance is that it potentially reduces the ability of tort liability to create incentives for care.[32]

In terms of incentives, insurance has a similar effect as the judgment proof problem by shielding the insured party from some or all of the damages that he or she causes. Although the injurer paid a premium to purchase the insurance in the first place, the premium is a sunk cost at the time of the care choice. Thus, insurance will cause the injurer to take too little care from a social perspective. This moral hazard problem ultimately hurts the injurer, however, because insurance companies are aware of the problem and set the premium up front to reflect the actual risk.

Insurance companies have ways of mitigating moral hazard, however. One is to condition the premium, to the extent possible, on the risk-reducing behavior of insured parties. For example, insurance companies give discounts to those who maintain a good driving record and charge more to those who buy sports cars. Another response is to offer partial coverage. Most insurance policies include deductibles requiring the insured to pay some fixed amount before the insurance kicks in. The higher the deductible, the greater is the injurer's incentive to take care, and hence the lower is the premium. (Raising the deductible is like increasing α in [2.10].) The problem, however, is that this reduces the value of insurance in reducing risk. Optimal insurance coverage thus strikes an efficient balance between risk reduction and incentives (Shavell 1979).

3.8   Litigation Costs

Our discussion of accident costs in this chapter has occasionally mentioned administrative costs as one component of overall accident costs, but we have not explicitly considered how the cost of using the courts to resolve accident claims affects the operation of the tort system. In Chapter 8 we examine how legal costs affect the manner in which parties resolve legal disputes in general (for example, whether to settle or go to trial).[33] Here we examine the prior question of how these costs affect the incentives for injurer care, which determines the number of disputes that arise in the first place.

Generally speaking, litigation costs tend to reduce incentives for injurer care (Hylton 1990; Ordover 1978). To see how, consider the simple unilateral care model with strict liability. Observe first that when litigation is costly, the *efficient* level of care is higher compared to the model with zero litigation costs. This is true because the costs of an accident now include both the damages to the victim and the litigation costs of both the injurer and the victim. Thus, the marginal benefit of care increases while the marginal cost remains the same.

In the model with litigation costs, strict liability gives inadequate incentives for injurer care for two reasons. First, litigation costs will deter some victims from filing suit. Thus, injurers will not face liability for the full amount of damages that they cause (the logic is the same as for the judgment proof problem). Second, the injurer will ignore the litigation costs incurred by those victims who do file suit.

The outcome may be better under a negligence rule. In this case, if the injurer complies with the due standard of care, victims will be deterred from filing suit because they will not expect to recover any damages at trial. Thus, the zero-litigation-cost outcome is possible because no litigation costs are actually incurred. In reality, however, some victims do file suit under negligence, either because some injurers are in fact negligent, or because the court makes errors, as discussed in the next section. If the due standard of care continues to be set by the Hand rule without concern for litigation costs, then there will be underdeterrence in this case as well because injurers will have no incentive to take more care than is necessary to avoid liability.

3.9 Legal Error*

We have assumed to this point that courts implement the negligence rule without error. This requires both correct measurement of the injurer's actual level of care and correct calculation of the due standard. In reality, however, evidentiary uncertainty will cause courts to make two types of errors in applying the negligence rule: they will sometimes find an injurer nonnegligent when he actually violated the due standard (a type I error), and they will sometimes find an injurer negligent when he complied with the due standard (a type II error). It turns out that both types of errors reduce the incentives for care under negligence (Png 1986).

To see how, let q_1 be the probability of a type I error, and let q_2 be the probability of a type II error. Consider first an injurer who takes care. Under a perfectly functioning negligence rule, he would face no liability, but with error, he faces expected liability of $q_2 D$ (where D is the victim's damage). Similarly, an injurer who does not meet the due standard would face liability of D under a perfectly functioning negligence rule, but with error he only faces expected liability of $(1 - q_1)D$. Thus, the injurer's gain from taking care (that is, his savings in liability) is given by

$$(1 - q_1)D - q_2 D = (1 - q_1 - q_2)D. \tag{2.12}$$

Note that this expression is less than the gain from taking care in the absence of error, which is D. Further, it is clear from (2.12) that an increase in either type of error reduces the gain from taking care.

3.10 The Statute of Limitations for Tort Suits

A statute of limitations sets an upper bound on the period of time following an accident during which the victim can bring a legal action for compensation. There are two sorts of benefits associated with limiting suits in this way. The first has to do with limiting legal error, which presumably increases with the length of time between the accident and the trial due to fading memories and deteriorating evidence. The second is simply the savings in litigation costs because fewer suits are permitted (Baker and Miceli 2000; Miceli 2000).

Offsetting these benefits are the costs of a limited filing period, which consist of the reduced incentives for injurer care. In particular, as the statute length is shortened, injurers expect to face fewer suits and therefore have less incentive to take care. (A shorter statute therefore has the same effect as a lower value of α in [2.10].) The optimal statute length, L^*, therefore occurs where the marginal benefit of increasing L equals the marginal cost. This is shown graphically in Figure 2.9.

Figure 2.9

The Optimal Statute of Limitations for Tort Suits

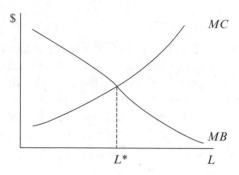

3.11   Intentional Torts

The focus of our analysis to this point has been on *accidental* harms, but there is also an area of tort law concerned with harms that are intentionally caused, such as assault and battery. In this section, we examine the economics of these so-called intentional torts.[34]

We begin by distinguishing two possible meanings of *intentional harm.* The first is harm that is the inevitable consequence of certain risky activities. In other words, the probability of harm from engaging in these activities is nearly certain, even though the activity itself is not meant to cause harm. An example is the manufacture and sale of a dangerous product like a chainsaw. The probability of harm from any single chainsaw might be relatively small, but if enough are sold, the probability approaches one.[35] The second meaning of intent is harm resulting from a single act whose primary objective is to cause an injury, like throwing a punch. In both of these cases, intent is reflected by a high probability of harm, but intuition tells us that they are different. The question is whether they should therefore be treated differently by the law.

From an economic perspective, one key difference between the two cases is that the injurer in the latter case (the one throwing the punch) is not investing in precaution to avoid an accident but is in fact making an effort to *increase* the probability of harm. Presumably he does this because he derives some benefit from inflicting the harm. Although one might claim that the chainsaw manufacturer is also deriving benefit from selling a product that it knows to be dangerous, the fundamental difference is that it is socially desirable for the manufacturer to invest in a positive amount of accident avoidance, whereas it is optimal for the puncher to invest zero effort to cause harm (assuming that the harm to the victim exceeds the benefit to the injurer).

Despite this difference, strict liability for compensatory damages would seem to achieve the proper level of deterrence in both cases since it forces injurers to internalize the full costs of their actions. In fact, punitive damages are probably called for in the second case for at least two reasons. First, intent to inflict harm implies forethought on the part of the injurer with the likely consequence that he will seek to avoid responsibility. (This is a second key difference between the two notions of intent described above.) As we have seen, when the probability of detection is less than one, punitive damages are needed to achieve optimal deterrence.[36]

Second, in some cases the benefit to the injurer of inflicting harm may exceed the cost to the victim, but the benefit is not socially valuable. Examples are acts of violence like rape and murder. In these cases, compensatory damages are insufficient to deter the injurer, so some additional sanction is needed. This example, combined with our discussion of the judgment proof problem above, also suggests why intentional torts are sometimes classified as crimes. If the injurer has insufficient wealth to pay damages, then the threat of imprisonment can provide the only deterrent. In Chapter 9 we provide further economic reasons for the use of criminal law, as opposed to (or in addition to) tort law, for the control of certain harmful acts.

3.12 Valuing Human Life and Safety

We conclude this introductory chapter on tort law with a few words on the problem of measuring damages. As we have noted, one of the functions of tort law is to compensate victims for their losses. This is straightforward when the damages are to property, which has a market-determined value, but it is more difficult in the case of personal injury or death. Since compensation necessarily takes the form of monetary damages, however, the court must place a dollar value on a victim's injuries or loss of life. Typically, courts seek to provide compensation for financial losses as well as for nonmonetary factors such as pain and suffering.[37]

Financial losses are ordinarily based on the present value of lost earnings of the victim, plus medical expenses (if any). In computing lost earnings, one takes account of the victim's educational attainment, life expectancy, fringe benefits, and the like, as well as the amount they would have spent on their own consumption plus the taxes they would have owed on their earnings (if the award itself is not taxed). The job of calculating this amount usually falls to an economist acting as an expert witness for the plaintiff.

Courts also award monetary damages for pain and suffering, though here the calculation is more subjective (and hence more controversial). A key factor in determining the amount of pain and suffering is the impact that the accident has on the victim's loved ones. The greater their perceived loss, the larger the award. Another rationale for awarding pain and suffering is to serve as an additional deterrent when compensation for lost earnings seems inadequate, such as when the victim dies or when the victim's losses are not highly valued by the market. Finally, pain and suffering may be appropriate when the injurer's actions were intentional. In this sense, pain and suffering and punitive damage awards serve similar economic functions.

The lost-earnings approach to valuing personal injury is practical, but it most likely underestimates total costs. For example, it ignores the value of leisure. Another approach is to survey people to find out how much they are willing to pay to avoid certain risks. Such "contingent valuation" surveys are useful when market information is lacking—thus, they are often used in valuing environmental damage, like loss of an endangered species. An interesting issue that arises out of surveys is the gap between willingness-to-pay (WP) and willingness-to-accept (WA) measures of value. It turns out that most people require more compensation to take on an increase in risk (WA) than they will pay to reduce risk by the same amount (WP) (Kahneman et al. 2000).

There is, however, a potentially more reliable way than surveys to get information about how people value risks to themselves—namely, wage premiums for risky occupations. Specifically, how much more do workers need to receive to work as, say, miners compared to safer jobs? The resulting measure, referred to as "hedonic damages," reflects the willingness-to-accept measure of risk. Although such studies are useful, they too are subject to bias. First, they only reflect people's valuation of small risks and cannot reliably be extrapolated to obtain a measure of the value of life. (For example, if a worker accepts a wage premium of $100 in return for a 1/10,000 risk of death, does that mean that he values his life at $1 million?) Second, people who accept risky jobs are ordinarily those who incur the lowest cost from the risk, or who may actually receive a benefit from it (for example, firemen and policemen). This will bias the risk-premium downward. Finally, as we will argue in the next chapter, people often misperceive risk, thereby distorting the ability of the market to adequately compensate workers for it. For these reasons, courts generally look skeptically on hedonic damage measures.

4   Conclusion

This chapter laid out the basic economic theory of tort law. At the center of the theory is the model of precaution, which prescribes that injurers and victims should invest in accident-reducing activities up to the point where the last dollar spent on care equals the marginal savings in accident costs. The role of the law is to provide incentives in the form of liability rules for the parties to meet this standard. We argued that the law of negligence, as embodied by the Hand test, conforms well to this ideal.

We also examined several factors that complicate the simple model. We first considered causation, which plays a prominent role in the law but fits somewhat uneasily into the economic model. We nevertheless proposed several economic explanations for the practical importance of causation. In addition, we showed that activity levels can have a significant effect on the risk of accidents but are not handled well by negligence rules.

Finally, we considered several departures of real-world accidents from the simple model—including legal error, injurer bankruptcy, the availability of liability insurance, and litigation costs—all of which tend to reduce the efficiency of the tort system. We will encounter several of these problems again in the next chapter in the course of applying the economic model to specific areas of tort law.

DISCUSSION QUESTIONS

1. We have argued in this chapter that the primary economic function of tort law is to deter unreasonably dangerous behavior, but a second function is to provide social insurance against accidental harm. In what ways are these objectives compatible, and in what ways are they incompatible?

2. Suppose that an accident has occurred. Which of the following does the victim *not* have to prove in order to recover damages under tort law: (1) that she sustained some harm; (2) that the injurer's actions were cause-in-fact of the harm; (3) that the injurer's actions were proximate cause of the harm; (4) that the injurer intentionally caused the harm?

3. State whether a rule of strict liability or negligence is preferred in each of the following situations:

    (a) The court makes errors in measuring the level of damages from an accident.
    (b) The court makes errors in measuring the injurer's care level.
    (c) The victim's care is an important determinant of accident risk.
    (d) The injurer's activity level is an important determinant of accident risk.

4. (a) Describe the test courts use to determine cause-in-fact.
    (b) Suppose that a train traveling at 35 mph collides with a car that was stalled at a crossing and injures the driver. The court determines that trains traveling faster than 25 mph are negligent, but it also determines that even if the train in question had been traveling at this slower speed, it could not have avoided hitting the car. Would the train's negligence be found cause-in-fact of the accident? Explain why or why not.

5. What is the economic rationale for a statute of limitations for tort suits? Based on this rationale, explain why it makes sense that there is no statute of limitations for serious crimes like murder.

PROBLEMS

1. Consider a unilateral care accident model in which the injurer can either take care at a cost of $50, or take no care. Further, suppose that if he takes care, there is zero risk of an accident, but if he does not take care, the risk is 0.1. Finally, suppose the victim's damages in the event of an accident are $750.

   (a) Use the Hand rule to determine if care is efficient in this case.

   (b) Suppose the victim cannot observe the injurer's care choice and therefore would be unable to prove negligence in the event of an accident. Would it be appropriate for the court to invoke the doctrine of *res ipsa loquitur* in this case? Explain why or why not.

2. A train passing a farmer's property emits sparks that sometimes set fire to the farmer's crops. The crop damage can be reduced, however, if the railroad installs spark arresters on its trains, if the farmer moves his crops, or both. The following table summarizes the cost of the various possible actions, and the crop damage (if any):

Action	Crop damage ($)	Farmer's cost ($)	RR's cost ($)
No action	150	0	0
Farmer moves crops	90	15	0
RR installs arresters	40	0	50
Farmer moves crops and RR installs arresters	0	15	50

   (a) Which action yields the socially optimal outcome?

   (b) What action will result under a rule of no liability? (Assume here and in subsequent questions that bargaining costs between the RR and farmer are high.)

   (c) What action will result under a rule of strict liability?

   (d) What action will result under a negligence rule where the due standard of care for the RR is to install arresters?

3. Consider the owner of a large tract of undeveloped land that is suitable for recreational use by campers, bikers, hikers, and so on. If the land is left open, users will enter and enjoy a benefit of $3,000, but they may suffer accidents. Specifically, if users enter and take no care, they will suffer expected damages of $2,000, whereas if they enter and take care of $200, they will suffer expected damages of $500. The owner of the land cannot take care to reduce the risk of accidents, but he can fence in the land at a cost of $1,000, which prevents entry altogether.

   (a) Calculate the net benefit from each of the following options: (1) owner fences land; (2) owner does not fence land, users enter and take no care;

(3) owner does not fence land, users enter and take care. Which is most efficient?

(b) Many states have passed laws that immunize owners of undeveloped land from liability if they open the land for recreational use. What outcome in (a) will result under this rule?

4. The case of *New York Cent. R. Co. v. Thompson* (21 N.E.2d 625, 1939) concerned a woman who accidentally caught her foot in some railroad tracks and was injured when a train failed to brake in time and struck her. Suppose the liability rule is negligence with a defense of contributory negligence.

   (a) Will the woman be able to recover her damages if the court determines that she was negligent for walking on the tracks?

   (b) Under what doctrine will the woman be able to recover, despite her negligence, if the court determines that the train saw her predicament and had time to brake but did not? Explain the economic rationale for this doctrine.

5. Suppose that an injurer escapes liability in three out of four accidents that he causes. Let the average damages per accident be $100,000 and assume the liability rule is strict liability.

   (a) In order for the injurer to face the correct incentives to take care, what should his total damages be in each case where he is held liable?

   (b) What portion of total damages is compensatory and what portion is punitive?

CHAPTER 3

APPLYING THE ECONOMIC MODEL OF TORT LAW

The preceding chapter focused on general principles of accident law that apply to a broad range of accident settings. In this chapter we apply these principles to several specific areas of tort law. We begin with products liability, or accidents caused by dangerous products. We devote the most attention to this topic, both because it has become an important area of tort law and the source of much dissatisfaction with the operation of the tort system, but also because it raises some new conceptual issues for the economic theory of accident law, the primary one being the distinction between accidents involving "strangers" and accidents involving parties to a contract. Following our discussion of products liability, we examine (in a more cursory fashion) workplace accidents, environmental hazards, and medical malpractice.

1 Products Liability

The number of products liability suits increased markedly during the decades of the 1980s and 1990s. To get an idea of the numbers involved, look at Table 3.1, which shows the number of products liability cases filed in U.S. district courts from 1980 to 2005. Despite some fluctuations during the 1990s, the trend is predominantly upward, even when measured as a percentage of all civil cases filed during this period (see Figure 3.1).[1] One result has been an increase in the price of certain consumer products, another the withdrawal of some from the market altogether. These trends have led to a number of proposals for tort reform, some of which we discussed in the preceding chapter (for example, the call for a cap on punitive damage awards).

TABLE **3.1**   **Data on Products Liability Cases Filed in U.S. District Courts, 1980–2005**

Year	Total cases filed	Cases as a % of all civil cases
1980	6,876	4.07
1981	8,028	4.45
1982	7,908	3.84
1983	8,026	3.32
1984	7,677	2.94
1985	12,507	4.57
1986	12,459	4.89
1987	14,145	5.92
1988	16,166	6.75
1989	13,408	5.74
1990	18,679	8.57
1991	12,399	5.97
1992	10,769	4.75
1993	16,545	7.24
1994	23,977	10.16
1995	17,631	7.38
1996	38,170	14.00
1997	23,294	8.79
1998	28,325	10.84
1999	17,196	6.84
2000	15,349	5.84
2001	12,569	4.96
2002	35,074	13.08
2003	24,255	9.53
2004	29,089	11.27
2005	35,615	12.60

SOURCE: *Viscusi (1991, Tables 2.1, 2.2); Statistical Abstract, various years.*

We begin our discussion of product-related accidents in this chapter by briefly reviewing the history of products liability law in the United States. We then extend the model from the previous chapter to show the impact of the market relationship between the injurer and the victim. Our objective is to explain the historical trends in terms of the economic model and to evaluate the current status of the law.

1.1   A Brief History of Products Liability Law

In contrast to the modern image of products liability law as protecting defenseless consumers against manufacturers of dangerous products, the law in the nineteenth century was based on the belief that excessive producer liability would burden society with high administrative costs and threaten the economic viability of business.[2] The past 150 years, however, have witnessed a gradual evolution in the law in the direction of greater producer liability. This has occurred in several distinct phases.

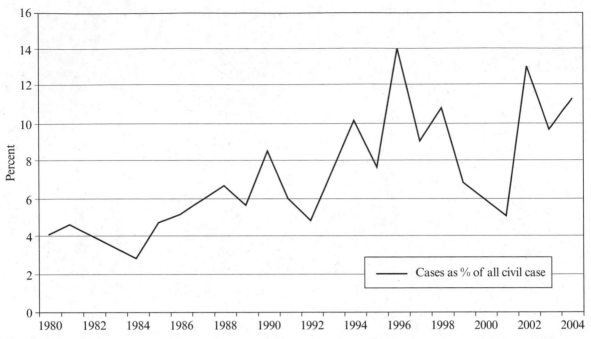

Figure 3.1

Products Liability Cases as a Percentage of All Civil Cases Filed in U.S. District Courts, 1980–2004

The first phase began in the mid-nineteenth century with the birth of the doctrine of "privity," which held that in the event of a product-related accident, the purchaser only had a cause of action against the immediate seller of the product—that is, the party with whom he had a direct contractual relationship.[3] For example, if an automobile accident occurred as a result of negligence on the part of the manufacturer, the victim could only seek recovery from the retailer.

Under privity, the allocation of risk from product-related accidents largely relied on contract rather than tort principles. Although we will see below that the chain of contractual relationships leading from the manufacturer to the ultimate consumer can theoretically serve to shift liability from immediate sellers back to the manufacturer, in reality this shifting occurs imperfectly. Thus, the doctrine of privity effectively insulated most manufacturers from liability.

The privity limitation nevertheless endured through the end of the nineteenth century until it was finally overturned in 1916 in the famous case of *MacPherson v. Buick* (217 N.Y. 382, 111 N.E. 1050, 1916). The case involved an accident that occurred when one of the wheels on the plaintiff's car broke off, causing him to be thrown from the car. Since the plaintiff had bought the car from a dealer, the doctrine of privity apparently barred the plaintiff from recovering against the manufacturer. Judge Benjamin Cardozo rejected this position, however, based on the argument that the manufacturer could clearly have foreseen the possibility of injuries to individuals other than the immediate purchaser of the car (in this case, the dealer). This did not automatically imply liability on the part of the manufacturer, however. The victim also had to prove negligence by the manufacturer (which he succeeded in doing in *MacPherson*). Nevertheless, the transition from no liability to negligence had occurred, thereby significantly expanding the scope of producer liability.

The next phase in the evolution of products liability law, which witnessed the transition from negligence to strict liability, occurred by two separate routes. The first was the result of a gradual increase in the standard of care owed by product manufacturers and sellers. A key case in this development was *Escola v. Coca-Cola Bottling Co.* (24 Cal.2d 453, 150 P.2d 436, 1944), which concerned an injury caused by an exploding Coke bottle. Although the plaintiff, who was a waitress in a restaurant, could offer no evidence of negligence on the part of the manufacturer, the court held the manufacturer liable based on the doctrine of *res ipsa loquitur.* Recall that under this doctrine, the fact of the accident itself is evidence of negligence—only a defective Coke bottle would explode. As noted in the previous chapter, the application of *res ipsa loquitur* in cases where due care does not entirely eliminate the risk of accidents amounts to a rule of strict liability.

The second route to strict liability occurred in the area of producer liability for breach of warranty. Under the theory of warranties, a branch of contract law, sellers were strictly liable for damages caused by products that failed to function as represented—considerations of negligence were irrelevant. However, the requirement of privity remained for these cases because warranties (implied or expressed) are a form of contract.

This changed with the 1960 case of *Henningsen v. Bloomfield Motors, Inc.* (32 N.J. 358, 161 A.2d 69, 1960). The case also concerned an automobile accident, this time caused by a failure of the steering mechanism. The new element of this case was that the sales contract between the plaintiff's husband and the manufacturer included a clause that expressly limited the latter's liability to the original purchaser and for only certain types of damages. The court rejected this type of contractual limitation, however, arguing that the implied warranty of fitness prevailed regardless of any expressed intentions of the parties to the contrary. Further, the court struck down the privity requirement, noting that, although the victim was not the purchaser, she was someone who "in the reasonable contemplation of the parties to the warranty, might be expected to become a user of the automobile. Accordingly, her lack of privity does not stand in the way of prosecution of the injury suit against the defendant Chrysler."

With the *Henningsen* decision, the tort and contract theories of products

liability had converged on a strict liability standard. This was explicitly recognized with the publication of the Restatement (Second) of Torts in 1965,
Section 402A of which says:

(1) One who sells any product in a defective condition unreasonably
dangerous to the user or consumer or to his property is subject to
liability for physical harm thereby caused to the ultimate user or
consumer, or to his property, if

(a) the seller is engaged in the business of selling such a product, and

(b) it is expected to and does reach the user or consumer without
substantial change in the condition in which it is sold.

(2) The rule stated in Subsection (1) applies although

(a) the seller has exercised all possible care in the preparation and
sale of the product, and

(b) the user or consumer has not bought the product from or entered
into any contractual relation with the seller.

Note that part (2)(a) excludes consideration of producer care (hence, liability
is strict), while part (2)(b) eliminates privity.

To say that liability is strict, however, is somewhat misleading because, in
addition to causation, plaintiffs must show that the product had a *defective
design*, or, if it is *inherently dangerous* (like cigarettes or dynamite), that
the manufacturer failed to warn consumers of the danger. Thus, there is an
element of negligence in strict products liability because manufacturers can
avoid liability by meeting the design standard or the duty to warn. Recent
trends, however, have made it harder to meet these standards. With the foregoing history as background, in the next section we develop a formal model
of products liability with the objective of explaining the broad trend in the law
toward strict producer liability. The crucial extension in the accident model
from the previous chapter will be to explicitly account for the contractual
relationship between the injurer (producer) and the victim (buyer).[4]

1.2   An Economic Model of Products Liability

We develop our analysis of product-related accidents in the context of a
simple model of perfect competition.[5] As a benchmark, we first consider a
product for which there is no risk of an accident. Let the aggregate inverse
demand curve for the "safe" product be given by $b(q)$, which represents the
amount consumers are willing to pay for a unit of the good as a function of the
number of units purchased, q. A downward-sloping demand curve (reflecting
diminishing marginal benefits) implies that $b(q)$ is decreasing in q, as shown
in Figure 3.2.

Figure 3.2

Equilibrium Output
and Price for a Safe
Product

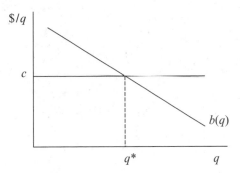

On the supply side, we assume, for simplicity, that marginal and average costs are constant and equal to c.[6] Thus, the supply curve is horizontal at c. Equilibrium output for the safe product occurs at the point where demand equals supply, or at q^* in Figure 3.2, while the equilibrium price is equal to the constant marginal cost, c. Algebraically, equilibrium output is defined by the equation $b(q^*) = c$.

1.2.1   Equilibrium Price and Output for a Dangerous Product

Now consider a product for which there is a risk of injury to the consumer, but which is identical to the safe product in all other respects. Assume that each unit of the product carries the same probability of an accident, p, and the same damages in the event of an accident, D. Thus, total expected damages are qpD (for now we suppress considerations of care, or the safety of the product). Note that this specification mirrors our discussion of activity levels in Chapter 2, where we assumed that expected damages were proportional to the injurer's (or victim's) activity level.

The existence of accident risk may affect either the demand or the supply sides of the market (or both), depending on how the law assigns liability between the manufacturer and the consumer. For purposes of the current discussion, we represent the liability rule as follows. Let s represent the share of accident costs borne by the manufacturer and $1 - s$ the share borne by the consumer, where s is between zero and one. Note that all of the rules from Chapter 2 emerge as special cases of this general formulation. For example, $s = 1$ corresponds to strict liability, $s = 0$ corresponds to no liability (also known as caveat emptor, or "buyer beware"), and conditioning s on the injurer's and/or the victim's care level can yield the various negligence rules.

Consider first the impact of the accident risk on the demand side of the market. In comparison to the safe product, we would expect consumers to reduce their willingness to pay for a unit of a risky product by exactly the amount of their expected accident losses. Thus, if consumers will pay $b(q)$ for a unit of the safe product, they will pay $b(q) - (1 - s)pD$ for a unit of the risky product, where $(1 - s)pD$ is the uncompensated portion of their expected

Figure 3.3

Equilibrium Output
and Price for a
Dangerous Product
Under Different
Liability Rules

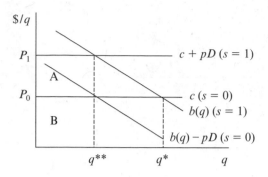

damages. This has the effect of shifting the demand curve down relative to that in Figure 3.2. This is illustrated in Figure 3.3 for the cases of strict liability ($s = 1$) and no liability ($s = 0$). Note that the demand curve for the risky product is equivalent to that for a safe product when the rule is strict liability because the consumer expects to be fully compensated in the event of an accident, but the curve shifts down by the full expected damages under a rule of no liability because the consumer expects to receive no compensation.

Now consider the impact of accident risk on the supply side. The marginal cost, or supply curve in this case, will equal marginal production costs plus expected liability per unit of output, or $c + spD$. Thus, under a rule of no liability ($s = 0$), the supply curve corresponds to that for the safe product, but under strict liability ($s = 1$), the supply curve shifts up by the full amount of expected damages. These two curves are also shown in Figure 3.3.

As before, equilibrium output and price are determined by the intersection of the relevant demand and supply curves. Figure 3.3 shows the equilibrium under strict liability and no liability. The first thing to note about these two equilibria is that *they result in the same level of output, q*** (which is less than the equilibrium output of the safe product, q^*). This is not a coincidence. In fact the result can be stated more generally: *equilibrium output in the model with accident risk is independent of the liability rule.* To prove this general result, equate the algebraic expressions for demand and supply to get

$$b(q) - (1 - s)pD = c + spD. \tag{3.1}$$

But note that terms multiplied by s on the left- and right-hand sides cancel, leaving the condition for equilibrium output:

$$b(q^{**}) = c + pD, \tag{3.2}$$

which is independent of s. Thus, no matter how the law assigns liability for accidents, equilibrium output occurs at the point where marginal consumption benefits for the good ($b[q]$) equals the *total* marginal costs, $c + pD$, which is the sum of marginal production and accident costs.

To see the intuition for this result, we first need to determine the equilibrium price. Note in Figure 3.3 that, unlike output, price is *not* independent of the liability rule. In particular, under strict liability ($s = 1$), the price is given by $P_1 = c + pD$, the full marginal costs (including expected accident costs), whereas under no liability ($s = 0$), the price is $P_0 = c$, or simply marginal production costs. The difference reflects the fact that, under strict liability, the manufacturer is selling the consumer the product *bundled with an insurance policy for the associated accident risk.* Thus, the price reflects the marginal production costs (c) plus the expected damages (pD), where the latter in effect acts like an actuarially fair insurance premium. In Figure 3.3, the insurance component of the price is therefore the difference between P_1 and P_0, while area A is the aggregate expected damages that the manufacturer expects to pay out. Algebraically, area A is given by the insurance premium, pD, multiplied by the aggregate output, q^{**}.

In contrast, when the rule is no liability (caveat emptor), the price simply reflects the marginal production costs because the manufacturer faces no liability in the event of an accident. Area B thus equals aggregate production costs. Consumers nevertheless must still pay for the expected damages, but now they expect to pay it out of their own pockets when an accident occurs. This is what causes the demand curve to shift down when $s = 0$, with the result that the equilibrium output remains at q^{**}. Although consumers cannot look to manufacturers to insure them against product risk in this case, most will have purchased some form of health insurance that will cover any damages due to product-related accidents. The discounted price for the product provides funds that can be used to purchase this insurance.

Alternatively, consumers can "self-insure" by setting aside an amount pD for every unit of the dangerous product that they purchase. Over the long run, this will provide exactly enough money to compensate them for their losses (again, area A in Figure 3.3). The problem with this approach is that if the first unit purchased results in an accident, the consumer will not have had time to accumulate enough resources. This is one important reason why consumers are better off purchasing market insurance rather than self-insuring. Firms, especially small ones, are susceptible to this same problem, so under a rule of strict liability they too usually purchase market insurance to cover their expected tort liability.

As an illustration of the preceding analysis, note that the availability of service contracts to cover the repair or maintenance costs of many durable goods represents a contractual analog to strict liability for product-related accidents. The key difference, however, is that when the law imposes strict products liability, consumers do not have the option to refuse coverage in return for a lower price.

EXERCISE 3.1

Let the aggregate inverse demand curve for a dangerous product be given by $b(q) = 20 - q$. Also, let

$c = \$5$

$p = .01$

$D = \$1,000.$

Derive the equilibrium output and price for the product under a rule of no liability ($s = 0$) and under a rule of strict liability ($s = 1$).

The discussion of products liability to this point, and in particular the fact that equilibrium output does not depend on the liability rule, represents an example of the Coase Theorem, discussed in Chapter 1. Recall that the Coase Theorem says that when parties to a legal dispute can bargain at low cost, they will allocate resources efficiently regardless of the particular assignment of liability. As Figure 3.3 and equation (3.2) show, the equilibrium level of output for a dangerous product occurs at the point where marginal consumption benefits equal total marginal costs, regardless of the liability rule. Output is thus invariant to the assignment of liability. The reason for this is the shifting of liability by means of the price.

As we will see below, however, when the price mechanism fails to function perfectly, the requirements for the Coase Theorem are no longer satisfied, and the liability rule will matter for efficiency. This was the case in the model of accidents between "strangers" in the previous chapter. "Strangers" in this sense means parties who had no contractual or market relationship prior to the accident. As a result, they had no opportunity to bargain over the allocation of liability, or at least the cost of doing so was prohibitively high. (When you get into your car, imagine the prospect of having to identify and bargain with all the motorists or pedestrians with whom you might have an accident.) In that case, the liability rule was crucial in determining the allocation of resources. Indeed, recall that our discussion of activity levels in the previous chapter ended with the conclusion that, for accidents between strangers, none of the standard liability rules could achieve efficiency of care and activity levels by both injurers and victims.

1.2.2 Care Choices by Manufacturers and Consumers

In focusing on equilibrium output, we have to this point ignored the care choices of the manufacturer and consumers. The question in this context is whether the irrelevance of the liability rule extends to care as well. In theory, the answer is yes, again as a result of the Coase Theorem. To see why, suppose initially that the rule is no liability. In the model of accidents between strangers, we saw that victims will take efficient care under this rule, but injurers will take no care. In the product model, however, suppose that the manufacturer and consumer can strike a bargain whereby the manufacturer agrees to produce a safe product in return for a higher price to reflect the extra cost.[7] If this bargaining exhausts all gains from trade, then the manufacturer will invest in safety to the point where the marginal reduction in accident risk just equals the marginal cost — in other words, he will invest in the efficient safety level.

A similar story holds for strict liability. Under this rule, the problem with the stranger model was too little victim care. To remedy this inefficiency, the necessary bargain would entail a promise by the consumer to use the product carefully in return for a price reduction by the manufacturer. Again, if the bargain exhausts all gains from trade, it will yield the efficiency level of victim care.

The preceding shows that the Coase Theorem holds for care as well as output, assuming that the market mechanism functions perfectly. In assessing whether these bargains will actually occur, however, the reader may have perceived an asymmetry in the two cases. Under no liability, the consumer will pay the higher price provided that she perceives that the product is indeed safer. In many cases, this will merely require careful inspection of the product prior to purchase. (In other cases, the increased safety will have to be taken on faith or may be misperceived, as discussed below.)

In contrast, the bargain under strict liability requires that the consumer must honor her promise to use the product carefully *after she has paid the lower price and taken possession.* Given the cost of care, this creates a situation in which the consumer may renege on her promise with little if any chance of detection by the producer. As a result, the producer is unlikely to be willing to engage in the proposed bargain in the first place. Such a "market failure" undermines the Coase Theorem in this case.

The preceding discussion suggests that a pure strict liability rule will probably not achieve efficiency regarding consumer care. That still leaves several candidates for a fully efficient rule, including no liability, the various negligence rules, and strict liability with contributory negligence. It turns out, however, that we can significantly narrow the list by considering another possible source of market failure — consumer misperceptions of risk.

1.2.3   Consumer Perceptions of Risk

Our discussion of the economic model of accidents, whether involving strangers or market participants, has assumed that the parties correctly estimate the risk of an accident. In fact, individuals tend to *misperceive* risk in a systematic way. Specifically, there is evidence that people tend to underestimate the probability that bad events (like a product-related accident) will happen to them. The apparent explanation for this "unrealistic optimism" is that it is adaptive; that is, expecting a favorable outcome increases the chance that such an outcome will occur (Jolls 2000, 292).

At the same time, people also sometimes overestimate risks. In particular, Jolls (2000) notes that they overestimate the probability of "highly visible" risks (for example, those that receive a lot of media attention, like a toxic waste spill), while Viscusi (1991, 64) suggests that they overestimate low-probability events (like being struck by lightning). Whatever the direction, we will see that misperception of risk has an important effect on our conclusions about the efficiency of the various liability rules (Spence 1977; Polinsky and Rogerson 1983).

To begin the analysis, we initially ignore care and focus on the determination of equilibrium output. Suppose that consumers potentially misperceive the probability of an accident, viewing it to be αp rather than p, where $\alpha > 1$ represents an overestimate, and $\alpha < 1$ represents an underestimate. Assume, however, that producers perceive p correctly, reflecting the superior knowledge they have about their product's risk, and assume that both consumers and producers correctly estimate the damages from an accident, D.

In this setting, the demand curve for an arbitrary legal rule becomes $b(q) - (1 - s)\alpha pD$, while the supply curve remains the same as before, $c + spD$. Equating these expressions yields the condition defining equilibrium output:

$$b(q) - (1 - s)\alpha pD = c + spD. \tag{3.3}$$

Note first that when $\alpha = 1$, (3.3) is identical to (3.1)—this is the case of no misperceptions where output is independent of the liability rule. However, when $\alpha \neq 1$, (3.3) and (3.1) will differ for any liability rule other than strict liability (that is, for any $s < 1$), meaning that equilibrium output in these cases will depart from the efficient level of output, q^{**}, depending on the specific liability rule and the nature of consumers' perceptions.

To illustrate, suppose that the rule is no liability ($s = 0$), which corresponds to the lower pair of supply and demand curves in Figure 3.3. Setting $s = 0$ in (3.3) yields

$$b(q) - \alpha pD = c. \tag{3.4}$$

If consumers overestimate risk, $\alpha > 1$, and the demand curve is below that in Figure 3.3. As a result, output is too low—consumers demand too little of the product. In contrast, if consumers underestimate risk, $\alpha < 1$, and the demand curve is above that in Figure 3.3. Output in this case is too high. This conclusion generalizes to the case of any $s < 1$; so long as consumers expect to bear some of their own losses, misperceptions will affect output in the directions just described, though the extent of the inefficiency decreases as s approaches one.

EXERCISE 3.2

Reconsider the example from Exercise 3.1, but now suppose that consumers misperceive risk. Assume that the rule is no liability ($s = 0$).

(a) Calculate the equilibrium output when consumers overestimate the risk to be .012 (rather than its true value of .01).

(b) Calculate the equilibrium output when consumers underestimate the risk to be .008.

The conclusion is different when the producer is strictly liable. In that case, we have seen that (3.3) reduces to (3.1) and output is efficient for any α. Misperceptions have no effect on output in this case because the consumer internalizes the expected damages through the market price, which accurately reflects the risk, given our assumption that producers have no misperceptions.

What this discussion shows is that when consumers misperceive risk, the liability rule matters for efficiency of the output level. The general conclusion is that *the party who more accurately perceives the risk should bear the liability in equilibrium*. This argument supports the historical trend toward strict liability in conjunction with the increasing complexity of most consumer products.

We now reintroduce care into the analysis. We saw above that strict liability induces efficient producer care but will not provide incentives for consumer care due to the high cost of enforcing contracts conditioned on consumer use of the product. Incentives for consumer care can be restored, however, by including a contributory negligence defense as discussed in the previous chapter.

1.2.4 A Note on Custom as a Defense

If a particular safety feature becomes widespread in an industry, it may achieve the status of "custom." The existence of industry custom provides a potential standard for applying a negligence rule in products liability cases.[8] For example, showing a manufacturer's failure to adhere to industry customs is an easy way for consumers to prove negligence, and courts have historically accepted such arguments. The question, however, is whether adherence to custom should be accepted as evidence that the manufacturer is *not* negligent.

The most famous custom case, *The T.J. Hooper* (60 F.2d 737, 2d. Cir. 1932) explicitly addressed this question. (Interestingly, the opinion was written by Judge Learned Hand of the *Carroll Towing* case.) The case concerned a tugboat that lost its barge and cargo during a coastal storm because it did not have a radio by which the captain could have been warned. The owner of the barge sued claiming negligence, but the tug owner argued that it was not customary for tugs to have radios, and hence his failure to have one was not negligence. Judge Hand rejected this argument, stating that

> in most cases reasonable prudence is in fact common prudence; but strictly it is never its measure; a whole calling may have unduly lagged in the adoption of new and available devices. It may never set its own tests, however persuasive be its uses. Courts must in the end say what is required; there are precautions so imperative that even their universal disregard will not excuse their use.

Judge Hand thus argued that cost-benefit principles trump custom in determining negligence. But why would market forces not compel an industry to adopt all cost-justified safety measures? (That is, why wouldn't the Hand test and custom arrive at the same solution?) The answer again may be consumer misperceptions of risk, which limit the ability of the market to enforce efficient safety standards. For this reason, custom is properly rejected by courts as a defense in products liability cases. (See the further discussion of this issue in the context of medical malpractice in Section 4.1 below.)

1.2.5   Recent Trends

Our conclusion to this point is that strict liability with contributory negligence is the most efficient liability rule for product-related accidents. Strict liability provides incentives for manufacturers to produce safe products and ensures that the market price accurately reflects the residual risk to consumers, while the contributory negligence defense gives consumers an incentive to use the product properly.

The general trend in the law toward strict liability during the first half of the twentieth century seems consistent with this conclusion. However, recent developments in the law appear to be stripping producers of some defenses against liability while holding them liable for some risks that were unforeseen or unknowable at the time of manufacture of the product. (An example is the risk from asbestos—see Section 3.3 below.) Some commentators refer to this emerging standard as "absolute" or "enterprise" liability. While this trend may be consistent with the view that the primary role of products liability is to compensate victims of product-related accidents, the economic model suggests that the result could be a reduction in efficiency for those products where consumer misuse is an important determinant of risk (Priest 1988).

1.2.6   Evidence on the Impact of Products Liability Laws

Most economic analysis of products liability is theoretical, but a couple of studies have examined the effect of products liability laws on prices. For example, in a study of the market for childhood vaccines, Manning (1994) found that wholesale prices for several vaccines have increased dramatically in the past few decades as a result of increasing producer liability. Further, a substantial portion of this increase has been due to litigation costs. Manning (1997) similarly found a liability premium in the cost of prescription drugs in the United States as compared to Canada, reflecting the significantly higher liability costs in this country. Although these studies confirm the prediction of a higher product price in response to greater producer liability, they cannot tell us whether consumers have received their money's worth in terms of safer products, and/or more efficient insurance against risk.

1.3   Concluding Remarks

We conclude the discussion of products liability by emphasizing the reasons why contract law is not an adequate remedy for most product-related accidents. Although the injurer and victim have a contractual relationship, which we have seen can fully internalize the accident risks, we have also seen that various sources of market failure can inhibit this mechanism from functioning perfectly. These include consumer misperceptions of product risk and the inability of producers to monitor consumer use of the product. Two further reasons are, first, the cost of writing contracts in the presence of remote risks, which, as Landes and Posner (1987, 281) observe, "may well be disproportionate to the benefit of a negotiated (as distinct from imposed-by-law) level of safety"; and second, imperfections in the insurance market, which may prevent consumers from acquiring adequate protection against product risks.

These conclusions illustrate the general principle, asserted in Chapter 1, regarding the role of the law in internalizing costs. In particular, when bargaining between the concerned parties can occur smoothly, the specific legal rules do not matter for efficiency—the primary role of the law is to enforce whatever contracts the parties write. This is the insight of the Coase Theorem. However, when bargaining fails, the law needs to be more interventionist in assigning liability. According to economic theory, this is where contract law needs to give way to tort law. The history of products liability law in the twentieth century seems to provide an example of this transition, though some would argue that recent developments have caused it to overshoot the mark.

2   Workplace Accidents

This section deals with accidents in the workplace, including accidents in which workers are injured on the job as a result of unsafe working conditions or negligence by a fellow worker, as well as accidents in which a worker causes an injury to a nonworker (a stranger) in the course of his or her employment. Many of the issues raised by the first type of accident—those in which the victim is a worker and the injurer is the employer or another employee—have already been discussed in our analysis of products liability. For example, in a perfectly functioning labor market, the wage will adjust to reflect the legal assignment of liability between the parties. Thus, contract rather than tort law principles can, in principle, govern these accidents, though market failures of the sort discussed above may again interfere with the attainment of an efficient outcome. In contrast, accidents involving a worker and a non-employee raise many of the same issues discussed in Chapter 2 in the model of accidents between strangers. The emphasis in this section will therefore be on unique aspects of the law governing workplace accidents.

2.1   Respondeat Superior

Under the doctrine of respondeat superior, an employer is strictly liable for accidents caused by his employees' negligence when committed in the course of their employment.[9] One possible rationale for this rule is that employees will often lack the resources necessary to compensate victims' losses (that is, they will be judgment proof). The law therefore allows victims to reach into the "deep pockets" of their employers. While this "vicarious liability" of employers makes sense regarding the compensation function of tort law, it may be an impediment to efficient accident avoidance since it insulates the injurer from responsibility for damages.

It is possible, however, that the employer can use his contractual relationship with the employee to give the latter an incentive to be careful. For example, the employer can supervise employees and threaten to fire those who perform their duties in a careless manner. As Landes and Posner (1987, 121) note, "Making the employer liable for his employee's tort serves to enlist the employer as a substitute enforcer of tort law where the primary enforcement mechanism, a tort action against the immediate tortfeasor is unworkable."

2.2   Accidents in Which the Victim Is an Employee

An important exception to the liability of employers for their employees' negligence concerns accidents in which the victim is also an employee. Historically, employer liability for these accidents was severely limited. The common law did impose a duty on employers to maintain a safe workplace and to warn of dangerous situations, but even an employer who was negligent in fulfilling these duties could defend himself by demonstrating contributory negligence or assumption of risk by the injured worker. As we saw in the previous chapter, a rule of negligence with a defense of contributory negligence provides efficient bilateral incentives for care, and, as we saw in the case of products liability, the wage will adjust to compensate workers for whatever losses they cannot recover from the tort system (as well as to achieve the efficient level of employment).[10]

A further defense was available to employers when an employee was injured as a result of the negligence of another employee. Although the doctrine of respondeat superior would seem to have imposed strict liability on the employer in this case, the so-called fellow servant rule actually absolved the employer of any liability, provided that the latter had not been negligent in hiring or inadequately supervising the negligent employee. The economic rationale for this rule is that it gives workers an incentive to monitor one another and to report careless behavior to the employer.

While the fellow servant rule might have been appropriate in small enterprises and shops where workers had close contact with one another, it seems less valid in large businesses where victims might be injured by the negligence of workers with whom they had never had contact (Keeton et al. 1984, 571). More cynical observers simply saw the rule as yet another pro-business rule that, like the privity limitation in products liability, insulated firms from liability. For whatever reason, the law governing workplace accidents changed dramatically in the early twentieth century.

2.3   Workers' Compensation Laws

Following the turn of the twentieth century, dissatisfaction with the common-law rules governing workplace accidents led to legislation by all states that instituted a form of strict employer liability. Employer negligence was no longer necessary for recovery, nor could the employer invoke contributory negligence or the fellow servant rule as defenses. The new laws differed from strict liability, however, in that the amount of compensation was set by fixed damage schedules for each class of injury. (A typical formula calls for replacement of two-thirds of wages for a set period of time.) In addition, agencies rather than the courts administered the rules.

In evaluating the efficiency of these laws, we can draw an analogy to products liability, where we argued that, although the price mechanism can in principle shift risks in such a way as to make the particular liability rule irrelevant (according to the Coase Theorem), market imperfections like misperceptions of risk make this mechanism unreliable in practice. In this setting, we argued that strict liability imposes the risk on the party who can best estimate it (the firm), and the wage or price can adjust appropriately.

A possible inefficiency in workers' compensation laws is the elimination of contributory negligence as a defense, which may result in too little care by workers. This problem may not be severe, however, for two reasons (Landes and Posner 1987, 310–11). First, employers can contract with workers to achieve the efficient level of safety by paying a higher wage for greater care. Second, the limitation on compensation mitigates the moral hazard problem associated with standard strict liability.

To see the latter point, suppose that in the event of an accident, a worker expects to receive fixed compensation equal to $\overline{D}$, while her actual damages would be $D(x, y)$, where, recall, x is the employer's care and y is the worker's care. The worker's choice of care will therefore solve

$$\text{minimize} \quad y + p(x, y)[D(x, y) - \overline{D}]. \tag{3.5}$$

It is possible to show that in this case, the victim will choose more care than under true strict liability (which, in this simple model, results in zero victim care), though she will choose less than optimal care. Intuitively, the victim has an incentive to take some care at the margin because by doing so, she reduces the amount of undercompensation.

Another inadequacy in workers' compensation laws is that the victim must prove that the injury is job-related. This is straightforward when the injury is the result of an accident, but for illnesses like cancer that have multiple causes, the burden is more difficult. The problem is one of "uncertainty over causation" as discussed in Chapter 2. Although this potentially attenuates the incentives for employers to provide a safe workplace, recall that efficient incentives can be maintained under two rules. The first imposes full liability on the employer if the conditional probability that the illness is work-related exceeds a threshold, and the second imposes liability on the employer in proportion to the conditional probability that the illness is work-related.

A further check on workplace safety is direct regulation by OSHA, the Occupational Safety and Health Administration. Established in 1970, this agency's goal is to assure "safe and healthful working conditions" for all workers. The most favorable evidence available, however, suggests that it has had only limited success in this effort. Specifically, Viscusi found that over the period 1973–83 OSHA regulations did not significantly reduce work-related injuries and illnesses, and they reduced lost workdays by only 1.5–3.6 percent (Viscusi 1986). One explanation for this is the high cost of monitoring compliance. Another may simply be that the threat of liability for workers' compensation had already given employers an incentive to take most cost-justified safety measures, so further improvements in safety were hard to come by.

3 Liability for Environmental Damages

This section discusses issues that arise in the use of tort law for internalizing environmental damages. The role of tort law in this context is generally limited to unanticipated releases of harmful substances like oil spills or toxic-waste leaks, referred to as "environmental accidents." In contrast, the continuous discharge of pollutants as the known by-product of a firm's production process is usually dealt with by means of taxes or direct regulation. (We will examine regulatory approaches to environmental policy in Chapter 7 as part of a general discussion of the control of externalities.)

3.1 Characteristics of Environmental Accidents

Environmental accidents are similar in many ways to other sorts of accidents, but they also present some unique problems. This section emphasizes those unique elements.

3.1.1 Multiple Victims

Many environmental accidents involve multiple victims. Examples include radiation discharges from nuclear power plants and oil spills. One problem created by the existence of multiple victims is that, while aggregate damages may be large, the damage suffered by any individual victim may be too small to justify the cost of filing suit against the injurer. This is referred to as the *dispersed cost problem*. To illustrate, suppose that n victims each suffer individual damages of D dollars, making aggregate damages nD. Also, let the cost to any one victim of filing suit be c dollars. If $D < c$, no victim will find it *privately* worthwhile to file suit, even though a suit is *socially* desirable, given that $nD > c$.

One solution to this problem is a class-action suit, in which all of the individual claims are bundled into one suit. This not only overcomes the disincentive of individual victims to bring suit, it also economizes on judicial resources by eliminating duplicative trials over the same set of factual and legal issues. In most cases, these benefits will more than offset the costs of identifying and notifying all victims (underinclusion), as well as preventing uninjured parties from claiming to be victims (overinclusion).

A second problem associated with multiple victims is that the likelihood of injurer bankruptcy increases. Suppose that the injurer has total assets of A out of which it can pay liability judgments. In the previous example, the injurer will not be able to cover all damages if $A < nD$, a situation that becomes more likely as n increases. Not only does this result in undercompensation of victims, but also, as we saw in the previous chapter, it potentially reduces incentives for injurer care, depending on the liability rule. When the rule is strict liability, the possibility of insufficient assets generally reduces the incentive for injurers to take care because their expected liability is less than the full damages that they impose.[11] (In particular, the injurer expects to pay liability of A dollars when damages are $nD > A$ dollars.) In contrast, under a negligence rule the injurer may still have an incentive to take efficient care because by doing so he avoids *all* liability. Thus, if the savings in liability from choosing due care, equal to A dollars, is larger than the cost of taking the additional care, then the injurer will do so.

The preceding suggests that a move toward strict liability may have the unintended effect of creating incentives for firms engaging in hazardous activities to alter their organizational structure so as to use bankruptcy as a shield against liability. There is in fact evidence that firms engage in this sort of strategy by contracting out particularly hazardous aspects of their business to smaller firms (Ringleb and Wiggins 1990).

3.1.2 Causal Uncertainty

A second distinguishing feature of environmental accidents is that the particular cause of the accident may not be easy to identify. One circumstance in which this causal uncertainty arises is when there are *multiple injurers*. For example, several polluters may dump hazardous waste into a landfill, which eventually seeps into the groundwater. Another example, not in an environmental context, is when two hunters fire at what they think is a deer, and one of their bullets hits a third hunter.[12] This situation, in which the actions of multiple injurers contribute to a single harm, is sometimes referred to as a *joint tort*.[13]

To illustrate the problems created by joint torts, consider the following example of two injurers whose actions create a risk of damages to a single victim. Let $p(x_1, x_2)$ be the probability of an accident as a function of the expenditures on care by the two injurers, and let D be the fixed damages in the event of an accident. Note that this resembles our model of bilateral care except that now it is the two injurers who take care rather than the injurer and the victim. As before, the social problem is to choose the care levels to

$$\text{minimize} \quad x_1 + x_2 + p(x_1, x_2)D. \tag{3.6}$$

By analogy to the bilateral care model, optimal care by both injurers in this case requires that each face the victim's full damages at the margin. In general, this will not be possible given the constraint that the total liability payments collected from the injurers cannot exceed the damages suffered by the victim. To illustrate, suppose that the rule is strict liability and that each injurer is responsible for a share of total damages. Specifically, suppose injurer one pays a share s_1 and injurer two pays a share s_2, where $s_1 + s_2 = 1$. The problem facing each injurer is therefore to

$$\text{minimize} \quad x_j + p(x_1, x_2)s_j D, \quad j = 1, 2. \tag{3.7}$$

Like the judgment proof problem, both injurers face less than full damages (that is, $s_j < 1$) and therefore take too little care. (Compare the problem in [3.7] to that in [2.10] in the previous chapter.)

How are the shares determined in actual law? The traditional common-law rule, referred to as "joint and several liability," is that the victim can collect her full damages from either injurer or from both. In the latter case, the victim can obtain the judgment in whatever proportions she chooses, usually based on which injurer is best able to pay. Under this rule, each injurer must form an expectation about his share of damages, but the constraint that the shares must sum to one implies that neither injurer will generally expect to face full damages. As a result, they will both tend to take too little care.

The conclusion is different under a negligence rule. In this case, it is possible to show that if the due standard of care is set at the efficient level for each injurer, then in equilibrium they will both meet the standard. The intuition is the same as in our earlier discussions of the negligence—each injurer has an incentive to meet the due standard in order to avoid any share of the victim's damages.

A second source of causal uncertainty is when there is a *long latency period* between the exposure to a toxic substance and the emergence of the illness. The problem here is that when the illness emerges, there may be no way to tell whether it was due to the accidental exposure or to a normal "background" or "natural" risk.[14] This is the situation we examined in the previous chapter under the heading of "uncertainty over causation." We showed there that efficient incentives for injurer care can be achieved by using ordinary strict liability or negligence rules with no limitation on liability to reflect the background risk.

We also showed that it is possible to maintain efficiency if liability is limited in one of two ways. The first is a threshold rule that holds the injurer liable only if the conditional probability that he caused the accident exceeds an appropriately chosen threshold. The second is a rule that holds the injurer liable for the proportion of the damages that he caused in a probabilistic sense, conditional on the fact that the illness actually occurred.

All of the preceding rules assign liability only after an exposure victim has actually contracted the illness. Another approach to causal uncertainty is to allow all victims of the exposure to file for damages *at the time of exposure*. In this case, the risk is itself at tort (a "tort for risk"), and damages are calculated to reflect reduced life expectancy, future pain and suffering, and future medical costs resulting from the exposure.[15]

To see how the proportional liability and tort-for-risk rules compare, suppose that damages from an illness, when contracted, are $150,000; the probability of getting the illness from the accidental exposure is .10; and the background probability is .05. The overall probability of developing the illness after exposure is therefore .15. Under the proportional liability rule, the share of damages the injurer pays equals the conditional probability that the exposure caused the illness, given that the illness has occurred. This probability is $(.10)/(.15) = 2/3$. Thus, at the time the illness occurs, the injurer pays $(2/3)(\$150,000) = \$100,000$. In contrast, under the tort-for-risk, the injurer would pay damages *at the time of exposure* equal to the contribution of the exposure to the expected losses from the illness, or $(.15 - .05)(\$150,000) = \$15,000$.

Although it may seem that the tort-for-risk rule imposes less cost on the injurer and therefore provides less incentive for care, recall that proportional damages are not paid to all victims, but only those who develop the illness. Thus, the injurer's expected cost under the proportional rule, as of the time of exposure, is $(.15)(\$100,000) = \$15,000$. The two rules therefore provide identical (and efficient) incentives. The rules are not identical in all respects, however. The chief advantage of the proportional rule is that it saves on litigation costs since not all exposure victims end up filing suit. The advantage of the tort-for-risk rule is that it avoids the risk that the injurer will be judgment proof at the time, possibly well in the future, when the illness occurs.

3.2 Superfund

An important area of environmental law concerns the cleanup of hazardous waste sites.[16] Despite the obvious risk to public health and the environment from these sites, there was little regulatory oversight of disposal practices prior to the 1970s. An important change occurred in 1980 with the enactment of the Comprehensive Environmental Response, Compensation, and Liability Act (CERCLA). The primary objective of this legislation was to clean up hazardous waste sites quickly and effectively and to impose the cost (when possible) on the responsible parties. To fund the cleanup of sites, CERCLA established a "superfund" to be financed in part by taxes but also by damage actions brought by the Environmental Protection Agency (EPA) against responsible parties. It is the liability aspect of CERCLA that is of interest to us here.

The extent of liability under CERCLA is broad. First of all, liability is strict, and in the case of multiple polluters, it is joint and several. As noted above, this means that any one of them can be held responsible for the entire cost of cleanup. Thus, "disposal of a thimbleful of hazardous waste at a large disposal site exposes an entity to enormous potential liability" (Menell 1991, 109). The resulting uncertainty has led to dramatically higher costs of insurance for environmental liability, when it is available at all.

In addition to holding polluters strictly liable, CERCLA extends liability to "innocent" buyers of a contaminated site. Many have criticized this provision as discouraging transactions that would otherwise lead to the beneficial redevelopment of old industrial sites—so-called brownfields. This negative conclusion is not necessarily true. Recall from our discussion of products liability that, in the absence of misperceptions about risk, the equilibrium output of a dangerous product is independent of the allocation of liability between the buyer and the seller. The same is true here; if land prices accurately reflect anticipated cleanup costs, then there should be no distortions in land transactions. However, if sellers have better information about the extent of contamination than do buyers, then too few transactions may occur as a result of adverse selection (Segerson 1997).

To illustrate, suppose that a contaminated site is worth V dollars to a buyer (developer) and R dollars to a seller, exclusive of cleanup costs, which equal C. Since someone must pay the costs whether or not a sale occurs, it is efficient for the buyer to acquire the site if $V > R$, which we assume is true. Let s be the share of costs that the buyer expects to incur. If P is the price, the buyer will purchase the site if

$$V - sC \geq P. \tag{3.8}$$

As for the seller, if no sale is made, she must pay the full cleanup costs (assuming she is solvent), yielding a value of $R - C$, whereas if she sells, she receives the price less her share of cleanup costs, or $P - (1 - s)C$. She will therefore sell if $P - (1 - s)C \geq R - C$, or if

$$P \geq R - sC. \tag{3.9}$$

A sale will occur if there exists a price that satisfies both (3.8) and (3.9), that is, if $V - sC \geq R - sC$, or if $V > R$, which is the condition for an efficient sale. This shows that, regardless of s, the efficient outcome will occur.

It should be easy to see, however, that if the parties hold different assessments of the size of C, this conclusion will no longer hold. Suppose, in particular, that the seller has a better assessment of C due to private information. In that case, the efficient transaction will only occur if the seller bears full liability (that is, if $s = 0$) since the buyer's criterion in (3.8) will be independent of C (except insofar as it is reflected in the price). Note that this conclusion mirrors the above argument that strict products liability is efficient because it imposes liability on the party with better information about risks (the seller). However, it appears contrary to the imposition of liability for environmental contamination on "innocent" buyers ($s = 1$).

Under the original provisions of CERCLA, lenders could also be held liable for cleanup if the owner was insolvent (Segerson 1993). Again, if credit markets operate perfectly, this creates no distortions and in fact helps to mitigate the incentive problems due to insolvency of the injurer. However, if there is asymmetric information between the borrower (injurer) and lender, an adverse selection problem of the sort described above arises. In addition, if the injurer makes some or all of its abatement (care) decisions *after* the loan is made, and the terms of the loan cannot be made contingent on the level of care (for the same reason that the seller of a dangerous product cannot condition the price on the buyer's care after purchase), then the injurer will have an incentive to underinvest in abatement.

The discussion in this section has pointed to several problems in the use of tort liability and its statutory counterpart for internalizing environmental harm. In some cases, these problems can be overcome by redesigning liability rules in ways that we have discussed, but in others, a liability approach is inherently flawed. As a result, an efficiently designed approach to the control of environmental externalities will likely involve a combination of liability and safety regulation, a topic to which we return in Chapter 7.

3.3   Case Study: Asbestos

Asbestos is a product that was widely used in the United States in a variety of industrial settings, as well as in schools and homes. The link between exposure to asbestos and severe illnesses like lung cancer, asbestosis, and mesothelioma, however, apparently was not known until the 1930s. Tort suits against asbestos manufacturers began in the 1970s, slowly at first, but by the 1990s, they had expanded to the point where they comprised a substantial fraction of all products liability cases filed in this country.

Asbestos litigation involves several of the problems that we have identified with the use of the tort system for internalizing risk (Dewees 1998; White 2006). These problems largely stem from the long latency period of asbestos-related illnesses, usually ten to thirty years. First, it is difficult for plaintiffs to prove causation given the existence of multiple background risks unrelated to exposure. Second, plaintiffs may be unable to establish which of several manufacturers or suppliers was responsible for their exposure. And even if they could, the responsible party may have gone bankrupt by the time the illness arises. As we have seen, these factors weaken the deterrence function of tort law.

Asbestos is also an interesting case study because it combines aspects of products liability, workplace safety, and environmental risk. Initially, workers' compensation provided the sole remedy for work-related exposures to asbestos, but since compensation is limited under this system, plaintiffs' law-

Figure 3.4

Asbestos Cases Filed in U.S. District Courts, 1974–2005

yers early on sought to circumvent that system. They succeeded in 1973 by suing manufacturers (rather than employers) under products liability principles.[17] This success resulted in a surge of tort claims in the 1970s that has continued into the 1990s. (See Figure 3.4, which shows the trend in asbestos cases filed in U.S. district courts from 1974 to 2005.) Evidence that manufacturers knew of the risks of asbestos and failed to warn workers in many cases resulted in punitive damage judgments against defendants. The resulting financial pressure caused several bankruptcies, the most notable being that of the largest manufacturer, the Manville Corporation, in 1982.

Today, the risk of new asbestos exposures has been greatly reduced, partly as a result of this litigation. One could therefore argue that the law has succeeded in its deterrence function. Most would agree, however, that it has been much less successful in compensating victims, while at the same time imposing high costs on the legal system.

One reform, noted above, that could improve the compensation function of tort law in mass-exposure cases would be to allow victims to file at exposure for expected damages, rather than having to wait until actual symptoms arise. We have seen that the advantage of this rule is that all victims would receive some compensation, which they could use to purchase health insurance or precautionary medical treatment. The drawback is the likely "flood" of litigation (Robinson 1985). To date, some states have taken the limited step of allowing exposure victims to collect medical monitoring expenses, but none has gone so far as the allow a full-blown "tort for risk."[18]

4   Medical Malpractice

Following the trend of other forms of tort litigation, patient claims against physicians for malpractice have risen significantly in recent decades. Beginning in the late 1960s and continuing through the 1970s and 1980s, malpractice claims rose at roughly 10 percent per year, while damage awards and malpractice insurance costs correspondingly increased (Danzon 1991). (See Figure 3.5, which shows the trend in malpractice insurance premiums.) Though some of this increase can be attributed to wider availability and use of certain higher-risk medical procedures, the general trend mirrors the growth

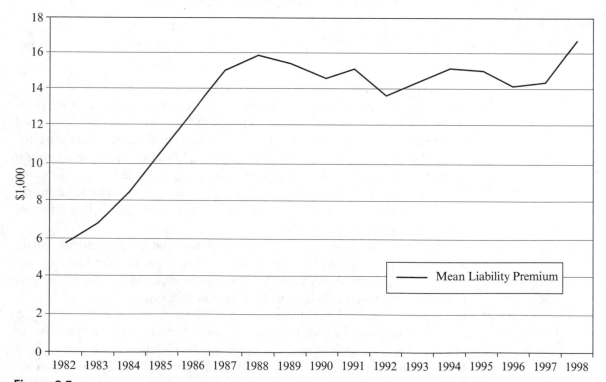

Figure 3.5
Mean Liability Premium ($1,000s), All Physicians, 1982–1998

in products liability and other tort claims over the same period. In response to this "medical malpractice crisis," many states enacted reforms, including caps on awards, a shorter statute of limitations for malpractice claims, and regulation of legal fees (Keeton et al. 1984, 192–93).

The economic analysis of medical malpractice resembles products liability and workplace accidents in the sense that the injurer and victim have a preexisting market relationship. Thus, contractual principles can theoretically govern the assignment of liability. In most cases, however, consumers of medical care, especially high-risk care like surgery, are infrequent purchasers. Further, they lack the knowledge to evaluate the quality and/or safety of care. The likely misperception of risk therefore prevents an efficient contractual solution for reasons noted above.

Another source of inefficiency that precludes a contractual solution in this area is insurance—the majority of consumers have either private or public health insurance that pays most of their medical expenses. Because the price consumers face is therefore "too low" (and the provision of care is not otherwise rationed), the consumption of medical services is distorted, apart from considerations of risk.

4.1 Customary Practice and Informed Consent

The actual liability rule applied to malpractice cases is negligence, with the due standard based on "customary practice." Specifically, "the doctor must have and use the knowledge, skill and care ordinarily possessed and employed by members of the profession in good standing" (Keeton et al. 1984, 187). Thus, a successful finding of negligence generally requires expert testimony by another physician. Some criticize this standard as giving the medical profession (and other professions subject to the same standard) the right to establish their own standards of conduct (especially given the reluctance of physicians to testify against one another). Further, we argued above that custom as a defense is unlikely to establish an efficient standard when consumers are poorly informed about available technologies. One difference here is that physicians have a code of professional ethics to provide the best possible care for their patients, a factor that may outweigh the profit motive.

A more recent duty imposed on physicians also helps to mitigate the problem of asymmetric information between doctors and patients. It is the duty of doctors to inform patients of the risks involved in receiving a particular treatment—the *doctrine of informed consent*. Disclosure is costly, however, so the law only compels physicians to inform the patient of "material risks," defined as risks that a reasonable person would find significant. This reflects an effort by courts to efficiently balance the costs and benefits of information.

4.2 Do Physicians Practice Defensive Medicine?

The increasing costs of malpractice litigation have led many to ask whether physicians practice "defensive medicine." According to Danzon (1991, 54), "Defensive medicine should be defined as liability-induced changes in medical practice that entail costs in excess of benefits and that should not have occurred in the absence of liability." Generally speaking, one might interpret defensive medicine as excessive care by physicians ($x > x^*$) in response to an expectation of liability in excess of actual damages imposed.[19] A difficulty in measuring the extent of such activities is that the moral hazard problem associated with consumer health insurance can also result in too much care from the demand side, as noted above.

The logical limit of defensive medicine is that many physicians simply stop performing high-risk procedures. This reflects an inefficiently low activity level, assuming that the benefit of the activity exceeds the risk. Unfortunately, the only evidence on the extent to which physicians alter their practices (too much care and/or too little activity) in response to the threat of liability comes from surveys and anecdotal evidence, neither of which is a good basis for drawing general conclusions or for formulating public policy.

Continuing dissatisfaction with the malpractice system has led to renewed calls for reform. One interesting alternative is to institute a no-fault system along the lines of workers' compensation. Under this proposal, strict liability would replace negligence, and adjudication would be taken out of the tort system and transferred to an administrative agency. The intended benefits would be reduced delay in the litigation process, better compensation of victims, and greater predictability of physicians' liability. In addition, it is consistent with our conclusion above that strict liability is preferred to negligence when consumers misperceive risk.

5 Conclusion

This chapter applied the economic model of accidents to products liability, workers' compensation, environmental accidents, and medical malpractice. While these areas of tort law differ in many respects, we showed that economic theory can go a long way toward explaining their basic features.

An important methodological issue that arose in our discussion of products liability (but applied to other areas as well) was the role of the contractual relationship between injurers and victims in internalizing accident risk. We showed, in particular, that when parties correctly perceive risk and can bargain with one another, the output of the product will be efficient regardless of the liability rule; only the equilibrium price will adjust to reflect the assignment of liability. This was in contrast to accidents between "strangers" (parties who cannot bargain), or where the market failed to operate efficiently, in which case the liability rule matters for efficiency. This distinction between disputes where the parties can bargain and those where they cannot will be a recurrent theme in the chapters ahead.

DISCUSSION QUESTIONS

1. Discuss the difference between accidents between strangers and accidents in which the injurer and victim have a preexisting economic (contractual) relationship.

2. Propose an answer to the following "economic puzzle of products liability law: the injurer and the victim have a contractual relationship, so why shouldn't they be left to work out the optimal combination of safety precautions contractually?" (Landes and Posner 1987, 280).

3. Describe the economic functions (if any) of the privity doctrine in products liability and the fellow servant rule in workplace liability. What was the rationale for their elimination?

4. Discuss the shortcomings of tort liability as the sole means of controlling environmental hazards.

5. Discuss the following statement regarding medical malpractice: "Altruism, professional or ethical concerns may motivate physicians to act as better agents for patients than would be predicted from models that assume purely self-interested income maximization" (Danzon 1998, 624).

PROBLEMS

1. Consider the market for a dangerous product in which the supply curve is *upward sloping.*

   (a) Use a supply and demand diagram to show the irrelevance of the liability rule for equilibrium output.

   (b) Show that when the rule is no liability, consumer perceptions of risk affect both output and price.

2. An automobile manufacturer designed a car with the gas tank in the rear, the effect of which was to create a one in four risk of fire from rear-end collisions. An alternate design would have reduced the risk of fire to one out of twenty collisions, but at a cost of $10 per car. Suppose that one out of

five thousand cars are rear ended at least once during their lifetime, and the average damage from a fire is $100,000. Use the Hand rule to determine if the manufacturer should be held negligent for failing to use the alternate design.

3. Suppose that there are two consumers who derive benefits from consuming one unit of a dangerous product. Consumer A derives total benefits of $200; consumer B derives total benefits of $100. The risk of an accident from consuming the product is .01, and the damages from an accident are $5,000. Finally, the firm's cost of producing the product is constant at $75 per unit.

   (a) Is it efficient for the firm to produce and sell the product to consumer A? What about consumer B?

   (b) Suppose that both consumers (and the firm) correctly perceive the risk of an accident. What is the price of the product, and which consumer(s) purchases it under a rule of no liability? Under strict liability? Which rule (or rules) yields the efficient outcome? (Assume the firm is competitive and sets the price equal to its full expected cost per unit.)

   (c) Now suppose that both consumers misperceive the risk of an accident to be .001. How does this change your answer to (b)? (Assume the firm continues to perceive the risk correctly.)

4. Consider the case of *Helling v. Carey* (84 Wash.2d 514, 519 P.2d 981, 1974), which was a medical malpractice suit brought by Barbara Helling against Dr. Thomas Carey and his partner, who were ophthalmologists. The plaintiff, who was thirty-two years old, claimed that she suffered permanent and severe damage to her eyes as a result of the doctors' failure to test her for glaucoma. The defendants countered that the standards of their profession did not call for routine glaucoma tests in patients under the age of forty. Evidence at trial revealed that the incidence of glaucoma in patients under forty is 1 in 25,000.

   (a) Suppose that the average loss from blindness in people under forty is $1,000,000, and the test for glaucoma costs $35. Use the Hand rule to determine if the professional standard of not testing those under forty is efficient.

   (b) What factors may account for the persistence of an inefficient professional standard?

5. Consider two identical parcels of land, each of whose surface value is $1,000 to a potential buyer. The owner of each parcel values the surface at $800, but one of the parcels has contamination that will cost $500 to clean up. The owners know whether their parcels are contaminated, but the buyer does not (that is, the parcels look identical to the buyer).

(a) Is it efficient for the buyer to acquire one of the parcels? Explain.

(b) What is the buyer's best offer for a parcel if sellers are fully responsible for cleanup costs? What is the buyer's best offer if the buyer is responsible?

(c) Show that the seller of the uncontaminated parcel will accept the buyer's best offer only if sellers are responsible, but the seller of the contaminated parcel will accept the buyer's best offer under either rule for cleanup costs.

4

THE ECONOMICS OF CONTRACT LAW I:
The Elements of a Valid Contract

Contract law provides the legal means by which people enforce promises to one another. Promises come in all varieties, including promises to provide a good or service in exchange for money, promises of marriage, promises to quit drinking or smoking, and campaign promises by political candidates. But people who make promises often wish to break them. The basic question underlying contract law, therefore, is what sorts of promises should be *legally* enforceable. The next two chapters seek to answer this question.

It should be obvious that economic theory has a lot to say about this question. After all, most promises involve some kind of exchange, and exchange is fundamentally an economic activity. Indeed, much of microeconomic theory is concerned with finding ways to promote efficient exchange. The economic theory of contract law examines the role of the legal system in achieving this goal.

This chapter begins the analysis by describing the elements of a valid contract. In effect, it answers the question of what must be true of a promise for it to be legally enforceable. The next chapter then examines the conditions under which someone who has made a contract can legally break it (that is, "breach" the contract), and what the penalty should be for doing so.

1 Contracts and Efficient Exchange

The economics of contract law is concerned with promoting efficient exchange, by which we mean the movement of goods and services from lower- to higher-valuing users. For example, if I value your car at $2,000, and you value it at $1,500, then the value of the car is increased by $500 if I acquire it. When such a potential increase in value exists, it can be realized by means of a market exchange that gives both of us a share of the "gains from trade." For example, I agree to pay you $1,750, and you agree to give me the title to the car. (The increased value can also be realized if I steal the car; we address this type of "exchange" in Chapter 9.)

A contract is a legal agreement, explicit or implicit, between two parties to a transaction that allows either party to go to court to enlist the power of the state to enforce the other's promise. When is a contract needed to bring about an efficient exchange like the one described above? Probably not in a world where the exchange is instantaneous and information is perfect. If I hand you cash and you give me the title to the car, and if I am certain that it has no hidden defects, then we both get exactly what we expected and there are no surprises. Most everyday transactions are of this sort, so contract law plays no role.

But suppose that I pay you with a check (which may bounce when you try to cash it), or the car turns out to be stolen or to have a hidden defect. Alternatively, suppose that, after we made the deal to transfer the car but before we complete the exchange, I decide that I don't really need the car after all, or you realize that you do need it. Now we have a situation where one party wants to complete the contract according to the original terms, while the other wants to alter the terms or back out altogether. In other words, we have a dispute that may have to be resolved by application of the law of contract.

What has led to the dispute? The examples all involve some unforeseen change in circumstances that makes one of the parties unhappy with the terms of the exchange as originally specified. (If both parties become unhappy and want to terminate the exchange, then a dispute does not arise.) The fact that the change was unforeseen is important, because if it were foreseen, then the terms of the contract could have been structured to account for the change. For example, we could have specified in the contract that the seller will pay for any defects that arise within the first month after the sale. In this case, there is no need for legal intervention.

Unforeseen contingencies, however, cannot be accounted for in the contract. And, in some cases, the parties will choose not to account for some *foreseeable* contingencies because the likelihood of such circumstances is so remote that it is not worth incurring the costs of preparing for them. For example, you and I would not likely discuss how to deal with the possibility that the government might outlaw the internal combustion engine the day after I buy your car.

When contracts do not provide for all possible contingencies, for whatever reason, we say that they are *incomplete*. The economic theory of contract law says that courts provide the missing terms of incomplete contracts so as to maximize the gains from trade. The way they do this is by answering the hypothetical question: How would the parties have provided for the contingency if they could have bargained over it costlessly at the time of formation and in a perfectly competitive contracting environment?

The paradigm underlying the economic theory of contract law is therefore the competitive market. This is based on the well-known result from microeconomic theory, the Invisible Hand Theorem, which says that competitive markets maximize the gains from trade. We will see that many of the doctrines of contract law can be interpreted as efforts to replicate the competitive paradigm in actual contracting environments. It is therefore worth reviewing here the conditions that characterize a competitive market.

The first and most basic assumption is that contracting parties are *rational*. That is, they pursue their self-interest subject to whatever constraints they face. This typically involves maximization of utility (or wealth) subject to a budget constraint. The second requirement of a competitive contracting environment is that there be *no externalities*, or third-party effects. Third-party effects lead to market failure in the sense that some inefficient transactions may occur (in the case of a negative externality) because the parties to the transaction ignore the costs borne by third parties. Contract law proceeds under the assumption of no third-party effects (though, as we saw in Chapters 2 and 3, third parties can seek compensation for external costs by suing for damages in torts).

Market failure is also caused by *monopoly*. Contract law therefore looks unfavorably on transactions in which it appears that one party has an undue amount of bargaining power, or where one of the parties has entered the contract involuntarily, as a result of some coercion.

Another characteristic of a competitive market is *perfect information*. That is, both parties to a transaction must be fully informed about the nature of the exchange to ensure that both receive a benefit. For example, I probably would not have bought your car if you had told me that it needed a brake job (or at least I would have offered a much lower price). This suggests that full disclosure of information prior to exchange promotes efficiency and that contract law should therefore encourage it. But the efficiency of disclosure rules is more subtle than this case suggests. For example, suppose that I am an expert on antiques and I routinely go to tag sales looking for bargains. Should I be compelled to notify the seller of any underpriced items that I see? Generally, the law does not require me to do so for reasons that we will discuss.

A final issue concerns *transaction costs*. These include any costs associated with the writing and enforcing of a contract. In competitive markets, these costs are assumed to be zero, but in the real world they can often be considerable. Since transaction costs reduce the benefits from a transaction, it is in the parties' mutual interests to minimize them. Indeed, this is one reason why they often write incomplete contracts in the first place, even when there is no uncertainty.

Transaction costs also provide a reason why contract law must supply remedies for contract disputes after the fact. If a contract is silent about what should happen in the event of some contingency, why can't the parties simply renegotiate the contract if and when that contingency arises? According to the Coase Theorem, such bargaining should always lead to the efficient resolution of the dispute, and there is no role for contract law other than to enforce whatever agreement they reach. The reason contract law matters is that such bargaining is often costlier than seeking a court-imposed remedy. We take up this line of reasoning again in the next chapter in our discussion of specific performance versus money damages as alternative remedies for breach of contract.

2   The Elements of a Valid Contract

Having described the ideal contracting environment, we are now ready to confront the question of what contracts are enforceable. According to the law, an enforceable contract must, first and foremost, constitute a *bargain*. That is, it must arise out of a mutual agreement between the two parties. This makes economic sense since agreement by both parties signifies that each expects to realize some benefit from the transaction.

But how does the law decide when there are mutual gains? Traditionally, three elements must be present: *offer*, *acceptance*, and *consideration*. The first two, offer and acceptance, are straightforward—one party (the *promisor*) has made an offer to provide a service or deliver a good to the other party (the *promisee*), and the latter has accepted the offer. When this happens, we say that there is a "meeting of the minds." The contract is not complete, however, unless the promisee gives something in return—usually a promise to pay some money to the promisor. *Consideration* is the legal term used to describe the promisee's "return promise"; this is what makes the transaction mutual and hence enforceable.

Although consideration usually takes the form of a promise by the promisee to pay for the good or service being provided, it need not. To illustrate, consider the following two promises:[1]

1. An uncle promises to pay his nephew $5,000 on the day that the nephew turns twenty-one.
2. An uncle promises to pay his nephew $5,000 on the day that the nephew turns twenty-one, provided that the nephew refrains from drinking and smoking until that time.

First, is either one of these promises a legally enforceable contract? The answer is that only the second one is. While both have offer and acceptance, only the second has consideration. But what form does the consideration take? It is the nephew's promise to refrain from drinking and smoking until he turns twenty-one. Presumably, these are activities that the nephew enjoyed, yet his acceptance of the uncle's offer implies that he valued them at less than $5,000. At the same time, the uncle must have placed a value above $5,000 on seeing his nephew give up these activities, at least until he turned twenty-one. Thus, both expected to receive a benefit. This is what makes the promise mutual and thus enforceable.

But there is a further point. One might object that $5,000 is a lot of money (especially in 1891) to pay someone to give up drinking and smoking (and only temporarily at that!), and on this basis, the court should not enforce this promise. In fact, courts will not ordinarily engage in such second-guessing, provided that when the promisor (the uncle) made the promise, he did so willingly and in his right mind.[2] Consider the following excerpt from the court's opinion in *Hamer v. Sidway* (124 N.Y. 538, 27 N.E. 256, Court of Appeals of New York 1891):

> The promisee [the nephew] used tobacco, occasionally drank liquor, and he had a legal right to do so. That right he abandoned for a period of years upon the strength of the promise of the [uncle] that for such forbearance he would give him $5,000. We need not speculate on the effort which may have been required to give up the use of these stimulants. It is sufficient that he restricted his lawful freedom of action within certain prescribed limits upon the faith of his uncle's agreement, and now, having fully performed the conditions imposed, it is of no moment whether such performance actually proved a benefit to the promisor, and the court will not inquire into it.

This general rule—that courts will only inquire about the *presence* of consideration but not about its *adequacy*—reflects an important economic principle: namely, that the parties to a transaction are the best judges of their individual benefits therefrom. Thus, third-party attempts to alter the terms of the transaction after the fact, absent specific evidence of irrationality, coercion, or other market failure, will hinder rather than enhance freedom of contract.

3   Reasons for Invalidating Contracts

To this point we have identified the elements of an ideal contracting environment, and we have argued that courts should simply enforce contracts that meet that ideal. In this section, we discuss how contract law deals with those contracts that fail to meet the ideal. In general, our discussion will involve various rules that specify the conditions that must be met for a contract to be enforceable. We will see that in many cases, the rules can be interpreted as straightforward attempts to eliminate sources of market failure as described above. However, we will also see that in some cases the most efficient rule will be far from obvious.

3.1 Mental Incapacity or Incompetence

Courts will not enforce contracts made by parties judged to be mentally incompetent or otherwise unable to exercise rational judgment. This includes parties who are mentally impaired, or who are too young to act in their own best interest. This rule clearly makes economic sense as a way of ensuring rationality, which, as we noted above, is a fundamental prerequisite for parties to engage in mutually beneficial transactions.

Generally, the legal burden of proving incompetence is placed on the party alleging it as a reason for voiding a contract. That is, the law presumes competence unless it is proven otherwise. This reduces the opportunistic use of this doctrine by parties seeking to avoid performance simply because the terms of the contract are no longer favorable to them. (We will see below, however, that there are other ways of avoiding performance in the face of unforeseen contingencies.)

3.2 Coercion or Duress

Courts will also invalidate contracts that a party signed under duress or as a result of coercion. The presence of coercion or duress clearly violates the requirement of voluntariness, which, like rationality, is a prerequisite for a mutually beneficial transaction. But what constitutes coercion from a legal perspective? Suppose that someone approaches a business owner and proposes the following bargain: "If you pay me $100 a week, I will refrain from burning down your store." The store owner may well accept this bargain for fear that the police would not be able to provide adequate protection against the threat. However, a court would never enforce such a contract because the store owner's acceptance of the deal was made under duress; that is, it was not truly voluntary.

The preceding was an easy case. What about the following situation? I offer my car for sale at $1,000. A prospective buyer shows up and says, "If you lower your price to $800 I'll buy it, but if not, I'll take my business elsewhere." I accept the $800 offer but later seek to invalidate the sale claiming that I accepted under duress. Technically, I may be right, but legally, I don't have a leg to stand on. The court will enforce the sale at $800.

The difference between this case and the previous one is that here, the buyer's "threat" promotes competition because it gives buyers the freedom to seek the lowest possible price, thus preventing the formation of monopolies. Enforcement of the contract legitimizes the buyer's actions in this case because they serve to enhance efficiency. In contrast, the protection money example involved a bargain whereby the owner was forced to buy something that he already legally owned—namely, the right to be free from damage to his store. Enforcement would therefore only encourage threats to impose such damage.

The issue of duress arises in a less obvious way in cases involving contract modifications (Aivazian et al. 1984; Posner 1977). Contract modifications are changes to a contract, made after formation but prior to performance. The question is, when are such changes enforceable? The traditional legal rule, referred to as the *preexisting duty rule*, holds that they are only enforceable when accompanied by new consideration. In ordinary circumstances, this rule is self-enforcing. For example, if a hardware store requests an additional shipment of snow shovels during an unexpectedly harsh winter, the supplier will only comply if the store promises to pay for the extra items. In this case, both parties benefit from the modification.

In other cases, however, circumstances cause a party to agree to a modification that he later regrets, thus raising the question of duress. Consider, for example, the case of *Alaska Packers' Assn. v. Domenico* (117 F. 99, 9th Cir. 1902), in which the defendant hired a crew of sailors to go on a salmon-fishing expedition off the coast of Alaska. Prior to the voyage, the crew agreed to a set wage, but once at sea they refused to fish unless the wage was raised. Since the defendant was in no position to fire the crew and hire substitutes, he agreed to their demands (under duress) but later reneged on the agreement. The sailors sued for the higher wage but lost on the grounds that the promised wage increase was unsupported by additional consideration. That is, what the sailors offered in return for the wage increase was merely to complete the job for which they were initially hired. Thus, according to the preexisting duty rule, the modified wage was unenforceable—the defendant only owed the original wage.

Another case of modification under duress, *Goebel v. Linn* (47 Mich. 489, 11 N.W. 284, 1882), concerned a contract between an ice company and a brewery for supplying ice during the summer. When an unseasonably warm winter caused a short supply of ice, the ice company requested a price increase, and the brewery, which had a supply of beer that would have spoiled, agreed.[3] (The contract did provide for a modest price increase in the event of short supply, but the ice company requested a larger increase.) The brewery later reneged on the price increase, claiming that it was unenforceable because the ice company had offered no new consideration—it simply complied with the original promise to supply ice.

On the face of it, this also seems to be a straightforward application of the preexisting duty rule. The problem is that the court enforced the modification in this case! Its reasoning was that the price increase was necessary to prevent the ice company from going bankrupt in the face of a genuine change in economic circumstances, and if it had gone bankrupt, the brewery (and probably other customers) would have lost their ice supply. This is in contrast to the fishing case, in which the only change was that the sailors gained substantial bargaining power once the ship left the port, given the absence of substitute workers. Their demand for a wage increase was therefore purely opportunistic, rather than a response to a true increase in costs (that is, performance continued to be viable at the original wage). Another way to say this is that the supply curve shifted up in the ice case but not in the fishing case.

These cases show that "economic duress" is really about the prevention of monopoly power. Nonenforcement of modifications like that in *Alaska Packers'* therefore enhances the value of contracting by discouraging opportunistic nonperformance. At the same time, enforcement of modifications reflecting true cost increases, as in *Goebel*, enhances the value of contracting by promoting beneficial exchanges that might otherwise have been foregone.

A case intermediate between the opportunistic modification in *Alaska Packers'* and the legitimate modification in *Goebel* occurs when a seller threatens to terminate a contract with buyer A because buyer B offers a higher price for the same goods. Hold-outs by professional athletes fall into this intermediate category. On the one hand, the higher offer by B represents a genuine economic change (an increase in the seller's opportunity cost), but on the other, failure by buyer A to offer a matching price increase would probably not result in the need for the seller to breach. If this is true, then the only question is whether the seller or the original buyer (buyer A) should benefit from the higher offer made by buyer B. This is an example of a purely *distributional*, rather than a *productive*, question, a distinction that we examine in the next section.

3.3 Mistake and the Duty to Disclose Private Information

The contract doctrine of mistake refers to situations in which the parties formed a contract based on mistaken beliefs. For example, suppose I make a contract to sell one of my cars to my neighbor, but when we are about to complete the deal, we discover that he was expecting to buy my new Mercedes while I had intended to sell him my ten-year-old Ford. Courts will properly refuse to enforce contracts based on this sort of *mutual mistake* because there is a fundamental disagreement about a material aspect of the contract (that is, there is no "meeting of the minds").

A harder question arises when only one of the parties is mistaken about some aspect of the contract, a so-called unilateral mistake. To illustrate, suppose that a collector of baseball cards goes into a shop and buys a certain card that turns out to be greatly underpriced. He then resells it for a large profit. When the shop owner finds out, he sues claiming that the original sale was invalid based on the doctrine of mistake (Kull 1992). Although courts invalidate contracts when the mistake is mutual, they ordinarily enforce them when the mistake is unilateral. Given this rule, however, note that the shop owner has an incentive to argue that both parties were mistaken, while the buyer has an incentive to argue that he knew the card's value all along, whether or not this is true. Since the beliefs of the parties are unobservable, the distinction between mutual and unilateral mistake is not helpful in deciding such cases.

The economic issue here is imperfect information, and when a party should have a duty to disclose private information. We said above that competitive markets require full information to function efficiently. Thus, economic theory would seem to suggest that legal rules relating to mistake should promote the maximal production and disclosure of information. This conclusion is too easy, however; the problems created by imperfect information are more complicated than that.[4] In this section, we attempt to untangle some of the issues. To provide a context for the analysis, consider the famous case of *Sherwood v. Walker* (66 Mich. 568, 33 N.W. 919, Mich. 1887).

The case concerned a contract for the sale of a cow by Mr. Walker, a cattle breeder, to Mr. Sherwood, a banker and farmer. The parties agreed to a price of $80 based on the apparent belief that the cow was infertile and hence only valuable for slaughter. Before delivery, however, Walker discovered that the cow was pregnant, and hence worth much more—between $750 and $1,000—as a breeder. He therefore refused to deliver the cow to Sherwood, who brought suit seeking enforcement of the contract.

The court in this case sided with the defendant, Walker, based on the doctrine of mutual mistake. Citing evidence presented by Walker "tending to show that at the time of the alleged sale it was believed by both the plaintiff and themselves that the cow was barren and would not breed," the court rescinded the contract. In the majority opinion, the court stated the traditional rule of mutual mistake:

> It must be considered as well settled that a party who has given an apparent consent to a contract of sale may refuse to execute it, or he may avoid it after it has been completed, if the assent was founded, or the contract made, upon the mistake of a material fact,—such as the subject matter of the sale, the price, or some collateral fact materially inducing the agreement; and this can be done when the mistake is mutual.

A dissenting judge, however, expressed doubt that the mistake was in fact mutual:

> There is no question but that the defendants sold the cow representing her of the breed and quality they believed the cow to be, and that the purchaser so un-

derstood it. And the buyer purchased her believing her to be of the breed represented by the sellers, and possessing all the qualities stated, and even more. He believed she would breed. There is no pretense that the plaintiff bought the cow for beef, and there is nothing in the record indicating that he would have bought her at all only that he thought she could be made to breed. Under the foregoing facts, . . . it is held that because it turned out that the plaintiff was more correct in his judgment as to one quality of the cow than the defendants, . . . the contract may be annulled by the defendants at their pleasure. I know of no law . . . which will justify any such holding.

The majority and dissenting opinions in this case therefore differed regarding the beliefs of the buyer: Did he or did he not believe that the cow was fertile? As a result, they reached different conclusions regarding enforceability of the contract. As we noted above, however, the beliefs of the parties do not provide a useful basis for resolving this case because they are unobservable and hence subject to misrepresentation. An economic theory of mistake instead asks what rule enhances the efficiency of contracting in the presence of asymmetric information.

We begin with the distinction between *socially valuable information* versus *purely distributive information* (Hirshleifer 1971; Shavell 1994). The difference is that socially valuable information has the potential to increase economic value (that is, enlarge the size of the pie), while purely distributive information simply affects the distribution of a fixed value (that is, changes the way the pie is cut). We can use the facts of *Sherwood v. Walker* to illustrate this difference and show how it affects the choice of contract enforcement rules (both the application of the mistake doctrine and the duty to disclose information prior to contracting).

3.3.1 Purely Distributive Information

We begin with an example of purely distributive information. Consider a seller who offers a cow, believed to be infertile, for sale. In 10 percent of such cases, however, supposedly infertile cows are revealed to be fertile prior to slaughter through no action by either the buyer or seller. Further, both parties are aware of this possibility. Suppose that fertile cows are worth $1,000, and infertile cows are worth $100, so the price of the cow is $190 = (.1)($1,000) + (.9)($100).

The facts of this example are similar to those in *Sherwood v. Walker*. The dispute arises in the state where the cow turns out to be fertile because the seller realizes that she has underpriced the cow, resulting in a windfall for the buyer. (Of course, the buyer has overpaid in the state where the cow is infertile—wouldn't he have an equally legitimate claim against the seller?) Note that it doesn't matter whether the information is revealed before or

TABLE **4.1**   **Purely Distributive Information—Contract Enforced**

State	Buyer's profit	Seller's profit	Social value
Fertile	$1,000 − $190 = $810	$190	$1,000
Infertile	$100 − $190 = −$90	$190	$100
Expected value	(.1)($810) − (.9)(90) = $0	$190	(.1)($1,000) + (.9)($100) = $190

after delivery, so long as it is revealed *after the price is set, but before slaughter*.

What will be the effect of the court's enforcement decision in this case? Assume first that it enforces the contract. Table 4.1 shows the resulting profits for the buyer and seller, and the joint (social) returns when the cow is revealed to be fertile (first line), and when it is infertile (second line). The third line shows the expected values. Note that the buyer receives a windfall profit of $810 in cases where the cow is fertile, a loss of $90 in cases where the cow is infertile, and an expected profit of zero, while the seller receives a profit of $190 in all states. (This is because the price already reflects the expected value of the cow.)

Suppose, in contrast, that the court rescinds the contract in cases where the cow turns out to be fertile (in our example, the only case that results in a dispute). The outcome is shown in Table 4.2. Note that in this case, the buyer will only pay $100 for the cow since he knows he will have to return any cows that turn out to be fertile. Thus, his expected return is zero in all cases. The seller, however, receives profit of $1,000 in cases where the cow is fertile (since she resells the fertile cow to a breeder), $100 in cases where the cow is infertile, and, as before, an expected profit of $190. Further, in both cases the expected social value of the contract remains the same: $190. We conclude that *the court's enforcement decision affects the distribution of gains from the contract, but it does not affect the expected value of the transaction.*[5]

To this point, the analysis has provided no argument for or against enforcement based on efficiency; but consider a slightly altered version of the example. Suppose that the buyer can spend $50 prior to contracting to learn the cow's type with certainty. This could involve an investment in some training that allows buyers to ascertain a cow's type on inspection (or, in the baseball card case, it would be the cost of becoming a baseball card expert). One might suppose that it would be socially valuable for buyers to make this sort of investment in the interest of improving information, but this conclusion turns out to be false in the current case. For purposes of the example, suppose that sellers do not know whether the buyer has made the investment prior to contracting. (If sellers knew that the buyer conducted the test, they could infer the outcome from the buyer's behavior.)

TABLE **4.2**   **Purely Distributive Information—Contract Not Enforced**

State	Buyer's profit	Seller's profit	Social value
Fertile	$0	$1,000	$1,000
Infertile	$100 − $100 = $0	$100	$100
Expected value	$0	(.1)($1,000) + (.9)($100) = $190	(.1)($1,000) + (.9)($100) = $190

Assume first that the court enforces contracts in which there is private information (that is, it does *not* require disclosure). The example in Table 4.1 can be used to calculate the buyer's expected gain from investing the $50. If he identifies the cow as fertile, he will conceal that fact and buy it for $190, receiving a gain of $810. In contrast, if he identifies it as infertile, he will not buy it. The buyer's expected gain at the time he invests the $50 is therefore

$$(.1)(\$810) + (.9)(0) - \$50 = \$81 - \$50 = \$31. \tag{4.1}$$

Since he expects a net gain of $31, he will make the investment. Note that the source of the net gain is the buyer's ability to avoid buying infertile cows, which are overpriced at $190.

The buyer's net gain in this case, however, is *purely private* in the sense that it does not change the use of the cow but simply redistributes the gains. In particular, note that the seller's profit in the state where the cow is fertile continues to be $190 (as in Table 4.1), but the seller's profit in the infertile state is now $100 because he is unable to sell it. The seller's expected profit is thus

$$(.1)(\$190) + (.9)(\$100) = \$109. \tag{4.2}$$

The expected social return is the sum of the buyer's return in (4.1) and the seller's return in (4.2):

$$\$31 + \$109 = \$140, \tag{4.3}$$

which is just the expected value of the cow in Table 4.1, $190, less the buyer's investment of $50. We conclude that *the investment produces no social benefit and is therefore wasteful.*

The buyer in this example was able to capitalize on this investment because the court allowed him to conceal his private information. Suppose instead that the court requires disclosure—that is, it will invalidate contracts in which there is a unilateral mistake. The buyer will no longer have an incentive to invest the $50 because if he tries to purchase a cow that he knows to be fertile at $190, the seller can simply reclaim the cow when this information becomes public (as happened in *Sherwood v. Walker*), thereby wiping out the $810 gain.

If the buyer chooses not to become informed and courts invalidate contracts based on mistake, then we are back in the situation of Table 4.2. But this is desirable from a social perspective because the buyer's investment to learn the cow's type produces no social benefits. This implies the following rule: *When information is purely distributive, courts should require disclosure of private information.*

3.3.2 Socially Valuable Information

We now consider a situation in which information is socially valuable. To do this, we continue with the cow example, but change the facts slightly. In particular, suppose that both parties are convinced that the cow is infertile (although there remains a 10 percent chance that she can breed), and information about her type will *not* become public knowledge unless the buyer invests the $50. Thus, if the buyer does not invest, he will buy the cow for $100 and slaughter her. The resulting social value is $100.

Now suppose that the buyer invests the $50 prior to contracting and can identify the cow's type. Also, suppose the court enforces contracts based on private information. Table 4.3 provides the relevant data. If the cow turns out to be fertile, the buyer realizes a windfall of $850, whereas if it is infertile, he suffers the loss of his sunk investment of $50. (Note that he is indifferent between buying the cow and not buying it in this state.) Since his expected value is $40, he will make the investment.

The buyer makes the investment in this case because it is privately profitable, but unlike the above example of purely distributive information, it is also socially valuable. In particular, note that the social return in this case is $140, which exceeds the $100 value when the buyer did not invest. The reason for the difference is that the buyer's investment *may alter the use of the cow.* Specifically, it allows the cow to be used for breeding in those states where it turns out to be fertile. The buyer's private gain thus coincides with a social gain, which is what makes his investment socially valuable. In contrast, when information was purely distributive, the buyer's investment had no effect on the use of the cow because the information would have become public before the cow was slaughtered. His investment simply allowed him to learn its type *earlier*—and thereby profit from it.

It should be clear that if courts required disclosure of private information

TABLE **4.3**   **Socially Valuable Information—Contract Enforced**

State	Buyer's profit	Seller's profit	Social value
Fertile	$1,000 − $100 − $50 = $850	$100	$1,000 − $50 = $950
Infertile	$100 − $100 − $50 = −$50	$100	$100 − $50 = $50
Expected value	(.1)($850) + (.9)(−$50) = $40	$100	(.1)($950) + (.9)($50) = $140

in this case, the buyer would be discouraged from investing. Since information in this case is socially valuable, this would result in a social loss. Thus, *when information is socially valuable, courts should not require disclosure of private information.*

3.3.3 Casual Versus Deliberate Acquisition of Information

To this point, we have distinguished between two types of information, purely distributive and socially valuable, and we have shown that they imply different enforcement rules. Another useful distinction concerns the manner in which information is acquired: whether it was the result of *deliberate search*, or was acquired *casually*, that is, with no expenditure of effort. The above cases where the buyer acquired information about the cow's type are examples of deliberate acquisition because the buyer invested resources with the specific purpose of being able to distinguish between fertile and infertile cows.[6] Our earlier conclusions therefore suggest that *courts should impose a duty to disclose deliberately acquired information when it is purely distributive but not when it is socially valuable.*

Casually acquired information is different in that the party acquiring the information did not invest any resources to obtain it; she merely came upon it by accident or chance. In cases like this, the disclosure rule will, by definition, have no effect on behavior, regardless of whether information is distributive or socially valuable. This implies that *when information is casually acquired, the disclosure rule is irrelevant for efficiency; its impact will be purely distributive.* The following exercise illustrates the distinction between deliberate and casual acquisition of information.

EXERCISE 4.1

A buyer makes a contract to purchase a parcel of land for residential use for $10,000. In the process of preparing for development, however, the buyer discovers a mineral deposit worth $500,000. The seller learns about the discovery and sues to invalidate the contract, claiming mistake.

  (a) Is the discovery of the mineral deposit socially valuable?
  (b) Did the buyer discover the information deliberately or casually?
  (c) Will a decision by the court to invalidate the contract affect the discovery of valuable mineral deposits in the future?

Now suppose that, prior to making the contract, the buyer had conducted an aerial survey of the property that indicated a high probability of a mineral deposit. The buyer then went ahead with the purchase for $10,000 without revealing his discovery to the seller.

(d) How does this change affect your answers to the above questions?

Table 4.4 summarizes the conclusions we have reached so far in our analysis of disclosure rules. It says that when information is deliberately acquired, courts should only compel disclosure when the information is purely distributive. As we have seen, such a rule encourages the production of socially useful information while discouraging wasteful production of distributive information. However, when information is casually acquired, the disclosure rule is irrelevant for efficiency. Thus, the rule can be chosen purely on the grounds of fairness or justice.

3.3.4   Disclosure of Unfavorable Information

The discovery that a cow thought to be infertile can breed and that a baseball card is worth more than initially believed are examples of the discovery of *favorable* information. In some cases, however, *unfavorable* information is discovered. For example, suppose that after purchasing a house, the buyer discovers that it is infested with termites. How do our conclusions regarding disclosure of information change in this case?

To be concrete, consider a contract for the sale of a house that may be infested with termites. Suppose that if termites are detected, the cost of extermination is $500, but if they are not detected, they will cause $2,000 worth of damages. Further, suppose that the fraction of houses with termites is one in ten. Clearly, information about the presence of termites is socially valuable in this case because of the expected cost savings, $(0.1)(\$2,000 - \$500) = \$150$. Thus, so long as this information can be acquired at a cost less than $150, it is socially valuable to do so.

Suppose that only the buyer can acquire information prior to sale (the case we have been considering). If he discovers termites, he will reveal that fact, whether or not the law compels him to do so, in order to receive a discount for

TABLE **4.4**   **Efficiency of Disclosure Rules Depending on the Type of Information and Manner of Acquisition**

		Type of information	
		Socially valuable	Purely distributive
Manner of acquisition	Deliberate	Do not require disclosure	Require disclosure
	Casual	Disclosure rule irrelevant for efficiency	Disclosure rule irrelevant for efficiency

the resulting costs. In contrast, if the seller discovers termites, she might not reveal it because it lowers the price that she can charge. Thus, the law should, and does, impose on sellers a duty to disclose unfavorable information.[7]

The preceding discussion reveals an apparent asymmetry between buyers and sellers regarding disclosure.[8] In our discussion of the cow case, we focused on acquisition of favorable information by buyers and concluded that the disclosure rule affects buyers' incentives to acquire such information prior to sale. In contrast, when sellers can acquire favorable information prior to sale, they will reveal it voluntarily, so a disclosure rule will not affect their decisions. (Thus, a seller of cows will voluntarily reveal the fertility of cows thought to be infertile.) In the case of unfavorable information, however, the situation is reversed: buyers will reveal the information voluntarily, but sellers must be compelled to do so. This difference reflects the fact that only the party who benefits from new information (the seller if it is favorable and the buyer if it is unfavorable) will disclose it voluntarily.

3.4 Unconscionability

The final reason for invalidating a contract is referred to as *unconscionability*. Under this doctrine, the court will invalidate contracts whose terms appear to be grossly unfair to one of the parties. The idea is that a party would not have voluntarily accepted such terms and therefore must have been either incompetent or the victim of duress (in the sense described above) or of fraud (Epstein 1975). However, under unconscionability, proof of these specific problems is not required. Instead, the court infers their presence from the terms of the contract and then imposes on the defendant the burden to prove that the contract was fair at the time it was formed. Unconscionability therefore does not introduce a new reason for invalidating a contract; it merely shifts the burden of establishing the fairness of the contract from the plaintiff to the defendant.

This shift in burden, however, has a practical impact. On the one hand, some contracts will be *properly* discharged because fraud, duress, or incompetence was present, but the plaintiff could not easily have proved it. On the other hand, some contracts that were fairly formed but turn out to be unfavorable to one party after the fact will be *improperly* discharged. In evaluating the desirability of unconscionability, therefore, the key question is the relative frequency and costs of these offsetting effects.

As an example, consider "add-on clauses" of the sort that the court ruled were unconscionable in *Williams v. Walker-Thomas Furniture Co.* (350 F.2d 445, D.C. Cir. 1965). Add-on clauses were sometimes used in contracts where consumers purchased durable goods like furniture on credit from the seller. The clause specified that if the buyer defaulted in paying for any particular item, the seller could repossess that item as well as any items the buyer had previously purchased and finished paying off. The court ruled such clauses unconscionable because they appeared to be grossly unfair to low-income buyers. Such a decision reflects the view that these clauses are manifestations of the superior bargaining power of sellers and hence a form of economic duress.

But economists take a different perspective by asking whether add-on clauses may have been a response to, rather than a source of, some kind of market failure. For example, suppose that poor consumers are unable to obtain bank loans for the purchase of durable goods owing to lack of collateral. The availability of add-on clauses might make sellers willing to extend credit to these buyers because, once an item is paid for, it can serve as collateral for the purchase of additional items. Thus, rather than being disadvantaged, buyers actually benefit from add-on clauses by gaining access to credit that they otherwise could not have obtained.

This is not to say that consumers are never taken advantage of by complex contract terms that they don't fully understand. It does, however, indicate the trade-off that courts face in deciding whether to invoke unconscionability. An important factor in evaluating this trade-off is whether examination of the terms of the contract provides good evidence one way or the other. A problem with sole reliance on the terms of the contract is its potential for circularity: "The party is ruled incompetent because the deal is bad, while the deal is ruled bad because the party is incompetent" (Craswell and Schwartz 1994, 338). To avoid this problem, evidence of incompetence, duress, or fraud should ideally be external to the contract itself. Otherwise, the threat of opportunism will be high, thereby reducing the expected value of contracting. At the same time, if certain contractual practices systematically arise in the presence of cases of unequal bargaining power (as may have been the case with add-on clauses), then the use of unconscionability to strike them down may be appropriate. If use of the doctrine is restricted to these sorts of cases, then it can serve a useful economic purpose.

4   Conclusion

This chapter began the economic analysis of contract law by reviewing the role of contracts in promoting efficient exchange. Using the competitive market as the paradigm for determining the elements of a valid (enforceable) contract, we interpreted legal reasons for invalidating contracts as responses to various forms of market failure. We first examined the rule invalidating contracts entered under duress and argued that the proper economic function of this doctrine is to prevent monopoly. We then turned to the tangled doctrine of mistake, which concerns the duty to disclose private information prior to contracting. At first glance, one might expect maximal disclosure to be most conducive to efficient exchange, but when incentives for information acquisition are taken into account, the issue becomes less clear. Our analysis of some simple examples suggested that efficient disclosure rules turn on two key dimensions: whether the information is socially valuable, and whether it was acquired deliberately or casually.

Finally, we considered the doctrine of unconscionability, which allows the court to invalidate contracts that appear to be grossly unfair. We argued that, while this doctrine might result in the proper invalidation of some contracts that were truly unfair but where plaintiffs lack evidence of fraud or coercion, it also might result in the improper invalidation of contracts that were fairly formed but simply turned out to be unfavorable to the plaintiff. The economic desirability of the doctrine depends on the relative frequency of these two outcomes.

This chapter focused on the enforceability of contracts. The next turns to the design of remedies for breach of contract. The key questions in that discussion are: When is it efficient to breach an enforceable contract? and, What legal remedies encourage breach only in those circumstances?

DISCUSSION QUESTIONS

1. In contract law, promises are enforceable if supported by consideration—that is, if they are mutual. In contrast, promises to give gifts are not generally enforceable unless the intended recipient incurs some expenses in anticipation that the promise will be honored. Discuss this distinction from an economic perspective.

2. Scheppele (1988, 84) argues that courts require disclosure of "deep secrets," those about which the uninformed party has no idea, but not "shallow secrets," those about which the uninformed party has some "shadowy sense." Does this rule make economic sense?

3. Posner (1998a, 114) notes that the facts of *Sherwood v. Walker* provide "some evidence that [the cow's] sale price included her value if pregnant, discounted (very drastically of course) by the probability of that happy eventuality." Should this evidence affect the court's decision regarding enforcement of the original contract?

4. The Statute of Frauds requires contracts for the sale of very valuable goods (like real estate) to be in writing. Provide an economic rationale for this rule based on the trade-off between the cost of drafting contracts and the risk that transactions will not be completed due to opportunism or legal error.

PROBLEMS

1. Consider the following two cases of contract modification:

   In *Recker v. Gustafson* (279 N.W.2d 744, 1979), the Reckers agreed to pay the Gustafsons $290,000 for a farm. Prior to closing, however, the Gustafsons demanded an additional $10,000 after informing the Reckers that they were "willing to go to court to get out of the [original] agreement and that litigation was expensive." The Reckers agreed to the price increase but later sued to have it refunded, claiming coercion.

In *Blakeslee et al. v. Board of Water Com'rs of City of Hartford* (139 A. 106, 1927), the plaintiff sought and obtained a price increase when the cost of building a dam rose unexpectedly due to the diversion of workers and materials at the outbreak of WWI. The city later sued to have the original price reinstated.

(a) Did the promisors offer new consideration in support of the requested price increase in either of these cases?

(b) Does economic theory provide any basis for distinguishing between the two cases? Explain.

2. Consider a contract for the sale of a parcel of land from seller S to buyer B at a price of $15,000. After the sale is complete, the local government announces plans to build a highway near the property, which raises its value to $100,000. S sues to have the contract invalidated on the grounds of mistake. Suppose it is learned at trial that the land would only have been worth $5,000 if the highway had not been approved. What does this information tell you about S's claim that the mistake was *mutual*?

3. The plaintiff in a breach of contract case sought to invalidate a contract in which he sold mineral rights in his land after he learned that the buyer found a valuable deposit. Suppose it was revealed at trial that the buyer had conducted aerial surveys of the site prior to purchase and had discovered evidence of the deposit, yet he had withheld the information from the seller. Should the court invalidate the contract on the grounds that the buyer had a duty to disclose the information? Is the information socially valuable or purely distributive?

4. The famous case of *Laidlaw v. Organ* (15 U.S. 178, 1817) concerned a contract in which a merchant in New Orleans, after receiving private information about the treaty ending the War of 1812, ordered a quantity of tobacco at a preset price. When the information became public, ending the naval blockade of New Orleans, the price of tobacco shot up, and the seller sought to invalidate the contract. Is the buyer's early knowledge of the treaty socially valuable or purely distributive? (Assume the buyer did nothing with this information besides forming the contract.) How should the court rule in this case? How would your answer be affected (if at all) by knowledge about the manner in which the information was acquired?

CHAPTER 5

THE ECONOMICS OF CONTRACT LAW II:
Remedies for Breach

The preceding chapter examined the question of what contracts are legally enforceable. We argued there that the various formation defenses ensure that the law will only enforce contracts that were formed voluntarily and, hence, promise a mutual benefit. Contracts that appear mutually beneficial at the time of formation, however, may not be when the date of performance arrives. The reason is the occurrence of some unforeseen contingency that reduces the value or raises the cost of performance for one of the parties. If the contract is judged to be enforceable—that is, if the party seeking to avoid performance fails to convince the court that the contract was invalidly formed—then the court must decide on a remedy. Designing an efficient remedy for the breach of enforceable contracts is the subject of this chapter.

We begin the analysis by arguing that breach of contract is efficient in those cases where the cost of performance turns out to exceed the benefit of performance. An efficient remedy for breach should give contractors an incentive to breach only in those circumstances. In addition, we will examine the incentives breach remedies create for parties to make investments in preparation for performance. These *reliance investments* are desirable because they enhance the value of performance, but they are often nonsalvageable in the event of breach. Thus, we examine the role of breach remedies in preventing contractors from overrelying on performance. Finally, we consider the role of breach remedies in assigning the risk of breach in an optimal way.

In examining the above issues, we will focus primarily on money damages since that is the standard remedy employed by courts. However, we will also examine specific performance, a remedy that is used less often, but one that we will argue ought to be used more often. Finally, we will examine remedies designed by the parties themselves, including liquidated damage clauses and product warranties.

1   The Efficient Breach Model

We begin with several examples of efficient breach.[1] The general setting concerns a contract between a buyer and a seller for the production and delivery of some good. Let V be the value of the good to the buyer and let C be the variable cost of production for the seller. (We will assume that the seller has zero fixed costs.)

Example 1: Uncertainty over Production Costs.   Suppose that the seller's cost of production is uncertain at the time the contract is made, due, for example, to uncertainty over energy, labor, or material costs. When the value of C is realized, the seller must decide whether to go ahead with production of the good. The efficient rule is to produce the good if $C < V$ but to breach the contract if $C > V$. Breach is efficient in the latter case because the cost of resources needed to complete production is greater than the value of performance. Thus, production would entail a net loss of $C - V$.

Example 2: Uncertainty over the Value of Performance to the Buyer.   In this case, suppose that the value of performance to the buyer is uncertain. For example, a factory orders a machine that it may not need if the demand for its product falls. Although the uncertainty is over V rather than C in this example, the condition for efficient breach (and the rationale) is the same as in example 1: that is, it is efficient to breach if $V < C$, and it is efficient to perform if $V > C$.

Example 3: Uncertainty About Offers from Alternative Buyers.   Suppose that the seller has completed production of the good (given that $V > C$), but before he can deliver it to the original buyer, a second buyer arrives and offers a higher price. In this case, efficiency dictates that the good should end up with the buyer who values it most. Thus, if V' is the valuation of the second buyer, then it is efficient for the seller to breach the original contract and sell to the second buyer if $V' > V$. (But see the discussion of this type of case in Section 2.3 below.)

These examples illustrate the conditions for *efficient breach*, but they say nothing about *actual breach*. In general, the breaching party will not base her decision on efficiency, but rather on how it affects her private return, in the same way that injurers made their care decisions based on private rather than social costs. The role of breach remedies, like tort damages, will therefore be to align the interests of the breaching party with those of society. The next section shows how this is done.

1.1 Money Damages and Efficient Breach

In the remainder of this chapter, we will rely primarily on example 1 (uncertainty over production costs) to illustrate the economic theory of breach. To be concrete, consider a contract for the construction of a house. Let the value of the house to the buyer be V, which is known, but suppose that the seller's actual cost of production is uncertain at the time the contract is made. For example, suppose the he is unsure how costly it will be to dig the foundation. However, he *expects* his costs to be less than the contract price P, which is less than the buyer's valuation. Thus, both parties expect to enjoy a positive gain from the contract.

Suppose further that in preparation for performance of the contract, the buyer made a *reliance investment* of R. For example, suppose that she hired a moving company to deliver her furniture on a certain date. The reason for making the investment is to enhance the value of performance in the event that the contract is completed (thus, V depends on R in a way that will be made explicit below), but the cost is that the investment will be lost if the contract is breached (for example, a non-refundable deposit paid to the moving company will be lost, or the furniture will have to be stored). We say that the investment of R is nonsalvageable.[2] The fact that the buyer invests R *before* the seller makes his breach decision is therefore crucial; if she could wait, she would clearly only spend R in the performance state. In many cases, however, waiting will not be possible or desirable. For purposes of the current analysis, we treat R as a fixed expenditure. Below, we examine the optimal choice of R by the buyer.

Finally, let D be the court-imposed damage payment that the seller must pay to the buyer in the event of breach. Our goal will be to determine the value of D that induces the seller to breach efficiently. Table 5.1 summarizes the payoffs to the buyer, the seller, and the joint (social) payoffs in the performance and breach states.

Before proceeding, recall that the condition for efficient breach in this example is

$$C > V, \tag{5.1}$$

or that the cost of performance exceeds the value of performance. Note that the reliance investment is irrelevant for this condition because it is a sunk cost at the time production costs are realized. To see this, note from column three

TABLE **5.1** **Breach of Contract Example**

State	Buyer's return	Seller's return	Joint return
Performance	$V - R - P$	$P - C$	$V - R - C$
Breach	$D - R$	$-D$	$-R$

of the table that the joint return from breach exceeds the joint return from performance if $-R > V - R - C$. The R's cancel, leaving $C > V$.

Now consider the actual breach decision by the seller. It is clear from column two of the table that, once production costs are realized, the seller will breach if $-D > P - C$, or if

$$C > P + D. \tag{5.2}$$

The left-hand side of this condition is the benefit of breach—the savings in production costs, while the right-hand side is the cost of breach—the foregone price plus damages. The seller will breach when the benefit exceeds the cost.

Remember that our objective is to give the seller an incentive to breach only when it is efficient. Thus, we want the seller's private breach condition in (5.2) to coincide with the social condition in (5.1). This will be true if the right-hand sides of the two conditions are equal, or if

$$D = V - P, \tag{5.3}$$

which says that damages should equal the difference between the buyer's valuation and the price (known as the buyer's surplus).

This damage measure was derived with the specific goal of inducing efficient breach. The next question is how it relates to actual remedies employed by courts in breach of contract cases. By far the most popular measure of damages is *expectation damages*, which is defined to be an amount of money that leaves the promisee (the victim of breach—in this case the buyer) as well off as if the contract had been performed. That is, it leaves the promisee indifferent between breach and performance. We can thus calculate this measure from Table 5.1 by equating the two rows in the buyer's column and solving for D. The result is $D = V - P$, which is identical to the measure in (5.3)! Thus, expectation damages gives sellers exactly the right incentives for efficient breach.

On reflection, this conclusion should not be surprising. Because expectation damages fully compensates the buyer for her losses as a result of breach, the seller is forced to internalize those losses and therefore makes the socially correct breach decision. Note the similarity to strict liability in torts, which likewise fully compensates victims for their losses from an accident and therefore induces injurers to take efficient care. The current model of efficient breach is therefore analogous to the unilateral care model of accidents from Chapter 2.[3]

Another measure of damages occasionally used by courts is *reliance damages*, defined to be an amount of money that leaves promisees as well off as if the contract had never been made. Like expectation damages, this measure is meant to fully compensate victims of breach, except that the reference point is their precontract status rather than their postperformance status. Since the returns in Table 5.1 are measured as net gains, the buyer's precontract status is zero profit. Thus, equating the buyer's return in the breach state to zero yields $D = R$. Reliance damages thus reimburse the buyer for her nonsalvageable reliance expenditures.

What are the seller's incentives for breach under the reliance measure? Substituting $D = R$ into (5.2) yields the breach condition:

$$C > P + R. \tag{5.4}$$

The seller will therefore breach *too often* if $P + R < V$ and *too little* if $P + R > V$. But note that $V - R - P > 0$ in order for the buyer to receive a positive return from performance of the contract (see the first row in the buyer's column). Thus, $P + R < V$ and *the seller breaches too often under reliance damages*.

Finally, we consider the seller's incentives for breach under *zero damages* ($D = 0$). Under this measure, the seller will breach whenever $C > P$, or whenever he incurs a loss from performance. Since breach will occur even more frequently under zero damages than under reliance damages (given $R > 0$), breach must also be excessive in this case. We return to zero damages in our discussion of the impossibility defense below. Figure 5.1 summarizes our conclusions regarding breach by showing the ranges of production costs over which breach occurs under the various damage measures compared to the efficient range.

Figure 5.1

Ranges Where Breach Occurs Under Various Damage Measures

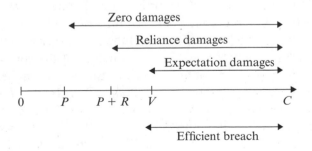

EXERCISE 5.1

Consider the following numerical example of the above construction contract. Let

$V = \$100{,}000$

$R = \$5{,}000$

$P = \$75{,}000$

(a) Calculate expectation damages and reliance damages for this example.

Suppose the builder's production costs, C, are uncertain at the time the contract is made.

(b) Over what range of C is it *efficient* for the builder to breach?

(c) Over what ranges of C will the builder *actually* breach under expectation damages, reliance damages, and zero damages?

1.2   Incentives for Efficient Reliance

We now extend the model to allow the buyer to choose the level of reliance. In order to do this, we need to be explicit about the relationship between the reliance choice, R, and the buyer's value of performance, V. As noted above, reliance investments are made prior to the contract to enhance the buyer's value of performance. Thus, we suppose that V is increasing in R but at a decreasing rate, reflecting the usual assumption of diminishing returns. Figure 5.2 shows $V(R)$ graphically.

If performance of the contract were certain, then the socially efficient level of reliance would maximize the net value of performance. That is, R would be chosen to

$$\text{maximize} \quad V(R) - R. \tag{5.5}$$

Let R^* be the solution to this problem. In Figure 5.2, R^* occurs at the point where the vertical distance between the $V(R)$ and R curves is greatest. (This is also the point where the slopes of the two curves are equal.)

As we saw above, however, performance of the contract is not certain if the seller's costs turn out to be high. To capture this in the simplest way, suppose that the seller will realize either *high costs* (C_H) or *low costs* (C_L), where $C_H > C_L$, and that performance is only efficient when costs are low.[4] Further, suppose that when the contract is made, both parties know that the probability of low costs is q. Thus, the probability of efficient breach is $1 - q$.

Figure 5.2

Efficient Reliance
When Performance Is
Certain (R*) and When
It Is Uncertain (R̂)

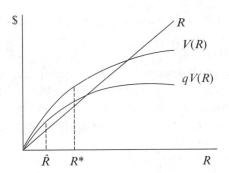

What is the buyer's optimal reliance given this uncertainty over performance? Return to Table 5.1. The final column shows the joint return from the contract in the performance and breach states (where now V should be viewed as a function of R). Weighting the first line by q, the probability of performance, and the second line by $1 - q$, the probability of breach, yields the expected joint (social) value of the contract:

$$q[V(R) - C_L] - R = qV(R) - qC_L - R. \tag{5.6}$$

The efficient level of reliance, denoted $\hat{R}$, maximizes this expected value. It is important to note that the $-qC_L$ term in this expression does not affect $\hat{R}$ since it is just an additive constant. Thus, $\hat{R}$ also maximizes the expression $qV(R) - R$. This outcome is shown in Figure 5.2. Note that $\hat{R} < R^*$, reflecting the fact that the buyer should invest less when performance is uncertain in order to reduce the loss in the breach state (given the nonsalvageability of R). Indeed, it should be clear from the graph that as the probability of performance decreases (i.e., as q falls), so should $\hat{R}$.

So far we have derived the efficient level of buyer reliance in a world of uncertain performance. The next step is to consider the buyer's actual choice of reliance. In order to do this, we need to reintroduce the damage remedy. Since our hope is to induce the buyer to invest in the efficient level of reliance while retaining incentives for efficient breach, we begin with the expectation damage remedy. In the current version of the model, this measure is given by $D = V(R) - P$. Note that the buyer's damages in the event of breach therefore depend on her choice of reliance because, as she invests more reliance, her loss in the event of breach increases.

As we showed above, the seller will make the efficient breach decision under expectation damages. Thus, the buyer expects the seller to breach when costs are high, and to perform when costs are low. From Table 5.1, we can therefore calculate the buyer's expected return to be

$$q[V(R) - R - P] + (1 - q)(D - R). \tag{5.7}$$

Substituting $D = V(R) - P$ in to this expression yields

$$q[V(R) - R - P] + (1 - q)[V(R) - R - P] = V(R) - R - P. \qquad (5.8)$$

Note that the level of reliance that maximizes this expression is R^*, the efficient level of reliance when performance is certain. Thus, *expectation damages causes the buyer to overinvest in reliance.* Intuitively, expectation damages fully insures the buyer against the risk of breach; hence, she behaves as if performance were certain. In other words, expectation damages creates a moral hazard problem for the buyer.

Earlier, we drew an analogy between expectation damages and strict liability in torts. Recall that in bilateral care accident models (that is, models in which both the injurer and victim can take care), strict liability gave injurers the correct incentives for care, but because victims were fully compensated for their losses, they had no incentives to take care. We may also describe the current contracting model as a "bilateral care" model because both the buyer and seller make choices that affect the value of the contract. In this context, the problem of overreliance by buyers under expectation damages directly corresponds to the problem of underinvestment in care by accident victims under strict liability (Cooter 1985).

We resolved this bilateral incentive problem in torts by switching from strict liability to negligence. Thus, we could similarly try to define a negligence-type rule for breach of contract that sets a threshold for efficient reliance. Such a rule, for example, would require sellers to pay full damages for breach if the buyer invested in the efficient level of reliance and no damages if the buyer overrelied. In equilibrium, buyers would invest in efficient reliance in order to ensure compensation in the breach state, and sellers would breach efficiently because they expected to pay full compensation.

The problem with this scheme is that there is apparently no analog to negligence in contract law.[5] Fortunately, there is a doctrine in contract law that addresses the problem of overreliance by a different method. We will refer to it as the *Hadley v. Baxendale* rule after the case in which it was first proposed.[6]

The facts of this case are easily stated. The plaintiffs operated a mill that was forced to shut down when the crank shaft broke. Because the design of the shaft was specific to the plaintiffs' mill, they needed to ship the broken one back to the manufacturer to serve as a pattern for construction of a new one. Accordingly, they hired the defendant, a carrier company, to transport the shaft. The defendant promised delivery to the manufacturer the following day, but delivery was "delayed by some neglect," which caused the mill to be shut down for several days. The plaintiffs sued for the lost profits resulting from the delay. The defendants conceded that they were negligent in delaying delivery, but they claimed that the requested damages were too high because the need for the mill to shut down was a "remote" possibility.

In deciding this case, the court stated the following general rule:

Where two parties have made a contract which one of them has broken, the damages which the other party ought to receive in respect of such breach of contract should be such as may fairly and reasonably be considered either arising naturally, i.e., according to the usual course of things, from such breach of contract itself, or such as may reasonably be supposed to have been in the contemplation of both parties, at the time they made the contract, as the probable result of the breach of it.

The implication of this rule is that damages for breach of contract will be *limited* to a reasonable level. One way to interpret this limitation is that damages will be limited to the losses that result from a reasonable (efficient) level of reliance. In terms of our model, expectation damages under the *Hadley v. Baxendale* rule would therefore be written

$$D = V(\hat{R}) - P. \tag{5.9}$$

Note that this differs from the *unlimited* expectation damage measure in (5.3) in that here, damages are based on the efficient level of reliance, whereas in (5.3), damages were based on the actual level of reliance.

The difference between limited and unlimited expectation damages is illustrated in Figure 5.3. Suppose the plaintiff invested in reliance of $R' > \hat{R}$. Under the unlimited measure, she would receive the full amount of the difference between $V(R')$ and P, whereas under the limited measure, she would receive the smaller amount $V(\hat{R}) - P$ (shown by the darkened segment in the graph). Thus, she would not be compensated for the value of reliance in excess of $\hat{R}$.

What is the impact of this limitation on the buyer's choice of reliance? Return to the buyer's expected return in (5.7), but now substitute the damage measure in (5.9) for D. The resulting expression, after rearranging, is

$$qV(R) - R - P + (1 - q) V(\hat{R}). \tag{5.10}$$

Note that the final two terms in this expression are constants—that is, they are independent of R. Thus, the value of R that maximizes (5.10) is the same

Figure 5.3

Comparison of Limited and Unlimited Expectation Damages

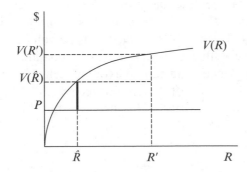

as that which maximizes $qV(R) - R$, which is $\hat{R}$, the efficient level of reliance. Thus, *under the limited expectation damage measure, the buyer invests in the efficient level of reliance.*[7]

Mathematically, this result arose because the first and last terms in (5.10) cannot be combined to eliminate the q since $V(R)$ is a *function* while $V(\hat{R})$ is a *number* (a single point of the function $V(R)$). Intuitively, the buyer has no incentive to invest in reliance beyond $\hat{R}$ because she will receive zero compensation for any losses that result. (In this sense, limited expectation damages is a threshold rule like negligence.) The moral hazard problem associated with full compensation is thereby eliminated.

In some cases, buyers may have unavoidably high reliance, perhaps because they underestimated the likelihood of breach, or simply because there is some variation in the value of performance across buyers. (For example, there are high and low V's in the population of buyers: some mills have spare shafts and some don't.) The court in *Hadley v. Baxendale* also addressed this possibility by placing the burden on high-value plaintiffs (those who have a lot to lose from breach) to communicate this information to defendants. If they do, then the damages in the event of breach "would be the amount of injury which would ordinarily follow from a breach of contract under these special circumstances so known and communicated." However, if the plaintiffs failed to communicate their higher than normal value of performance, then the damages would be limited to the "injury which would arise generally, and in the great multitude of cases not affected by any special circumstances, from such a breach of contract."

In other words, the law limits the ability of promisees to collect so-called consequential damages, defined to be damages that were unforeseeable to the promisor at the time of breach. From an economic perspective, limiting damages in this way serves to encourage communication between the parties prior to contracting. This is desirable because it allows defendants to exercise extra care in those cases where the cost of breach is unusually high.[8]

In sum, the *Hadley v. Baxendale* rule serves two important economic functions in breach of contract cases. First, when buyers can choose the level of reliance prior to contracting, it prevents them from overrelying by limiting the damages to the amount that buyers would lose if they had invested efficiently. Second, when buyers vary in their valuation of performance, it encourages those with higher than normal valuations to communicate that fact so sellers can take extra care to avoid breach. Thus, the court in *Hadley* held that the mill's lost profits were not recoverable because the mill owner had not informed the carrier of his need to shut down for lack of a spare shaft.

1.3   Mitigation of Damages

A related limitation on expectation damages concerns the duty to mitigate damages following breach (Goetz and Scott 1983). Suppose, for example, that the owner of a duplex house agrees to rent an apartment to a college student for twelve months at a monthly rent of $300, but after six months, the student abandons the apartment. At the end of the twelve-month term, the landlord files suit for the unpaid rent of $1,800. The student admits to breaching the contract, but claims that a friend had offered the landlord $200 a month for the remaining six months of the lease, which the landlord refused. The student therefore claims that landlord is only entitled to $600, the difference between the aggregate unpaid rent and the amount that the landlord could have received by re-letting the apartment to the friend.

In this case, the court would agree with the student. The general principle is that contractors have a duty to take any reasonable (cost-effective) efforts to mitigate the damages from breach. This rule promotes efficiency by preventing resources from being wasted or, in the apartment example, from being left idle. The way that courts enforce the duty to mitigate is by limiting damages to the losses that the mitigator could not have avoided by reasonable efforts. In contrast, avoidable losses cannot be recovered.[9] Thus, the landlord can only collect damages of $100 per month since he could have re-let the apartment for $200.[10]

Note that the *Hadley v. Baxendale* rule, which limits damages to prevent overreliance or to encourage revelation of unusually high reliance, also promotes a form of mitigation. In this case, contractors take steps to minimize expected damages before breach. Note that this type of "anticipatory mitigation" resembles victim precaution in bilateral care accidents. In the next section, we explicitly introduce the idea of optimal "precaution" against breach.

1.4   Impossibility and Related Excuses

The economic theory of breach of contract remedies is based on the recognition that changed circumstances can sometimes make breach of contract more efficient than performance. The fact that promisors should be excused from performance in some cases, however, does not imply that they should suffer no penalty for doing so. Indeed, we have shown that promisors will breach too often unless they must pay damages equal to the expected losses of promisees (expectation damages). There are circumstances, however, in which the court excuses performance without imposing any damages. This section discusses the economic basis for these so-called performance excuses.

The prototypical performance excuse is *impossibility*.[11] Under this doctrine, a promisor is excused when performance is no longer physically possible. A closely related excuse is *frustration of purpose*, which applies when performance is physically possible, but the purpose of the bargain is no longer attainable. Finally, *commercial impracticability* is invoked when performance is possible and the purpose of the contract is attainable, but the cost of performance has become much higher than originally anticipated. We focus on the first two excuses here, and then turn to commercial impracticability in Section 1.4.2. below.

The problem we need to address with regard to impossibility and frustration of purpose is not the desirability of breach, but why courts sometimes allow breach *without penalty*. To do this, we introduce the notion of efficient risk sharing.

1.4.1 Efficient Risk Sharing

To this point, we have ignored the problem of optimal risk sharing in contract settings. But an important purpose of contracts, in addition to promoting efficient breach and reliance, is to allocate the risk of unforeseen contingencies between the parties to the exchange (Polinsky 1983).

If a contract spells out the allocation of a particular risk—for example, by providing for price adjustments in the face of cost increases—then courts should enforce that allocation since the parties were presumably in the best position to assign the risk optimally. The more interesting problem is when the contract is silent about the risk. Then the court must decide, after the fact, how the parties would have assigned the risk had they planned for it. This is a hard problem, but economic theory provides a basis for solving it—namely, *assign the risk to the superior risk bearer*. Generally, optimal risk bearing involves two elements: prevention and insurance.

Prevention.   A party can be the superior risk bearer if she is in the best position to *prevent the risk*. The issue is closely related to the idea of precaution against accidents in tort law, where the "accident" in this case is an unforeseen event that causes a breach of contract.[12]

To illustrate this "prevention model" of breach, consider the following hypothetical case.[13] A printer contracts with a manufacturer of printing machinery for the construction of a machine to be installed in the printer's premises. After the machine is completed but prior to installation, a fire destroys the printer's premises. Since the machine is custom-made and therefore has no salvage value, the manufacturer sues for the full price, while the printer seeks discharge of the contract on the grounds of impossibility. (He could just as well claim frustration of purpose.)

How can we use the prevention model to resolve this dispute? Suppose that the printer can undertake precaution of x to reduce the probability of a fire, given by $q(x)$. Also, let V be the value of performance to the printer, P the price, and C the cost of building the machine. From a social perspective, the efficient level of precaution by the printer maximizes the expected value of performance:

$$(1 - q(x))V - C - x, \tag{5.11}$$

where $1 - q(x)$, the probability of performance, is increasing in x. (Note that the cost of construction in this expression is sunk and therefore has no effect on the optimal level of precaution.) Let x^* be the value of x that maximizes (5.11).

Now consider the actual incentives of the printer. His expected profit is given by

$$(1 - q(x))(V - P) - q(x)D - x, \tag{5.12}$$

where D is the damage payment. Suppose first that zero damages are awarded to the manufacturer (as the printer requests). In this case, (5.12) reduces to $(1 - q(x))(V - P) - x$. The printer therefore underestimates the value of performance and hence chooses too little effort to prevent breach. In contrast, if the printer is required to pay the full price for the machine (the measure of expectation damages for the manufacturer in this case), that is, if $D = P$, then (5.12) becomes $(1 - q(x))V - P - x$, which is identical to (5.11) except for the additive constants. The printer therefore chooses x^*, the optimal level of precaution. Thus, although performance is impossible, the printer should *not* be excused from paying damages. The conclusion is therefore the same as in our earlier discussion of efficient breach: impose expectation damages on the party who either intentionally breaches the contract, or who is in the best position to prevent breach.

In many cases, however, breach will not be preventable. Perhaps the fire could not be avoided despite all reasonable steps by the printer. When this is true, the focus shifts to providing optimal *insurance* against the risk.

Insurance.   Economists typically assume that individual economic agents are risk averse, which means that they are willing to pay some amount of money to avoid uncertainty. For example, consider the decision of a home-owner to purchase fire insurance. Suppose that the probability of a fire in a given year is one in one thousand (.001), and that the loss from a fire would be $100,000. The expected cost per year is thus $100. A risk-averse homeowner, however, would be willing to pay more than $100 per year (say $120) to buy an insurance policy to cover the loss.

Why would the insurance company be willing to sell the policy? Suppose that it sells one thousand of the above policies to identical homeowners. Its total revenue would be $120,000, and it would expect to have one claim costing $100,000. Thus, it would expect to earn a profit of $20,000. The insurance company is willing to take on the risk because it can rely on the large number of uncorrelated risks to result in a (fairly) predictable cost from year to year. Thus, market insurance provides a benefit to both the insured individual (who avoids uncertainty), and the insurance company (which expects to earn a profit).

The discussion so far has focused on *market insurance*, but parties facing a risk can also *self-insure*.[14] For example, the above homeowner could set aside some money every year in a fund to be used in case of fire. More commonly, people self-insure against small risks, such as the loss of a cheap watch. In general, we expect individuals to choose whichever form of insurance is cheaper for the particular risk that they face.

The preceding discussion suggests that, in the case of the risk from breach of contract, courts should apply the following principle: *assign the risk to the party that can insure against it at lowest cost.* To illustrate this principle, consider a couple of examples.

Consider first the printer example from above. If the fire could not be prevented, then the determination of damages must rest on the abilities of the parties to insure against the loss. On the one hand, the printer could purchase fire insurance against the loss of its business, including any outstanding contractual obligations. It seems less likely that the manufacturer could purchase market insurance against breach due to fires in its customers' premises. However, the manufacturer may be able to self-insure by charging a small premium to all of its customers to cover the risk of breach. Given these two possibilities, optimal risk sharing dictates that the court should enforce payment for the machine if the printer can acquire market insurance at lower cost, and it should discharge the contract if the manufacturer can self-insure at lower cost. The answer will depend on the facts of the particular case.

As a second example, consider a contract for the delivery of an agricultural product that may be rendered impossible by adverse weather conditions like a flood or drought.[15] Clearly in this case, prevention is not an issue so the question again becomes, which party, the buyer or the seller, can better insure against bad weather? Suppose first that the seller is a farmer and the buyer is a large grocery store chain. In this case, the buyer can reduce the risk of nondelivery due to bad weather by diversifying its purchases geographically, something that the farmer cannot do.[16] Thus, the court should discharge the contract because the buyer is the superior risk-bearer.

The story is different when the seller is a wholesaler because he can similarly reduce the risk of nondelivery by diversifying his purchases. Indeed, the grocery store may deal with a wholesaler precisely because the latter is in a better position to diversify. In this case, the court should not discharge the contract.

The preceding cases suggest how courts can apply the principle of optimal risk sharing. That does not mean that the cases will be easy; there will almost always be cross-cutting effects that will have to be weighed on a case-by-case basis. Nevertheless, economic theory at least provides a consistent framework to apply to these cases.

1.4.2   Commercial Impracticability

Our discussion to this point has focused primarily on situations in which performance is made physically impossible as a result of an unforeseen contingency. Courts will also discharge contracts when performance is *physically* possible but has become *economically* burdensome; performance in this case is said to be *commercially impracticable*.[17] Risk sharing can also justify this action, but only at a cost, given our earlier conclusion that setting damages at zero will lead to excessive breach. A proper formulation of the commercial impracticability defense, however, turns out to be consistent with efficient breach and also to provide an advantage over simple (unlimited) expectation damages.

To see this, note that the impracticability defense is *not* equivalent to zero damages, as we defined it above. Rather, it is a conditional rule that discharges performance without penalty only when costs are exceptionally high. To illustrate, recall the above example of a construction contract where the builder faces uncertain costs. Suppose now that his costs can take one of three values, high (C_H), medium (C_M), or low (C_L). Further, suppose that breach is efficient only when costs are high: $C_H > V > C_M > C_L$, where V is the buyer's value of performance (ignore for now the buyer's choice of reliance). Suppose, however, that the builder only earns a profit when costs are low: $C_H > C_M > P > C_L$. (Note that these two assumptions are compatible given $V > P$.)

As we saw in our analysis of breach, expectation damages will lead to efficient breach, and zero damages will result in too much breach. Thus, in the current example the builder will breach under expectation damages ($D = V - P$) if $P - C \leq (V - P)$, or if $C > V$, which only holds for high costs; but he will breach under zero damages ($D = 0$) if $P - C < 0$, which holds for high and medium costs.

Now consider the following formulation of the commercial impracticability defense:

$$D = \begin{array}{ll} V - P, & \text{if } C = C_L \text{ or } C_M \\ 0, & \text{if } C = C_H. \end{array} \tag{5.13}$$

Note that under this rule, the builder is only discharged if he realizes high costs; if he realizes low or medium costs he is still subject to expectation damages in the event of breach. He will therefore perform when costs are low or medium (even though he incurs a loss in the medium-cost state), and breach only in the high-cost state—exactly the efficient outcome. And although it will appear that the builder is being excused from paying damages whenever he breaches (that is, that he is paying zero damages), it is actually the threat of positive damages in the low- and medium-cost states that prevents him from breaching too often. The impracticability defense when formulated in this way thus functions exactly like a negligence rule in torts.

The fact that both expectation damages and impracticability induce efficient breach parallels our conclusion that both strict liability and negligence induce efficient injurer care in accident models. The primary advantage of negligence in the tort context was that it also created incentives for victim care. Thus, the corresponding question here is whether the rule in (5.13) can simultaneously induce efficient reliance by buyers.

To answer this question, let q be the probability that costs are low or medium and $1 - q$ be the probability that costs are high. Thus, q is the probability of efficient performance. Since the buyer correctly anticipates efficient breach by the builder under the rule in (5.13), and also that she will receive no damages in the event of breach, she will choose reliance to maximize

$$q[V(R) - P] - R. \tag{5.14}$$

You should recognize by now that the solution to this problem is the efficient level of reliance, given that the term $-qP$ is additive and independent of R. Thus, the impracticability rule in (5.13) does indeed achieve bilateral efficiency. That is, it simultaneously induces efficient breach by the builder and efficient reliance by the buyer.

Of course, we have already seen that the *Hadley v. Baxendale* rule also achieves bilateral efficiency in breach of contract cases. The choice between the two rules therefore depends on which is easier for the court to implement. Both place high information demands on the court, though the required information is different. The *Hadley v. Baxendale* rule requires the court to determine the efficient level of buyer reliance in order to calculate the correct level of expectation damages, while the impracticability rule requires the court to set the threshold for discharge at the level of builder costs where breach becomes efficient. Since either burden may be easier to meet in a given case, we cannot assert that one rule is generally superior to the other.

There is one final point to make regarding commercial impracticability. Under the Uniform Commercial Code (UCC), defendants cannot invoke the defense if they have assumed the risk of the cost increase either *directly* or *indirectly*. Direct assumption of risk means that the contract contained explicit language to the effect that the defendant will bear any cost increases. But if the contract is silent about a risk, what evidence might the court use to infer that the defendant has indirectly assumed it?

Consider a contract for the digging of the foundation for a house. Suppose the contractor quotes a price of $5,000, but when he encounters difficult soil conditions (ledge, large boulders) he demands an increase of $2,000 to complete the job. In deciding whether to grant the increase, suppose the court learns that when soil conditions are "normal," foundations of this sort cost $4,000, but when difficult conditions are met, the cost is $7,000. The fact that the contractor quoted a price higher than the cost of a normal job but lower than the cost of a difficult job suggests that he is charging all customers the cost of an *average* job. In other words, he is self-insuring (in the manner described above) against the risk of high-cost jobs.[18] The court could use this as evidence that the contractor has indirectly assumed the risk of high costs and hence refuse to grant the price increase (or discharge if that is the desired remedy).

2   Specific Performance

Money damages is by far the most common form of court-imposed remedy for breach, but in cases where money damages are thought to provide inadequate compensation—generally, contracts involving land or "unique goods"—the court will order specific performance. That is, the court will order the promisor to perform the contract as written. The attractiveness of specific performance in these cases is apparent, but, given the centrality of efficient breach to the economic theory of contract law, one might suppose that economists would support its limited use, fearing excessive performance. To the contrary, some economists have argued for the wider use of the remedy.[19] This section lays out the economic arguments in favor of specific performance over money damages in the context of the efficient breach model.

The first point to emphasize is that specific performance is *not* inconsistent with efficient breach of contract. Consider a contract for the sale of a parcel of land for $50,000. Suppose that the buyer values the land at $60,000, but before closing, another buyer arrives and offers $65,000. It is efficient for the second buyer to acquire the land because she is the highest valuer, and this outcome will be achieved under expectation damages. Specifically, the seller will breach the contract with the first buyer, pay damages of $10,000 (= $60,000 − $50,000), then sell to the second buyer for $65,000, producing a net gain of $5,000 for the seller.

What will happen under specific performance? First, the court will order the seller to honor his promise to sell to the first buyer. Then, one of two things will happen. If the first buyer is aware of the second offer, she will likely enforce the original sale, but then resell to the second buyer for a net gain of $5,000. If she is not aware of the offer, the seller will offer some amount of money greater than $10,000 (the first buyer's surplus) and less than $15,000 (the premium above the original price offered by the second buyer) to cancel the contract. The first buyer will accept, and the seller will then sell the land to the second buyer.

The important point is that the efficient outcome occurs in both of these scenarios; the only difference is how it is achieved. Under expectation damages, the court sets the price that the seller must pay to breach the original deal; the original buyer can only accept the damages. In contrast, specific performance allows the original buyer to participate in setting the terms of the breach, either by enforcing the original deal and reselling, or by bargaining with the seller over the price of a "buyout." In general, it will always be true (according to the Coase Theorem) that when breach is efficient, bargaining between the original contractors can yield the same result. This basic insight is the starting point for our evaluation of specific performance.

EXERCISE 5.2

Return to the construction contract from Exercise 5.1 where

$V = \$100,000$

$P = \$75,000$

Suppose the builder's cost of production turns out to be $125,000. Describe the bargaining between the buyer and the builder under a specific performance remedy. Will performance occur?

2.1 Transaction Costs

One criticism of specific performance is that transaction costs might inhibit the sort of renegotiation that needs to take place to achieve the efficient disposition of the contract. Such costs are not required under money damages because the court sets the terms of breach. But in their place are the litigation costs involved in court determination of the correct amount of damages. Assuming that both methods (money damages and specific performance) reach the efficient outcome (an assumption that we question below), the choice depends on a comparison of these costs.

Let's tally the likely transaction costs under the two remedies to see which is lower. If the above transaction for sale of land is governed by a damage remedy, a breach by the seller will entail two further "transactions": (1) litigation over damages owed to the first buyer, and (2) resale to the second buyer. Although the transaction costs of resale are probably low, the costs involved in determining damages for the first buyer may be quite high. Recall that it requires measurement of the value of performance, which is the buyer's private information and is therefore subject to misrepresentation. (See the discussion of the *Peevyhouse* case below.) Measuring it accurately could be a difficult factual inquiry.

Under specific performance, there are also two transactions needed to get the land to the second buyer: (1) a court proceeding, initiated by the first buyer, to enforce the contract, followed by (2) the sale from the original buyer to the new buyer. There seems no good reason to believe that the transaction costs of resale will be any higher in this case, but there is reason to think that the litigation costs will be lower under specific performance because of the absence of factual issues. (It is the same argument that we used to claim that litigation costs would be lower per case under strict liability compared to negligence in torts.) Further, the seller may be less inclined to breach in the first place under specific performance because he expects to realize no gains from doing so, whereas he realizes all of the gains from breach under expectation damages (see Section 2.3 below). In this case, the litigation costs involved in enforcement are replaced by the transaction costs of the original sale, almost certainly a savings.

What if breach involves nonperformance, as in the production cost model? In this case, there is no resale following breach; there are only the litigation costs of determining the amount of damages under a damage remedy compared to the negotiation of a buyout price under specific performance (plus the enforcement costs, if any) (see Exercise 5.2 above). While the comparison is an empirical question, one supposes that the costs of renegotiation will generally be low because the parties have already demonstrated the ability to bargain with one another when they first negotiated the contract.

2.2 Subjective Value and Efficient Breach

The preceding discussion focused on the transaction costs of money damages compared to specific performance while assuming that efficient breach would occur under both remedies. But there is reason to believe that in some cases specific performance will also result in more efficient breach decisions. This point is best made in the context of the well-known case *Peevyhouse v. Garland Coal & Mining Co.* (382 P.2d 109, *cert. denied*, 375 U.S. 906, Okla. 1962).

This case concerned a contract between the Peevyhouses, owners of a farm containing coal deposits, and a mining company. The contract allowed the mining company to conduct a strip mining operation for a period of five years, after which it was required to perform "certain restorative and remedial work . . . at a cost estimated by expert witnesses at about $29,000." When the mining company failed to repair the land, the Peevyhouses sued for damages. At trial, the mining company admitted to having breached the contract, arguing that the cost of performance was substantially larger than the mere $300 reduction in the market value of the farm resulting from the failure to do the repairs. The court agreed and awarded the Peevyhouses $300 in damages.

According to our efficient breach model, breach appears to have been the efficient outcome in this case since the cost of performance, $29,000, far exceeded the value of performance, $300. And, by setting damages equal to the value of performance, the court established the correct incentives. So what's wrong with this decision?

The problem is that the measure of damages is based on the *market value* of the repairs rather than the value to the Peevyhouses. To see the difference, note that market value measures the maximum amount that someone would *offer* for a piece of property, while the value to the owner is the minimum amount he or she would *accept*. You often hear the expression that "everyone has their price." The value to the owner is that price, and the owner will only sell when the market value is greater. Refusal to sell is therefore a signal that the owner's value exceeds the market value. This difference is sometimes referred to as the owner's *subjective value.*[20]

It seems likely that in this case the Peevyhouses attached a significant subjective value to repairs. (Some evidence is that this case was an appeal of an earlier damage award of $5,000.) What does that have to do with efficient breach? The answer is that economic exchange, voluntary or involuntary, should respect subjective value. The whole point of voluntary exchange is that owners are free to turn down offers that they find unacceptable *for any reason*. And since market exchange is the paradigm for efficient breach (an involuntary exchange), remedies for breach should account for subjective value. If they do not, there will be too many breaches.

To illustrate, suppose that the true value of performance to a promisee is V, which is greater than the market value of M. If the court sets damages equal to M, then promisors will breach when $C > M$ rather than when $C > V$. Thus, inefficient breach will occur over the range where $M < C < V$.

The argument to this point suggests that the problem of excessive breach can be solved by setting damages equal to V rather than M. How is this an argument for specific performance? The problem with setting damages equal to V is that subjective value is unobservable to the court. Further, the court cannot simply ask the Peevyhouses how much they value performance because they would have an incentive to overstate it. Specific performance overcomes this problem by placing the breach decision back in the hands of the parties where they will resolve it through negotiation (assuming that bargaining costs are low). If the cost of performance is truly greater than V, then the mining company will be able to offer an amount between V and $29,000 to breach the contract, and both parties will be better off (recall Exercise 5.2). In contrast, if V exceeds the cost of performance, then performance will occur, as it should.

2.3 The Value of Consent

The final argument in favor of specific performance is not based on efficiency but instead on fairness. Return to the above example of a contract for the sale of land from seller S to buyer B1 for a price of $50,000. Before closing, buyer B2 arrives and offers $65,000, which exceeds B1's value of $60,000. Table 5.2 summarizes the returns to S and B1 under money damages and specific performance. First, under money damages, S breaches the contract with B1, pays damages of $10,000 (assuming that the court can observe V), and then sells to B2 for $65,000. S thus receives a net gain of $5,000 compared to the original contract with B1. (This net gain is obtained by subtracting $50,000 from S's return to reflect the opportunity cost of breaching the contract with B1—see table 5.2.) B1, in contrast, receives a net gain of zero; she is no better or worse off as a result of the breach. In this case, S receives all of the gains from the arrival of the second buyer.[21]

Now consider specific performance. If B1 knows about B2's offer, she will enforce the original contract and resell to B2 herself. In this case, B1 receives the gain of $5,000, while S receives no gain. Both remedies therefore achieve the efficient outcome, but differ in the distribution of the net gains. The advantage of specific performance is that it does not allow S to benefit from his breach, which is a legal wrong. This sentiment is expressed by the dissenting judge in the *Peevyhouse* case, who argued for specific performance because damages "would be taking from the plaintiffs the benefits of the contract and placing those benefits in defendant which has failed to perform its obligations."

Let us consider the difference between the two remedies further. Buyer B1 receives no gain under money damages because she cannot object to the breach; she can merely sue for expectation damages. Thus, she cannot obtain any portion of the $5,000 net gain created by B2's arrival. In contrast, she

TABLE **5.2** **Money Damages Compared to Specific Performance**

Remedy	S's return	B1's return	Joint return
Damages	$65,000 − $10,000 − $50,000 = $5,000	$0	$5,000
Specific performance	$0	$65,000 − $60,000 = $5,000	$5,000

obtains all of the gain under specific performance because she has the right to enforce the original contract; the seller must obtain B1's *consent* before breaching. In this example, the $5,000 net gain represents the "value of consent" to B1.

More generally, the value of consent will depend on the bargaining abilities of the parties. For example, suppose that the value of performance to the Peevyhouses is $15,000. If the court employs specific performance, the mining company must obtain the Peevyhouse's consent to breach. Thus, depending on the bargaining abilities of the parties, it will pay a price between $29,000, the cost of performance, and $15,000, the value of performance. If they split the difference, then the mining company will pay the Peevyhouses $15,000 + $7,000 = $22,000. In contrast, the mining company will only have to pay $15,000 under money damages (assuming again that V is observable). Thus, $7,000 is the value of consent in this case.

The importance of consent goes beyond concerns about fairness. As we shall see in the next chapter, it is central to the fundamental problem of designing an efficient framework for exchanging legal entitlements.

3   Self-Enforcement of Contracts

Our analysis of breach of contract in this chapter has so far focused exclusively on court-imposed remedies. Some contracts, however, provide their own remedies for breach. In this section, we discuss two types of self-imposed remedies: liquidated damage clauses and product warranties. We conclude by discussing the self-enforcing nature of long-term contracts.

3.1   Liquidated Damage Clauses

There are several reasons why the parties to a contract might want to specify their own damage remedy rather than rely on a court-imposed remedy.[22] First, they may wish to avoid the litigation costs that are involved. Second, the court may have difficulty in measuring the loss from breach, especially if it includes subjective value (though, as we have noted, this problem can be addressed by use of specific performance rather than money damages). Finally, the parties may want to structure damages to share the risk of breach in an optimal way (Polinsky 1983, 436).

Regardless of the reason, economists argue that courts should enforce liquidated damage clauses because they reflect the wishes of the parties at the time of contracting. Courts generally follow this advice with one notable exception—they refuse to enforce damages that appear to be excessive, so-called penalty clauses. The remainder of this section examines the economic basis for this rule.

Liquidated damages are specified by the parties at the time the contract is made. If the objective is efficient breach (the rationale that we focus on), then the damage amount should be set equal to the *expected loss* of the victim of the breach. For example, consider a mill that hires a transport company to ship a damaged crank shaft back to the manufacturer for repairs. Suppose that the mill has a spare crank shaft that it can use temporarily, but if there is a delay, it will have to shut down at an expected cost of $500. Knowing this, the mill insists on a clause in the contract saying that the transport company will pay the mill $500 in the event of a delay. Note that this clause gives the transport company exactly the right incentives for breach: if the cost of avoiding delay is less than $500, it will perform on time, but if the cost exceeds $500, it will delay. Further, the parties will avoid a costly legal proceeding in the event of breach.

The problem is that when the contract is written, the best that the parties can do is form an expected value of the loss from breach. The *actual loss* may turn out to be higher or lower. In the latter case, the specified damage amount could appear excessive. For example, suppose that the transport company breaches, and the mill's actual losses turn out to be $200 because of a bad harvest, which results in a lower than expected demand for its services. The mill owner nevertheless seeks enforcement of the $500 damage payment. How should the court rule? For purposes of efficient breach, the court should enforce the damage amount as written so long as $500 was a reasonable estimate of the mill's loss *at the time the contract was made*.[23] The amount of the actual loss doesn't matter for efficiency because it could not have affected the transport company's decision. The fact that the mill is overcompensated by $300 is purely distributional (and is offset in expected terms by the possibility that the actual loss could have been greater than $500, resulting in undercompensation).

The actual practice of courts partially conforms to this view. Courts do not enforce damages that are unreasonably high at the time of contracting (higher than the expected loss). However, depending on the jurisdiction, they may or may not enforce damages that are reasonable at the time of contracting but turn out to be too high at the time of breach.

Are there any circumstances in which it would be efficient to enforce damages that are excessive, even in *expected terms*? One might be when breach is hard to detect, as in the case of employee shirking or malfeasance. To deter inefficient breaches of this sort, damages would have to be multiplied by the inverse of the probability of detection, like punitive damages in torts. Other efficiency rationales for enforcing excessive damages have been offered as well.[24]

An argument in support of the nonenforcement rule is that excessive damages may be a signal of mutual mistake or unconscionability (Rea 1984). It is a signal of mutual mistake if both parties miscalculated the loss from breach, and it is a sign of unconscionability if one party miscalculated and the other took advantage of that miscalculation. In either case, nonenforcement is justified.

3.2 Product Warranties*

Product warranties are guarantees that a product will perform as advertised, backed by a promise of full or partial compensation for the costs of product failure (repairs or damages). Express warranties are explicit guarantees made by the producer and thus represent a form of self-imposed remedy for breach. Implied warranties, in contrast, are imposed by a court after the fact and thus represent a form of court-awarded damages. We examine both types of warranty in this section.

3.2.1 Express Warranties

In this section we examine two economic models of express product warranties. In the first, warranties provide incentives for contractors to invest in optimal precaution against product failure; in the second, they serve as signals of the probability of failure.[25]

Prevention Model. Our earlier prevention model of breach provides a useful framework for examining the role of warranties in providing incentives to avoid product failure (Cooper and Ross 1985). For example, consider the purchase of an automobile that includes a warranty for repair of certain defects. Let $q(x)$ be the probability of a defect, which is decreasing in the producer's expenditure on prevention (care), x. For example, x could be the additional production costs (monitoring, testing) needed to reduce the probability of a defect. Also, let K be the cost of repairing the defect. The socially optimal level of prevention, denoted x^*, minimizes the expected costs

$$x + q(x)K. \tag{5.15}$$

Now consider contracting between the producer and consumer. This involves both the choice of x by the producer and the fraction, w, of the repair costs that the warranty will cover ($0 \leq w \leq 1$). Suppose initially that the consumer can observe the level of producer prevention so the price of the car can be conditioned on x.

In a perfectly competitive market, the producer will maximize the consumer's expected return subject to a zero profit constraint.[26] The consumer's expected return is

$$V - q(x)(1 - w)K - P, \qquad (5.16)$$

where V is the value of a nondefective car, and $q(x)(1 - w)K$ is the consumer's expected share of the cost of a defect. The producer's profit is

$$P - C - [x + q(x)wK], \qquad (5.17)$$

where $q(x)wK$ is the producer's share of repair costs, and C is the cost of production other than prevention costs. Setting the expression in (5.17) equal to zero and substituting the resulting value of P (which depends on x) into (5.16) yields the following return for the consumer:

$$V - C - [x + q(x)K]. \qquad (5.18)$$

Note that w drops out of this expression. Thus, maximizing (5.18) is equivalent to minimizing (5.15). As a result, the producer chooses the efficient level of prevention, x^*, *regardless of the level of warranty coverage.*

This conclusion mirrors the irrelevance of the liability rule in products liability cases when producers and consumers can bargain over care levels.[27] It is important to emphasize, however, that it relies on the ability of consumers to correctly perceive the producer's actual level of prevention so that the price can adjust accordingly. But this is not a realistic assumption for complex consumer products, which are the ones most likely to include warranties.

When consumers cannot observe x, producers will choose x to maximize profits in (5.17) treating the price as a constant. Thus, they will only choose efficient prevention if warranty coverage is complete ($w = 1$); that is, if they are strictly liable for the repair costs. Although the parties are in a contractual relationship, the liability rule matters here because of the unobservability of the producer's prevention, which represents a form of market failure. Recognizing this, the parties will rationally choose full warranty coverage to maximize the gains from contracting. Recall that we made a similar argument in Chapter 3 for strict products liability when consumers cannot accurately observe product risks.

Most warranties, however, do not offer complete coverage. The likely reason is that product failures, like product accidents, depend on consumer as well as producer efforts. And, as we argued in the products liability context, consumer efforts, because they occur after the product has been sold, are nearly impossible for producers to monitor. One explanation for partial warranties, therefore, is to give producers and consumers alike an incentive, albeit imperfect, to take care against product failure.[28]

Signaling Model.   Another economic theory of warranties is that they provide consumers with a signal of the probability of product failure: the greater is the coverage, the lower is the probability of failure (Spence 1977). In this model, producers vary in their chosen levels of product reliability, which we

Figure 5.4

Signaling Equilibrium
of Product Warranties

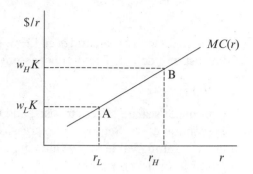

define by r, which is the probability that the product will *not* fail.[29] Consumers cannot observe the product's actual reliability, however, so producers of more reliable products (those with higher r) try to signal that fact by offering greater warranty coverage. This implies that in equilibrium, the unobserved variable r must be an increasing function of the observed variable w, the degree of warranty coverage.

Under what conditions will this type of equilibrium exist? Let $C(r)$ be the cost of producing a product of reliability r, where C is increasing in r. That is, more reliable products are costlier to produce. Further, suppose that the costs of making a product more reliable increase at an increasing rate. Thus, the marginal cost of r, denoted $MC(r)$, is also increasing as shown in Figure 5.4. The producer's expected profits in this case are

$$P - C(r) - (1 - r)wK. \tag{5.19}$$

The price cannot be a signal of r in this model (for reasons noted below), so the producer chooses r to maximize (5.19), treating P as a constant. At the optimum, the producer therefore sets the marginal cost of greater reliability equal to the marginal reduction in its share of repair costs, or

$$MC(r) = wK. \tag{5.20}$$

Note that Equation (5.20) does not define a unique value of r, but rather a set of (r, w) pairs, all of which are consistent with profit maximization. Figure 5.4 shows two such pairs: point A represents a product with low reliability and low warranty coverage, while point B represents a product with high reliability and high warranty coverage. A signaling equilibrium is possible as long as consumers' expectation about the relationship between r and w is consistent with equation (5.20). Note that the positive relationship between r and w is a consequence of the positively sloped marginal cost function.

The preceding analysis showed what must be true on the supply side for a signaling equilibrium to exist. On the demand side, there must be a variation in consumer preferences such that consumers demand different bundles of product reliability and warranty coverage. That is, some consumers must prefer product A (low reliability, low price) while others must prefer product B (high reliability, high price).

Finally, we consider the question of why price cannot serve as a signal of product reliability. In particular, why can't producers of more reliable products simply raise their prices? The reason is that producers of less reliable products will also have an incentive to raise their prices because there is no cost of doing so. Thus, a higher price is not a believable signal of higher quality. This problem does not exist for warranties because it is costly for producers to increase their coverage. Price will vary with product reliability in equilibrium (because a more reliable product is costlier to produce), but consumers cannot use it as a signal.

3.2.2 Implied Warranties

Not all products carry express warranties, but, as we saw in Chapter 3, developments in products liability law in the twentieth century resulted in courts finding implied warranties of product fitness (Epstein 1980). Under an implied warranty, producers are strictly liable for damages caused by defective or unreasonably dangerous products. Thus, products liability law represents the intersection of contract and tort approaches to product-related risks.

The economic rationale for court-imposed warranties is the same as for express warranties: to encourage manufacturers to invest in prolonging the life of products, and to insure against losses from product failures and accidents. The advantage of an implied warranty is that it saves the parties the cost of negotiating the assignment of liability for product failure in every transaction. In this respect, an implied warranty is similar to a standard form contract, or a default rule, and is based on the belief that the manufacturer is generally the optimal risk-bearer.

For some products, however, the manufacturer may not be the optimal risk-bearer, as when consumer care is the primary reason for product failure. Although manufacturer disclaimers of liability would appear to be efficient in this case—and are allowed under the Uniform Commercial Code—courts view them with considerable skepticism. The reason is probably the same one that we offered in Chapter 3 for the trend toward strict products liability in torts—namely, the inability of most consumers to accurately assess the risk of product failure. In the presence of this sort of market failure, voluntary contracting is inferior to court-imposed liability (Landes and Posner 1987, 138–39). Based on this principle (which we will explore in greater detail in Chapter 6) it is not surprising that the tort and contract approaches to product-related accidents have converged on the same solution.

3.3 Long-Term Contracts*

Long-term contracts involve ongoing relationships between trading partners. One obvious benefit from such relationships is that the parties save the cost of negotiating each transaction anew. Another, more interesting benefit is that they potentially provide an enforcement structure in which parties can make transaction-specific investments (analogous to reliance investments) without fear of losses from the sort of opportunistic behavior that can plague short-term contracts.[30]

To illustrate the gains from transaction-specific investments, and the potential for opportunism, consider the example of an employment relationship. Suppose unskilled workers have a value of marginal product (VMP) equal to $100, but if a firm hires a worker for two periods and invests $100 in training in the first period, her VMP rises to $300 in the second period.[31] Assume all workers retire after two periods. Note that training is efficient in this example because an investment of $100 yields a gain of $200. The question is whether contracting between the firm and worker will yield this result.

Suppose initially that the firm offers to hire the unskilled worker for two periods at a wage of $125 per period and promises to train the worker. The worker will accept this contract because she earns a lifetime income of $250, as compared to the $200 she could earn from two one-period contracts at $100 per period. The firm also benefits because it earns total profit of $100 + $300 − $100 − $250 = $50, as compared to zero from hiring an unskilled worker at $100 in both periods. So far, there seems no need for the firm and worker to form any special relationship.

The problem is that investment in training by the firm will often give workers skills that are at least partially *transferable* to other firms. This creates the potential for worker opportunism because, once the firm's investment is sunk, the worker can threaten to quit unless the firm matches the wage offer of competing firms. To illustrate, suppose in our example that trained workers have a VMP of $200 in other firms (that is, half of the value of training is transferable). And because these other firms have not incurred the cost of training, they will offer up to $200 to attract trained workers. The original firm will therefore have to match this offer to retain the worker—that is, it will have to raise the worker's second-period wage from $125 to $200. The resulting lifetime income for the worker is now $125 + $200 = $325, while the firm's profit falls to $100 + $300 − $100 − $325 = −$25.[32] The worker has thus succeeded in extracting a larger share of the gains from the firm's investment.

It is easy to show that the threat of worker opportunism results in an inefficient equilibrium in which firms choose not to invest in training. The payoff matrix in Table 5.3 shows the two-period payoffs to the firm and worker, as

TABLE **5.3**   **Payoff Matrix for Employment Example**

		Firm	
		Invest	*Not invest*
Worker	Not threaten	$250, *$50*	*$200*, $0
	Threaten	*$325*, −$25	*$200*, *$0*

derived above, from the various strategies (the first number in each cell is the payoff to the worker and the second is the payoff to the firm). The strategies for the firm are "invest" and "not invest," while the strategies for the worker are "not threaten" to leave and "threaten" to leave. The entries in italics show the optimal strategies for each party given the strategy of the other party.

Consider, for example, the worker's optimal strategy. If the firm invests, the worker will threaten to leave ($325 > $250), but if the firm does not invest, the worker will be indifferent ($200 either way). As for the firm, it will invest if it does not expect the worker to threaten to leave ($50 > $0), but it will not invest if it expects the worker to threaten ($0 > −$25). The Nash equilibrium occurs when each party's expectation about the other's strategy is fulfilled. In this case, the only Nash equilibrium is for workers to threaten to leave and firms not to invest in training. Thus, the threat of opportunism causes the parties to forego the mutual gains from the investment.

In the presence of these gains, we would expect the parties to devise some contractual or other means of forestalling opportunism. Two types of contractual solutions are (1) explicit long-term contracts enforced by the court, and (2) implicit contracts that rely on self-enforcement. Explicit contracts depend on court-imposed breach remedies to prevent opportunism, but they entail "costs of specifying possible contingencies and the policing and litigation costs of detecting violations and enforcing the contract in the courts" (Klein, Crawford, and Alchian 1978, 303). These costs are likely to be especially high in long-term contracts where there is an ongoing threat of breach.

When the costs of explicit contracting become too high, parties will rely instead on implicit, or "self-enforcing," contracts.[33] Self-enforcement can take several forms, for example, mutual threats to terminate a long-term relationship if a breach occurs, or the posting of a bond that is forfeitable in the event of breach. The important point is that third-party detection and enforcement are not required under these measures. In a classic study, Macauley (1963) provides evidence that this sort of informal approach to contracting is widely used in business relationships.

As an illustration of a self-enforcement mechanism in the above employment example, suppose that the firm offers unskilled workers a two-period "increasing wage" contract that pays $50 in the first period and $200 in the second. The worker is indifferent between this contract and the "flat wage" contract offering $125 per period because both offer the same lifetime income. Similarly, the firm is indifferent because its total wage costs remain the same. But unlike the flat wage, the increasing wage scheme deters opportunism because the trained worker has no incentive to leave the firm in the second period. In effect, the worker posts a bond in the first period (the difference between the $50 first-period wage and $100 spot wage) that is forfeited if she leaves the firm prematurely. As a result of this increasing wage structure, the parties are able to achieve the efficient outcome without the need for court intervention.[34]

Another solution would be for employers to agree not to negotiate with workers from other firms. Professional baseball maintained such a system throughout most of its history until courts struck down the so-called reserve clause in 1976.[35] Under the reserve system, all player contracts included an implicit provision that bound the player to the team that drafted him for life. Although viewed by most as an anticompetitive practice among owners, the current analysis suggests that this system may have also served as a way for owners to make binding commitments to one another ("tying their hands"), thereby encouraging efficient investment in player development.[36]

A final solution to the problem of worker opportunism would be for workers to pay their own training costs. This eliminates the problem of opportunism because workers internalize both the costs and the benefits of training. Thus, they can move freely without imposing a cost on the firm that trained them. In professional baseball, this would be equivalent to a system in which players financed the cost of the minor leagues. In most cases, however, this is not a viable solution because workers are generally wealth-constrained, and capital market imperfections make financing of such investments costly.

But this solution does point to an alternative response to opportunism in contracting—namely, vertical integration. Vertical integration occurs when a buyer and seller who formerly engaged in market exchange consolidate into a single firm.[37] For example, an automobile manufacturer merges with the firm that supplies it with custom-made body parts, or a brewery merges with an ice company to ensure a steady supply of ice during the summer. By consolidating, the parties save on the transaction costs of enforcing contracts, but they now incur the costs of internal organization. Thus, the boundary between transactions *within* firms (intrafirm) and transactions *across* firms (interfirm) is determined by the relative costs of these alternative organizational structures.[38]

4   Conclusion

This chapter began by asking when it is efficient to breach an enforceable contract. Although a contract may have promised mutual gains at the time of formation, unforeseen changes can cause the cost of performance to exceed the value of performance, in which case breach is the efficient course of action. The role of the court in fashioning remedies for contract disputes is to create incentives for the parties to breach only when it is efficient to do so. Using an adaptation of the model of precaution, we showed that expectation damages (a form of strict liability) achieves exactly this outcome. Unlimited expectation damages does not, however, provide efficient incentives for reliance, nor does it necessarily share risks optimally. We therefore discussed alternative remedies aimed at achieving these goals.

Besides money damages, courts sometimes order specific performance. Typically, this remedy is limited to contracts involving unique goods (like land), but economists have argued for its wider use, both to lower the transaction costs of resolving disputes and to protect subjective value.

Court-imposed remedies are costly to employ, so parties often provide their own "self-help" remedies as part of the contract, the most common being liquidated damages. This type of remedy is especially beneficial in long-term or repeated contracts where the parties can develop a reputation for honoring promises. Economic theory says that courts should generally enforce such self-imposed remedies since they reflect the parties' efforts to maximize the value of the contract.

DISCUSSION QUESTIONS

1. Consider the following theory of contractual obligations, due to Charles Fried: "There exists a convention that defines the practice of promising and its entailments. . . . By virtue of the basic Kantian principles of trust and respect, it is wrong to invoke that convention in order to make a promise, and then to break it" (Craswell and Schwartz 1994, 14). Contrast this view with the economic theory of contract breach.

2. Discuss the implications of the Coase Theorem (see Chapter 1) for the choice of an efficient breach of contract remedy.

3. Traditional contract law treats breach of contract and discharge due to impossibility or commercial impracticability as distinct problems. Explain the sense in which economic theory views them as variants of a single problem where the relevant question is the amount of damages for nonperformance.

4. The case of *Siegel v. Eaton & Prince Co.* (46 N.E. 449, 1896) involved a contract for the installation of an elevator in a department store. When the

store burned down, it sought to invalidate the contract on the grounds of impossibility. Discuss the issues that are relevant to an economic analysis of this case.

5. Friedmann (1989) argues that the logic of efficient breach of contract, when extended to property rights, amounts to "efficient theft." Discuss.

6. As noted in Chapter 2, one response of firms to increasing corporate liability for hazardous activities has been to spin off such activities to subsidiary firms whose liability is limited (Ringleb and Wiggins 1990). In other words, the firm replaces an internal transaction with a market transaction. Discuss this strategy as an optimal response to a change in the costs of organization relative to the costs of enforcing contracts.

7. Discuss the following statement: "Almost any tort problem can be solved as a contract problem, by asking what people involved in an accident would have agreed on in advance with regard to safety measures if transaction costs had not been prohibitive. . . . Equally, almost any contract problem can be solved as a tort problem" (Posner 1998a, 272–73).

PROBLEMS

1. Consider a contract between buyer B and seller S for delivery of a good that S must produce. Suppose that the value of performance to the buyer, V, non-salvageable reliance by the buyer, R, and price, P (payable on delivery), are

    $V = \$1,000$

    $R = \$100$

    $P = \$650$

    Suppose that, at the time the contract was made, the cost of production, C, was uncertain. However, when the time of production arrives, it takes one of four values:

    $C = \{\$500, \$700, \$900, \$1,100\}$

    After observing C, the seller must decide whether to produce and deliver the good, or not produce it and breach the contract.

    (a) For which values of C (if any) is it efficient to breach the contract?
    (b) For which values of C will the seller breach under expectation damages? under reliance damages? under zero damages? How do your answers compare to (a)?

2. Suppose that the value of a contract to a buyer, V, is a function of her investment in nonsalvageable reliance, R. Specifically, the buyer can invest either $100 or $200 with the resulting impact on V as follows:

R	V
$100	$400
$200	$550

The contract price, payable on performance, is $75.

(a) Assume initially that performance of the contract will occur with certainty. What level of reliance maximizes the buyer's net return from the contract?

(b) Now suppose that the buyer anticipates a breach of the contract with probability .5, in which case her reliance investment is lost (though she does not have to pay the price). What choice of reliance maximizes the buyer's expected return in this case (ignoring damages)?

(c) What level of reliance will the buyer choose under unlimited expectation damages? How does your answer compare to your answers in (a) and (b)? Explain.

3. The case of *Kerr S. S. Co. v. Radio Corp. of America* (245 N.Y. 284, 157 N.E. 140, 1927) concerned a message sent by the plaintiff to its affiliate in the Philippines regarding the loading of a ship with cargo. The message was sent in code to prevent its competitors from reading it. The defendant, however, negligently failed to send the message, costing the plaintiff nearly $7,000, which it sought in damages. The defendant countered that it should only be liable for $27, the cost of sending the message. Under what conditions, if any, should the plaintiff recover the $7,000? What case should the court invoke as precedent in making its decision?

4. A buyer hires a manufacturer to build a specialized machine for delivery on a certain date. The value of the machine to the buyer is $2,000, and the price, payable on delivery, is $1,500. Suppose that after the machine is completed but before delivery, a second buyer arrives and offers the manufacturer $2,500 for it.

(a) From a social perspective, who should get the machine?

(b) Calculate the value of expectation damages for the first buyer and show that it gives the seller the correct incentives regarding breach of the original contract.

(c) Suppose the first buyer sought and obtained a specific performance remedy. How will this affect the ultimate ownership of the machine compared to expectation damages? (Assume that the first buyer is aware of the second buyer's offer and that the two buyers can bargain.)

(d) The arrival of the second buyer created a "surplus" of $500 (the excess of his offer over the valuation of the first buyer). Describe how this surplus is divided between the seller and first buyer under the two breach remedies.

6

THE ECONOMICS OF PROPERTY LAW:
Fundamentals

From an economic perspective, property law is the most fundamental of the three major areas of the common law. This is true, first of all, because the assignment and protection of property rights provide the legal background for the production and distribution of wealth in an economy. But it is also true in a broader sense because we will see that the principles of property law provide a general framework for understanding the economic approach to law. For this reason, I have chosen to treat property last because doing so allows us to bring together several themes that have run throughout the preceding chapters.

This chapter begins with a general discussion of the nature and function of property rights, focusing on their importance for economic incentives and on the emergence and protection of property rights. We will see that the primary function of property rights is to internalize externalities. Thus, the foundation of the economic analysis of property law is Coase's (1960) classic treatment of the problem of externalities.

Of course, economists studied externalities long before Coase, but his insights substantially altered their perspective. Most important, the Coase Theorem highlighted the impact of the assignment of rights and of transaction costs on both the allocation and distribution of resources. His conclusions have important implications for the design of efficient legal rules for enforcing property rights, which is the primary focus of this chapter. In the process of examining enforcement rules in the context of property, however, we will see that many of the conclusions we reached in our earlier discussions of torts and contracts will emerge naturally from the property rights–transaction cost framework that Coase established. This illustrates one of the ways in which economics provides a unifying theory of the law.

1 The Nature and Function of Property Rights

Property rights are a creation of society: they delineate the boundaries between what individuals can and cannot do with assets under their control.[1] Although we will focus mostly on property rights over tangible assets like land and automobiles, the basic principles also apply to intangible assets like labor services, inventions (intellectual property), and personal safety. (For example, a tort can be interpreted as an unlawful infringement of the victim's right to safety.) In this section, we provide an overview of the following aspects of property rights: (1) how they are defined; (2) their impact on economic incentives; (3) how property rights emerge; and (4) how they are protected. This overview sets the stage for the subsequent analysis of property law and previews several issues that we will address later in more detail.

1.1 The Definition of Property Rights

Both lawyers and economists view ownership of an asset as consisting of a "bundle of rights." This bundle includes:

1. The right to *use* the asset (for example, to obtain the monetary gains that the asset produces);
2. The right to *exclude* others from using the asset; and
3. The right to *dispose* of the asset (that is, to sell it).

Thus, for example, the owner of farmland can grow and sell crops, exclude trespassers, and sell the land to a willing buyer.

The law enforces the above rights, but only up to the point where they become incompatible with the rights of other individuals. Incompatible rights is just another way of saying "externality," and the law will generally limit property rights in the presence of externalities. For example, a court may limit a farmer's right to use certain fertilizers on his land if chemicals in the fertilizer seep into his neighbor's well, or it may force him to prevent his cattle from straying onto his neighbor's land.

Individuals may also *choose* to limit their property rights in order to enhance the value of the asset. For example, a landowner may lease his land to tenant farmers, thereby contractually dividing the above rights between the landlord and the tenants. Specifically, the tenants have the rights of use and exclusion, but the landlord retains the right to dispose.[2] Or, several ranchers may choose to hold some grazing land in common. Thus, no single owner can exclude other owners from use, but collectively they can exclude nonowners or sell the land.

Much of this chapter will be concerned with efficient limitations of rights, both coercive and voluntary. Before undertaking this task, however, it is necessary to understand the impact of property rights on incentives.

1.2 Property Rights and Incentives

One way property rights create efficient incentives is by internalizing externalities. An externality exists when a decision maker does not internalize the full costs or benefits of his activities. A familiar example is the polluting factory that does not account for the cost its smoke imposes on nearby residents. One way this externality can be internalized is to make the factory pay damages to the residents, a solution analogous to liability in tort law. We will see, however, that other remedies are possible and that some may be more efficient than others.

A useful way to think about externalities is that they exist when property rights are not completely defined. Incomplete property rights lead to inefficiencies of both *exchange* and *production*. Exchange efficiency requires that resources end up with the party who values them most. Well-defined property rights promote this outcome by allowing market exchange: if you value my property more than I do, then you will offer a price that I will accept. For this to happen, however, you have to be confident that I alone have the legal right to sell my property, and that once you acquire it, you will have the exclusive rights to use it. Thus, people are reluctant to buy property they believe to be stolen (because the true owner could show up to claim it) and are skeptical of someone trying to sell the Statue of Liberty.

Property rights also create efficient incentives for production. People will only invest resources to produce goods if they have the exclusive rights to sell what they make. As a general rule, therefore, exclusive property rights are necessary to ensure adequate production (though we will see some examples below where time limits on exclusive rights may nevertheless be desirable).

The lack of well-defined property rights, however, can also lead to *overproduction*, as in the case of an open-access resource. The excessive depletion of an open-access resource, referred to as the "tragedy of the commons" (Hardin 1968), results when several producers have unrestricted access to the resource. Suppose, for example, that a large underground pool of oil is discovered beneath land whose ownership is divided among several oil companies. Each company has an incentive to extract the oil as fast as possible before the pool is depleted. The result is excessive extraction and surface storage. An efficient outcome requires the firms to agree on an extraction rate and division of the resulting revenues—in other words, to define property rights to the resource.[3] (Alternatively, they could consolidate, which accomplishes the same purpose by concentrating the divided property right.) The same problem arises for other common resources like fishing or hunting grounds and mineral deposits. In the next section, we provide some examples of how property rights actually emerge in these sorts of settings.

1.3 The Emergence of Property Rights

As we have noted, the economic function of property rights is to internalize externalities. Property rights will therefore emerge "when the gains from internalization become larger than the costs of internalization" (Demsetz 1967, 350). The gain is the greater efficiency of exchange and production as described above; the cost is the cost of enforcement. The following examples illustrate the emergence of property rights in various settings.

Primitive Property Rights.   The best place to start is with primitive society, where, in contrast to the conventional image of early peoples living in a lawless "state of nature," anthropological evidence shows that they actually developed sophisticated property rights systems (Bailey 1992; Rubin 2001). On reflection, this is not surprising since the pressures of subsistence placed a high premium on structuring property rights efficiently. An important insight of this research is that group ownership (common property) often took precedence over private property. (Since observers often mistake group ownership for no ownership, this may have led to the misperception that primitive societies lacked property rights.) This was especially true of hunting and gathering societies, where exclusive ownership of individual parcels of land made little sense. In contrast, peoples who engaged in agriculture generally did have property rights in the land used for growing crops. Even in these societies, however, sharing of food was often practiced as a form of social insurance against famine or other fluctuations in food supply.

A particularly interesting example of sharing within a system of private property was the practice of "potlatching" by Indians in the Pacific Northwest. Although kinship groups held exclusive rights to salmon-fishing territories, groups that were particularly successful shared their bounty with less successful groups (Johnson 1986). This system reflects a fairly sophisticated attempt to balance the competing economic goals of risk sharing and incentives.

The Gold Rush and Mining Rights.   In more modern times, Umbeck (1981) described the emergence of property rights to gold deposits in California in the years following the discovery of gold at Sutter's Mill in 1848. When gold was first discovered, government-enforced property rights to the land being mined did not exist. Thus, individual miners initially enforced their claims privately. Following the gold rush of 1849, however, when land became scarce and the threat of violence increased, the miners found it advantageous to enter into explicit contractual arrangements that gave individual miners exclusive rights to their "claims." Further, groups of miners formed districts to help one another enforce their rights against claim "jumpers."

In the absence of formal legal institutions, however, the threat of violence was the ultimate means of enforcing contracts. For example, Umbeck noted that all miners carried guns, representing an implied warning to any prospective jumpers. Apparently, this threat worked well, because little violence actually occurred.

In 1872, Congress passed mining legislation aimed at consolidating the various territorial laws and customs. The Mining Law allowed miners to stake claims on federal land and, if they wished, to obtain federal patents for these claims. A patent offered more secure property rights but also entailed significant administrative costs. Thus, economic theory predicts that miners facing higher enforcement costs would have been more likely to seek patents, and this is what in fact happened (Gerard 2001).

Homestead Laws.   A third example of the emergence of property rights is homesteading, the practice of awarding property rights to land on a "first come, first served" basis. By the 1850s, the United States had acquired more than 1.2 billion acres of public land in the west. The Homestead Act of 1862 awarded rights to surveyed tracts of this land to squatters, conditional on payment of a $10 entry fee and a promise to reside on the land continuously for five years. This method for allocating land is often regarded as inefficient because it "causes farmers to rush to the land in an effort to preempt other potential farmers and, in the process, dissipate the value of the land" (Allen 1991, 1). In other words, it appears to suffer from the tragedy of the commons.

If this is true, why did the United States maintain such a policy for more than seventy years? (Homesteading officially ended in 1934.) Allen (1991) argues that it was in fact a rational response of the U.S. government to the cost of enforcing property rights to western lands. Land ownership on the frontier was indeed a risky proposition. Competing claims potentially came from other settlers, but also from Native Americans, who were understandably hostile to expropriation of their land by the settlers. The government was able to provide some protection in the form of a military presence, but like the gold rushers, settlers wishing for greater security invested in various forms of self-enforcement, including threats of violence.

One interpretation of homesteading is that it lowered the overall cost of this mix of public and private enforcement methods:

> The sudden arrival of tens of thousands of people into given territory destroyed much of the Indian way of life and forced the Indian tribes to accept reservation life or to join the union. The selective and intensive settlement caused by homesteading also reduced the cost of defending any given settlement. (Allen 1991, 5)

Thus, although homesteading may have resulted in inefficiencies due to the commons problem, when viewed in the larger perspective of *establishing* and *enforcing* property rights, it looks like a value-maximizing policy.[4]

First Possession.   The preceding examples of the gold rush and homesteading both illustrate the general rule of establishing property rights by *first possession*.[5] First possession has historically been the dominant method for establishing property rights in the law, but it also pervades less formal modes of behavior according to rules like "finders keepers" and "first come, first served." To the philosopher John Locke, the rule was justified on the grounds that, when an individual combines his labor with property, 99 percent of the realized value is due to the labor (Epstein 1985, 10–11).

As noted, however, economists generally emphasize the inefficiencies of first possession, either because of the wasteful race to acquire exclusive use of a resource (including the use of violence or force), or the excessive depletion of an open-access resource (the tragedy of the commons).[6] But as the homesteading example illustrates, this view ignores potentially offsetting benefits of the rule (as there must be, given its pervasiveness).

It also ignores ways in which the law seeks to mitigate dissipation. To illustrate, consider the two ways in which a rule of first possession can be applied to an oil pool. Either ownership of the *entire pool* can be granted to the discoverer, or ownership of *individual barrels* can be granted to drillers who first pump them to the surface (referred to as the rule of capture).[7] In economic terms, the first rule confers ownership of the *stock*, while the second confers ownership of the *flow*. Dissipation can occur under both rules but in different ways. If ownership applies to the flow, competitors will deplete it too rapidly, whereas if ownership applies to the stock, would-be owners will race for discovery.

The extent and nature of dissipation can therefore be partially controlled by the particular form of the first possession rule. For example, when users are few and the resource abundant, no individual will find it profitable to enforce a right to the entire stock, and the rule of capture will result in minimal dissipation. However, if dissipation becomes severe, laws that grant exclusive rights to a single user or group of users, or that limit access to the stock (for example, by defining a hunting season or limiting the "take"), can overcome the tendency to overexploit the resource (Lueck 1989). We return to these and other ways of controlling dissipation (such as time-limited rights) in our discussion of alternative ownership regimes in Section 4 below.

1.4   Enforcement of Property Rights

Assigning ownership of an asset is only part of the process of establishing a property right—equally important is the rule for protecting that assignment.

We therefore conclude our discussion of property rights by examining methods of enforcement. When property rights first emerge, they are often protected, at least partially, by private threats of violence or force. But in modern societies, they are primarily protected by the government, which holds a monopoly on the (legal) use of force.

Nozick (1974) provides a classic discussion of the transition from private to public enforcement of rights.[8] In the absence of government, private enforcement is the only option, but this method puts the greatest power in the hands of the strongest according to the principle of "might makes right." The technology of warfare can level the playing field—as Umbeck (1981, 100) notes, the six-gun was referred to as the "equalizer" in the gold fields—but the result is often a world in which the violation of rights "leads to feuds, to an endless series of acts of retaliation and exactions of compensation" (Nozick 1974, 11).

In an effort to gain an advantage in this setting, individuals are likely to form associations in which members pledge to protect one another's rights (like mining districts during the gold rush). This has the benefit of exploiting scale economies in protection—because deterrence is a public good—but it also is subject to free riding. Further, competing associations may become entangled in "turf wars" (not unlike gang wars in modern cities) for control of a given area. Once again, violence is the ultimate arbiter, and a dominant association eventually emerges. Nozick (1974, 16–17) characterizes the process as follows: "Out of anarchy, pressed by spontaneous grouping, mutual-protection associations, division of labor, market pressure, economies of scale, and rational self-interest there arises something very much resembling a minimal state or group of geographically distinct minimal states."

The transition to a state further requires that the dominant association acquire monopoly control over its use of force. However, this is a case where monopoly is probably efficient, both because of the scale economies in protection (a natural monopoly) and the destructive nature of "competition" among associations vying for control. As with any monopoly, however, there exists the risk of abuse. Democratic states therefore take additional steps to ensure "legitimate" use of the government's monopoly on force, including creation of a constitution to limit the government's powers and periodic review of its performance by means of elections. Dictatorial states use other methods to legitimize their power, such as assertions of divine right or appeal to nationalistic or ideological fervor, but they are also more susceptible to popular revolt.

In modern societies, individuals still invest in private protection of their property, mainly as a supplement to public protection. For example, people install security systems in their houses or cars, and businesses hire private security companies. (See Section 2.9 in Chapter 9.) For the most part, however, protection of private property is a function of the government.

2   Fundamentals of the Economics of Property Law

We have argued that the primary economic function of property rights is to internalize externalities. Traditionally, economists viewed externalities as a problem that governments had to correct by coercive means, for example, by imposing a tax or other regulation. According to this "Pigovian" view (named after the famous economist Arthur Pigou), the government first identifies the "cause" of the externality—for example, a polluting factory—and then imposes a tax on the factory equal to the external harm. The factory thereby internalizes the harm and operates at the efficient level.

Note that by this action, the government eliminates the externality by assigning property rights in a particular way. Specifically, it gives people harmed by the pollution the right to be free from the harm and then requires the factory to "purchase" that right if it wishes to continue operating. While there is nothing wrong with this solution, it turns out that it is not the only one, and maybe not the best one. This is the key insight of Ronald Coase's analysis of externalities and is a fundamental element of the economic approach to property law (Coase 1960). We provided an introduction to the Coase Theorem in Chapter 1; here we examine it in more detail.

2.1   The Coase Theorem

Coase's critique of the Pigovian approach to externalities challenged two of its underlying assumptions (as embodied in the polluting factory example): first, that there is a well-defined cause of the external harm (that is, that there is a clear injurer and victim); and second, that government intervention is required to internalize the externality. Coase also pointed out the importance of transaction costs when thinking about alternative remedies.

The best way to illustrate Coase's argument is in the context of his rancher-farmer example. Suppose a farmer and rancher occupy adjoining parcels of land, and cattle from the rancher's herd occasionally stray onto the farmer's land, damaging his crops. Assume that the number of acres cultivated by the farmer is fixed, but the size of the rancher's herd can vary.

Figure 6.1 graphs the marginal benefit to the rancher (MB) and marginal cost to the farmer (MC) as functions of the rancher's herd size (x). The MB curve is downward sloping, reflecting a diminishing marginal return to cattle ranching. The point where marginal benefits equal zero corresponds to the rancher's profit-maximizing herd size (that is, the point where the last steer yields zero profit), and is labeled x_p in the graph.

The MC curve reflects the crop losses that straying cattle impose on the farmer. The socially optimal herd size, x^*, occurs at the intersection of the two curves, or the point where the marginal benefit of an additional steer to

Figure 6.1

The Farmer-Rancher Example

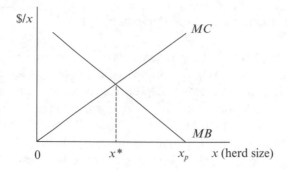

the rancher equals the marginal cost in terms of lost crops to the farmer. This is the herd size that a farmer-rancher would choose if he owned both operations. When the operations are owned separately, however, the rancher may ignore the farmer's costs and choose a herd size of x_p, which is too large.

According to the Pigovian approach to externalities, this problem is resolved by making the rancher liable for the farmer's costs by means of a tax or court-imposed damages. The rancher will then choose the optimal herd size because he is forced to internalize the marginal cost that additional cattle impose on the farmer.

Note that this solution adopts the causal relationship implicit in the polluting factory example—that is, there is a single cause of the damage, the rancher, who imposes harm on the farmer. Another way of saying this is that the rancher is viewed as the "injurer" and the farmer as the "victim." Thus, the rancher is required to pay compensation for the victim's damages.

From a property rights perspective, this solution to the straying cattle problem is equivalent to assigning the farmer the "right" to be free from straying cattle, and requiring the rancher to "purchase" that right by compensating the farmer for his crop damage. Since the rancher internalizes the farmer's loss, he purchases just the right amount of "straying" rights and ends up with an efficient herd size.[9] Note that this assignment of rights corresponds to an initial "entitlement point" of $x = 0$. That is, the rancher cannot allow any cattle to stray without incurring an obligation to pay damages to the farmer. This assignment not only results in an efficient amount of ranching, but it conforms to most people's common-sense notions of causation because, after all, it is the rancher who is "physically" causing the harm to the farmer, so he should pay.

Common sense is often a good guide to policy, but in this case it limits one's ability to perceive other solutions to the externality. To illustrate, suppose that the rancher were not liable for any damages. That is, suppose the rancher initially holds the right to allow his cattle to stray. According to the Pigovian view, this assignment of rights will lead the rancher to expand his herd to x_p because he can ignore the farmer's losses. It turns out, however, that this conclusion is not necessarily correct.

The reason that the herd size may not end up being too large in this case is that there is room for bargaining between the farmer and rancher. To see why, suppose the rancher initially has a herd of size x_p. The last steer yields a return of zero to the rancher (since $MB = 0$) but imposes a large cost on the farmer, equal to the height of the MC curve at x_p. The farmer would therefore be willing to offer up to this amount to the rancher if he agreed to reduce his herd by one, while the rancher would accept any amount greater than zero (the marginal value of the last steer) to do so. This transaction is mutually beneficial because the farmer places a higher value on the last steer than does the rancher.

By this same logic, the parties will continue bargaining to reduce the rancher's herd so long as the farmer values the last steer more than the rancher—that is, so long as the MC curve is above the MB curve. Bargaining will therefore end when the herd has been reduced to x^*, the efficient size. Further reductions will not occur because for smaller herds (that is, herd sizes to the left of x^* in Figure 6.1), the rancher values the marginal steer more than the farmer does.

In this example, property rights in straying cattle were initially assigned to the *rancher*, and the farmer purchased them so long as he valued them more than the rancher. This is the reverse of what happened under the Pigovian solution where the farmer initially held rights to the straying cattle (specifically, the right to be free of them) and the rancher purchased them. The outcome in both cases, however, is efficient. This conclusion has become known as the Coase Theorem, which we have already encountered in Chapter 1 and which we restate here:

> The Coase Theorem: *When property rights are well-defined and transaction costs are low, the allocation of resources will be efficient regardless of the initial assignment of property rights.*[10]

When we say property rights are well-defined, that simply means that both parties know the initial assignment. This is important because it determines the nature of the transactions, if any, that are needed to reallocate rights toward the efficient point. So long as both parties know the starting point, then bargaining of the sort described above can proceed. The other qualification—that transaction costs are low—is also necessary for the requisite bargaining to occur. We return to this point in detail below.

Now recall the two assumptions implicit in the Pigovian view of externalities: that there is a unique cause of the harm, and that government intervention is needed to produce an efficient outcome. The Coase Theorem shows that neither is necessarily true. First, both parties are simultaneously causes of the harm in the sense that the presence of both farming and ranching are necessary for crop damage to occur. (That is, both parties satisfy the "but-for" test for causation from Chapter 2.) Further, assigning rights to either party will result in an efficient allocation without intervention of the government, provided that the parties can bargain. The government need only assign rights and enforce whatever transactions the parties arrange. In this sense, the Coase Theorem is an "irrelevance result" because it says that the initial assignment of rights is irrelevant for the final allocation, which will be efficient.

Although the Coase Theorem seems surprising at first, it becomes intuitively clear when we recognize that it is really a version of Adam Smith's Invisible Hand Theorem, which states that the competitive market will "guide" self-interested agents toward an efficient allocation of resources, provided that externalities or other forms of market failure (like monopoly) are absent. The Coase Theorem shows that when transaction costs are low, even the presence of externalities need not preclude an efficient outcome.

2.1.1 The Assignment of Rights and the Distribution of Wealth

Although the initial assignment of rights does not matter for efficiency when transaction costs are low, it does matter for the distribution of wealth. This should be clear from the nature of the bargaining between the farmer and rancher under the two assignments described above. For example, when the farmer initially had the right to prevent straying cattle (that is, starting from $x = 0$ in Figure 6.1), it was the rancher who paid the farmer for the right to increase his herd size up to the efficient point, x^*. In contrast, when the rancher initially had the right (that is, starting from x_p in Figure 6.1), the farmer paid the rancher to reduce his herd to x^*. In both cases, the herd size ended up being the same, but the distribution of wealth favored the party who held the initial right.

This is not surprising once we recognize that the property right in this case is valued by both parties. The rancher values the right to allow his cattle to stray (as measured by the MB curve in Figure 6.1), and the farmer values the right to prevent straying cattle (as measured by the MC curve in Figure 6.1). Thus, whoever receives the right first is better off. This is an important point because it implies that when the conditions of the Coase Theorem are met, the legal system does not face a trade-off between equity and efficiency in assigning property rights in externality situations. In other words, courts can assign property rights to achieve a desired distribution of wealth without sacrificing efficiency.

This conclusion mirrors another well-known result from welfare economics, the Second Fundamental Theorem of Welfare Economics, which says that any efficient allocation of resources can be achieved as a competitive equilibrium by suitably altering the initial allocation. Coase's analysis shows that this conclusion holds for property rights as well.

An interesting application of the above conclusions concerns the impact of railroads on the development of tort law in the United States during the nineteenth century. In particular, the emergence of negligence law closely coincided with the industrial revolution and the age of machines. As Lawrence Friedman (1985, 300) notes, "The railroad engine swept like a roaring bull through the countryside, carrying out an economic and social revolution; but it exacted a tremendous toll—thousands of men, women and children injured and dead." One (controversial) argument for the emergence of negligence law during this time was to promote industrialization by limiting the liability of railroads and other enterprises in the face of this explosion of accidents.[11]

Recall from Chapter 2 that a negligence rule bars recovery by victims if the injurer invested in the efficient level of care. This provides a powerful incentive for the injurer to meet the due standard of care, but we argued that it also creates an incentive to overinvest in the harmful activity. Thus, so long as the railroad makes sure each train operates safely (for example, obeying the speed limit and stopping at crossings), it can run as many as it wishes without fear of liability.

When bargaining between the railroad and victims is possible, however, the number of trains will be efficient because, in the same way that the farmer paid the rancher to reduce his herd size, potential victims of railroad accidents could pay the railroad to reduce the number of trains to the point where the marginal damage to victims from the last train equals the marginal revenue for the railroad. If courts are confident that such bargaining will occur, then, according to the Coase Theorem, the switch to negligence law provides a way to subsidize railroads without increasing the accident rate. Of course, this interpretation only makes sense if transaction costs between the railroad and potential accident victims are low, a situation that we have argued is highly unlikely in cases of accidents between strangers.[12] Later, therefore, we offer an alternative interpretation of the use of negligence law for railroad and other accidents in the presence of high transaction costs.

2.1.2   Examples of the Coase Theorem

As the railroad example illustrates, most real-world externality settings do not have low transaction costs, which suggests that the Coase Theorem, like the perfectly competitive market, represents an important benchmark but has little practical relevance. While this is largely true, there are some notable examples of the Coase Theorem in action. We provide four in this section.

Example 1: Pollution Rights.   Pollution represents the prototypical example of an externality that results in market failure. Historically, pollution control in the United States has therefore been conducted by means of direct regulation—so-called command and control. Recently, however, economists have urged the creation of tradable pollution rights in the hope that Coasian bargaining among polluters will result in an efficient allocation of these rights (Tietenberg 1985). Such a program was in fact established for the control of sulphur dioxide emissions (the cause of acid rain) as part of the Clean Air Act of 1990. To date, the program has proven quite effective in reducing emissions, thus demonstrating its superiority over traditional methods for controlling pollution (Schmalensee et al. 1998).

Tradable permits work because they involve bargaining among a small number of polluters. Polluters and victims can also trade rights to pollute, but transaction costs usually preclude this (see the discussion of the *Boomer* case below). In one interesting case, however, an electric generating plant in Cheshire, Ohio, completed a deal with 221 nearby residents in which the residents sold their houses to the plant and signed pledges not to sue for damages in return for $20 million.[13] Although highly unusual, this case provides a striking illustration of how Coasian bargaining can internalize externalities, even in a large-numbers case, without the need for government intervention.

Example 2: The Reserve Clause in Major League Baseball.   Prior to 1976, professional baseball players were contractually bound to the team that drafted them. Under this "reserve system," owners could automatically renew a player's contract and could trade or sell the player at will, but players did not have the right to negotiate with other teams. Their only alternative to negotiating with the owner was to threaten not to play. The decision of an arbitrator's panel in 1976, however, introduced a limited form of free agency into major league baseball whereby players with a minimum amount of major league experience could negotiate with other teams.

Owners had justified the reserve system by arguing that it was essential to maintain competitive balance in the league. Under free agency, they argued, the richest teams would end up with the best players. In contrast, economists have argued that free agency should not change the distribution of player talent. To see why, note that under free agency, players would move to the team that placed the highest value on their services, whereas under the reserve system, owners would sell (or trade) players to the team that placed the highest value on their services. The only difference between the two systems is who owns property rights in the players' services: under the reserve system it is owners, while under free agency it is players. Thus, the Coase Theorem implies that free agency should not change the distribution of talent, only the distribution of wealth.[14]

It is possible to test this proposition by looking at the records of major league teams before and after the onset of free agency. Table 6.1 looks at two measures of competitive balance for both the American and National

TABLE **6.1**   **Impact of Free Agency on Competitive Balance in Major League Baseball**

	Pre–free agency (1963–1976)	Post–free agency (1977–1990)
Average range of winning percentage		
American League	.241	.249
National League	.251	.211
Average standard deviation of winning percentage		
American League	.071	.070
National League	.066	.064

SOURCE: *Quirk and Fort (1992, 285).*

Leagues during fourteen years before (1963–1976) and fourteen years after (1977–1990) free agency (Quirk and Fort 1992).[15] The first measure is the average range of winning percentages (that is, the average of the difference between the teams with the highest and lowest winning percentages), and the second is the average standard deviation of winning percentages. Both measures indicate that no significant change occurred in the competitive balance of either league as a result of free agency. There is little doubt, however, that it has shifted the distribution of wealth toward players.

Example 3: Order Without Law.   Robert Ellickson (1991) provides an interesting illustration of the Coase Theorem in action in his case study of how residents in a rural county of California deal with the problem of straying cattle. Prior to 1945, most of the county in question was "open range." That is, cattle ranchers were not liable for damages caused by straying cattle. In 1945, however, the county enacted a "closed range" statute in some areas, making ranchers strictly liable for cattle damage. This regime change offered a unique opportunity, in the context of Coase's own example, to evaluate the impact of a change in property rights on the allocation of resources.[16]

Ellickson found that neighbors were in fact strongly inclined to cooperate with one another to resolve their disputes. In this sense, the parties achieved the outcome predicted by the Coase Theorem, namely, a mutually beneficial outcome without the need for government intervention. Surprisingly, though, they did not reach this outcome by bargaining from established legal rules. Instead, they did it "by developing and enforcing adaptive norms of neighborliness that trump legal entitlements" (Ellickson 1991, 4). This finding shows that, in some circumstances, even the minimalist role of government implied by the Coase Theorem—that is, of defining rights as a background for bargaining and enforcing any reallocations—is not necessary to achieve an efficient outcome. Although we saw that property rights similarly emerged without government intervention in mining, that was a prelude to formal government enforcement, rather than a substitute.

Example 4: Experimental Evidence for the Coase Theorem.   A final example of the Coase Theorem in practice is provided by experimental evidence. Hoffman and Spitzer (1982) report the results of a set of controlled experiments that tested the predictions of the Coase Theorem in two- and three-person interactions. In each experiment, the parties made pseudoproduction decisions that affected each other's payoffs (as in externality cases), and they were allowed to bargain over the outcome and division of the proceeds. The results turned out to be efficient in 89.5 percent of the experiments, providing clear support for the Coase Theorem in small numbers (that is, low transaction cost) settings.

2.1.3   The Role of Transaction Costs

The preceding examples show that the Coase Theorem has some practical significance. However, many, if not most, externalities involve large numbers of individuals, in which case the assumption of low transaction costs is not likely to be satisfied. When transaction costs are present, the assignment of property rights will matter because some assignments will involve lower transaction costs than others. Thus, we state:

> Corollary 1 to the Coase Theorem: *When transaction costs are high, the assignment of property rights matters for efficiency.*

As an illustration of how the law matters, return to the above example of the response of tort law to the proliferation of railroad accidents in the nineteenth century. We suggested there that, if transaction costs between injurers and victims are low, then the liability rule will not affect efficiency, only the distribution of wealth. Thus, one could interpret the shift from strict liability to negligence as an effort to subsidize railroads—thereby promoting economic development—without affecting the accident rate.

The assumption of low transaction costs in this setting, however, is not very realistic. As we noted above, railroad accidents involve accidents between strangers who have little if any ability to bargain before an accident. Thus, the liability rule is likely to have an important bearing on how much the parties invest in the prevention of such accidents. Seen in this light, and using the insights from Chapter 2, we can see that the shift from strict liability to negligence probably had offsetting effects on efficiency. On the one hand, negligence creates an incentive for potential victims to take precaution, thus reducing the accident rate, and it also reduces litigation costs by discouraging some lawsuits. On the other hand, strict liability is better at inducing injurers to choose the correct activity level (for example, to run the efficient number of trains), and the costs of litigating a strict liability case are lower.

The point of this example is not to suggest which rule is more efficient (it is an empirical question), but to illustrate that the rule *matters* for efficiency (Demsetz 1972). In other words, the irrelevance of the Coase Theorem is gone. (And, as a result, a trade-off between efficiency and equity emerges.) This is a fundamental insight because it defines the scope for legal intervention. We expand on this idea in our discussion of enforcement rules in the next section.

2.1.4 Loss Aversion and the Endowment Effect

The preceding discussion has highlighted transaction costs as the primary impediment to Coasian bargaining, but there is another effect that can prevent the exchange of property rights even when transactions are costless. Experimental evidence has demonstrated the existence of the *endowment effect*, which says that individuals place a higher dollar value on the loss of a particular property right than they would be willing to pay to acquire it. This effect is attributed to *loss aversion*, which is the idea that individuals weigh losses more heavily than commensurate gains.

The implication of these effects for the Coase Theorem is that, even when transaction costs are low, the assignment of property rights may affect the ultimate allocation of resources by increasing the minimum amount that the party receiving the right would be willing to accept in return for it. As a result, the ultimate allocation of resources will not be independent of the initial assignment of rights, as our discussion so far has implied (Kahneman et al. 2000). It does *not* follow, however, that the endowment effect prevents resources from being allocated efficiently. Indeed, if the party receiving the right truly values it more than a prospective buyer by virtue of possessing it, then it is efficient for him or her to retain possession. The endowment effect merely implies, therefore, that the efficient allocation of resources cannot be defined independently of the initial assignment of rights.

2.2 Enforcement Rules

So far we have focused on the assignment of property rights, but the rules for enforcing property rights are also important for determining the allocation of resources because they dictate how property rights can be (legally) transferred and what remedies are available for infringements. In this section, we examine the economic implications of the choice of enforcement rules.

2.2.1 Property Rules and Liability Rules

The classic treatment of this problem is presented by Calabresi and Melamed (1972) in a paper that is second only to Coase in its importance for the economic analysis of law.[17] The two basic rules that Calabresi and Melamed identify are *property rules* and *liability rules*. The best way to distinguish them is by means of an example. Suppose party A initially holds the right (or the *entitlement*) to plant a tree that blocks B's view of the ocean. If A's right is protected by a property rule, then B can only prevent him from planting the tree by offering an amount of money that A is willing to accept. That is, B must purchase the right in a consensual transaction. In contrast, if A's right to plant the tree is protected by a liability rule, than B can acquire the right without A's consent—for example, by chopping the tree down—so long as he pays damages to A as set by the court.

As this example illustrates, the rules differ in terms of how the price for the transaction is set. Under a property rule, the price is set by the parties through bargaining. Property rules therefore form the basis for market exchange. If I want to buy my neighbor's car, then I must offer an amount that he is willing to accept, and we are both free to back out of the deal at any time. The key is the presence of *consent*, which ensures that all transactions are mutually advantageous. Property rules in market settings are enforced by laws against theft, while in nonmarket interactions, they are enforced by *injunctions*—that is, court orders to do, or refrain from doing, something (like chopping down a tree) backed by the threat of force.

Under liability rules, in contrast, the party seeking to acquire the right can do so without first obtaining the holder's consent, provided that the acquirer is willing to pay compensation for the holder's loss. The transaction is therefore nonconsensual, and the price is set by the court after the fact rather than by bargaining.

An example of a liability rule is strict liability in tort law. Under strict liability, injurers are responsible for all losses suffered by victims of an accident. In effect, the injurer is required to compensate the victim for having "taken" her right to be free from an accident. Another example is expectation damages in contract law. Under this remedy, a promisor is free to breach a contract without first obtaining the promisee's consent, provided that he pays for the promisee's losses.

Contrast this with a specific performance remedy for breach. Recall that specific performance is an order by the court that the promisor must perform the contract as written. This does not mean that breach will never occur; rather, it means that the promisor can only breach by first obtaining the promisee's *consent*. Specific performance is therefore an example of property-rule protection of the promisee's right to performance of the contract.

2.2.2   The Choice Between Property Rules and Liability Rules

If property rules guarantee that all transactions will be mutually beneficial, then why would it ever be more efficient to use liability rules? The answer is that, if consent were always required, transaction costs would sometimes prevent otherwise beneficial exchanges from occurring. Suppose, for example, that people have the right to be free from accidents caused by trains, and that this right is protected by a property rule. Railroad companies would then have to identify and negotiate with all potential accident victims over the assignment of liability *before any accidents happen*, a prospect that would prevent most trains from ever leaving the station. In contrast, a liability rule would allow the railroad to compensate victims after the fact. And so long as compensation were set equal to the victim's damages, the efficient number of trains would run.

This example suggests that when transaction costs are high, liability rules are preferred over property rules. The advantage of liability rules is that they allow the court to coerce beneficial exchanges of rights when transaction costs prevent the parties from doing so in a consensual manner. This advantage, however, must be weighed against the cost of using liability rules. These include litigation costs and the possibility of court error in setting damages.

To illustrate the latter problem, consider the following example of the rancher-farmer conflict. Suppose the farmer sustains damages of $120 from straying cattle that the rancher could prevent by fencing in his cattle at a cost of $100. It is therefore efficient to prevent straying. (Alternatively, the farmer could "fence out" straying cattle; but assume that this costs more than $100.) Also suppose that the farmer has the right to be free from damages, and this right is protected by a liability rule. If the court sets damages correctly at $120, then the efficient outcome will arise: the rancher will spend $100 to fence in the herd rather than paying damages of $120. However, if the court errs and sets damages too low—say, at $80—then the rancher will allow the cattle to continue straying, resulting in a net social loss of $20.

This sort of inefficiency is always possible under liability rules, but so long as the court does not err too severely, the gains from coercing efficient inframarginal transactions will more than offset the losses that arise at the margin as a result of too many or too few transactions. We will see, however, that there is one situation in which the losses from court error can be high—namely, when a large component of the victim's loss is subjective value. An earlier example of this in the context of contract law was the *Peevyhouse* case. Recall that when the promisor breached a contract to repair the Peevyhouses' property after a strip mining operation, the court awarded damages based on the market value of the damages, although their actual losses were probably substantially higher. We therefore argued that the promisor had an excessive incentive to breach, which would have been eliminated by replacing money damages (a liability rule) with specific performance (a property rule). (We return to this issue below in the context of title systems for land, and again in the next chapter in our discussion of takings law.)

One reason for favoring a property rule in the *Peevyhouse* case was that the transaction costs between the parties were presumably low. A simple application of the Coase Theorem, however, establishes that when transaction costs are low, *the enforcement rule doesn't matter for efficiency*, even if the court makes systematic errors in measuring damages under a liability rule (Kaplow and Shavell 1996, 732). The following exercise asks you to verify this claim in the context of the above farmer-rancher example.

EXERCISE 6.1

Consider the above example where a rancher can spend $100 to prevent straying cattle from causing $120 in damages to a farmer. Assume that the farmer has the right to be free from damages, and transaction costs between the parties are zero so they make all mutually beneficial trades. Describe the transactions (if any) in each of the following situations:

(a) The farmer's right is protected by a property rule.
(b) The farmer's right is protected by a liability rule and damages are correctly set at $120.
(c) The farmer's right is protected by a liability rule and damages are underestimated at $80.

There may be one basis for choosing between property rules and liability rules in the low-transaction-cost case, namely, administrative costs. Under property rules, the administrative role of the court is limited to enforcing transfers of rights, whereas under liability rules, the court has to establish the initial terms of trade (which the parties may later adjust) by measuring the victim's damages. Thus, the administrative costs of liability rules are likely to be higher. This conclusion, coupled with the above results for the high-transaction-cost case, yields the following prescription regarding the choice of enforcement rules:

> Corollary 2 to the Coase Theorem: *Use property rules when transaction costs are low, and liability rules when transaction costs are high.*

This result provides a normative theory for the choice of enforcement rules in externality cases. The next section applies this theory to the law of trespass and nuisance.

2.2.3   Trespass and Nuisance

Trespass and nuisance are the primary common-law doctrines designed to protect a property owner's right to exclude other users, which is one of the three fundamental rights associated with ownership.[18] The distinction between the two is stated as follows in a leading casebook: "Trespass is an invasion of the plaintiff's interest in the exclusive possession of his land, while nuisance is an interference with his use and enjoyment of it" (Keeton et al. 1984, 622). Examples of trespass include squatting on another's land and boundary encroachment; examples of nuisance include pollution, foul odors, and noise.

In terms of remedies, a victim of trespass has the right to seek an injunction against the trespass (as well as compensation for any damages caused by it).[19] Even if the trespasser values the invasion more than it costs the landowner, the trespasser can only continue by seeking permission from the owner. In other words, the owner's right to exclude invasions is protected by a property rule.

The law of nuisance is more complicated. First, the victim cannot bring legal action unless the harm is substantial. In some cases, the demonstration of substantial harm only entitles the victims to damages, a liability rule. In other cases, the victim can seek an injunction against the harmful activity, but such a remedy requires the further demonstration that "a reasonable person would conclude that the amount of the harm done outweighs the benefits served by the conduct" (Keeton et al. 1984, 630). Thus, injunctive relief from a nuisance is only available if the plaintiff can satisfy a cost-benefit test that resembles the Hand rule for negligence. This is in contrast to trespass, where an injunction is virtually automatic.

The differing remedies for trespass and nuisance make sense in terms of the property rule–liability rule framework if trespass cases involve low transaction costs and nuisance involves high transaction costs. On the whole, this appears to be the case. Cases of trespass ordinarily involve a small number of parties and, hence, have low transaction costs. Thus, a property rule is efficient. For example, in the case of boundary encroachment, the owner's unqualified right to exclude the encroacher encourages the latter to locate and bargain with the owner before erecting a structure or otherwise improving the land.

In contrast, nuisance cases tend to involve high transaction costs. For example, cases of air or water pollution will generally cause harm to large numbers of individuals, making bargaining between the polluter and victims impractical. In cases like this, liability rules are preferred.

It is interesting to note that the distinction between trespass and nuisance, and more generally, between property rules and liability rules, marks the boundary between property law and tort law. As noted above, the right to exclusion embodied in trespass is a fundamental component of the ownership of property, whereas liability for damages is the basis for tort law. The economic approach to law reveals that these two areas of the law simply reflect alternative solutions to the general problem of designing an efficient "transaction structure." Specifically, rules of property law govern exchanges in settings of low transaction costs, and rules of tort law govern exchanges in settings of high transaction costs.

The preceding discussion illustrates an important theme of this book—namely, the ability of economics to provide a unifying theory of the law. The study of boundaries between different areas of the law is especially fruitful in this regard. The property rule–liability rule distinction is an important example; another is the evolution of products liability from a species of contract law to one of torts (a change that we previously argued was largely due to transaction costs).[20] Below we will argue that the law of leases occupies the nexus between contract and property law. The point is that there is much to be learned by examining boundaries, for that is where alternative solutions to common problems reveal the law's underlying economic logic.

The Boomer Case.   The well-known case of *Boomer v. Atlantic Cement Company* (26 N.Y.2d 219, 309 N.Y.S.2d 312, 257 N.E.2d 870, Court of Appeals of New York 1970) provides another illustration of the choice between property rules and liability rules in a classic externality setting. The case involved a group of landowners who sought an injunction against a large cement company because of the dirt, smoke, and vibration that it produced. The court denied the request for an injunction and instead awarded the plaintiffs damages of $183,000. The court reasoned that an injunction would have been an overly drastic remedy, causing the plant to shut down with the loss of three hundred jobs and the present value in profits arising from an original investment of $45 million. In contrast, money damages allowed the plant to continue operating while at the same time compensating victims and providing an incentive for the plant "to research for an improved technique to minimize nuisance."

The court thus favored a liability rule over a property rule in this case. The analysis in this section suggests that this was the efficient result because of the prospect of high transaction costs. In particular, if the court had issued an injunction, the plant owner would have had to bargain with each victim for permission to continue operating. Not only would this have required multiple transactions, there also existed a potential hold-out problem because any one owner could have enforced the injunction. Thus, each had monopoly power and could have sought to extract a large fraction of the plant's value.[21]

Even if there had been only one victim in *Boomer*, however, transaction costs may still have been high because of the presence of a bilateral monopoly problem. To illustrate, recall that the plant stood to lose the present value of its profits if it shut down, while the residents would have suffered $183,000 in damages if it continued to operate. Thus, any price between these two amounts should have made both sides better off while allowing the plant to continue operating (the efficient result). The problem is that the bargaining range is so large, each side would have had an incentive to invest a large amount of effort to secure as much of the surplus as possible. This sort of "rent seeking" represents a potential impediment to bargaining, even in small-numbers cases, and therefore provides a further justification for the use of a liability rule in this case.[22]

EXERCISE 6.2

Consider a different set of facts in the *Boomer* case. Suppose that Atlantic Cement Co. has proposed building a factory worth $45 million in a predominantly residential area, but nearby residents, anticipating damages of $183,000, obtained an injunction preventing construction. Further, suppose that Atlantic has an alternate site for the factory where it will be worth $44 million but will impose no external costs. Describe the nature of the bargaining between Atlantic and the residents (as a group) over enforcement of the injunction. How does it compare to the actual case?

2.2.4   A Note on Inalienability of Property Rights

We have focused on property rules and liability rules as the primary mechanisms governing the legal transfer of property, but the law also prohibits some transfers of property altogether. Calabresi and Melamed (1972) refer to such prohibitions as *inalienability rules.* Examples include constitutional protections of certain basic freedoms (speech, religion, and the right to vote), as well as laws against the sale of body parts, cultural artifacts, and children. Minimum wage and rent control laws are examples of limited inalienability rules.

At first glance, inalienability rules seem inconsistent with the goal of promoting efficient exchange of property rights because they forbid even consensual transactions. An efficiency rationale for inalienability must therefore rely on the existence of externalities associated with the transfer of certain goods. For example, the sale of some drugs, though consensual on the part of the buyer and seller, may deprive the buyer of his or her free will due to the drug's addictive nature, and may also cause buyers to commit crimes in order to support their habit. Similarly, a free market in organs, body parts, or children might lead to a greatly increased rate of kidnapping for profit, thereby imposing substantial costs on victims and generally increasing the costs of law enforcement (Friedman 2000, 242). A similar argument justifies laws against involuntary slavery.

It is more difficult, however, to rationalize on purely efficiency grounds laws against voluntary slavery (for example, indentured servitude and debtors' prisons), as well as other transactions (like prostitution) that apparently involve no third-party effects. In many cases, however, the objections to these transactions are based on moral or political, rather than economic, considerations. Finally, restrictions on market exchange like minimum wage and rent control laws, though inefficient, are primarily aimed at goals other than efficiency, such as attaining a fairer distribution of wealth.

2.3 The General Transaction Structure

The Coase Theorem and its two corollaries provide a general theoretical framework for organizing the exchange of property, a framework that we will refer to as the *transaction structure*.[23] As Table 6.2 shows, the structure involves the choice of an *assignment* of rights and an *enforcement rule*. In terms of the farmer-rancher conflict, the right is either assigned to the rancher (the "producer" of the harm), or the farmer (the "recipient" of the harm), and it is protected by a property rule or a liability rule.

We return to our earlier numerical example to illustrate how each of the four possible combinations internalizes the external harm from straying cattle. Recall that the farmer suffers a loss of $120 if the cattle stray, but the rancher can prevent straying by erecting a fence at a cost of $100 (which is the efficient result). For purposes of the current discussion, we assume that both parties have initial wealth of $200.[24] Thus, in the efficient outcome, aggregate wealth is $300, which equals the initial wealth of $400 minus the cost of the fence.

Under combination I, the rancher has the right to allow his cattle to stray, and the right is protected by a property rule. In this case, the farmer can only prevent straying cattle by bargaining with the farmer. Assume that the parties split the surplus from any bargain evenly. Thus, the farmer pays the rancher $110 and the rancher erects a fence. The resulting returns to the two parties are as follows:

Farmer:	$200 − $110 =	$ 90
Rancher:	$200 − $100 + $110 =	$210
Aggregate:		$300

Under combination II, the farmer has the right to be free from straying cattle, protected by a property rule. In this case, the farmer can obtain an injunction

TABLE **6.2**   **The General Transaction Structure**

		Assignment	
		Rancher	*Farmer*
Enforcement rule	Property rule	(I) Rancher is free to impose harm	(II) Farmer can seek an injunction against harm
	Liability rule	(III) Rancher can seek damages for cost of reducing harm	(IV) Farmer can seek damages for harm suffered

against straying cattle, so the rancher has to purchase the right to let his cattle stray. However, since the farmer will demand an amount in excess of $120 (his damage from straying cattle), the rancher will simply build the fence for $100. The resulting returns are

Farmer:		$200
Rancher:	$200 − $100 −	$100
Aggregate:		$300

Consider next combination III, which awards the right to the rancher protected by a liability rule. In this case, the rancher has the right to let his cattle stray, but the farmer can force him to erect a fence by paying "damages" of $100 (the cost of the fence). The returns are

Farmer:	$200 − $100 =	$100
Rancher:	$200 =	$200
Aggregate:		$300

Finally, combination IV awards the right to the farmer protected by a liability rule. The rancher thus has the choice to let his cattle stray and pay damages of $120, or to erect a fence. Since the fence is cheaper, he will erect it, yielding returns of

Farmer:		$200
Rancher:	$200 − $100 =	$100
Aggregate:		$300

This example has shown how each of the four combinations of an assignment of rights and an enforcement rule can achieve the efficient allocation of resources. Combinations I and II relied on bargaining between the par-

Figure 6.2

Distribution of Wealth
in the Four Cases

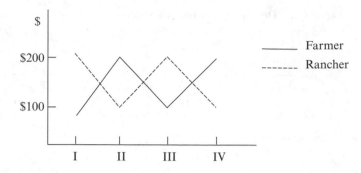

ties (though no actual transaction took place under II) and therefore required low transaction costs, while combinations III and IV relied on court-imposed damage payments. Aggregate wealth was invariant across the cases as required by the Coase Theorem, but the distribution of wealth varied depending on the initial assignment of rights. This is shown in Figure 6.2, which graphs the wealth of the farmer and rancher in each of the cases. Clearly, the farmer is better off when he receives the right (combinations II and IV), while the rancher if better off when he receives the right (combinations I and III).

Exercise 6.3

Reconsider the farmer-rancher example, but now let the cost of erecting a fence be $140. Show how the efficient outcome is achieved in each of the four cases.

The general transaction structure as just described represents the foundation of the economic approach to law. We illustrate its generality with several applications from tort, contract, and property law.

Note first that the Pigovian approach to externalities corresponds to combination IV, where the producer of the externality is viewed as the cause of the harm, and the recipient is entitled to compensation. That is, the recipient, or victim, has the right to be free from harm, protected by a liability rule. The *Boomer* case similarly falls into this category, as does the law of nuisance (provided that the harm is substantial) and all the liability rules from tort law. Finally, a money damage remedy in contract law fits combination IV, where the "victim" of the breach has the right to performance of the contract protected by a liability rule.

Combination II adopts the same assignment of rights (namely, the recipient has the right) but protects it with a property rule. Thus, a victim of harm can obtain injunctive relief, as under the law of trespass. For example, in the case of *Hadacheck v. Sebastian* (239 U.S. 394, 1915), the court ordered a brickyard to shut down when residential development began to encroach on it and residents became "seriously incommoded by [its] operations." The case is similar to *Boomer* in terms of the assignment of the right, but the court enforced it with a property rule rather than a liability rule. According to the theory, this choice was efficient provided that bargaining costs between the brickyard owner and victims were low (or if the court was confident that shutting down the brickyard was efficient).

In the area of contract law, the use of specific performance corresponds to combination II. Under this remedy, the victim of breach has the right to performance enforced by a property rule. Thus, breach can only occur as a result of bargaining between the contracting parties.

Combinations I and III represent an assignment of rights to the producer of the external cost. Under combination I, the producer's right is protected by a property rule. This combination fits the common-law doctrine of "coming to the nuisance," under which preexisting land uses are protected against suits filed by encroaching newcomers (Wittman 1980). For example, in *Mahlstadt v. City of Indianola* (251 Ia. 222, 100 N.W.2d 189, 1959) the court overturned an injunction shutting down a dump that had been impinged on by residential development. This case is the thus flip side of *Hadacheck*. Most states properly reject the coming to the nuisance doctrine, however, because high transaction costs would likely prevent the parties from internalizing the costs through bargaining (Posner 1998a, 70–71). Indeed, much of nuisance law has been replaced in the United States with public regulation for this and other reasons that we discuss in Chapter 7.[25]

Finally, combination III corresponds to an assignment of rights to the producer of the external harm, protected by a liability rule. This combination fits the well-known case of *Spur Industries, Inc. v. Del E. Webb Development Co.* (494 P.2d 701, Ariz. 1972). The case involved a developer who encroached on a preexisting feed lot and then sued to have the lot shut down as a nuisance. The court allowed the coming-to-the-nuisance defense by assigning the right to the feed lot, but it protected it with a liability rule rather than a property rule. Specifically, the court ordered the lot to cease operating but required the developer to "indemnify Spur for a reasonable amount of the cost of moving or shutting down."

The coming to the nuisance doctrine reflects the relative nature of the labels "injurer" and "victim." In the case of encroaching land uses (*Spur* and *Mahlstadt*), it is reasonable to treat the preexisting use as the victim, even when it is the physical producer of the harm. However, the pairing of coming to the nuisance with a liability rule, as in *Spur*, represents an efficient response to the high transaction costs that characterize most nuisance cases.

3 Consensual Transfers of Property

Having completed our description of the general transaction structure, we now turn to a more detailed discussion of the legal aspects of the exchange of property. We first examine consensual, or market, exchange; in the next chapter, we turn to nonconsensual, or involuntary, exchange.

3.1 The Legal Protection of Ownership

The primary role of the legal system in promoting market exchange of property is the protection of ownership rights (Baird and Jackson 1984). In a world of perfect information, possession is sufficient to establish legitimate ownership because prospective buyers are confident that all previous transfers of the property occurred by consensual means. Thus, there is no risk that a previously defrauded owner will arrive and assert a claim. In reality, however, information is not perfect, and buyers always face the risk of past theft or error. An important function of property law, therefore, is to minimize this cloud of uncertainty, thereby improving the efficiency of market exchange.

Since information is costly, however, legal protection of ownership, or "title," will generally not be complete. Rather, an efficient system will protect title up to the point where the marginal benefit of increased security of ownership equals the marginal cost. To illustrate, consider the following simple model.[26]

For concreteness, we consider ownership of a parcel of land, though the model generalizes to other sorts of property. Suppose that, in the absence of ownership risk, the parcel in question is worth V dollars in its best use. However, there is a risk that a past owner will assert a claim based on error or fraudulent transfer. Let $p(c)$ represent the probability that the current owner will retain title (thus, $1 - p(c)$ is the probability of a successful claim), where c is the cost devoted to ensuring title. For example, c could represent the cost of consulting a public record of all past transfers, or the cost of establishing a security system. We assume that p is increasing in c, though at a decreasing rate, reflecting diminishing marginal returns to security. The $p(c)$ function is shown graphically in Figure 6.3.[27]

The owner's problem is to maximize the expected value of the property, given by $p(c)V - c$. The resulting optimum occurs at the point where the marginal benefit in terms of increased security from the last dollar spent equals the marginal cost ($1). Graphically, this optimum is the point where the slope of the $p(c)$ function equals $1/V$, the reciprocal of the value of the parcel.[28] Two optima, reflecting two different values of V, are shown in Figure 6.3, where the straight lines have a slope equal to $1/V$. The tangency between $p(c)$ and the flatter line (point B) therefore corresponds to the higher-valued property.

Figure 6.3

The Optimal Level
of Title Protection

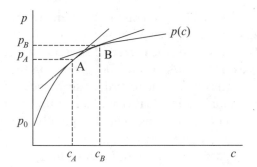

It follows that owners of more valuable property will incur a higher cost ($c_B > c_A$), and in return obtain greater security of ownership ($p_B > p_A$), compared to owners of less valuable property.

Actual ownership systems vary by type of property. All states maintain a public recording system for land (with some variation across jurisdictions, as discussed below), and, to a lesser extent, for cars. For most other goods, however, would-be buyers invest little or no effort in verifying the seller's rightful ownership. The owner's possession of the good and a reputation for not dealing in stolen property are usually sufficient evidence. This variation seems consistent with the predictions of the model that people will invest more resources in security of ownership as the value of their property increases. For example, land might correspond to point B in Figure 6.3, cars to point A, and most other goods to the point labeled p_0 on the vertical axis.

3.2 Should the Law Protect the Possessor or the Claimant? An Analysis of Land Title Systems*

The preceding analysis showed that in a world of costly information, buyers and sellers will not choose to verify ownership with certainty before transacting, even for very valuable property. As a result, owners will sometimes be deprived of their property by fraud, theft, or error. If the deprived owner later asserts a claim for the property, the law confronts a fundamental problem: Should it protect the rights of the current possessor (who acquired the property in a legal manner), or should it protect the rights of the claimant (the last rightful owner)? In this section, we try to provide an answer to these questions based on economic theory. Although the questions are general and arise for any type of property, we focus on how the law has answered it in the specific context of land claims (Miceli and Sirmans 1995b).[29]

3.2.1 Land Title Systems: Recording Versus Registration

Common-law countries have historically employed two types of systems for protecting title to land. By far the most common in the United States is the *recording system*, which is based on the maintenance of a public record of all consensual transfers of a piece of property. Prospective buyers can consult this record for evidence that the current possessor has legitimate title, but the record itself does not establish title. Depending on the thoroughness of the search, errors or omissions in the record, or differences in lawyers' interpretations, there may remain a residual risk of a claim. As a result, buyers search the record anew with each transfer and generally purchase title insurance against the possibility of a future claim.[30]

The other major title system is the registration, or Torrens, system. This is the predominant system in England, and it has been used sporadically in the United States.[31] Under the registration system, a landowner registers her property with the government at the time of purchase, at which point there is a judicial inquiry into the status of the title. If no outstanding claim is found, the government issues a certificate that is good against most future claims. If a claimant does appear, he is usually only entitled to seek monetary restitution from a public fund financed by registration fees.

In general terms, therefore, the primary difference between the two systems is this: in the event of a claim, the registration system awards title to the possessor and monetary compensation to the claimant, whereas the recording system (with title insurance) awards title to the claimant and monetary compensation to the possessor. The two systems therefore provide opposing solutions to the fundamental problem of title protection under uncertainty. The question is, does the particular solution matter for efficiency or is it purely a distributional (fairness) issue? A simple graphical analysis allows us to answer this question.

Consider two parties, the *possessor* of the land in question, and a *claimant*. The possessor has a utility function, $U(L, W)$, that depends on her holding of land, L, and wealth, W. Suppose that, prior to the arrival of the claimant, the possessor holds L_0 units of land and W_0 dollars in wealth. Further, suppose that this reflects an optimal portfolio in the sense that she cannot increase her utility by buying or selling any amount of land at the market price of p. The possessor's initial portfolio is thus shown by point A in Figure 6.4, which occurs at a tangency between her indifference curve, labeled U_0, and the budget line, whose slope is $-p$.

It is worth emphasizing that the convexity of the indifference curve indicates that the possessor does not view land and wealth as perfect substitutes. Note, for example, that if she were required to give up her entire holding of land, the minimum amount of wealth she would require in order to maintain the same level of utility (that is, to remain on the indifference curve labeled U_0) is given by the vertical segment BW_0 in Figure 6.4. In contrast, the market value of the land is given by the smaller segment, $\overline{W}W_0$. Thus, if she were forced to sell her land at the market value, her utility would fall from U_0 to U_1.

Figure 6.4

Comparison of
Recording and
Registration
Systems for
Protecting Title
to Land

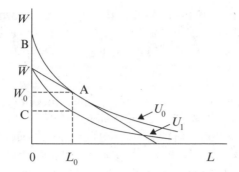

The higher utility associated with point A as compared to point $\overline{W}$ reflects the possessor's subjective value of the land—that is, her valuation of the land in excess of its market value (given by segment $B\overline{W}$). Although we encountered this idea in the previous chapter in the context of breach of contract, subjective value is more often associated with possession of land.[32] As the great American judge Oliver Wendell Holmes once observed, "Man, like a tree in the cleft of a rock, gradually shapes roots to its surroundings, and when the roots have grown to a certain size, can't be displaced without cutting at its life."[33] This suggests that possession and subjective value are inextricably linked, and that subjective value likely grows over time as the possessor occupies the land. (The idea is the same as that underlying the endowment effect discussed above.) This would be reflected by an increase in the convexity of the possessor's indifference curve over time, which would cause a corresponding increase in the distance $B\overline{W}$ (holding point A fixed).

Now suppose a claimant arrives and asserts a claim for the land. The claimant similarly has utility over land and wealth, but because he is not currently occupying the land (and maybe never has), it is reasonable to suppose that he has little or no subjective value. In that case, he will value the land at roughly its market value. In other words, his indifference curves will be straight lines with slope equal to $-p$ (that is, they will be parallel to the budget line).

The important implication of this difference in preferences between the possessor and the claimant is that the possessor will strictly prefer a title system that allows her to retain title rather than receiving its market value as compensation. In contrast, the claimant will most likely be indifferent between the two options. As a result, economic theory would seem to favor the registration system over the recording system because it leaves the land in the hands of the higher valuer (the possessor).

There are two qualifications to this conclusion. First, if compensation were adjusted to account for subjective value, then the possessor should be indifferent between receiving the land and receiving compensation. The problem with this solution is the difficulty in measuring subjective value, which is one of the drawbacks of liability rules in general.

The second qualification is that, although the recording system *initially* awards title to the claimant, the former possessor may be able to repurchase it from him. To see why, note that starting from point $\overline{W}$ (after compensation has been paid), the former possessor will pay up to $\overline{W}\,C$ to reacquire the land (that is, $\overline{W}\,C$ is the maximum amount she can pay and remain on indifference curve U_1), while the claimant will accept any amount greater than the market value (still given by $\overline{W}\,W_0$) to sell it. And since $\overline{W}\,C > \overline{W}\,W_0$ a mutually beneficial bargain is possible. (The actual sale price will depend on the bargaining abilities of the parties.) Thus, so long as transaction costs between the parties are low, the original possessor will reacquire the land, thereby achieving the value-maximizing outcome.

Of course, this conclusion—that both title systems will result in the land being allocated to the higher valuer—is just an example of the Coase Theorem. In this case, the impact of the title system is purely distributional. (Each party prefers the system that assigns title to him or her.)

When transactions between the parties are costly, however, the title system will matter for efficiency (Corollary 1 to the Coase Theorem). In that case, the efficient system is the one that minimizes impediments to bargaining. With regard to land claims, this criterion would seem to favor registration because in most cases it initially assigns the land to the higher valuer—no further transactions are necessary.

Land claims are infrequent, however. Thus, a better measure of exchange efficiency for the vast majority of cases is the relative cost of completing ordinary transactions under the two systems. Below, we offer some evidence on this question based on the coexistence of the recording and registration systems in some jurisdictions in the United States.

3.2.2   Land Title Systems in the United States

The predominant title system in the United States is the recording system, but as many as twenty-one states have experimented with title registration. The most notable of these experiments was the adoption of the Torrens registration system in Cook County, Illinois, following the Great Chicago Fire of 1871, which destroyed the public land records.[34] Although Cook County has since abandoned the Torrens system for lack of use, its coexistence with the recording system for more than one hundred years provides a unique opportunity to compare the day-to-day operation of the two systems.

One of the purported advantages of the Torrens system, according to its advocates, is that it saves on transaction costs by eliminating the need to search the title history of a property with each sale. Janczyk (1977) used data from Cook Country from 1938 to 1967 to estimate the resulting savings in transaction costs. His results are shown in column one of Table 6.3. (All data in the

TABLE **6.3** **Comparison of Transfer Costs Under Torrens and Recording Systems**

	Janczyk	Shick and Plotkin
Registration cost	$442.54	$574–$774[a]
Average transfer cost		
Torrens	$173.54	$269–$332[a]
Registration	$335.29	$332

SOURCE: *Janczyk (1977); Shick and Plotkin (1978).*
[a] *Ranges reflect differences in lawyers' fees and variation in practices.*

table are based on 1976 dollars.) He found a substantial savings in transfer costs under the Torrens system ($335.29 − $173.54 = $161.75) which, he argued, justified the one-time registration cost of $442.54. In fact, he estimated that if all property in Cook County were converted to the Torrens system, the present value in net savings would be $76 million in 1976 prices.

Shick and Plotkin (1978) undertook a similar cost comparison of the Torrens and recording systems, but arrived at a less favorable assessment of the advantages of Torrens. Their results, based on 1976 data, are shown in column two of Table 6.3. They reveal little if any savings in transfer costs and a higher registration fee. The apparent increase in the cost of Torrens between 1967 (the last year of Janczyk's data) and 1976 may account for the declining use of the system over that period.

Measuring cost differences, however, does not tell the whole story. An important advantage of the Torrens system is that it clears title to land for which the risk of a claim is high, as when records are poor, incomplete, or lost. Thus, when both the recording and registration systems coexist, we would expect owners of high-risk properties to choose the registration system, even if the transaction costs are higher. A recent study of land transactions in Cook County found that this was in fact how landowners sorted themselves into the two systems (Miceli et al. 2002). Further, once this "self-selection" effect is taken into account, land values in the sample were higher under the Torrens system than under the recording system. The declining use and eventual repeal of Torrens in Cook County in the twentieth century therefore most likely reflects the declining number of high-risk properties on the market as the effects of the Chicago Fire fade into history.

3.3 Title Protection and Economic Development

Economists have recently begun to examine the role of land title systems for economic development. For example, the economist Hernando de Soto (2000) has argued that an important impediment to growth in many developing countries is the absence of well-functioning capital markets that would allow entrepreneurs to transform assets, primarily land, into financial capital. The problem is not insufficient resources—de Soto estimates that developing countries have $9.34 trillion in available assets—but rather the lack of a formal, government-backed title system that would allow landowners to use these assets as collateral to "unlock" the embedded capital.[35] Although most countries have informal systems for securing ownership, these systems do not provide the ease of transfer that is necessary for efficient markets and that is essential if banks are to use land as security for loans.

De Soto's evidence is mostly informal, but there is some empirical support for his argument. For example, Alston, Libecap, and Schneider (1996) found a statistically significant effect of formal title on land values and investment in Brazil, and Besley (1995) found a significant, though somewhat weaker, effect of land title in Ghana. Finally, Miceli, Sirmans, and Kieyah (2001) found that in Kenya, where the government has long encouraged title registration, owners of more valuable agricultural land (as measured by rainfall potential) are the most likely to enter their land into the government system.

Why have landowners in developing countries not taken full advantage of the economic benefits of title registration, even when it is made available to them? One explanation is that a formal title system is a public good in that many of its benefits are external to individual landowners: everyone benefits from more efficient markets (Miceli and Kieyah 2003). Thus, in the absence of coercive government action, title registration will likely remain underutilized in developing countries.

4 Limited and Divided Ownership

The discussion of consensual transfers has to this point focused on simple transactions in which an individual owner of property contracts to transfer ownership (title) to another individual owner. In this section, we examine more general settings in which ownership can be divided or limited. We first consider one of the most common forms of divided ownership: the leasing arrangement. A lease involves a voluntary agreement to divide ownership over time, such as when a landlord temporarily transfers possession of his land to a tenant farmer. Such agreements can enhance value (otherwise the parties would not enter into them), but we will see that the law plays a role in achieving this outcome.

Although we have said much in praise of private ownership in this chapter, we conclude by showing that limits on private property can sometimes promote efficiency. For example, we will argue that under certain conditions it is more efficient for property to be held collectively than privately, or for private ownership to be subject to a time limit, after which it becomes public. In the next chapter, we look at other ways that the law limits private property.

4.1 Leasing

The ability of owners to transfer partial interests in their property potentially creates economic gains from specialization. For example, a lease of agricultural land allows the tenant to specialize in farming while the landlord specializes in bearing the risk of land value fluctuations.[36] The division of ownership, however, creates incentives for inefficient behavior by both parties. For example, the tenant will have little incentive to make improvements or repairs that outlast the term of the lease. Similarly, the landlord will have no incentive to invest in maintenance that primarily benefits the tenant. Thus, the law potentially plays an important role in overcoming these incentive problems, thereby promoting an efficient allocation of property rights.

4.1.1 The Lease: A Contract or Conveyance?

The law of leases for land arose in the agricultural economy of the middle ages, during which time leases were governed by the law of property.[37] Specifically, the lease was viewed as a *conveyance* of an interest in the land whereby the tenant acquired the rights of use and exclusion in return for a promise to pay rent. Even if the tenant failed to pay the rent, the landlord could not enter the property or evict the tenant; instead, he could only sue for recovery of the rent. At the same time, the landlord had no duty to maintain the premises. The lease thus provided strong legal protection of the tenant's possessory interest in the land; in effect, the tenant became the temporary owner during the term of the lease.

In contrast, modern real estate leases, which are primarily for housing, are interpreted by most courts as contracts rather than conveyances. This change in the law has had two important effects. First, courts have found an "implied warranty of habitability" in leases, and second, the obligation of tenants to pay rent is dependent on landlords' fulfillment of this warranty obligation.[38] Thus, tenants can withhold rent if a landlord fails to invest in reasonable maintenance of the property, but symmetrically, the landlord can evict a tenant for failure to pay rent. The obligations of the landlord and tenant, like those of contracting parties, are therefore mutual: each is dependent on the other.

From an economic perspective, this evolution in the law makes sense (Miceli, Sirmans, and Turnbull 2001). Historically, land was leased primarily for agriculture use. Thus, tenants supplied the primary inputs for production (besides the land). In this context, security of possession was paramount so that the tenants could be assured of receiving the benefits of their efforts. The law provided this security by effectively giving tenants ownership rights during the term of the lease, even against the landlord. Thus, for example, landlords were not allowed to retake possession after crops were planted but before harvest.

Over time, however, tenants began to lease property primarily for shelter, which required the landlord to provide a continuous flow of maintenance and other housing services. But because landlords had no incentive to provide this effort under the traditional law of leases, tenants needed an enforcement mechanism. The law provided it by transforming the lease into a contract with an implied warranty of habitability on the part of landlords. Tenants could therefore legally withhold rent if the landlord breached his duty to maintain the premises. The mutuality of obligations, however, gave the landlord a symmetric right to evict tenants who failed to pay rent. Thus, tenants gave up some security of tenure in return for the ability to ensure landlord maintenance.

4.1.2   Mitigation in Leases

Another change that accompanied the transformation of leases from conveyances to contracts concerns the duty to mitigate damages. Under property law principles, landlords had no duty to mitigate damages arising from a tenant's breach of the lease. If a tenant failed to take possession or abandoned the leased property, the landlord had no obligation to re-let it; he could simply sit back and sue the tenant for the rent for the entire term (Cribbet 1975, 190). (This was a by-product of the rule barring landlord entry.) Many states, however, have begun to adopt the rule from contract law that requires the victim of breach to take reasonable steps to mitigate the damages.[39] According to this interpretation of leases, a landlord who failed to re-let the premises following tenant breach would only be entitled to the difference between the original rent and the rent that he could have obtained by reasonable efforts.

The economic benefit of mitigation is that it prevents property from being left idle when the original tenant abandons it. There are at least two reasons, however, why the no-mitigate rule may be better for leases. First, the tenant may be in a better position than the landlord to find a replacement tenant. Second, tenant absence is not always a sign that she has truly abandoned the property. In many cases, absentee use is very valuable. For example, a farmer may wish to leave certain fields fallow as part of a practice of crop rotation, or a commercial user may hold land for storage or in reserve for use in certain contingencies. In these instances, the duty to mitigate could result in inefficient re-letting of the property to a lower-valuing user.

Again, the evolution of the law seems to have reflected these offsetting economic factors. The old no-mitigate rule prevailed during the period when land was used primarily for agriculture, and it continues to apply in many states for commercial leases. As noted, these are exactly the contexts in which absentee use is most likely to be valuable. In contrast, the modern rule, which requires mitigation, applies to residential leases in most states. This also makes sense since residential use generally entails continuous occupation of the property and makes absence a good signal of the tenant's intention to abandon. Thus, the risk of incorrectly re-letting the property is low.

4.1.3   The Law of Waste

As noted, an important incentive problem that arises in landlord-tenant relationships is that tenants have inadequate incentives to invest in efficient maintenance of the unit during the term of the lease. This problem, sometimes referred to as the "rental externality," arises because tenants do not internalize the benefits of their efforts beyond their tenancy (Henderson and Ioannides 1983).

To illustrate, consider a lease of fixed duration, where $T(x, y)$ is the value of the property to the tenant during the lease period, and $R(x, y)$ is the present value of the *reversion*, that is, the value of the property after it reverts to the landlord. The variable x represents the cost of maintenance by the landlord, and the variable y represents the cost of maintenance by the tenant. Thus, the overall present value of the property as of the start of the tenancy is given by

$$V = T(x, y) + R(x, y) - x - y. \tag{6.1}$$

The tenant, however, will choose y to maximize her private return, given by

$$T(x, y) - y - r, \tag{6.2}$$

where r is the rent, which is fixed. The tenant therefore invests in too little maintenance because she does not account for the impact of y on the landlord's reversion. Figure 6.5 compares the tenant's choice of maintenance (y_t) to the social optimum (y^*) for a given level of landlord maintenance.

The law addresses this problem with the doctrine of waste.[40] According to this doctrine, a tenant has a duty to invest in reasonable (that is, efficient) maintenance of the property and also to refrain from inflicting damage or otherwise altering the nature of the reversion.[41]

We also noted above that the landlord's choice of maintenance is subject to inefficiency because the landlord does not internalize the benefit of x for the tenant. Specifically, the landlord will choose x to maximize $R(x, y) + r - x$ rather than V. As previously suggested, the law has addressed this problem by imposing an implied warranty of habitability. Thus, the law of waste is to

Figure 6.5

The Rental Externality

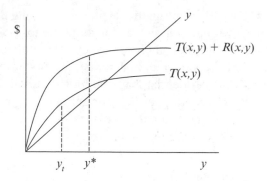

the tenant what the warranty of habitability is to the landlord: "A landlord can expect his tenant to maintain the leased premises and sue in waste if he doesn't; the tenant can expect his landlord to, at least, comply with housing codes and sue for breach of an implied covenant of habitability (or defend a suit for [unpaid] rent) if he doesn't" (Cribbet 1975, 210–11).

In combination, the law of waste and the warranty of habitability therefore work much like negligence with contributory negligence in torts to create efficient bilateral incentives for care by both the landlord and tenant.

4.1.4   Sharecropping

Sharecropping represents a contractual response to the problems associated with divided ownership of farmland (Allen 1998). Under such a contract, the landlord and tenant physically divide the crops rather than dividing the revenue from their sale (which is what happens under an ordinary lease). A typical contract involves an equal sharing of the output (50–50).

Economists have long studied the efficiency properties of cropshare contracts. The most famous analysis was by Cheung (1969), who argued that such contracts were a way to share the risk of uncertain crop yields. To understand this argument, consider two alternatives to cropsharing: a fixed rental contract and a fixed wage contract. Under the fixed rental contract, the tenant pays the landlord a fixed rent and retains the residual revenue from selling the crops. Thus, the *tenant* bears all of the risk from fluctuations in output or prices. Under a fixed wage contract, in contrast, the landlord pays the tenant a fixed wage and retains the residual revenue. Thus, the *landlord* bears all of the risk. In a world where both the landlord and tenant are risk averse, however, there is an economic gain from assigning some of the risk to each party. A cropshare contract accomplishes this by dividing the output between the landlord and tenant.

A pure risk-sharing argument, however, ignores the impact of the contract on incentives for effort. As Stiglitz (1974) showed, a trade-off often emerges between risk sharing and incentives because the party who receives the residual return will have the right incentives to supply effort but will also bear all of the risk. Thus, for example, if the tenant is the primary supplier of effort but the landlord is the better risk-bearer, then the fixed rent contract is best for incentives, but the wage contract is best for risk sharing. In this case, the cropshare contract may be a good way to balance these offsetting factors.

The problem with the preceding arguments, however, is that recent empirical work has provided no evidence that risk sharing considerations are an important factor in contract choice, or that landlords are better risk-bearers than tenants (Allen and Lueck 1995). Even if risk sharing is not an important consideration, however, cropsharing may nevertheless be an efficient contract if both landlords and tenants supply inputs into agricultural production (as in bilateral care models) (Eswaran and Kotwol 1985). In that case, fixed rent contracts will provide no incentive for landlord effort and fixed wage contracts no incentive for tenant effort, but cropshare contracts will elicit some effort (though less than the efficient level) from both.[42] In a world where contracting is costly, this may be the best possible solution.

4.2   Private Versus Group Ownership

In landlord-tenant relationships, ownership is divided over time, but at any point in time, a single individual controls the property. In situations of common, or group, ownership several individuals simultaneously hold ownership rights. The extreme case is an open-access resource where no one is excluded. In other cases, a particular group of individuals has access to the property, while nonmembers of the group are excluded.

The problem with group ownership, as we have noted earlier, is that individual owners have an incentive to overuse the property because they do not internalize the cost that their use imposes on other owners. Despite the potential inefficiencies, however, group ownership can offer advantages over individual (private) ownership. The next section examines how these advantages, when balanced against the costs, determine the optimal scale of ownership.

4.2.1   The Optimal Scale of Ownership

From an economic perspective, the social objective of an ownership regime for property is to minimize the costs of "inducing people to 'do the right thing' with the earth's surface."[43] The benefits of private ownership of land in achieving this goal have been emphasized throughout this chapter. The primary benefit of private ownership is that it equates the private and social returns to actions taken within the boundaries of the owned property. The Coase Theorem implies that this same outcome can be achieved with multiple owners, but this solution will ordinarily involve the cost of negotiating and enforcing agreements among owners to prevent inefficiencies. Generally, this will make group ownership less efficient than individual ownership.

Individual ownership is not without costs of its own, however. One is the cost of erecting and policing boundaries between neighboring parcels, which is the counterpart to internal bargaining under group ownership.[44] Another is the possibility that actions by owners on their own property may impose spillover effects (externalities) on their neighbors. This will happen when the *scale* of the activity is too large compared to the size of the parcel.

In the farmer-rancher case, for example, the problem of straying cattle suggested that the rancher's parcel size may have been too small. One solution is for the rancher and farmer to bargain; another is simply for the rancher to consolidate his land with the farmer's, thereby internalizing the damage caused by the cattle. The optimal solution depends on the cost of Coasian bargaining between the rancher and farmer (or possibly multiple farmers) compared to the cost to a single individual of managing a larger holding of land.

Another benefit to group ownership, besides exploiting scale economies in parcel size, is risk sharing. A sole owner bears all of the risk associated with land ownership, such as uncertain crop yields, accidents, or fluctuations in prices. Group ownership spreads this risk across all owners. It therefore provides a form of insurance when market or other insurance mechanisms (such as government welfare) are unavailable. The Pilgrim colony at Plymouth, Massachusetts, offers an example of the insurance function of group ownership. At the start of the colony, both livestock and agricultural land were primarily held on a communal basis. Although this curtailed output due to shirking, it protected less able members of the community from the severe risks associated with settlement in a remote and potentially hostile location. Later on, as the community became more established, it transitioned to a private property regime, and output greatly increased.

Private property increases aggregate output by improving incentives, but it reduces equality if individual members of a community vary in ability or cost of effort. Thus, a final reason for group ownership is to satisfy a group's preference for egalitarianism, or equal sharing of output. As Ellickson (1993, 1351) notes, however, "The absence of material incentives increases the need for pervasive controls against shirking, and may prompt the most skillful workers to consider pursuing greater rewards outside the commune." Successful communes are therefore rare and usually rely on a strong ideological or religious commitment to help maintain incentives (Cosgel, Miceli, and Murray 1997).

An alternative way to achieve greater distributional equality is to combine private property with a public welfare system that redistributes wealth. Such a "mixed" system is subject to the distortionary effects of taxation (that is, there remains a trade-off between equity and efficiency), but for large groups it is almost certainly more efficient than a strictly communal system.

4.2.2   Public Goods

We noted above that the internalization of cost spillovers may be a reason to increase the scale of ownership. The same may be true of benefit spillovers. Suppose that a good, once provided, can be consumed by everyone, even those who have not contributed to its production. An example is defense—once the palisade was built around the Plymouth colony, all inside were protected.

Economists refer to these types of goods as *public goods*. An important characteristic of public goods is that private ownership will result in under-production because the producer will not be able to capture the full con-sumption benefits. For this reason, the government usually takes on the task of providing public goods in order to fully exploit the scale economies in production.[45] At the same time, the government acts to prevent free riding by coercing all members of the community to contribute to the provision of public goods by means of taxation.

4.2.3   The Anticommons Problem and the Right to Partition*

As noted, the problem with an open-access resource where no one can be excluded is that it may be overused. We referred to this above as the *tragedy of the commons*. At the other extreme, consider a piece of property with multiple owners, each of whom can exclude all of the others from use. In this case, the failure of the owners to agree on a course of action can result in underuse of the property, a problem referred to as the *tragedy of the anticom-mons* (Heller 1998). The existence of this problem suggests that the scale of ownership may have become too large, but the same transaction costs that prevent coordinated action among the co-owners will likely preclude disag-gregation of the property into smaller parcels.

Fortunately, the law provides a solution in the form of the right to partition. According to the common-law version of this right, each co-owner can unilat-erally request a physical partition of the land (partition in kind) into separate, individually owned parcels. While this solution overcomes the transaction costs among the co-owners, it could result in excessive fragmentation if there are scale economies associated with the best use of the land that individual owners would not internalize. State partition statutes have addressed this problem by giving courts the discretion to choose between physical partition and sale of the undivided parcel (thus preserving its scale) with division of the proceeds among the owners.

The problem with a forced sale is that it pays nonconsenting owners the market value of their shares, thus depriving them of any subjective value that they may attach to the land. In effect, it substitutes liability rule protection of owners' shares for property-rule protection. From an efficiency perspective, the court therefore faces a trade-off between preserving the optimal scale of the property and protecting the subjective value of owners.

How should it resolve this trade-off? Subjective value is not observable, but empirical study of land markets reveals that scale economies tend to exist for small parcels while diseconomies exist for large parcels (Colwell and Munneke 1999). This suggests that partition in kind should be used for large parcels and that forced sale should be used for small parcels. The actual case law seems to accord well with this prescription (Miceli and Sirmans 2000).

5 Intellectual Property

Intellectual property (ideas, inventions, musical compositions, artwork, and so on) has the characteristics of a public good. That is, once created, it can be reused without diminishing its quantity. Our analysis above therefore implies that to achieve the maximum benefit, ideas should be freely available to the public (publicly owned). But this presumes the existence of the idea. In fact, ideas and other creative works are costly to produce, and common ownership will prevent the originator from capturing the returns. (This is sometimes referred to as the appropriability problem.) Consequently, there is a trade-off between the benefits of public ownership of ideas, on the one hand, and the need for incentives to invest in producing them, on the other. In this section, we examine various ways in which the law of intellectual property has resolved this trade-off, including patents, trade secrets, copyright, and trademarks.[46]

5.1 Patents

Ideas and inventions are different from private goods like apples. A farmer can capture the returns on his investment in apple trees by charging a price for his apples and denying consumption to nonpayers. In contrast, it is often very difficult for inventors to prevent nonpayers from using their ideas. Thus, they will have little incentive to produce the ideas in the first place. The patent system solves this problem by awarding exclusive property rights in ideas to inventors (Kitch 1977). But while this solves one problem, it creates another: monopoly. As the sole producer of the patented invention, the inventor will have an incentive to restrict output, thereby depriving society of the full benefits from the use of the idea.

Figure 6.6

The Impact of a Patent

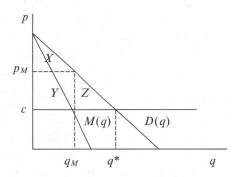

The impact of the patent is illustrated in Figure 6.6. The inverse demand curve for the patented invention is shown by the downward-sloping line labeled $D(q)$, where q is the output. This reflects the social value of the invention.

Suppose that the marginal (= average) cost of producing the additional units of the invention (as distinct from the cost of creating the original idea) is a constant c. Thus, the efficient level of output, that which would be achieved by a competitive industry, occurs at the intersection of the demand curve and the marginal cost curve. The resulting output is denoted q^*, and price equals marginal cost. The measure of welfare under the competitive outcome is the consumer surplus, given by the triangle $X + Y + Z$ (producer surplus is zero given constant marginal costs).

In contrast, a monopolist would produce at the point where the marginal revenue curve, labeled $M(q)$, intersects marginal costs. The resulting output and price are denoted q_M and p_M. The monopolist therefore restricts output and raises price relative to the competitive outcome. As a result, the monopolist earns a profit shown by the rectangle labeled Y, consumer surplus shrinks to the triangle X, and there is a deadweight loss from underproduction given by triangle Z.

Despite the welfare loss from the patent, it is still better than the competitive outcome, which would result in no invention at all (hence, zero consumer surplus). The reason is that the competitive price would cover the marginal production costs of the invention, but not the initial cost (now sunk) of creating the idea.[47] This is shown by means of an example.

EXAMPLE

Suppose the inverse demand curve is given by $D(q) = \$150 - q$, marginal revenue is $M(q) = \$150 - 2q$, and $c = \$50$.[48] We can then calculate: $q^* = 100$, $q_M = 50$, $p_M = \$100$, $Y = \$2,500$, and $X = Z = \$1,250$.

Now suppose that the fixed cost of the invention is $K = \$2,000$. If the firm expects to receive a patent, it will make the investment because its profit will be $Y - K =$ \$500. Social welfare in this case is given by the sum of the consumer surplus (area X) and the firm's profit, or \$1,250 + \$500 = \$1,750.

It is possible, however, to improve on the monopoly outcome by imposing a time limit on the patent.[49] In fact, the law limits most patents to twenty years. The trade-off is as follows. As the patent life is extended, the inventor's return (area Y in Figure 6.6) increases (because he has monopoly power for a longer period of time), thus increasing his incentives to invest in ideas. The offsetting effect is that the welfare loss from monopoly (area Z in the graph), which is due to the restricted use of the ideas, endures for a longer period of time. The optimal patent life just balances these two effects. Ideally, the length of a patent should be different for every invention—for example, those requiring larger initial investments or offering substantial social benefits should have longer lengths. The law does not attempt to tailor patent length in this way, however, given the high information costs of doing so.

Patent Races.   To this point, we have assumed that there is a single potential originator of an idea. In fact, individuals or firms may simultaneously be seeking the same idea, and the patent is awarded to the first one who demonstrates its usefulness. Because the patent is valuable (owing to the monopoly returns), this may generate a *patent race* that actually results in overinvestment in research and development.[50] Note that this is an illustration of the inefficiency, noted above, associated with the assignment of property rights by a rule of first possession. The possibility of a patent race provides a further reason (along with the loss from monopoly) to shorten the life of a patent. An offsetting factor, however, is that patent races may hasten the development of new technologies and lead to the unintended discovery of others (an external benefit). Thus, the overall effect of a patent race on efficiency is ambiguous (Blair and Cotter 2005, 18).

Rewards Versus Patents.   An alternative to patents for stimulating inventive activity is a government system of rewards paid to innovators (Shavell and Ypersele 2001; Wright 1983). The prospect of the reward provides the incentive for innovation, but unlike a patent, the invention would immediately become public property. Thus, rewards have the advantage over patents of eliminating the deadweight loss from monopoly. The disadvantage is that the government may lack the information necessary to set the appropriate reward, thereby possibly leading to inefficient investment incentives. In particular, innovators will have better information about their costs and probably better information about the social value of an invention.[51] A reward system therefore does not appear to offer a clear advantage over a patent system.

The Scope of Patents. The strength of patent protection depends not only on *duration* but also on *scope*, that is, the extent to which "imitation" products represent infringements of the original patent. The basic trade-off in determining the optimal scope, or breadth, of a patent is the same as that determining its optimal length: a broad patent offers greater protection to inventors, thereby spurring investment, but it also limits the ability of rivals to develop new and useful products. From a legal perspective, patent scope is not as clearly defined as patent length in the sense that there is no set rule for determining when an infringement has occurred. Thus, courts can tailor decisions on patent scope to the characteristics of individual inventions or fields. Blair and Cotter (2005, 22) note, for example, that U.S. courts confer broader protection on so-called pioneering inventions.

An interesting theoretical question concerns the optimal trade-off between the duration and scope of patents. Some scholars advocate long and narrow patents (Klemperer 1990), while others argue that patents should be short and broad (Gallini 1992). Unfortunately, there does not exist any empirical evidence to resolve this debate.

5.2   Trade Secrets

An alternative way for a firm to protect an invention is by means of a trade secret. The main advantages of a trade secret over a patent are, first, that the inventor does not need to reveal the nature of the invention, as he must when seeking a patent application, and second, the secret is (theoretically) of unlimited duration. The chief disadvantage is that trade-secret law offers less protection than a patent. Although disclosures by "improper means" (such as by employees or by espionage) are forbidden and punishable, competitors can legally appropriate the idea by means of independent discovery or reverse engineering. In this way, the duration of the secret is effectively limited. These characteristics of trade secrets suggests that they will be most useful to inventors whose ideas will take longer than the legal length of a patent to discover (and which will not be revealed by use of the invention), or for inventions that are not worth the cost of patenting. Trade-secret law therefore supplements patent law by offering a lesser degree of protection, and at a lower cost, for less valuable information (Blair and Cotter 2005, 26; Shavell 2004, 160–61).

5.3   Copyrights

Copyright law provides legal protection to writing, music, artistic works, and other creations (Landes and Posner 1989). Like patent protection, copyright protection is of a limited duration, specifically, the life of the creator plus seventy years. This time limit reflects the same basic trade-off described above: it encourages production of creative materials without overly limiting their use.

Copyright law differs from patent law, however, in several respects. First, unlike patents, copyrights do not preclude independent discovery, only copies. (In this sense, copyrights are more like trade secrets.) The likely reason is that the probability of unintentional duplication is remote. (What is the likelihood of two authors writing the same novel?) A second difference is that copyright protects the *expression* of an idea, rather than the idea itself. For example, I can get a copyright for this particular law and economics book but not for the idea of writing a law and economics book in general. This limited protection makes sense since protection of the idea would greatly impede the production of creative works by requiring each prospective producer to obtain the holder's consent. (Good ideas are scarce but they can often be usefully expressed in various ways—how many versions of the Romeo and Juliet theme are there?) Finally, although patents protect ideas, the length of protection is much shorter than is provided by a copyright.

Fair Use. Another limit on copyright protection is the "fair use" doctrine, which allows limited copying for certain purposes, for example, for educational use or in a review. (In this sense, fair use is similar in scope to patent protection.) The proper economic standard for allowing fair use, according to Gordon (1982), involves asking whether, in a world of zero transaction costs, the copyright holder would have consented to the use in question. In this way, fair use imposes a market test on the transfer of copyrighted ideas. Examples of fair use include limited photocopying of copyrighted material for educational use and recording of television programs for later viewing.

A more difficult case concerns the recent development of computer technology that allows consumers to freely download copyrighted music—is this "fair use" or an infringement of the copyright? The creator of the technology may claim that it is fair use because it allows consumers to sample individual songs, thereby increasing demand for the full album (the market test). But if companies viewed this as a valuable form of promotion, they could have released the songs themselves for free distribution, in the same way that they promote radio play of songs. The fact that they didn't is evidence that they view the practice as detrimental to the value of the copyright. Apparently, the court agreed (Klein, Lerner, and Murphy 2002).[52] This type of case points out the need for courts to continually adjust the scope of fair use in the face of technological change so as to maintain the proper balance between incentives to produce new ideas and the benefits of making them widely available (Adelstein and Peretz 1985; Miceli and Adelstein 2006).

5.4 Trademarks

Trademark law protects symbols, phrases, or any other distinctive signs that uniquely identify a product or service. Legal protection of a trademark only requires that the owner be the first to use it commercially, though protection may be limited to the geographic region in which the product or service is advertised. Wider protection requires the owner to register the trademark with the federal government. Unlike patents and copyrights, legal protection of a trademark endures for as long as the owner uses it, though in the case of a registered trademark, the owner must periodically renew the registration.

The economic function of trademark protection differs from that of patents, trade secrets, and copyrights. Principally, trademarks help to lower consumer search costs by making it easier for buyers to distinguish high-quality products from inferior competitors. To serve this function, however, trademarks must be a credible signal of product quality. Thus, owners of trademarks must have an incentive to invest in product quality as a way of maintaining the commercial value of the trademark. Trademark law provides this incentive by awarding owners exclusive rights in use of the trademark.

5.5 Remedies

The primary legal remedy available to owners of intellectual property, whether it be a patent, trade secret, copyright, or trademark, is injunctive relief against infringers. Thus, intellectual property rights are protected by property rules rather than liability rules (though owners may sometimes also be able to seek damages for lost profits due to the infringement). This makes sense according to our earlier discussion of the choice between property and liability rules, first, because transaction costs tend to be low in disputes involving intellectual property given the small number of parties involved (typically, only the would-be infringer and the rightholder); and second, because courts would have a hard time setting the correct terms of exchange given the specialized nature of the property in question (Blair and Cotter 2005, 40).

One situation where property-rule protection might prove problematic, however, is when a prospective user of intellectual property would need to bargain with several rightholders, as in the case where multiple patents for genetic information are needed to produce a particular drug. Here, property rules can impede transactions by promoting strategic behavior of the sort identified in our discussion of the *Boomer* case. In settings like this, compulsory licensing (a liability rule) might be preferred (Blair and Cotter 2005, 40).

6 Conclusion

Property law is the most fundamental area of common law from an economic perspective because well-defined property rights are essential for market exchange and investment. The role of property law in this context is to assign and protect property rights as a background for economic activity. In addition, when markets fail, property law needs to internalize externalities, either by establishing property rules as a point of departure for Coasian bargaining (if transaction costs are low), or by imposing an assignment of rights and protecting it with a liability rule (if transaction costs are high).

With this basic transaction structure as backdrop, we focused in this chapter on consensual exchange. In that context, we examined legal rules aimed at defining ownership and facilitating the voluntary transfer or division of property. We also examined factors affecting the optimal scale of ownership, as well as reasons why we might want to limit ownership of certain goods. In the latter context, we examined patents and copyrights as examples of time-limited property rights for intellectual property.

In the next chapter we shift emphasis to nonconsensual transfers in the presence of high transaction costs. In that connection, we will examine various ways in which the government regulates or coercively acquires property, and conclude by comparing public (regulatory) versus private (common law) responses to externalities.

DISCUSSION QUESTIONS

1. Contingent fees in effect give lawyers partial property rights (typically a one-third share) in plaintiffs' legal claims. What economic function might such contracts serve?

2. The law, however, forbids plaintiffs from selling complete property rights in their legal claims. Explain this restriction as a means of preventing excessive competition among lawyers.

3. What is the economic rationale for limiting the length of the fishing season, and limiting the daily catch of fishermen?

4. Discuss the following statement: The Coase Theorem defines the boundary between markets (voluntary exchange) and law (involuntary exchange).

5. Explain why the rental externality tends to make renting an asset more expensive than buying it (all else equal).

6. Residential developers often include restrictive covenants in deeds of sale that limit the actions of present and subsequent owners. Why would buyers willingly accept such covenants and possibly pay a premium for them?

7. Researchers studying human DNA have succeeded in obtaining patents for mapping individual sequences. Discuss the costs and benefits of allowing such patents. Is there a relevant distinction between scientific "discoveries" and "inventions"?

8. According to the economic theory of fair use, book reviewers are allowed to quote brief passages from the book being reviewed because the author and publisher, if asked, would consent to such a use. But on this theory, quotations in *unfavorable* reviews would not qualify as fair use. Why would such a distinction probably not be efficient?

PROBLEMS

1. Classify each of the following as a form of *property rule* or *liability rule*:

   (a) negligence

   (b) expectation damages

   (c) specific performance

   (d) an injunction

   (e) \   eminent domain (see Chapter 7 for a definition).

2. A railroad can operate zero, one, or two trains a day along a certain stretch of track that borders a farmer's field, but the trains occasionally emit sparks that set fire to the crops. The following table shows the railroad's total profit and the farmer's total fire damage (in dollars) as functions of the number of trains:

No. of trains	RR's profit	Farmer's fire damage
0	0	0
1	150	100
2	200	125

   (a) What is the socially optimal number of trains?

   (b) Assume bargaining costs between the railroad and farmer are zero. Describe the outcome under the following two situations:

      (i) The railroad has the right to operate any number of trains, protected by a property rule;

      (ii) The farmer has the right to be free from crop damage, protected by a property rule.

   (c) Assume bargaining costs between the railroad and farmer are high. Describe the outcome under the following situations:

      (i) The railroad has the right to operate any number of trains, protected by a liability rule;

      (ii) The farmer has the right to be free from crop damage, protected by a liability rule.

3. In the case of *Pendoley v. Ferreira* (345 Mass. 309, 187 N.E.2d 142, 1963), a residential development encroached on an established pig farm, causing

residents to complain about the offensive smell. The residents sought an injunction to have the farm shut down.

(a) Suppose transaction costs between the residents and the farmer are low. Does it matter for efficiency whether the court grants or denies the injunction? Explain.

(b) Now suppose transaction costs are high. What information does the court need to know to decide whether granting the injunction will lead to an efficient outcome?

(c) Propose a remedy based on a liability rule. What information does the court need to know for your proposed remedy to achieve the efficient outcome?

4. Consider a piece of property that is jointly owned by two individuals, each with one-half share. Suppose that, in order to sell, owner 1 requires $3,000 for his half share, but owner 2 requires $6,000 for her half share. A buyer arrives and offers $10,000 for the entire property.

(a) If the two owners can bargain with each other costlessly, do you expect a sale to occur (assuming both owners have to give their consent)?

(b) Suppose instead that the two owners cannot bargain with each other (for example, they are a divorcing couple). If each is entitled to one half of the proceeds, do you expect a sale to occur in this case?

(c) Describe the trade-off involved in a rule that allows either one of the parties to "force" a sale of jointly owned property when they cannot come to an agreement.

5. Under the ancient law of admiralty, the finder of an abandoned shipwreck becomes the owner according to the "law of finds."

(a) Discuss the incentives (both good and bad) that this rule creates for would-be treasure hunters. (Hint: Relate lost shipwrecks to patentable inventions.)

(b) The Abandoned Shipwreck Act of 1987 (43 U.S.C. 2101–2106) abrogated admiralty law for wrecks found in U.S. waters, awarding ownership instead to the state in whose waters a wreck is found. The state can then design its own reward scheme. Suggest what an optimal reward scheme might look like.

CHAPTER 7

INVOLUNTARY TRANSFERS AND REGULATION OF PROPERTY

We argued in the previous chapter that efficient exchange of property is most often achieved by first defining and protecting property rights, and then facilitating voluntary (market) transfers based on property rules. When markets fail to operate smoothly because of transaction costs or externalities, however, some form of coercive action may be required to promote efficiency. In this chapter, we examine both involuntary (forced) exchange by means of liability rules and restrictions on exchange.

The first section considers transactions between private parties. Here we discuss problems associated with uncertain boundaries between properties and intergenerational transfers of property (inheritance rules). Subsequent sections turn to transactions between the government and private property owners.

The Constitution gives the government the power to take private property for public use without the owner's consent provided that it pays just compensation (the *eminent domain clause*). This power raises several questions: Why should the government have a power that is generally denied to private buyers? What is the proper measure of just compensation? Does the compensation requirement extend to government regulations like zoning, where the government restricts property use but does not acquire title? We examine these and other questions associated with government acquisition or regulation of property.

Government regulation is a public response to an externality. In earlier chapters we examined private responses based on the common law of torts or nuisance. We conclude our discussion of property by examining the appropriate economic scope for these two approaches to the control of externalities. This discussion serves as a good summary of the economic approach to property law as discussed in this and the previous chapter.

1   Involuntary Transfers and Restrictions on Transfers Between Private Parties

This section examines coercive transfers, or restrictions on transfers, between private parties. The first two topics—adverse possession and mistaken improvement—concern the occupation or development of someone else's property without their permission. The questions we address in these cases are: What is the appropriate legal remedy? and, Does it matter whether the encroacher acted intentionally or innocently?

We then turn to inheritance rules. Generally, property owners are free to bequeath their property as they see fit, a freedom consistent with the efficiency of voluntary exchange. There are, however, some restrictions on that freedom. We examine two: one that was historically important (primogeniture), and one that continues to be valid (the rule against perpetuities).

1.1   Adverse Possession

Adverse possession is a curious doctrine that on its face seems to legitimize the theft of land. Under the doctrine, the occupier of a piece of land who is not the true owner acquires title after a statutorily defined number of years if the occupation is hostile to the owner's interests, open, and continuous. Further, the displaced owner cannot seek to recover the land, or even compensation, if he has failed to act within the statutory period. Thus, although adverse possession is an involuntary transfer of land, it is not a liability rule because of the absence of a right to compensation. Rather, it is a statute of limitation on the owner's right to enforce a property rule.

Adverse possession represents a particularly severe challenge to the economic theory of law since it seems to undermine the very basis of market exchange—namely, secure property rights. Nevertheless, economists have formulated theories to explain the doctrine as a response to various forms of market failure.[1]

One common theory is that it deters owners from leaving their land idle. Economically speaking, this is not a good reason because irreversibilities in land development often make it optimal to wait until a future date to develop. Another reason is the standard argument for statutes of limitations: as time passes, memories fade and evidence becomes stale, making litigation over disputed title costlier.[2] This argument is more plausible, but still it seems

Figure 7.1

The Optimal Statute
of Limitations for Land
Claims Under Adverse
Possession

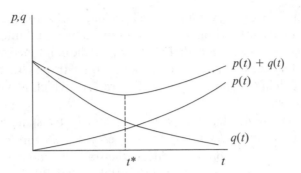

a frail reason for weakening a landowner's rights, especially given modern methods of record keeping.

A better theory for adverse possession concerns the uncertainties of ownership discussed in the previous chapter in connection with land title systems. Recall from that discussion that even an efficient title system cannot entirely eliminate the risk that landowners face from past claims. One way to limit an owner's risk, and hence to strengthen his property rights, is to put a limit on the time period during which a claim can be asserted. Adverse possession accomplishes this by extinguishing any claims filed after the statutory period has elapsed. In the extreme, a statutory period of length zero would eliminate virtually all claims. (Note that this is in effect what the Torrens registration system does—see Section 3.2.1 in the Chapter 6.)

Figure 7.1 illustrates this argument by graphing the risk of a past claim, $p(t)$, as a function of the statute length, t. When $t = 0$, this risk is (essentially) zero (some exceptions usually exist), but it is increasing in t. (That is, as the statute length becomes longer, the risk of a claim rises.) If the goal is to maximize the security of title (that is, minimize the risk of a claim), and hence to promote the marketability of land, why is zero not the optimal statute length?

The answer is that we have only considered one source of ownership risk, based on a backward-looking view. When we take a forward-looking view, we see that the current owner may himself be subject to the risk of dispossession by boundary encroachment, squatting, or other expropriations in the future, especially if he is an absentee owner (which, we have argued, is often efficient). Note that the risk of this sort of loss is reduced by a longer statutory period because the owner has a longer period of time during which he can eject squatters and thereby reestablish his legitimate title. This is also shown in Figure 7.1, where $q(t)$, the risk of dispossession, is shown as a decreasing function of t.

We have therefore seen that there are competing risks to ownership that have offsetting effects on the desired statute length. On the one hand, the risk of past claims, $p(t)$, is minimized by a length of zero, but on the other, the risk of future dispossession, $q(t)$, is minimized by an infinite length. The optimal statute length—the length that minimizes the combined ownership risk, $p(t) + q(t)$—balances these effects at the margin. In general, this will result in a finite length (as shown by t^* in Figure 7.1), which is what we observe in all fifty states.

Actual statute lengths vary considerably by state, ranging from one to thirty years with a mean length of 13.63 years.[3] Empirical studies have shown that this variation broadly reflects the trade-off implied by the above model (Netter, Hersch, and Manson 1986; Baker et al. 2001).

1.2   The Mistaken Improver Problem*

An issue related to adverse possession is the mistaken improver problem, which arises when an individual improves a piece of land owned (wholly or partially) by someone else. Typically, the problem arises in one of three situations: (1) the improver believed that he owned the land in question but later found that his title was defective; (2) the improver was mistaken about the location of a boundary; or (3) the improver intentionally improved another's land. We discuss the first two cases, which involve true errors, reserving until later discussion of the case of intentional "errors."

In the previous chapter we saw that in a world of costly information, buyers and sellers of land will not find it optimal to verify ownership with certainty before transacting. The same is true for potential improvers. Thus, some mistakes will occur, just as some accidents occur under efficient tort rules. The economic problem is to design the law of mistaken improvement so that landowners have an incentive to invest efficiently in determining ownership prior to making irreversible investments.

The law pertaining to mistaken improvement is old, dating back at least to Roman times (Casad 1968; Dickinson 1985). According to the Roman law of accession, for example, materials affixed to land became the property of the landowner; mistaken improvers could at most seek compensation for the increased value of the owner's land (a form of liability rule). The common law of England and America incorporated the doctrine of accession, but greatly curtailed improvers' right to recover damages. Most states, however, have enacted so-called betterment acts that provide more generous remedies. Although the remedies vary by state, the most common gives the owner an option: he can either retain the land and pay for the improvements (as under the Roman rule), or require the improver to buy the land at its unimproved value. This turns out to be an ingenious remedy that gives improvers exactly the right incentives to avoid mistakes.

To prove this claim, consider the following model (Miceli and Sirmans

1999). An individual (the "improver") wishes to improve a piece of property (erect a building, cut down some trees) but is unsure if he owns the land in question. For example, suppose a "neighbor" may hold title. The uncertainty matters because if the land turns out to belong to the neighbor, the cost of undoing the improvement would be very high. Let p be the probability that the improver owns the land. Also, let s be the cost of a survey that, if conducted, would reveal the true ownership with certainty.

The social benefit of establishing ownership can be described as follows. Suppose the value of the improvement is V, while the value of the unimproved land to the neighbor is R. If $V > R$, the improvement is efficient regardless of ownership, but if $V < R$, the land is best left unimproved. In a world of certainty and low transaction costs, the efficient outcome will always arise, regardless of ownership, according to the Coase Theorem. But recall that one requirement for the Coase Theorem is that property rights be well defined. Uncertainties about ownership violate this requirement and may lead to inefficient land use.

To illustrate, suppose that R varies across landowners. Specifically, suppose a fraction q place a high value on undeveloped land, R_H, while the remaining fraction, $1 - q$, place a low value, R_L, where $R_H > V > R_L$. Thus, it is only efficient for the improver to develop if the neighbor has a low value. We assume that this outcome will be achieved if the improver surveys prior to developing; that is, the parties will engage in Coasian bargaining following determination of ownership. (In other words, the higher valuer will acquire the land and put it to its highest use.) As a result, the expected social value of a survey is $EV_S = qR_H + (1 - q)V - s$. If instead the improver proceeds without a survey, the value of the land is fixed at V, regardless of who turns out to be the owner. Thus, a survey is socially valuable if $EV_S > V$, or if

$$q(R_H - V) > s. \tag{7.1}$$

The left-hand side of this condition is the expected benefit from preventing development when the land is more valuable to the neighbor in its unimproved state. (Note that condition (7.1) is independent of the improver's assessment of his probability of ownership, p. This reflects the fact that, from a social perspective, the efficient land use is independent of ownership.)

In general, however, the improver will not have the correct private incentives to survey any more than an injurer will take efficient precaution against accidents, absent the threat of a legal sanction. We thus examine the improver's incentives under the "owner's option" remedy described above. Consider first the case where the improver proceeds without a survey. If the land belongs to him, no further action occurs and his return is V. However, if the land belongs to the neighbor, the neighbor has two legal options. She can retain the land and pay for the value of the improvement (that is, pay $V - R$), or force a sale for the unimproved value of the land, R. If she has a high value of the unimproved land, she will clearly prefer to sell for R_H rather than keep the land, given $R_H > V$. In this case, the improver realizes a return of $V - R_H$. In contrast, if the neighbor has a low value, she will be indifferent between the two options since selling the land yields R_L while retaining it and paying $V - R_L$ yields $V - (V - R_L) = R_L$. Either way, the improver receives a return of $V - R_L$ in this case (either from the land itself or as compensation).

The resulting expected return for the improver if he proceeds without a survey is given by

$$EV_{NS}^I = pV + (1 - p)[q(V - R_H) + (1 - q)(V - R_L)]. \tag{7.2}$$

Note that, regardless of ownership, the land use is fixed given the irreversibility of the improvement.

Now consider the outcome if the improver surveys. If he turns out to be the owner, two cases are possible. If the neighbor has a low value, the improver will go ahead with the development for a return of $V - s$, but if the neighbor has a high value, she will buy the land to block development. This yields the improver a return of $R_H - s$.[4] As we assumed above, when ownership is known with certainty prior to investment, Coasian bargaining will ensure the efficient land use.

The same conclusion arises if the survey reveals that the neighbor owns the land. In this case, a low-valuing neighbor will sell to the improver, while a high valuer will not sell. The improver's return is $V - R_L - s$ in the first case, and $-s$ in the second. Combining all of these cases and weighting them by the appropriate probabilities yields the improver's expected return from conducting a survey:

$$EV_s^I = p[qR_H + (1 - q)V] + (1 - p)(1 - q)(V - R_L) - s. \tag{7.3}$$

The improver will conduct the survey if $EV_s^I > EV_{NS}^I$. Some tedious algebra reveals that this condition reduces to (7.1). Thus, the improver faces exactly the right incentives to conduct a survey under the "owner's option" remedy. This is true because this remedy forces the improver to internalize the expected cost of his actions in the face of ownership uncertainty.

It may not be enough, however, for the law to give improvers the right incentives to survey. Consider finally an improver who *knows* he is not the owner of the targeted land but proceeds with development anyway in an effort to avoid bargaining with the owner. That is, the improver seeks to "bypass the market"—in effect, to substitute a coercive transfer for a voluntary one.[5] The unobservability of the improver's intent prevents the court from treating such cases differently from those involving genuine errors. Thus, the question is how profitable this strategy is.

To answer this question, note that the improver's return in the event that his mistake is discovered is given by the term in square brackets in expression (7.2) (since the probability that he is the true owner is zero), and that this value may be positive or negative given $R_H > V > R_L$. Suppose instead that the improver chooses to bargain. If the neighbor (the true owner) turns out to value the undeveloped land at R_L, the improver will buy it, yielding a return of $V - R_L$. However, if the neighbor values the land at R_H, no deal will occur. Thus, the improver's expected return prior to bargaining is $(1 - q)(V - R_L)$, which is strictly positive and greater than the return from the mistaken improvement. The bargaining strategy is therefore better because it allows the improver to avoid forced sales that turn out to be unprofitable.

This optimistic conclusion, however, assumes the mistaken improvement is discovered in a timely manner. One factor that works against discovery is the statute of limitations under adverse possession. If the statutory period runs out before discovery, the owner may be barred from seeking a remedy. A study of adverse possession cases by Helmholz (1983), however, suggests that when there is evidence of intentional encroachment, courts are reluctant to award title, even after the statutory period has run.[6] This policy suggests that courts do in fact recognize the importance of deterring efforts to bypass the market in cases where transaction costs are probably low.

1.3 Inheritance Rules

Inheritance rules govern the intergenerational transfer of wealth. The objective of these rules is to balance the goal of honoring the wishes of decedents regarding how to dispose of their wealth, against the need to impose some limits on the extent to which the "dead hand" can control the use of property. Although Anglo-American law gives testators significant freedom, it has imposed some limitations. Our discussion in this section will focus on two: primogeniture and the Rule Against Perpetuities.[7]

1.3.1 Primogeniture

In English common law as well as other cultures, the predominant rule of inheritance has historically been primogeniture, which says that all land in a decedent's estate passes to the eldest son. The most common explanation economists have offered for this rule is that it prevents land from being fragmented into inefficiently small parcels (Posner 1998a, 554). This is especially important in an agricultural economy where land is the primary source of wealth. Thus, in the United States, primogeniture survived until revolutionary times in the southern colonies, which relied on large estates, but was largely rejected in the New England colonies (L. Friedman 1985, 66).

There are two objections to the scale economies rationale for primogeniture. The first is that the land market should enable entrepreneurs to reassemble inefficiently small parcels if there are gains from doing so. However, this presumes well-functioning land and credit markets, which are relatively modern institutions that may have been absent when primogeniture was first adopted (Baker and Miceli 2005).

Second, even if scale economies in land use are important, why not let the testator bequeath the undivided estate to the best-qualified heir rather than to the eldest son? Such a rule preserves the scale economies while expanding the discretion of the testator. There is an offsetting benefit, however, from restricting the discretion of testators. If potential heirs know that the estate will be given in its entirety to the "best qualified," they may engage in costly competition, or rent-seeking, for the prize (Buchanan 1983; Baker and Miceli 2005). Primogeniture, or any other fixed rule, prevents this sort of competition by removing the testator's discretion. The general decline in primogeniture probably reflects several factors, including the diminishing importance of land as a source of wealth and the development of land markets, which, as noted, permit the reassembly of land (though some impediments to assembly remain, as discussed in Section 2 below).

1.3.2 The Rule Against Perpetuities

Another issue regarding the discretion of testators is how far into the future they can control the use of land. The Rule Against Perpetuities limits this control to the lifetime of anyone alive at the time of the bequest plus twenty-one years. In seeking an economic justification for this limitation, Stake (1998, 319) notes, "The purpose of the rule . . . is to prevent people from even attempting to control ownership beyond the generation they know well, their children." Thus, testators can restrict the actions of heirs known to be spendthrifts, but they cannot extend their control into the uncertain future. This makes sense, in terms of both allowing future generations to respond to contingencies that are unforeseeable to their forebears and not limiting the marketability of land for long periods of time (Miceli and Sirmans 2005).

2 Government Acquisition of Property Under Eminent Domain

In the remainder of this chapter, we consider interactions between private individuals and the government. In the current section we consider government takings of private property under eminent domain and, in the next, government regulation of property.

In examining these powers of the government, it is important to keep in mind the conception of the government as an economic agent whose objective, ideally, is to reflect the preferences of the citizenry, however those preferences are aggregated. This implies certain roles for the government as well as limitations on its power in the Lockean sense of a social contract. As Epstein (1985, 13) describes it, "Every transaction between the state and the individual can thus be understood as a transaction between private individuals, some of whom have the mantle of sovereignty while others do not." This concept of limited government power is well exemplified by the eminent domain clause.

2.1 The Eminent Domain Clause

The Fifth Amendment to the U.S. Constitution contains a clause, referred to as the eminent domain, or takings, clause, that says: "Nor shall private property be taken for public use, without just compensation." The clause thus grants the government limited powers to take private property without the owner's consent. The limits are twofold: the property must be put to *public use*; and the government must pay *just compensation*. The vagueness of these terms, however, leaves considerable room for interpretation in their application. In this section we shall see what economists have to say about these limits.

2.1.1 Public Use and the Scope of the Takings Power

The power of eminent domain lies in its coerciveness: landowners do not have the right to refuse a sale to the government as they normally do if the buyer is a private party. Eminent domain is therefore a form of liability rule. The question is how broadly or narrowly the government should be able to use this power.

The public use limitation will serve as the basis for our examination of this question (Merrill 1986). The phrase "public use," however, is somewhat misleading in this respect. For example, it suggests that eminent domain should only be used by the government, and perhaps only then to provide public goods. It turns out that neither interpretation is correct, legally or economically. Our goals in the remainder of this section, therefore, will be (1) to develop a theory of public use that appropriately defines the scope of eminent domain, and (2) to compare that theory to actual legal practice.

We begin by considering the provision of a good or service that requires the acquisition of land as an input. Two questions regarding the provision of such a good will bear on our discussion: Is it a *public good*? and, Does it require the *assembly of land*? Before proceeding, we therefore need to review the economics of public goods and land assembly.

Public Goods.   Public goods have the characteristic that, once provided, their benefits are available to all consumers, including those who have not contributed to the cost of provision.[8] Examples of this are national defense and lighthouses. Because the nonexcludability, or free-rider, problem makes it difficult for producers to exact payment from consumers, the market will generally underprovide public goods. Thus, the government usually provides them and uses its powers of taxation to coerce consumers to contribute to their cost. Government provision of public goods is therefore justified as a response to market failure on the *demand side* of the market.

Land Assembly.   Some large-scale goods require the assembly of several contiguous parcels of land whose ownership is dispersed. Examples include public projects like parks and highways, but also private ventures like shopping centers, railroads, and residential developments. The problem facing the provider in all of these cases is that, once the assembly becomes public knowledge, each landowner realizes that he or she can impose a substantial cost on the provider by refusing to sell. Imagine, for example, that a road builder has decided on the optimal path for a public highway and has begun to assemble properties along that route. If any single owner refuses to sell, the cost of completing the project would increase greatly. This knowledge confers significant monopoly power on individual owners, who can hold out for prices well in excess of their true valuations.[9] In contrast to public goods, therefore, land assembly involves a failure on the *supply side* of the market.

Figure 7.2 provides a graphical illustration of the assembly problem. The downward-sloping curve is the marginal benefit of the project, say a road, which is drawn as a function of the number of parcels acquired (q). Its negative slope reflects a diminishing marginal benefit. Assume that the marginal cost, which reflects the true reservation price of landowners, is constant at *MC*. The optimal number of parcels to be acquired is thus q^*, which occurs at the intersection of the marginal benefit and marginal cost curves. Note that the surplus from the project, if completed, is given by the triangle *abe*.

Figure 7.2

Example of the Holdout Problem

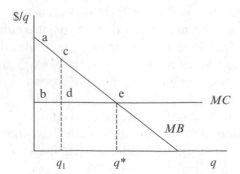

Now suppose that q_1 parcels have been acquired, and the assembler begins negotiation with the next owner. If this owner knows that without her land, the project will not proceed further, she can ask for a price that reflects her true reservation price, given by the height d, *plus the entire remaining surplus, given by triangle cde.* Moreover, every subsequent owner can similarly hold out for the remaining surplus. Worse still, if the project cannot be *begun* until all parcels are assembled, then each owner (starting with the initial one) can hold out for the *entire surplus, abe.* Clearly, this problem poses a serious impediment to the completion of the project.

It is important to note how this problem differs from the situation of a single landowner seeking the best price for his or her property, which is sometimes mischaracterized as a holdout problem. Suppose that instead of a highway, the government wished to buy q^* geographically dispersed parcels in order to build a series of post offices. Since no single parcel affects the purchase of any other, individual sellers can only seek a price that reflects the surplus value *from their particular parcel.* For owner q_1 in the graph, this surplus is the vertical distance cd. But bargaining over this surplus is possible in any market transaction and ordinarily poses no special impediment since both buyer and seller stand to gain from a sale. Moreover, failure to complete this sale has no adverse consequences for other transactions. The unique feature of the assembly problem, therefore, is the interconnectedness of the transactions and the absence of other options for the buyer once the project commences.

One solution to the assembly problem is to allow forced sales. That is, replace property-rule protection of each owner's land (the right to refuse a sale) with liability-rule protection. Owners therefore have no choice but to sell at the price set by the court. Logically, this suggests that takings power should be granted to any buyer—public or private—facing the assembly problem, a conclusion that seems contrary to the plain meaning of public use. We address this issue in the next section.

The Means-Ends Distinction.   Merrill (1986) refers to the proposition that the government alone should have takings power, and only when it provides public goods, as the "ends approach" for defining public use because it concerns the *use* to which the land will be put. He contrasts this with the "means approach," which concerns the method by which the land is acquired. Specifically, is land assembly involved?

Our discussions of public goods and land assembly revealed that these are separable categories. Public goods require tax financing to overcome free riders but do not require forced sale of the needed land unless assembly is necessary. In contrast, assembly requires forced sale of land to overcome the holdout problem but does not require tax financing unless the project being produced is a public good. Table 7.1 shows the four possible cases. We begin with cases I and IV since the means and ends approaches yield

TABLE **7.1**   **Categories Implied by the Means-Ends Distinction**

		Assembly Problem?	
		No	Yes
Public good?	No	(I) No tax financing No forced sales	(II) No tax financing Forced sales
	Yes	(III) Tax financing No forced sales	(IV) Tax financing Forced sales

the same conclusions regarding the use of eminent domain. Case I involves a private good with no assembly problem (for example, a private residence). Thus, neither the means nor the ends approach justifies the granting of eminent domain power to the provider. The transaction should therefore go through the private market, even if one of the parties is the government. At the other extreme is case IV, which involves a public good with an assembly problem (a highway). In this case, both approaches justify the use of eminent domain.[10]

The means and ends approaches yield different conclusions in cases II and III. Consider first case III. Here, the ends approach justifies the use of eminent domain because the good is public, but the means approach does not because there is no assembly problem. To determine which argument is correct, recall that the inefficiency associated with public goods is the free-rider problem, which the government overcomes by means of its powers of taxation. Once the funds are raised, however, there is no reason to allow the government to use eminent domain to obtain the resources necessary to produce the good, absent an assembly problem. Instead, it should be required to buy them on the market.[11]

For example, the government properly uses taxes to finance a police force that protects all citizens, but it should not be allowed to use its takings power to acquire the land for the police station, or to conscript police officers.[12] Instead, it should acquire these resources on the market, just as a private security company must. And it usually does this because of the high cost of using the power of eminent domain. As Fischel (1995b, 74) notes, "In markets lacking the holdout problem, in which eminent domain would be inappropriate, the transaction costs of using the market are typically less than that of using eminent domain." Thus, the risk of overuse of eminent domain by the government is apparently small.

Finally consider case II, which involves a private good requiring land assembly. In this case, the means approach justifies the use of eminent domain, but the ends approach does not. Historically, courts have tended to act in accordance with the means approach, for example, by giving takings authority to private parties like railroad and canal builders, but they nearly always attempt to justify their action in terms of the ends approach (Merrill 1986, 67).[13] This sometimes results in strained reasoning.

For example, in *Kelo v. City of New London* (125 S.Ct. 2655, 545 U.S. 469, 2005), the U.S. Supreme Court held that the use of eminent domain as part of a comprehensive economic development plan satisfied the constitutional requirement of public use, even though the bulk of the economic benefits of the project went to private interests. In support of its decision, the Court cited the spillover benefits to the public in terms of new jobs and an enhanced tax base. In other words, it justified its decision in terms of the ends approach. At the same time, the project involved significant land assembly, suggesting that eminent domain was also defensible in terms of the means approach. Indeed, most large private developments both involve land assembly, and promise significant spillover benefits, implying that the means and ends approaches will often coincide. To the extent that this is true, courts will generally arrive at the right decision, if for the wrong reason.[14]

The difficulty courts have in defending the delegation of eminent domain to private parties in public use cases, however, is somewhat odd in view of the fact that they routinely permit "private takings" without apology in other areas of the law. As we saw in the previous chapter, for example, in *Boomer v. Atlantic Cement Co.* a polluting factory was allowed to continue operating, despite objections by neighboring landowners, so long as it paid their damages. The court in effect gave the plant owner the right of eminent domain in order to overcome the high transaction costs of bargaining with multiple residents. Although this case did not involve land assembly, the owner clearly would have faced a similar holdout problem in seeking to assemble pollution rights if the court had issued an injunction (Goldberg 1985). The *Boomer* decision therefore embodies the logic of the means approach to takings but without the need to frame it in public use terms.

Peevyhouse v. Garland Coal & Mining Co. is another example of a private taking, but one that does not fit the logic of the means approach. Recall that the court awarded the Peevyhouses monetary damages after a mining company breached its contractual obligation to repair their land following a strip-mining operation. The fact that the court did not order specific performance of the contract in effect allowed the mining company to take the land in exchange for its market value. The means approach does not justify this decision because there was no apparent obstacle to bargaining between the parties. Thus, as we argued, the use of a liability rule was not justified.[15]

Our discussion to this point has suggested that the proper scope for eminent domain is provided by the means approach. That is, takings power should be extended to any party, public or private, facing a holdout problem.[16] Although this conclusion may be at odds with the literal meaning of the term *public use*, we have seen that it is consistent with actual practice across a range of legal contexts.

Kelly (2006) offers a different perspective, arguing that the takings power should be limited to public projects. His conclusion is based on two fundamental differences between private and public projects. First, private developers can often use secret buying agents to avoid the holdout problem, whereas the government, because of its need for openness, cannot. Second, the concentrated benefits from private projects create the threat of corruption as developers seek to influence the political process to grant them the power of eminent domain. In contrast, this threat is less severe for public projects precisely because the benefits are widely dispersed.

2.1.2   The Meaning of Just Compensation

Eminent domain is a liability rule that requires payment of just compensation following a taking. U.S. courts have interpreted this to mean "fair market value." We argued earlier, however, that market value almost certainly undercompensates landowners because it fails to account for their subjective value.[17] This point has been made in the context of takings by Knetsch and Borcherding (1979) and Fischel (1995a), among others, who note that market value can sometimes be significantly less than what the owners would willingly accept to part with their land. The problem with a "willingness to accept" measure of compensation, however, is that it is not observable and hence is subject to misrepresentation on the part of owners. In contrast, market value is an objective measure that is relatively easy to observe. It is the use of market-value compensation, however, that makes eminent domain a forced sale.

In addition to undercompensating owners, market-value compensation has a further drawback. By undervaluing land in private use, it potentially leads to excessive public acquisition (Munch 1976). For example, in Figure 7.3 (which reproduces Figure 7.2), the *MB* curve represents the value of land in public use, while the *MC* curve represents its value in private use, including the owner's subjective value. The efficient transfer of land to public use occurs so long as $MB > MC$, or up to q^*. In contrast, the curve representing the market value of the land—what buyers would pay for it—is lower than *MC*, as shown by the curve labeled *MV.* If the government makes its acquisition decisions based on a comparison of the public value of the land to the *amount it actually has to pay* (rather than to the true opportunity cost), then it will acquire q' parcels, which exceeds the efficient level. (We pursue the question of the government's criterion for acquiring land in more detail below.)

The loss from overacquisition can be measured as follows. In Figure 7.3, the loss in subjective value to owners is given by the rectangle *acfd*, which is

Figure 7.3

Overacquisition of
Private Property as a
Result of Market Value
Compensation

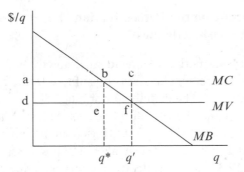

the area between the *MC* and *MV* curves over the parcels taken. The resulting gain in public value is given by the trapezoid *abfd*. Part of this gain is simply a transfer from owners to the public over the parcels up to q^* (rectangle *abed*), and part is the gain from the additional parcels taken (triangle *bfe*). However, the private loss exceeds the social gain by the triangle *bcf*. This triangle is the deadweight loss.

An interesting example where the discrepancy between market value compensation and value to owners was not lost on policymakers is the mill acts enacted by many states during the nineteenth century (Epstein 1985, 170–76). These laws authorized private mill builders to erect dams for the purpose of creating mill ponds, the power source for water-powered mills. The statutes further required the builders to compensate upstream landowners, sometimes requiring a payment in excess of the land's market value. For example, the New Hampshire Mill Acts required payment of 150 percent of market value.

The mill acts represent an example of the private use of eminent domain in a situation where the builder likely faced a potential holdout problem. Thus, like the granting of takings power to railroads, it was justifiable according to the means approach described above. The novel aspect of these laws, however, was the requirement of above-market compensation. One explanation is that the government was seeking, in a crude way, to protect the subjective value of owners.

In the case of government acquisition of land, Richard Epstein (1985, ch. 18) has suggested that the use of taxes to finance compensation is itself a form of taking from taxpayers for which they receive in-kind benefits from the resulting public goods. Fischel (1995b, 211) has therefore argued that landowners whose land is subject to takings risk, but who are also taxpayers and consumers of public goods, may view market-value compensation as the best way to balance their twin concerns about undercompensation in the event of a taking, on the one hand, and the higher taxes that would accompany a more generous compensation rule, on the other. According to this argument, the use of fair market value as the legal definition of just compensation for takings may be about right.

2.1.3   Case Study on the Determination of Just Compensation: "The Assassin's Bequest"

Following the assassination of President Kennedy in 1963, the government took title to various personal possessions of Lee Harvey Oswald as part of its evidence collection.[18] The statute authorizing this action, however, required that just compensation be paid to Oswald's widow, Marina Oswald Porter. The district court awarded her $3,000 based on the fair market value of items that were "similar in kind" to those taken, but the appeals court increased the award to $17,729.37, which reflected the market value of the actual items as enhanced by their connection to the infamous crime.[19]

Which measure of market value is the appropriate one? One reason that the district court cited for refusing to award the higher amount was the fear that it would only increase the incentive for individuals to commit unlawful acts. By denying this gain, at least the monetary incentive to commit such crimes would be removed. This is a good economic argument. Of course, Oswald's widow, who actually stood to gain from the enhanced value in this case, was not herself culpable, but Oswald may have acted out of a bequest motive. These incentive effects therefore argue for the lower award of $3,000.

EXERCISE 7.1

A Dallas dressmaker named Abraham Zapruder captured the assassination of John F. Kennedy on a home movie camera. In 1997, the government took possession of the now-famous "Zapruder film," declaring it a public record, and a three-judge panel awarded the family $16 million in compensation. Is $16 million an appropriate measure of compensation in this case (assuming it is the film's market value)? How does this compare to the Oswald case?

2.2   Eminent Domain and Land Use Incentives

Economic theory has contributed much to the vast literature on eminent domain, but the area where this contribution has been greatest is in its impact on land use incentives. In particular, how does the risk of a taking, and the nature of the compensation rule, affect the decisions of a landowner to invest in developing his land? The classic treatment of this question is an article by Blume, Rubinfeld, and Shapiro (1984), which arrived at the controversial conclusion that one way to induce landowners to invest efficiently in the face of a takings risk is to pay no compensation at all! As we will see, this is not the only rule that will lead to efficient investment, but it has understandably received the most attention. We will also see that the conclusion, while initially surprising, is perfectly consistent with results that we have obtained earlier in our analyses of both tort and contract law.

2.2.1   The No-Compensation Result

In this section we develop a simple version of the Blume, Rubinfeld, and Shapiro model in order to derive the no-compensation result. Consider a parcel of vacant land that will be worth $V(x)$ to the owner if he makes an irreversible investment of x dollars in developing it. (In this section, we do not distinguish between market value and value to the owner.) Assume that $V(x)$ is increasing in x but at a decreasing rate. In the absence of a takings risk, the owner would therefore choose x to maximize $V(x) - x$, which yields the solution x', as shown in Figure 7.4. This is the privately optimal level of investment.

Now suppose that there is a probability p that the government will take the land for public use, in which case it will provide a social benefit of B (after demolishing any private development), and will pay the owner compensation of $C(x)$. In the face of this risk, the socially optimal level of development is the solution to

$$\text{maximize} \quad pB + (1 - p)V(x) - x. \tag{7.4}$$

The optimal development level thus accounts for the possibility that the private value $V(x)$ will be lost with probability p. (Note that it is not unrealistic to require the landowner to choose x before the takings decision is made because the risk is ever present.) Optimal development does not, however, depend on the amount of compensation, which is simply a transfer payment. Note that, since B is independent of x, the solution to (7.4) is the same as the value of x that maximizes $(1 - p)V(x) - x$, which is x^* as shown in Figure 7.4.[20]

Figure 7.4

Moral Hazard Problem Associated with Full Compensation

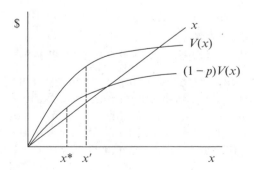

Because of the risk of a taking, the owner should invest less than he would if there were no risk.

But what level of investment will the owner actually make? His private problem is to choose x to solve

$$\text{maximize} \quad pC(x) + (1 - p)V(x) - x. \tag{7.5}$$

Note that, unlike the social problem, the solution to this problem does hinge on the nature of the compensation rule. If it is fair market value, then $C(x) = V(x)$, in which case (7.5) becomes

$$\text{maximize} \quad V(x) - x. \tag{7.6}$$

But as we saw above, the solution to this problem is x', which is too high from a social point of view. The reason is that the owner is fully compensated for his loss and therefore overinvests.

Of course, this is exactly the same moral hazard problem that arose under unlimited expectation damages for breach of contract. In that context, promisees overrelied on performance because they were fully compensated for their losses in the event of breach. (Note in particular the similarity between Figure 7.4 here and Figure 5.2 in Chapter 5.) Similarly, full compensation for victims under strict liability in torts removed their incentives to take care against the occurrence of an accident.

It should be easy to see that this problem can be corrected by setting $C(x) = 0$, for in that case, the landowner will maximize $(1 - p)V(x) - x$, which yields the efficient solution. This is the basis for the "no-compensation result." The following exercise, however, shows that this is not the only solution to the moral hazard problem.

EXERCISE 7.2

Explain why any lump-sum compensation rule—that is, any rule where C is independent of x—will result in the efficient level of investment by the landowner.

2.2.2   Arguments Against the No-Compensation Result

Despite the efficiency of the no-compensation result, it is both unappealing on fairness grounds and inconsistent with the law. Fortunately, there are several economic arguments against it. The first concerns the question of whether the government will act efficiently absent incentives to do so. Economists often assume that it will, as when it enacts policies to correct market failure, but a more realistic view is that the government responds to incentives just like any other economic agent. Thus, when not required to pay for the resources it uses (or, as discussed above, when required to pay too little), it will likely take too much. Full compensation is necessary to prevent this form of government moral hazard.

But since full compensation is not consistent with efficient investment incentives by the landowner, a trade-off exists between the incentives of the government, on the one hand, and of landowners, on the other. Several authors have examined the implications of this trade-off for the design of a compensation rule. We consider two proposals here.[21]

The first is suggested by our analysis of an efficient breach of contract remedy in Chapter 5, where we faced a similar bilateral care–type problem. In that context, we needed to design a rule that simultaneously gave promisors an incentive to breach efficiently and promisees an incentive to invest in efficient reliance. The solution was a limited expectation damage rule that restricted the promisee's recovery to her losses at the efficient level of reliance.[22]

The analog in the context of takings is to set compensation at the full market value of the land *evaluated at the efficient level of investment*—that is, set $C = V(x^*)$ (Miceli 1991a). Note that this will lead to the correct taking decision by the government since it will only take land if the value of the public project exceeds the cost, or if $B > V(x^*)$. As for the landowner, he will choose x to

$$\text{maximize} \quad pV(x^*) + (1 - p)V(x) - x, \tag{7.7}$$

which will also yield the efficient outcome because the first term is constant and hence has no effect on the optimal level of investment. One might object that $V(x^*)$ is difficult for the court to calculate and is therefore impractical, but a good rule of thumb is to base compensation on the level of development of similarly situated parcels.[23]

A second response to the no-compensation result is based on a very influential article on takings by Frank Michelman (1967).[24] According to Michelman's criterion, compensation turns on a comparison of two costs: settlement costs (S) and demoralization costs (D). *Settlement costs* represent the administrative costs of actually paying compensation (including the costs associated with moral hazard), while *demoralization costs* are the costs of not paying. They include the dollar cost of the disutility suffered by those whose land is taken without compensation, as well as the disutility of those who realize that they may be subject to the same treatment in the future. Demoralization costs thus arise from the political risk that the majority will use the powers of the government to expropriate the property of the minority; and compensation serves as public insurance against this risk (Blume and Rubinfeld 1984). However, compensation should only be paid if demoralization costs exceed settlement costs (if $D > S$). Otherwise, no compensation should be paid.

As a final point on the incentive effects of compensation, note that the extent of the moral hazard problem for landowners depends on the magnitude of the takings risk, p. (Specifically, the larger is p, the greater is the difference between x^* and x'.) In reality, p is near zero for most landowners, in which case the problem becomes inconsequential. Further, from a legal perspective the requirement of compensation is unquestioned. When we turn from physical takings to government regulation, however, the conclusion is different on both counts: the risk of regulation is high, and there is considerable debate about whether compensation should be paid.

3   Government Regulation of Property

To this point, our discussion of transactions between private individuals and the government has focused solely on government acquisition of property. Much more common, however, are government regulations that restrict the use of property. The primary economic justification for government regulation is to internalize external costs. For example, zoning ordinances segregate incompatible land uses (Fischel 1985), environmental laws restrict activities that generate pollution, and safety regulations limit unreasonable workplace risks. In addition, the government restricts private property for reasons unrelated to efficiency, for example, to protect the rights of the disabled or to ensure equal opportunity for disadvantaged groups.

Historically, courts have granted the government broad powers to enact regulations in the public interest, but occasionally, a regulation is so restrictive as to cause a substantial reduction in the value of the regulated property. When this happens, the question arises as to whether the regulation should be viewed as a taking for which compensation is due. In some cases, courts have answered this question in the affirmative, but there remains considerable debate over just where the dividing line is between noncompensable regulations and regulations that rise to the level of a taking—so-called regulatory takings. This section provides an economic perspective on this debate.

3.1   The Compensation Question

There is considerable case law and legal scholarship on the "compensation question." We begin by reviewing several of the tests that courts and scholars have used to distinguish between compensable and noncompensable regulations. The wide range of perspectives suggests both the difficulty of the question and the lack of a consensus on how to answer it. In light of this, our goal will be to develop a unifying economic approach. The basis for that approach will be an economic model of land use regulation that focuses on the trade-off, noted above, between the incentives of landowners, on the one hand, and government regulators, on the other.

3.1.1   Tests for Compensation

The Physical Invasion Test.   According to the physical invasion test, government actions that involve a physical invasion of private property are compensable, no matter how minor the invasion. For example, in *Loretto v. Teleprompter* (458 U.S. 419, 1982), the Supreme Court held that a state law allowing cable television providers to put wires and other equipment on a private building was a compensable taking. This test is of limited usefulness, however, because it says nothing about those regulations, comprising the bulk of government actions, that involve no invasion. The remaining tests address these sorts of regulations.

The Noxious Use Doctrine.   The case of *Mugler v. Kansas* (123 U.S. 623, 1887) concerned a state law, passed pursuant to a prohibition amendment to the Kansas constitution, that prohibited the operation of a brewery in the state. The owner of the brewery sued for compensation for the lost value of his property, but the U.S. Supreme Court denied it on the grounds that the state had the right to regulate, without compensation, so-called noxious uses—that is, activities deemed "injurious to the health, morals, or safety of the community."

The Diminution of Value Test.   The noxious use doctrine clearly authorized the government to enact a broad range of actions without running afoul of the takings clause, regardless of the loss in value to the landowner. (After all, what regulations cannot be seen as somehow protecting health, morals, or safety?) This changed, however, when the Supreme Court advanced a new test for compensation in what is probably the most famous regulatory takings case, *Pennsylvania Coal Co. v. Mahon* (260 U.S. 393, 1922).[25] The case concerned a law passed by the State of Pennsylvania, the Kohler Act, which required coal companies to leave a certain amount of coal in the ground in order to prevent damage to surface structures as a result of cave-ins. The Pennsylvania Coal Company brought suit for compensation on the grounds that the law was a taking of its mining rights. Although the law clearly satisfies the standard set forth in *Mugler*, the Court found for the coal company and awarded compensation.

Writing for the majority, Justice Oliver Wendell Holmes began by noting that the government has the right to regulate without compensation, for "Government could hardly go on if to some extent values incident to property could not be diminished without paying for every such change in the law." This was clearly a nod toward the prevailing noxious use doctrine, but he went on to note that a general rule of not paying compensation would, "given the natural tendency of human nature," result in overreaching by the government until "at last private property disappear[ed]." To limit this threat of government excess, Holmes therefore argued that "while property may be regulated to a certain extent, if regulation goes too far it will be recognized as a taking." Thus, the *impact of the regulation on the landowner* matters when deciding the compensation question. The Court did not go on to specify the precise point at which a regulation went "too far," leaving it instead to be decided on a case-by-case basis.

The ruling in *Pennsylvania Coal*, which has come to be known as the diminution of value test, marked an apparent watershed in takings law (L. Friedman 1986). Judge Louis Brandeis, another famous American judge, pointed this out in his dissent to Holmes in *Pennsylvania Coal*, noting:

> Every restriction upon the use of property imposed in the exercise of police power deprives the owner of some right theretofore enjoyed, and is, in that sense, an abridgement by the States of rights in property without making compensation. But restriction imposed to protect the public health, safety or morals from dangers is not a taking. The restriction here in question is merely the prohibition of a noxious use.

We will argue below that an economic approach to the compensation question can be used to reconcile the seemingly opposing perspectives of Holmes and Brandeis.

The Penn Central Standard.   The need to balance the purpose of the regulation against its impact on the landowner was made explicit in the case of *Penn Central Transportation Co. v. City of New York* (438 U.S. 104, 1978). The case involved the city's designation of Grand Central Terminal as an historic landmark, which prohibited structural alterations to the building without the approval of the Landmark Preservation Commission. When Penn Central's proposal to build a multistory office building above the terminal was turned down, it sued, claiming a taking of its development rights. In deciding against compensation, the Court articulated a three-pronged test for a taking. The first two prongs echoed the noxious use doctrine and the diminution of value test. Specifically, compensability of a regulation depended on a balancing of (1) the character of the government action (does it prevent actions harmful to the public?), and (2) the extent of the diminution of value.

The third prong, however, added a new element: Does the regulation interfere with the owner's "investment-backed expectations"? In other words, did the owner have a reasonable expectation of being allowed to proceed with the proposed land use? If so, the case for compensation was strengthened. We address the appropriate economic interpretation and application of this criterion below in Section 3.2.

The Nuisance Exception.   The final factor that we discuss in connection with the compensation question arose in the case of *Lucas v. South Carolina Coastal Council* (112 S.Ct. 2886, 1992). The case involved a developer who had purchased two beachfront lots with the intention of developing them for residential use. Subsequent to his purchase, however, the State of South Carolina passed a law prohibiting such development for the purpose of preventing erosion and other damage to the coastline. The developer sued for compensation, claiming nearly a total loss in the value of his land.

The case attracted considerable popular attention, arising as it did at a time of heated debate between environmentalists and property rights advocates. The case was seen as a test of the extent to which the government could enact regulations aimed at protecting the environment. Although the Court ruled in favor of the developer based on the extent of the diminution of value, it left an opening for the state to avoid paying compensation if it could show that the regulation prevented an action by the developer that would constitute a nuisance under the state's prevailing common law.

This so-called nuisance exception in effect allows the government to prohibit private activities judged to be socially harmful. It therefore echoes the noxious use doctrine, but goes beyond it to provide a standard by which to judge what constitutes a noxious use—namely, the law of nuisance as it has been defined by the common law of the state. This standard has been espoused by Epstein based on the proposition that government actions should be judged by the same legal principles that apply to private parties (Epstein 1985, ch. 9). Thus, just as a private individual can seek an injunction against a harmful activity under the law of trespass or nuisance, the government can use its regulatory powers to enjoin nuisances in the public interest. Below, we address the question of why regulation is needed given the availability of private (common-law) remedies.

Fischel has suggested a similar standard, which sets the benchmark for compensation at "normal behavior," defined to be "standards [for land use] exhibited by the community."[26] If a developer deviates from those standards, then the government is justified in prohibiting the use without compensation. Zoning ordinances segregating commercial, industrial, and residential uses are justifiable in this way.

Like the nuisance exception, normal behavior provides an operational basis for applying the noxious use doctrine.[27] It remains, however, to reconcile the noxious use doctrine with the diminution of value test. In particular, how should courts balance the purpose of the regulation against the impact on the landowner in deciding the compensation issue? The economic model in the next section seeks to answer this fundamental question.

3.1.2 An Economic Model of Regulatory Takings

This section develops a simple model of land use regulation for the purpose of answering the compensation question (Miceli and Segerson 1994, 1996). To be concrete, we will use the facts of the *Lucas* case as the basis for the model. Thus, consider a developer who has a parcel of vacant land for which there are two possible uses: use A, which we will refer to as development; and use B, which we will call recreation. Suppose that use A requires an initial, nonsalvageable investment of x dollars, which includes the cost of planning for development, site preparation, obtaining permits, and the like. This cost is similar to the landowner's investment in the takings model above, except that here, we treat it as a fixed amount. Once x has been spent, if the landowner is allowed to proceed with use A, his net return is therefore $V_A - x > 0$. Land use B, on the other hand, requires no preparatory investment and yields a private return to the landowner of $V_B \geq 0$. We assume that $V_A - x > V_B$, which implies that, in the absence of a regulatory threat, the landowner will maximize his profits by pursuing use A.

The purpose of regulation in this model is to prevent a possible external cost, denoted E, that is associated with development (use A). For example, development of beachfront land might result in beach erosion, toxic runoff, or damage to a wildlife habitat. The external cost does not occur with certainty, however. In particular, suppose that with probability p a high value of E is realized ($E = E_H$), but with probability $1 - p$ there will be no cost ($E = 0$). Further, suppose that the regulator only learns whether a cost will occur *after the landowner has spent x but before he begins development.* For example, once the developer signals his intention to develop by spending x, the regulator undertakes an environmental impact study, and, based on the results, decides whether or not to allow the development. In the case where it prohibits development (use A), the landowner is free to pursue use B but loses his investment of x.

Socially Efficient Behavior.   We begin the analysis of this model by characterizing the efficient land use and regulatory decisions. First consider the regulatory decision. Once the regulator learns E, it is efficient to prohibit development (use A) if the external cost is positive and exceeds the loss to the landowner; that is, if

$$E > V_A - V_B. \tag{7.8}$$

Note that the expenditure of x does not enter this condition because it is a sunk cost at the time the regulatory decision is made. We assume that (7.8) holds when E_H is realized—that is, regulation is efficient when external costs are high. Clearly, however, (7.8) will not hold when $E = 0$. Thus, from the landowner's perspective before the value of the external cost is known, the probability that use A will be prevented is p, the probability that $E = E_H$.

Now consider the efficient land use decision, which in this model amounts to the landowner's decision of whether or not to spend x, given uncertainty about the regulatory decision. Note first that if the developer spends x with the intention of pursuing use A, his expected return is $pV_B + (1 - p)V_A - x$. That is, with probability p, use A will be prohibited, yielding a return of $V_B - x$; but with probability $1 - p$, use A will be allowed, yielding a return of $V_A - x$. (Note, therefore, that the external cost is never incurred because use A is prohibited when that cost is positive.) In contrast, if the landowner chooses use B, he receives a return of V_B and the regulator never becomes involved. It follows that it is efficient for the landowner to spend x if $pV_B + (1 - p)V_A - x > V_B$, or if

$$(1 - p)(V_A - V_B) > x. \tag{7.9}$$

According to this condition, it is socially efficient for the landowner to spend x if the expected gain from use A over B, as discounted by the probability of a regulation, exceeds the cost. Note that this condition may or may not hold, depending on the magnitude of p.

Actual Regulatory and Land Use Decisions.   Now consider the actual decisions of regulators and landowners. Consider regulators first. As in our earlier discussion of eminent domain, we assume here that regulators do not necessarily act in the social interest, absent economic incentives to do so. In particular, we assume that the government will regulate efficiently when compensation is full (that is, when $C = V_A - V_B$), but it will tend to overregulate when compensation is zero.[28] Formally, let q be the probability of a regulation when compensation is zero, where $q > p$.

Now consider the landowner and assume initially that compensation is full (that is, $C = V_A - V_B$). In that case, the return from spending x is given by

$$p[V_B + (V_A - V_B)] + (1 - p)V_A - x = V_A - x. \tag{7.10}$$

Full compensation thus leaves the landowner unaffected by the regulation. He will therefore spend x if the expression in (7.10) exceeds V_B, or if

$$V_A - V_B > x, \tag{7.11}$$

which we assumed above always holds. Thus, full compensation induces the landowner to invest x, even though, according to condition (7.9), it may not

TABLE **7.2**   **Impact of Compensation Rules**

	Rule	
	Full compensation	*Zero compensation*
Government	Regulate efficiently	Overregulate
Landowner	Overinvest in development	Underinvest in development

be efficient for him to do so. In other words, the landowner *overinvests* in development. Intuitively, full compensation allows the landowner to ignore the possible external cost that development might cause. (Of course, this is the same moral hazard problem associated with full compensation in the model of eminent domain above.)

Now suppose that compensation is zero. In that case, the expected return from spending x is $qV_B + (1 - q)V_A - x$, where, recall, q represents the probability of regulation under zero compensation. The landowner will spend x if this return exceeds V_B, or if

$$(1 - q)(V_A - V_B) > x. \tag{7.12}$$

Comparing this condition to (7.9) shows that the landowner will spend x too infrequently given that $q > p$. That is, he *underinvests* in development. Although there is no longer a moral hazard problem on the part of the landowner, the threat of overregulation by the government reduces the landowner's return from spending x below the social return.

Table 7.2 summarizes the decisions of the government and landowner under the two compensation rules. Clearly, neither rule induces efficient decisions by both parties. This reflects the fundamental conflict between the incentives of the two parties—an issue that we have encountered in the context of both tort and contract models. It may also help to explain why courts and legal scholars have had such difficulty in settling the compensation question. This trade-off can be resolved, however, and our previous experience in designing efficient liability rules in torts and contracts will show us how to do it.

An Efficient Compensation Rule.   We begin by noting that the interaction between the landowner and regulator is a classic bilateral care problem like that between the injurer and victim in torts, and between the promisor and promisee in contracts. In both of those contexts, we have seen that a "threshold rule" can be used to induce efficient behavior by both parties. Thus, consider the following compensation rule for regulations:

$$C = \begin{cases} 0, & \text{if } V_A - V_B < E \\ V_A - V_B & \text{if } V_A - V_B > E. \end{cases} \tag{7.13}$$

The first line says that no compensation will be paid if the loss to the landowner from the regulation is less than the savings in external costs. In other words, *no compensation will be paid if the regulation was efficiently enacted.* In contrast, the second line says that full compensation will be paid if the loss from the regulation exceeds the benefit. That is, *full compensation will be paid if the regulation was inefficiently enacted.*

It is easy to see that this rule functions like a negligence rule in torts in achieving an efficient outcome. First, the government has an incentive to enact only efficient regulations (that is, those for which $V_A - V_B < E$) because, like the injurer, it wishes to avoid paying compensation. Given efficient regulatory behavior, the landowner expects that the probability of a regulation will equal the efficient probability, p, and further, he expects to receive no compensation. Thus, he makes the efficient investment decision. In equilibrium, therefore, both parties act efficiently.

3.1.3   Implications of the Efficient Compensation Rule

The foregoing efficient threshold rule for compensation has several implications for our understanding of the law of regulatory takings. First, note that the general form of the rule resembles the diminution of value standard advanced by Justice Holmes in *Pennsylvania Coal* in that it sets a standard, based on efficiency, for when a regulation "goes too far." Specifically, a regulation goes too far, and hence triggers compensation, when it is inefficiently enacted. In this sense, the diminution of value test establishes a sort of Hand rule for compensation.

Similarly, the compensation rule in (7.13) provides a standard for applying the noxious use doctrine. Specifically, if noxious uses are defined to be those that are efficiently regulated, then nonpayment of compensation for such regulations is consistent with efficiency. Based on this interpretation, the diminution of value test and noxious use doctrine are really two sides of the same coin: whereas the diminution of value test defines what regulations exceed the efficient threshold (and hence trigger compensation), the noxious use doctrine defines regulations that meet the efficiency standard.

With this perspective in mind, we can reinterpret the conflicting opinions of Holmes and Brandeis in *Pennsylvania Coal* as reflecting a *disagreement over facts rather than over law.* In particular, if we suppose that both judges were employing the rule in (7.13) to make their decision, then their opposing conclusions could simply reflect Holmes's belief that $V_A - V_B > E$—in which case the regulation was inefficient—and Brandeis's belief that $V_A - V_B < E$—in which case the regulation was efficient. Thus, they disagreed regarding compensation even though they agreed (according to this interpretation) about the applicable legal standard.

Similar reasoning suggests that the nuisance exception is also consistent with the rule in (7.13). Recall that the nuisance exception allows states to enact regulations without paying compensation if the regulation prohibits land uses that are considered nuisances under the prevailing common law. In Chapter 6, we noted that the common law determines what activities are nuisances by asking whether "a reasonable person would conclude that the amount of the harm done outweighs the benefits."[29] According to this definition, the nuisance exception establishes exactly the same threshold for compensation as does the rule in (7.13).

A final point regarding the efficient compensation rule concerns the case of *Keystone Bituminous Coal Assn. v. DeBenedictus* (480 U.S. 470, 1987), which was a takings case decided by the Supreme Court in 1987. The case is interesting because the facts are strikingly similar to those in *Pennsylvania Coal*. The regulation under review (the Subsidence Act) was again a state law requiring coal companies to leave sufficient coal in the ground to support the surface, but this time the Court awarded the plaintiffs no compensation. In an effort to justify this apparent reversal of the earlier decision, Justice Stevens, writing for the majority, noted that the law in *Pennsylvania Coal* only protected a few private landowners, whereas

> Here, by contrast, the Commonwealth is acting to protect the public interest in health, the environment, and the fiscal integrity of the area. . . . The Subsidence Act is a prime example that "circumstances may so change in time . . . as to clothe with such a [public] interest what in other times would be a matter of purely private concern."[30]

Apparently, the benefit of the current regulation was significantly larger than in the earlier case as a result of increased value of the surface rights. (In other words, the prevented harm, E, was larger in this case than in *Pennsylvania Coal*.) At the same time, the loss to coal companies was smaller due to the diminished value of coal in the economy.[31] As a result, what may have been an inefficient regulation in 1922 (at least, as Holmes reckoned it) had become efficient in 1987. Thus, the differing decisions in the two cases may be seen as resulting from a change in economic values rather than from a change in the controlling law.

3.2 Investment-Backed Expectations: Does the Market Eliminate the Need for Compensation?*

Our earlier discussion of the *Penn Central* case suggested that a relevant factor in deciding the compensation question is whether the regulation interfered with the claimant's "investment-backed expectations." From an economic perspective, expectations are important because they determine market values. For example, a piece of vacant land may sell for a very high price if the buyer expects to be able to develop it in the future. Similarly, the threat of a regulation preventing future development will depress the value of the property.

In his influential article, Michelman (1967) argued that this sort of market adjustment matters for the compensation question. In particular, if a developer purchased a piece property subsequent to the enactment of a regulation, his claim for compensation would be weak because he "got exactly what he meant to buy," namely, a parcel of land whose price reflected the risk of a regulation (Michelman 1967, 1238). Paying compensation to the buyer in this case would be like refunding the price of a losing lottery ticket.

This is a persuasive argument that has found its way into the law. For example, in *HFH Ltd. v. Superior Court* (542 P.2d 237, 1975), the court said, "The long settled state of zoning law renders the possibility of change in zoning clearly foreseeable to . . . purchasers of property, who discount their estimate of its value by the probability of such a change." The apparent implication of this argument is that the market renders the compensation rule irrelevant. To see this formally, consider the amount that a buyer would be willing to pay for the parcel in the above model of land use regulation, given that p is the risk of a regulation and C is the compensation amount:

$$p(V_B + C) + (1 - p)V_A - x. \tag{7.14}$$

This expression reflects the expected value of the parcel, including the expected compensation in the event of a regulation. Thus, if compensation were zero, the buyer would suffer no harm (in expected terms) from an uncompensated regulation because he would have discounted his offer for the land by the amount $p(V_A - V_B)$.

Several authors, however, have pointed out that this argument is flawed because it looks at the takings question at the wrong point in time.[32] While it is true that the *buyer* suffers no harm from an uncompensated regulation, the *seller* surely does. To see this, note that, prior to the existence of the regulatory threat, the above parcel is worth $V_A - x$ to the seller (the expression in (7.14) with $p = 0$), which is its value in development. However, once the threat became apparent, its value falls to the amount in (7.14), causing a loss to the seller of

$$p(V_A - V_B - C). \tag{7.15}$$

Only a rule of full compensation ($C = V_A - V_B$) eliminates this loss.

The preceding appears to be an argument for compensation of the seller, even though it is the buyer who owns the land at the time of the regulation.

However, paying compensation to the buyer eliminates the seller's loss as well because the market price rises by the expected amount of compensation, thereby shifting compensation back to the seller.

The logic of the preceding argument is illustrated in the following exercise.

EXERCISE 7.3

Consider the owner of a parcel of beachfront land, which, if developed, would yield a net value of $100,000. The owner plans to sell the land to a developer, but before he does, the state passes a law that greatly curtails beachfront development. In particular, the probability that development will be permitted falls to 0.1. Suppose the value of the undeveloped land is $10,000.

   (a) Calculate the sale price of the land if no compensation is paid when development requests are denied. What is the loss suffered by the initial owner when he sells the land?
   (b) Calculate the amount of compensation under a rule of full compensation.
   (c) Calculate the sale price and the owner's loss when compensation is full.

3.3   Compensation and the Timing of Development*

Our earlier discussion of the impact of compensation on land use decisions showed that full compensation distorts incentives by causing excessive development. Here we discuss an offsetting inefficiency associated with zero compensation—namely, the possibility that landowners will develop prematurely in order to forestall a threatened regulation. For example, the owner of a stand of timber may cut it early for fear that an endangered species will be found living there, or a landowner may develop his land to prevent it from being declared a wetland.

A simple extension of the above model to allow two periods illustrates the problem (Lueck and Michael 2003). Consider a developer who owns a piece of undeveloped land. Let V_N be the value of the land if it is developed *now*, and let V_L be the value of the land if it is developed *later*. Assume that $V_L > V_N$, implying that the landowner would wait to develop, absent a regulatory threat. Now suppose that with probability p there is an external cost E associated with development, but it will only be known in period two whether this cost is realized. Further, suppose that $E > V_L$, implying that if the cost is realized, it is not efficient to develop the land if it was not developed in period one. However, assume that if the land was developed in period one, there is no way to prevent the cost retroactively. (This is what allows preemptive development.)

In this setting, the expected social return from developing now (in period one) is $V_N - pE$, while the expected return from waiting is $(1 - p)V_L$. It is therefore efficient to wait if $(1 - p)V_L > V_N - pE$, or if

$$(1 - p)(V_L - V_N) + p(E - V_N) > 0. \tag{7.16}$$

Note that both terms are positive implying that it is always efficient to wait. This is true both because it is privately profitable for the developer to wait (given $V_L > V_N$), and because waiting allows the external cost to be avoided.

Now consider the private decision of the landowner regarding the timing of development. If he develops now, his return is V_N, and there is no risk of a regulation. If he waits, his expected return is $(1 - p)V_L + pC$, where C is his compensation in the event of a regulation. He will therefore wait if $(1 - p)V_L + pC > V_N$, or if

$$(1 - p)(V_L - V_N) + p(C - V_N) > 0. \tag{7.17}$$

Clearly, if $C = 0$, this condition may not hold, in which case the landowner will develop early. Further, this possibility becomes more likely as p increases. (Note that in the extreme case where $p = 1$, early development is certain.) This shows that some amount of positive compensation is necessary to ensure that premature development never occurs. Note in particular that $C = E$ perfectly aligns private and social objectives, though any C that makes (7.17) positive will work.

4 Regulation Versus the Common Law

In this and the previous chapters, we have examined two responses to externalities: a private response based on the common law of nuisance, and a public response based on government regulation. In this section, we examine the choice between these two types of remedies.

Recall that the nuisance approach requires victims of a harm to initiate legal action against the injuring party by filing suit. This is the sense in which the remedy is private. It is also the source of an important limitation of the approach. Suppose that the harm imposed by, say, a polluting firm, while large in the aggregate, is sufficiently dispersed that no one victim finds it worthwhile to bring suit. The nuisance approach will therefore fail to internalize the harm. Although collective action can overcome this problem in the form of a class-action suit, organizational costs and free riding will often prevent this from happening (Landes and Posner 1987, 52). In that case, the government acts as an "agent" of the victims to regulate the harmful activity.

The economic argument for government regulation is therefore based on high transaction costs *among victims*. Note that this is different from the case of high transaction costs *between the injurer and victims*, which we previously argued was the basis for choosing liability rules over property rules in resolving private disputes (Miceli 1999a). The *Boomer* case illustrates the distinction. The number of victims in that case was apparently small enough to permit a private lawsuit, but the existence of a holdout problem created high transaction costs between the factory and victims, which the court avoided by use of a liability rule.

The point is that it is high transaction costs among victims, not between injurers and victims, that justifies a regulatory response. Of course, these problems will often be correlated, especially in the case of large-scale environmental harms. This helps to explain why "the common law of nuisance today has largely been superseded by public regulation" (Merrill 1998, 618).

Regulation, however, is not without its own limitations. One is that regulators do not necessarily act in the social interest, a problem that we have already discussed at length. Another is that regulators may lack sufficient information about localized harms to set efficient standards. When this is true, regulation and common law represent imperfect alternatives (Komesar 1994). As a result, either may be preferred, or it may be optimal to use them in combination.[33]

To illustrate, consider a simple unilateral care model in which injurers take care of x to reduce the probability of an accidental harm, $p(x)$. Assume that the harm suffered by victims, D, is independent of x but varies across victims. The optimal level of care for each type of victim therefore minimizes

$$x + p(x)D. \tag{7.18}$$

Let the solution to this problem be $x^*(D)$. Clearly, optimal care should be increasing in the amount of victim harm. This is shown by the upward-sloping curve labeled x^* in Figure 7.5.

Figure 7.5

Care Levels Under
Liability and Regulation

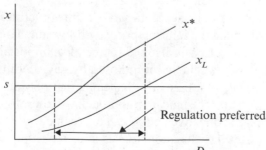

Figure 7.6

Injurer Care Under
Combined Liability and
Regulatory Regime

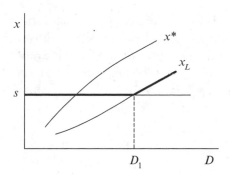

Now consider liability (common law) and regulation as alternative methods for inducing care by injurers. Under the threat of liability, injurers respond to victim-specific damage (given their localized knowledge), but only imperfectly because they sometimes avoid suit. This is true for the reasons just noted (dispersed costs and collective action problems), but also because injurers may be judgment proof due to limited wealth, or victims may have difficulty in proving causation. As a result, injurers will generally take too little care under a liability regime, though care will be increasing in victim damages. This is shown by the curve labeled x_L in Figure 7.5, where $x_L < x^*$ for all values of D.

Under a regulatory regime, in contrast, all injurers are required to meet a standard of safety, denoted s. Thus, compliance is complete, but the regulator lacks the information to tailor the standard to individual injurers. Consequently, the efficient standard is based on average damages and is the same for all injurers, as shown by the horizontal line in Figure 7.5.

The trade-off between liability and regulation is now clear. The advantage of liability is that it induces injurers to respond to information about victim-specific harm that is unavailable to the regulator. The advantage of regulation is that it overcomes the problem of noncompliance. Generally, the preferred regime will be the one that induces a level of care closer to the efficient level. Thus, in Figure 7.5, regulation will be preferred for intermediate levels of D (the range where s is closer to x^* than x_L), while liability will be preferred for very low and very high levels of D. Intuitively, the standard under regulation will be closer to the efficient standard for victims whose damages are near the average.

The preceding has viewed liability and regulation as alternatives, but in reality they can be (and are) used in combination. That is, injurers face a regulatory standard as well as the threat of liability. In this case, injurers will comply with s up to damage level D_1, at which point they voluntarily switch to a higher level of care (x_L) under the threat of liability. (The switch occurs at the point where $s = x_L$.)

Thus, for damage levels above D_1, the regulatory standard is nonbinding. This is shown by the darkened segments in Figure 7.6. An implication of this behavior by injurers is that the regulatory standard should be set fairly low because otherwise, injurers facing low-damage victims will be forced to comply with a safety standard well above their efficient level of care.

We conclude by noting that the analysis of government regulation in this section has focused exclusively on the goal of efficiency. Our conclusions about the appropriate scope of regulation therefore do not necessarily apply to actions aimed at other goals such as redistribution of income or protection of individual rights, which are motivated by other social values.

5 Conclusion

A central element of economic theory is the role of market (consensual) exchange in achieving an efficient allocation of resources. When externalities or high transaction costs cause markets to fail, however, nonconsensual exchanges in the form of court-imposed remedies or government regulations may be called for as (imperfect) alternatives. In this context, we began by examining coercive transfers of property between private individuals (for example, adverse possession), and restrictions on private transfers (inheritance law).

The bulk of the chapter, however, examined government takings and regulations of private property. Regarding takings, we asked why the government should have a power (eminent domain) that is generally denied to private citizens; what the proper scope of that power is; and what the measure of just compensation should be. Finally, we considered the impact of the compensation rule on private investment decisions.

Government regulation also raises the taking issue when a regulation substantially reduces the value of the targeted property. We reviewed the case law on the compensation question, and developed an economic model (an adaptation of the model of precaution) to determine where the dividing line should be between compensable and noncompensable regulations. We concluded the chapter by evaluating the relative merits of regulatory (public) versus common-law (private) responses to market failure.

DISCUSSION QUESTIONS

1. Contrast the economic rationale for patents and copyrights (time-limited property rights in ideas) with that for adverse possession (time-limited property rights in land).

2. Suppose the conditions of a charitable donation become illegal (for example, land donated for a city park to be open to whites only) or otherwise infea-

sible. The doctrine of cy pres allows administrators of the charitable foundation to adopt an alternate use "within the general scope of the donor's intent" (Posner 1998a, 557). Does this doctrine make economic sense?

3. The "harm-benefit" test for compensation says that compensation should be paid for regulations that confer public benefits, but not for regulations that prevent public harm. Does this distinction make economic sense? How might one draw a sensible line between a benefit conferred and a harm prevented?

4. In Chapter 1 we examined two efficiency criteria: Pareto efficiency and Kaldor-Hicks efficiency. Recall that Pareto allows projects to go forward only if losers are fully compensated, whereas Kaldor-Hicks allows them to proceed as long as aggregate benefits exceed costs, or if $B > C$ (that is, compensation of losers is not required). According to Michelman's (1967) criterion, projects can go forward if $B - C > \min(S, D)$, where, recall, S are settlement costs and D are demoralization costs. Given this formula, explain why Michelman is more permissive than Pareto but less permissive than Kaldor-Hicks.

5. Suppose a government agency takes part of an individual's land, say for a highway, for which it must pay compensation. The "benefit offset" principle would allow the government to reduce the amount of compensation by the increase in value of the remaining portion of the land. Does this make economic sense? What if the increase in value of the untaken land exceeds the value of the taken land?

6. In the case of *U.S. v. Miller* (317 U.S. 369, 1943), the Supreme Court said that the calculation of market value for purposes of paying compensation for a taking should not include any enhancement in the property's value arising from knowledge of the public project. What would be the effect of tying compensation to the value of the public project rather than to the value of the land in its current use?

PROBLEMS

1. The case of *Goldblatt v. Town of Hempstead* (369 U.S. 590, 1962) involved a takings claim by the operator of a gravel pit who was prohibited by a town ordinance from continuing to excavate from an open pit that had gone below the water table. Discuss how the court would evaluate the compensation question based on (1) the noxious use doctrine; (2) the diminution of value test; (3) the nuisance exception; and (4) the efficient threshold rule.

2. A developer owns a piece of beachfront land that he intends to develop for residential use. The private returns to the developer are as follows:

Return if developed $50,000

Return if undeveloped $10,000

Suppose that three nearby residents would sustain damages from beach erosion if the land is developed. Their damages would be as follows:

Resident 1: $20,000

Resident 2: $15,000

Resident 3: $10,000

(a) Is it efficient for the land to be developed?

(b) Suppose that the developer has property-rule protection of his right to develop. If bargaining costs between the developer and the residents are zero, describe the likely outcome.

(c) How does your answer to (b) change if it costs the three residents a total of $10,000 to organize and act collectively.

(d) Explain how the government can use its regulatory powers to overcome the problem of high bargaining costs.

(e) What amount of compensation should the developer receive if he is prohibited from developing the land and it is found to be a taking?

3. Suppose that a gas station plans to begin operation on a vacant parcel of land located in a residential neighborhood. The extra profit the station will earn at this location compared to its next best location is $500, but it will also impose an external cost of $10 on each of one hundred nearby residents.

(a) Is it efficient for the station to locate in the residential area?

(b) Two possible ways for the station owner and residents to resolve the externality are: (1) for the residents to organize and buy the property and then resell it to a residential user; or (2) for one or more of the residents to bring a nuisance suit to have the station shut down. Explain why each of these solutions is unlikely to work in this case.

(c) Use your answer to (b) to justify zoning ordinances used by most cities to segregate incompatible land uses.

4. A parcel of land in a commercial district is worth $500,000, but the city unexpectedly announces plans to rezone the land for residential use, in which case its value is $300,000. The owner sells the property after the announcement but before the rezoning occurs. How much would a buyer pay if she expects to prevail in a claim for compensation with probability .5? What is the resulting loss to the seller from the zoning change?

5. A developer buys several undeveloped parcels of land on a beachfront. At a later date, the state passes a law greatly restricting coastal development. When the developer's request for permission to develop is denied, he sues for

compensation under the Fifth Amendment, claiming he was denied all benefi-cial use of the land. (See *Palazollo v. Rhode Island*, 121 S.Ct. 2448, 2001).

(a) How would you decide this case? What other cases would you cite?
(b) Would it matter whether the plaintiff had bought the land *after* enactment of the statute restricting development?

8

THE ECONOMICS OF DISPUTE RESOLUTION

To this point, we have paid only passing attention to the costs of using the legal system to resolve disputes. In this chapter we remedy that neglect by examining in detail the economics of dispute resolution. For the purposes of the analysis, the specific nature of the dispute—whether it is in torts, contracts, property, or some other area—is not relevant. What matters is that one party, the plaintiff, is seeking a legal remedy against another party, the defendant. For the most part, we will focus on suits for monetary compensation (damages).

Economists are interested in the resolution of legal disputes for several reasons. First, the manner in which parties resolve their disputes—for example, whether they settle or go to trial—has important implications for the cost of operating the legal system. Second, economic theory can help to explain why some parties settle their disputes out of court while others end up at trial. It can therefore offer recommendations for lowering the cost of dispute resolution by encouraging settlements. Finally, the manner and cost of resolving disputes affects incentives for parties to avoid disputes in the first place.

In addition to affecting costs, the process of dispute resolution is of interest because it determines the way the common law evolves. Unlike legislation, changes in the common law arise from judicial decisions in private lawsuits. Cases that never reach trial therefore have no impact on the body of legal precedents because they never come before a judge. In fact, the vast majority of private disputes settle before reaching trial, which means that a small percentage of cases drives the common law. Thus, a theory of which cases settle and which go to trial is essential to an understanding of the nature of the common law.

Such an understanding is interesting in its own right, but also because it bears on two important economic issues. The first concerns empirical analysis of lawsuits. Since data are only available on cases that go to trial, if economists wish to draw inferences about the population of all disputes from publicly available data, they need to adjust for any biases arisising from the fact that cases that settle and cases that go to trial may be fundamentally different. The second issue is methodological. An important conjecture at the heart of the economic approach to law is that the common law evolves in the direction of efficiency. One of our tasks in this chapter will be to use the economic model of dispute resolution to evaluate this conjecture.

1 The Litigation Process

There is a common perception among Americans that people have become increasingly litigious.[1] The available data on litigation rates provide some support for this perception. For example, Figure 8.1 shows a rapid growth in the number of civil cases filed per capita in U.S. District Courts, especially during the 1970s and early 1980s.

One consequence of this increasing litigation rate is a growing demand for lawyers.[2] For example, Rosen (1992) noted that the "litigation explosion" was accompanied by a doubling of the number of lawyers from 1967 to 1979,

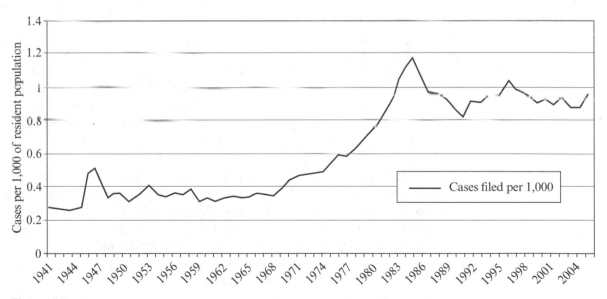

Figure 8.1
Civil Cases Filed in U.S. District Courts, per 1,000 of Resident Population, 1941–2004

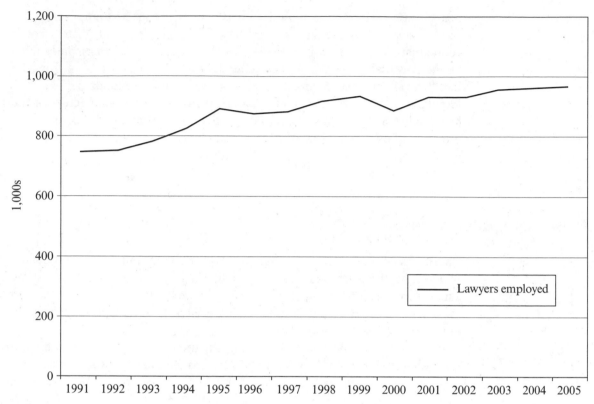

Figure 8.2

Number of Lawyers Employed in the United States (1,000s), 1991–2005

and another 50 percent increase between 1979 and 1987. Figure 8.2 shows that this increase has continued in the 1990s, albeit at a slower rate, even as the litigation rate has leveled off. As for lawyer income, Rosen found that earnings held fairly steady through the 1980s, suggesting that the entry of lawyers into the market matched the demand for legal services. According to this market test, at least, there are not too many lawyers.

Lawyers' fees, of course, are only a part of the overall cost of operating the legal system. In addition, there is the public cost, consisting of the salaries of judges and other court personnel, plus the cost of operating court facilities. A Rand study estimated this cost at more than $2.2 billion for all civil cases processed in state and federal courts in 1982 (Kakalik and Ross 1983), a figure that has undoubtedly grown considerably in recent decades.

The total social cost of resolving disputes, public plus private, is a form of transaction cost. Thus, one goal of the economic analysis of legal disputes is to reduce this cost so that the system operates more efficiently. Usually, this involves finding ways of promoting out-of-court settlement. Surprisingly, the vast majority of cases do in fact settle before reaching trial. As Table 8.1

TABLE **8.1**   **Trial Rates for Civil Cases in U.S. District Courts, 1988–1997 (numbers in 1,000s except for percentages)**

	1988	1989	1990	1991	1992	1993	1994	1995	1996	1997
Cases commenced	239.6	233.5	217.9	207.7	226.9	228.6	236.0	239.0	272.7	265.2
Trials	11.6	11.2	9.2	8.4	8.0	7.9	7.9	7.7	7.5	7.4
% Reaching trial	4.9	4.8	4.3	4.0	3.4	3.5	3.4	3.4	3.1	3.0

SOURCE: Statistical Abstract of the U.S., *various years.*

shows, of all civil cases filed in U.S. district courts between 1988 and 1997, less than 5 percent made it to trial, and the fraction seems to be falling. The numbers are similar for state court filings.

The high settlement rate turns out to be quite consistent with economic theory. In fact, the real question turns out to be, why do any cases go to trial? Answering this question is the first task of this chapter.

2   Why Do Trials Occur?

It may seem odd at first to ask why trials occur, especially when such a small percentage of suits actually end in trial. A little reflection, however, suggests why trials should be rare. If litigants are rational and have symmetric beliefs about the likely outcome of a trial, then they should always be able to replicate that outcome (in expected terms) in the form of a monetary settlement, thereby saving the cost and uncertainty of enduring an actual trial. In order to explain trials without invoking irrationality, we shall therefore have to relax the assumption of symmetric beliefs.

Before proceeding, we need to be clear about the basic structure of a lawsuit. This is shown schematically in Figure 8.3. The process begins with a dispute between two parties. This may involve an accident, a breach of contract, a property rights disagreement, or any other dispute in which one party, the victim, claims to have suffered damages at the hands of another party, the injurer. The victim then makes a decision whether or not to file a legal claim. Since lawsuits are costly, not all disputes end in a lawsuit. In fact, a Rand study found that, contrary to popular perceptions, victims of personal injury do not automatically turn to the liability system for compensation. In fact, "with the exception of motor vehicle accident victims, only a minority, even among those who are quite seriously injured, ever consider claiming; of those, just a small fraction use legal mechanisms" (Hensler et al. 1991, 110).

It is the fraction of victims who choose to file suit, however, that are of interest to us. At this point, they become plaintiffs in a lawsuit seeking monetary compensation from injurers, now defendants.[3] Once a suit is filed, the

Figure 8.3

The Structure of a
Legal Dispute

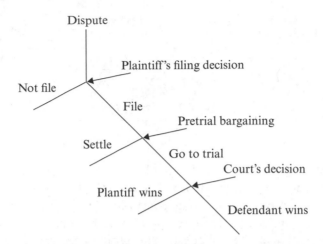

pretrial bargaining process begins. Here is where parties exchange information during the discovery process (to be discussed below), and where they
make offers and counteroffers in an effort to settle the dispute out of court. As
we saw above, better than 90 percent of civil disputes do in fact settle during
this period. It is easy to see why this occurs.

Suppose that a negligent injurer caused $50,000 in damages to a nonneg-
ligent victim, and the cost of going to trial would be $10,000 each. Thus, the
victim would accept any amount greater than $40,000 to settle out of court,
while the defendant would pay any amount less than $60,000. The difference
of $20,000 (equal to the combined costs of trial) represents the joint gains
from settling. Assuming that the parties can agree on how to share the gains, a
settlement should always occur. Risk aversion by litigants will only reinforce
the gain from settlement since the parties will prefer the certain outcome of a
settlement to the uncertain outcome of a trial.

But settlements do not always occur, so what explains why some cases
go to trial? One important factor is beliefs: the preceding example assumed
that the parties have symmetric beliefs regarding the outcome of trial. In
fact they may not for two reasons: they might have different *opinions* about
the outcome of a trial, or one party might have *private information* about a
relevant fact of the case. The principal economic models of litigation—the
optimism (or differing perceptions) model, and the asymmetric information
model (respectively), are based on these two reasons for disagreement. We
examine these models in turn.

2.1   The Differing Perceptions, or Optimism Model

The first model that was developed to explain the settlement-trial decision
is referred to as the optimism, or differing perceptions, model.[4] According

to this model, litigants can disagree about the outcome of a trial based on different opinions, for example, about the relevant law or how it will be applied. Suppose in the above model that the parties agree that the victim's loss is $50,000, but they disagree about the plaintiff's chances of winning. As the following exercise shows, this can lead to a situation in which settlement is no longer possible.

EXERCISE 8.1

Suppose that the victim believes her probability of winning is 90 percent, but the injurer believes the plaintiff's probability of winning is only 40 percent. Assume they agree that the victim's damages are $50,000, and the cost of trial to each is $10,000. Show that a settlement is not possible in this case.

To illustrate the implications of this model more generally, let P_p denote the plaintiff's assessment of her probability of winning at trial, and let P_d denote the defendant's assessment of this same probability. (In other words, P_d is the defendant's assessment of his probability of *losing* at trial.) Also let J equal the monetary judgment that the plaintiff will recover if she wins (an amount that both parties agree on), and let C_p and C_d be the costs of trial for the plaintiff and defendant, respectively.[5] For simplicity, we assume that settlement is costless, though our conclusions hold as long as settlement is less costly than trial (see Cooter and Rubinfeld 1989; and problem number 2 at the end of this chapter).

Using these variables, we can calculate the expected value of trial for the plaintiff to be $P_p J - C_p$, which is the expected monetary judgment at trial less the cost of a trial. We assume that this amount is positive, implying that the plaintiff would always go to trial if settlement negotiations failed. (We consider the case where this value is negative in our discussion of frivolous suits below.) However, the plaintiff would prefer to settle for any offer S such that $S \geq P_p J - C_p$.

We similarly calculate the expected cost of trial to the defendant as $P_d J + C_d$. Thus, the defendant will settle for any amount $S \leq P_d J + C_d$. We say that a settlement is *feasible* if there exists a settlement amount that is simultaneously preferred to trial by both parties; that is, if there exists an S such that

$$P_p J - C_p \leq S \leq P_d J + C_d, \tag{8.1}$$

or, equivalently,

$$P_p J - C_p \leq P_d J + C_d.$$

Thus, a settlement is feasible if the maximum amount the defendant will offer is at least as large as the minimum amount the plaintiff will accept. This can be rearranged to yield the condition

$$(P_p - P_d)J \leq C_p + C_d. \tag{8.2}$$

Note that if $P_p = P_d$, then this condition becomes

$$C_p + C_d \geq 0,$$

which always holds. This reflects the point made above that, if the parties have symmetric beliefs, a settlement is always feasible because they have a joint interest in avoiding the costs of trial.

A settlement is not *guaranteed* when (8.2) holds, however, because the parties may have difficulty in agreeing on how to share the surplus. Thus, one source of trials in this model is breakdowns in bargaining over division of the gains from settlement (Cooter, Marks, and Mnookin 1982). This is not much to hang our hats on, however, and would not be very convincing as the primary explanation for trials. A more general explanation is that (8.2) may not hold in some cases. The resulting *trial condition* is found by reversing the inequality in (8.2) to obtain

$$(P_p - P_d)J > C_p + C_d. \tag{8.3}$$

Several implications follow from (8.3). First, a trial is less likely the higher are the costs of trial, a perfectly intuitive result. Second, a trial is more likely the larger is the difference $P_p - P_d$. This reflects the role of optimism in encouraging trials. Specifically, a trial is more likely the larger is the plaintiff's assessment of her probability of winning and the smaller is the defendant's assessment of his probability of losing. Finally, given $P_p - P_d > 0$, a trial is more likely the larger is J, the expected judgment at trial. This implies that cases are more likely to go to trial the larger are the stakes of the case. We return to some of these implications at various points below.

Since the primary reason for trials in the optimism model is the fact that $P_p > P_d$, it is worth asking why this might be true. Experimental evidence suggests that it can be attributed to "self-serving bias"—the tendency for people to believe that the correct (or fair) outcome of a legal dispute, or any adversarial or bargaining situation, is the one that best serves their own interests (Babcock and Loewenstein 2000). (The idea is similar to "unrealistic optimism" as discussed in the context of risk perceptions in Chapter 3.) The result is that breakdowns in bargaining will occur more often than predicted by traditional rational choice models.

Most economists, however, are skeptical of models based on systematic biases in people's beliefs. Why, for example, would rational parties with equal access to legal counsel disagree about the expected outcome of trial? Note that this criticism is not based on a claim that the parties should be able to predict the court's behavior with certainty. Rather, it is a claim that neither party's prediction should be biased because they have access to the same information.

2.2 The Asymmetric Information Model

A more recent model of the settlement-trial decision sidesteps this criticism by proposing that trials result, not from biased perceptions, but from differences in information.[6] For example, in an accident case, the defendant may have private information about whether he was actually negligent, or the plaintiff may have private information about whether she was contributorily negligent. This asymmetry of information provides an alternative source of differing beliefs that can be used to explain why some cases go to trial.

To illustrate this in a simple setting, suppose that the plaintiff has private information about her probability of winning at trial. Specifically, suppose there are two types of plaintiffs in the population of plaintiffs, those with a high probability of victory at trial, P_h (plaintiffs who were not contributorily negligent), and those with a low probability of victory at trial, P_l (plaintiffs who were contributorily negligent), where $P_h > P_l > 0$. Plaintiffs know their own probabilities of victory, so they can calculate their expected returns at trial (where their private information will become public). For a "high" type, this return is $P_h J - C_p$, while for a "low" type it is $P_l J - C_p$, where $P_h J - C_p > P_l J - C_p$.

Defendants, however, cannot observe an individual plaintiff's type prior to trial, though they know the fraction of each type in the population. Let a be the fraction of high probability types. Thus, when facing a particular plaintiff, a defendant can only calculate the average probability of plaintiff victory, given by

$$\bar{P} = aP_h + (1 - a)P_l. \tag{8.4}$$

It follows that the defendant's expected cost of going to trial with a random plaintiff is $\bar{P}J + C_d$. ($\bar{P}$ thus takes the place of P_d from the optimism model.) As in the above model, a settlement will occur if the defendant is willing to offer an amount S that the plaintiff will accept rather than go to trial.

Note first that if the defendant offers an amount greater than or equal to the value of trial to a high-type plaintiff, $P_h J - C_p$, *both types will accept the offer and no cases will go to trial.* This type of outcome is referred to as a *pooling strategy* because the defendant treats both types of defendants alike. Assume that when the defendant employs this strategy, he offers exactly $S_h = P_h J - C_p$, which is the lowest amount that the high-type plaintiff would accept. Under this strategy, the defendant's average cost per case is just $P_h J - C_p$, and there are no trials.

The defendant may be able to lower his expected cost, however, by adopting a different strategy. Suppose, in particular, that he offers $S_l = P_l J - C_p$. Low-type plaintiffs are just willing to accept this amount, but high types will reject it and go to trial. This is referred to as a *separating strategy* because it treats the two types of plaintiffs differently (low types settle and high types go to trial). Since the defendant does not know which type of plaintiff he is facing when he makes the offer, his expected cost from this strategy is

$$a(P_h J + C_d) + (1 - a)(P_l J - C_p). \tag{8.5}$$

A third possible strategy is for the defendant to offer an amount less than S_l, in which case both types of plaintiffs will reject the offer and go to trial. His expected costs in that case will be $\bar{P}J + C_d$. It is easy to show, however, that this strategy is never cost minimizing for the defendant.[7] Intuitively, it is always cheaper to settle with at least one type of plaintiff since this saves the trial costs with that type.

We have seen that trials only occur under the asymmetric information model (and then only with high-type plaintiffs) when the defendant chooses the separating strategy over the pooling strategy. The defendant prefers the separating strategy if his expected costs in (8.5) are less than his costs under the pooling strategy, $P_h J - C_p$. This condition can be rearranged to yield:

$$\frac{1-a}{a}(P_h - P_l)J > C_p + C_d.\text{ [8]} \tag{8.6}$$

Note that this closely resembles the trial condition under the optimism model (condition (8.3)) and therefore has some of the same implications. For example, both models predict that trials become less likely as the costs of trial increase and more likely as the stakes increase. Both also imply that information sharing prior to trial will affect the settlement rate (though the nature of the information may differ). However, the models have different implications regarding the types of cases that will end up at trial. We pursue these last two points in more detail below.

2.3   The Social Versus Private Incentive to Sue

The analysis so far has focused on the settlement-trial decision, once a suit has been filed. In this section we consider the filing decision. A plaintiff will file a lawsuit if the expected gain from doing so exceeds the cost. The expected gain, of course, depends on the manner in which the suit is expected to be resolved. Plaintiffs who expect to go to trial will file if the expected return from trial, $P_p J - C_p$, exceeds the filing cost, f, while plaintiffs who expect to settle will file if the equilibrium settlement amount, S, exceeds f. We have not been explicit about the equilibrium settlement amount because it depends on the nature of the bargaining between the plaintiff and the defendant, but we did argue that plaintiffs would never accept less in a settlement than they expect to recover at trial. (That is, $S \geq P_p J - C_p$; see (8.1)). Thus, the prospect of settlement only enhances the plaintiff's incentive to file suit.[9]

Plaintiffs make their filing decision based on a comparison of their "private" costs and benefits. An important question is whether their decision is also "socially optimal." This can only be answered with reference to the social function of the legal system, which we have seen is to provide incentives for individuals to act in certain socially desirable ways. For example, in tort law, the threat of lawsuits induces injurers to take efficient precaution against accidents. Victims do not internalize this benefit, however, so their filing decisions do not necessarily coincide with the optimal decision.

To illustrate, consider a simple accident model in which an injurer chooses between taking care and not taking care (Shavell 1982a). If he does not take care, the probability of an accident is p_n, but if he does take care at cost x, the probability falls to $p_c < p_n$. The victim's damage in the event of an accident is D, and the costs of a lawsuit for the victim (plaintiff) and injurer (defendant) are C_p and C_d, respectively. (For the purposes of this example, we do not distinguish between trials and settlements regarding incentives for injurer care.) (See Polinsky and Rubinfeld 1988.) Finally, assume the rule is strict liability (the conclusions are similar for a negligence rule).

First consider the social value of a suit. If victims file suit and injurers respond by taking care, total social costs are

$$x + p_c(D + C_p + C_d), \tag{8.7}$$

which includes the cost of precaution, damages, and litigation costs. In contrast, if victims do not file suit, injurers will never take care, in which case social costs are

$$p_n D \tag{8.8}$$

Suits are therefore socially desirable if (8.7) is less than (8.8), or if

$$x + p_c(C_p + C_d) < (p_n - p_c)D. \tag{8.9}$$

The interpretation of this condition is that suits are desirable if the cost of care plus expected litigation costs are less than the expected reduction in damages. Note that the presence of litigation costs tends to make care less desirable compared to a zero-litigation-cost world because the threat of suits provides the only incentive for injurers to take care.

The private condition for victims to file suit, as noted above, is if the expected recovery at trial exceeds the litigation cost. In the current model, victims will therefore file if $D > C_p$. Clearly, this will not generally coincide with the social condition for trial in (8.9). The difference between the private and social incentives to sue arises from two effects. First, plaintiffs ignore the litigation costs borne by defendants; second, they ignore the incentives that lawsuits create for parties to invest in accident prevention. These effects can lead victims to file either too many or too few lawsuits, as the following exercise illustrates.

EXERCISE 8.2

Consider the following numerical example: $x = 1, p_n = .07, p_c = .02,$ $C_p = C_d = \$200$.

(a) Show that if $D = \$210$, it is both socially and privately desirable for victims to file suit.
(b) Show that if $D = \$190$, it is still socially desirable for victims to file suit, but it is not privately desirable.
(c) Now let $p_n = .04$. Show that it is no longer socially desirable for victims to file suit when D equals either \$210 or \$190. Does this change affect the victim's private filing decision?

---

3 Procedural Rules and Litigation Costs

An important policy objective of the economic analysis of dispute resolution is to find ways of reducing the costs of operating the legal system. In this section, we examine how different procedural rules can affect the magnitude of legal costs, including rules governing the disclosure of information prior to trial and rules for allocating legal costs among litigants and their lawyers. For the most part, we examine how these rules affect the settlement-trial decision. In addition, we examine two important problems with the legal process—frivolous suits and court delay—and conclude by considering alternative methods of dispute resolution.

3.1 Discovery

The rules of discovery allow the parties to a lawsuit to solicit information from each other prior to trial. The exchange of information can take the form of requests for documents, answers to a prepared list of questions (interrogatories), and deposition of witnesses. An important purpose of discovery is to promote out-of-court settlement of disputes by reducing the parties' uncertainty about the outcome of trial. This effect can be illustrated in both the optimism and asymmetric information models.

Recall that in the optimism model, the trial condition is given by (8.3), which is more likely to hold the larger is the "disagreement" term, $P_p - P_d$.

The model is not clear about the exact source of the disagreement, but to the extent that it is due to privately held information, discovery should increase the likelihood of settlement (Cooter and Rubinfeld 1994). In the case of the asymmetric information model, discovery should also increase settlement because trials in that model are entirely due to privately held information.[10]

In addition to affecting the likelihood of settlement, discovery can affect the settlement amount. As noted, it is difficult to specify this amount precisely because it depends on the bargaining abilities of the parties. One plausible assumption is that, when settlement occurs, the parties split the gains evenly. In the context of the optimism model, this would imply that S is exactly between the bounds in (8.1), or

$$ S = \frac{(P_P + P_d)\, J + (C_d - C_p)}{2}. \tag{8.10} $$

If the parties have roughly equal litigation costs, then the $C_d - C_p$ term drops out. It follows that, if discovery succeeds in aligning the beliefs of the two parties with each other and with the true merits of the case (that is, $P_p = P_d = P$), then the equilibrium settlement amount will reflect a "fair" resolution of the dispute (that is, (8.10) reduces to $S = PJ$).

Discovery is not without its drawbacks, however. Since requests for information are costly to comply with, parties can use them strategically to increase their opponent's costs, thereby gaining an advantage. Consider, for example, a plaintiff with an expected value of trial equal to $10,000. The plaintiff will therefore not settle for any lesser amount. But suppose that the defendant makes a discovery request that would cost the plaintiff $1,000 to satisfy. The plaintiff would now settle for as little as $9,000 rather than comply. As a result, the defendant has gained a strategic advantage from making the request (assuming it cost less than $1,000 to make), quite apart from any information it might yield.

3.2   The English Versus American Rule

Calls for reform of the legal system often include proposals to change the rule for allocating legal expenses from the American rule, under which litigants bear their own expenses regardless of the outcome of trial, to the English rule, under which the loser pays his own and the winner's expenses. Advocates of the English (or "loser pays") rule claim that it will lower overall litigation costs for two reasons. First, the greater cost it imposes on losers will discourage plaintiffs from filing meritless claims; second, the greater risk associated with trial will increase the likelihood of settlement among those cases that are filed. This section evaluates these claims theoretically using the litigation models developed above, and then offers some empirical and experimental evidence on these questions.

3.2.1   The English Rule and Settlement

We first ask how a switch from the American rule to the English rule affects the likelihood of settlement. In the context of the optimism model (Shavell 1982b; Cooter and Rubinfeld 1989), the plaintiff's expected value of trial under the English rule is

$$P_pJ - (1 - P_p)(C_p + C_d). \tag{8.11}$$

Thus, if the plaintiff wins, she receives the judgment J and is indemnified for her litigation costs, but if she loses, she receives nothing and must pay her own and the defendant's costs. Recall that the plaintiff's corresponding value of trial under the American rule is $P_pJ - C_p$.

The defendant's expected cost of trial under the English rule is

$$P_d(J + C_p + C_d). \tag{8.12}$$

Thus, if he loses, he pays the judgment J and both parties' litigation costs, but if he wins, he incurs no costs. His corresponding cost under the American rule is $P_dJ + C_d$.

As we argued above, settlement is feasible if (8.12), the maximum amount the defendant will pay to avoid trial, exceeds (8.11), the minimum amount the plaintiff will accept. After rearranging, this condition becomes

$$(P_p - P_d)(J + C_p + C_d) \leq C_p + C_d. \tag{8.13}$$

Now compare this to (8.2), the condition for settlement under the American rule. Note that the right-hand sides are equal, but the left-hand side of (8.13) is larger. This implies that the settlement range is smaller, making settlement *less likely* under the English rule. Intuitively, the stakes of the case are higher under the English rule because the outcome of the trial determines the allocation of legal costs as well as the defendant's liability. Thus, the effect of a switch to the English rule is the same as an increase in J. Since the asymmetric information model also implied that trials are more likely as J increases, it too predicts more trials under the English rule, holding other factors constant.

Other factors may not remain constant, however. For example, if litigants can choose their levels of spending at trial, they will likely spend more under the English rule because of the increased stakes (Hause 1989). And if the difference in the perceived probabilities of victory, $P_p - P_d$, does not change much as a result (and is small), then the increase in $C_p + C_d$ will tend to make settlement *more likely* under the English rule.

Risk aversion will also tend to promote more settlements under the English rule because it increases the range of outcomes, and hence the risk, of a trial

(Posner 1998a, 630). To illustrate, note that if the plaintiff wins under the American rule, she receives $J - C_p$, but if she loses, she pays C_p. The range is thus $J - C_p - (-C_p) = J$. A switch to the English rule increases this range to $J - (-C_p - C_d) = J + C_p + C_d$. A similar increase occurs for the defendant under the English rule.

Finally, Donahue (1991b) has argued that the settlement rate should be *identical* under the English and American rules. Using the logic of the Coase Theorem, he shows that, regardless of which cost allocation rule actually prevails, the parties will adopt the rule that maximizes their joint gains through private contracting. Of course, this requires the parties to recognize that they can override the existing rule and that bargaining costs are low enough relative to the gains that they actually strike the necessary bargains. The empirical evidence below suggests that they do not.

The preceding results do not provide a definitive prediction about the impact of the English rule on the settlement rate. Which of the offsetting effects dominates is therefore an empirical question.

3.2.2   The English Rule and the Incentive to File Suit

The other purported benefit of the English rule is that it discourages plaintiffs from filing meritless suits. We can evaluate this claim by comparing the plaintiff's expected value of trial under the two rules. Based on this comparison, we can conclude that a suit will be less valuable under the English rule as compared to the American rule (all else equal) if

$$P_p J - (1 - P_p)(C_p + C_d) < P_p J - C_p,$$

or, after rearranging, if

$$P_p < \frac{C_d}{C_p + C_d}. \tag{8.14}$$

Thus, plaintiffs with low probabilities of victory at trial will find their suits less valuable under the English rule. It follows that plaintiffs with $P_p > C_d/(C_p + C_d)$ will find their suits more valuable under the English rule.

The implication for plaintiffs' filing decisions is shown in Figure 8.4, which graphs the value of suits under the two rules for different values of P_p (Donahue 1991b). Suppose first that the cost of filing suit is f_1. In this case, a switch to the English rule will reduce the number of suits filed by raising the threshold value of P_p at which a suit becomes profitable. In contrast, if the filing cost is f_2, the English rule will increase the number of suits by lowering the threshold. Together, these results support the claim that the English rule tends to discourage low-value suits and encourage high-value suits.

Figure 8.4

Impact of the English
Rule on Plaintiffs'
Filing Decision

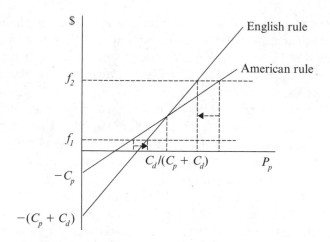

EXERCISE 8.3

Consider the following example: $J = \$1,000$, $C_p = C_d = \$200$, $P_p = .7$, and $P_d = .4$.

    (a) Calculate the expected value of trial for the plaintiff and the expected cost of trial for the defendant under the American and English rules. Is settlement feasible in either case?

    (b) How does the English rule affect the plaintiff's value of trial? How would it affect that value if $P_p = .45$? Explain the different outcomes.

3.2.3 Evidence on the Impact of the English Rule

The impact of the English rule could in principle be tested by statistical analysis of litigation and settlement data from the United States and England. This is not possible in practice, however, because it would be very difficult to control for all of the interjurisdictional differences that might influence decisions to file suit or settle, thus preventing the researcher from isolating the effect of the cost rule.[11]

Fortunately, there is some empirical evidence from a "natural experiment" conducted by the State of Florida, which mandated use of the English rule for medical malpractice cases between 1980 and 1985. In two studies, Snyder and Hughes used data from more than 10,000 cases to test the impact of the English rule (Snyder and Hughes 1990; Hughes and Snyder 1995). Their findings were as follows. First, the English rule increased the likelihood that parties would litigate rather than settle, as predicted by the simple optimism model. This was true even though defense expenditures per case rose. Second, the English rule increased the probability that a claim would be dropped, thus supporting the view that it discourages weak claims.[12] Third, the English rule increased the win rate of plaintiffs, as well as the judgment at trial and amount of compensation in settled cases. These findings provide further evidence that the English rule encourages plaintiffs to pursue higher-quality claims.

Evidence on the impact of the English rule is also available from "true experiments" of the litigation process conducted by Coursey and Stanley (1988). They found that the English rule increased the settlement rate, a result that they attributed to risk aversion on the part of the litigants. It is hard to know how much weight to put on these results, however, since the subjects were not involved in actual cases, nor did they have the benefit of legal counsel.

3.3 Rule 68*

Another cost allocation rule aimed at reducing litigation costs is Rule 68 of the Federal Rules of Civil Procedure. Under this rule, "a plaintiff who refuses a defendant's formal settlement offer and then obtains a judgment not more favorable than the offer must pay the defendant's postoffer costs" (Miller 1986, 93). The rule is clearly designed to promote settlement by penalizing plaintiffs who reject "reasonable" offers. In this section, we use the simple optimism model to see if it actually has that effect.[13] (We assume that the background rule for allocating legal costs is the American rule.)

In order to allow for the possibility that the plaintiff's recovery at trial will be less than the defendant's best settlement offer, S, we modify the model as follows. Suppose the judgment for the plaintiff in the event of victory at trial is a random variable that may take a high (J_H) or a low (J_L) value, where $J_L < S < J_H$. Thus, if the plaintiff wins and only receives J_L, Rule 68 dictates that she must pay her own and the defendant's trial costs. However, if she wins and receives J_H, or if she loses, both parties pay their own costs. Let a be the probability that the judgment is J_L, conditional on plaintiff victory. (The expected judgment at trial is therefore $J = aJ_L + (1 - a)J_H$, which both parties agree on.)

We can now calculate the plaintiff's expected value of trial under Rule 68 to be

$$P_pJ - C_p - P_paC_d,$$
(8.15)

where the final term is the expected sanction. The expected cost of trial for the defendant is similarly given by

$$P_dJ + C_d - P_daC_d,$$
(8.16)

where the final term is the expected reimbursement of costs. (Note that the expected transfer is different in the two expressions because the parties assess

Figure 8.5

Impact of Rule 68 on the Settlement Rate

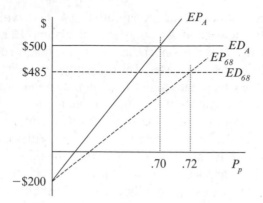

a different probability of plaintiff victory.) As above, a settlement is feasible if (8.16) is at least as large as (8.15). This yields the settlement condition

$$(P_p - P_d)J - (P_p - P_d)aC_d \leq C_p + C_d. \tag{8.17}$$

Compared to the corresponding condition in (8.2), this condition is more likely to hold because the right-hand sides are the same, but a positive term is subtracted from the left-hand side. This suggests when litigants are optimistic about trial (that is, when $P_p > P_d$), settlement is more likely under Rule 68. Intuitively, the expected sanction increases the cost of trial more for the plaintiff than it reduces the cost for the defendant, thereby expanding the settlement range.

EXAMPLE

To illustrate the impact of Rule 68, consider the following numerical example. Let $J = \$1,000$, $C_p = C_d = \$200$, $P_d = .3$, and $a = .25$. The expected cost of trial for the defendant is thus $ED_A = \$500$ under the American rule and $ED_{68} = \$485$ under Rule 68. These values are shown by the horizontal solid and dashed lines, respectively, in Figure 8.5. The figure also graphs the expected values of trial for the plaintiff under the American rule (EP_A) and Rule 68 (EP_{68}) as functions of P_p. Whenever the defendant's cost exceeds the plaintiff's value under the relevant rule, settlement is feasible. Settlement is therefore feasible for $P_p \leq .70$ under the American rule, and for $P_p \leq .72$ under Rule 68. Thus, the settlement range has expanded under Rule 68.

By promoting settlement, cost shifting under Rule 68 works in the opposite direction of the English rule. However, the two rules also have different distributional effects. Whereas the English rule penalizes plaintiffs and defendants symmetrically, Rule 68 only penalizes plaintiffs. In this sense, it is said to be "pro-defendant." To see the impact of this, assume as above that when settlement occurs, the parties split the surplus evenly. Thus, the equilibrium settlement is the average of (8.15) and (8.16), or

$$S_{68} = \frac{(P_p + P_d)J + (C_d - C_p) - (P_p + P_d)aC_d}{2}. \tag{8.18}$$

Compare this to the equilibrium settlement amount under the American rule in (8.10). The amount here is lower, reflecting the fact that Rule 68 lowers both the expected value of trial to plaintiffs and the expected cost of trial to defendants. The result is that lawsuits are less valuable for plaintiffs, who will therefore file fewer suits. Although this seems like a desirable outcome, it may have the offsetting effect of reducing incentives for defendants to take precautions to avoid disputes in the first place (Spier 1994). The net effect on caseloads is therefore ambiguous.

In their experimental analysis of the litigation process, Coursey and Stanley (1988) also evaluated the impact of Rule 68. They found that Rule 68 both increased the settlement rate compared to the American rule and shifted the settlement amount in favor of defendants, both in accord with the preceding theoretical predictions.

3.4   Contingent Fees*

To this point, we have only considered rules for allocating legal costs between the plaintiff and defendant, but rules for allocating costs between the plaintiff and her lawyer can also affect the outcome of litigation. In this section, we compare fixed and contingent fees. Under a fixed fee, the plaintiff pays a flat or hourly rate regardless of the outcome of the case, whereas under a contingent fee she pays a percentage (usually one-third) of her recovery.[14] Contingent fees are very common in the United States, especially for tort litigation. For example, a 1991 Rand study found that 87 percent of tort cases were brought under contingent fees (Hensler et al. 1991). In contrast, they were banned in England until recently and remain illegal in many countries. They nevertheless provide several benefits to potential litigants, which we review in the next section.[15] Later, we consider some criticisms.

3.4.1   The Benefits of Contingent Fees

Lawyer time and effort is probably the most important input into a lawsuit, but clients generally lack the requisite knowledge to evaluate this input. Thus, the most common argument for contingent fees is that they provide lawyers

Figure 8.6

Impact of a Contingent
Fee on Lawyer Effort

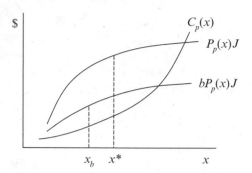

Figure 8.6

Impact of a Contingent
Fee on Lawyer Effort

an incentive to work hard for their clients by giving the lawyer a partial stake
in the outcome of the case.

To illustrate, suppose that a plaintiff's probability of victory at trial depends on how much effort her lawyer devotes to the case. If the lawyer's effort
is x, then the expected value of trial is

$$P_p(x)J - C_p(x), \tag{8.19}$$

where both $P_p(x)$ and $C_p(x)$ are increasing in x. (This assumes that the only
costs at trial are those incurred by the lawyer.) The socially optimal level of
effort (that is, the level that is best for a combined plaintiff-lawyer) maximizes (8.19) and is given by x^* in Figure 8.6.[16]

The lawyer, however, will make his actual choice of effort to maximize
his profit, which depends on the fee arrangement. Under an hourly or fixed
fee, he will internalize the cost but not the benefit of effort and will therefore
have little incentive to work hard. A contingent fee improves the situation by
allowing the lawyer to retain a fraction b of the judgment at trial. The lawyer
therefore maximizes

$$P_p(x)bJ - C_p(x), \tag{8.20}$$

which results in a positive level of effort, x_b, though still less than the optimal
level given $b < 1$ (see Figure 8.6).[17]

A second benefit of contingent fees is risk sharing. Under a fixed fee
arrangement, the plaintiff bears all of the risk of the outcome of the case,
whereas a contingent fee shares it between the plaintiff and lawyer. (Recall
that we made a similar argument for sharecropping contracts in agriculture.)
There are good reasons to believe that the lawyer is a better risk bearer than
the client. First, he can better estimate the prospects for success, thereby discouraging meritless claims (which an hourly-fee lawyer might accept). Second, he can diversify the risk of failure across his caseload.

The preceding conclusions regarding incentives and risk sharing suggest
that the most efficient contractual arrangement between the lawyer and client
would be for the lawyer to actually "purchase" the claim. That is, the lawyer

would pay the plaintiff a fixed amount up front (equal to the expected value of the case) and then retain any proceeds from a trial or settlement. This would have the dual benefit of creating efficient incentives for effort (because $b = 1$), while allocating all of the risk to the lawyer. Despite these benefits, the law forbids such contracts. Why? One reason is to prevent lawyers from stirring up litigation (a point that we discuss below in connection with frivolous suits). Another is the concern that plaintiffs have insufficient information to properly evaluate their claims, potentially causing the market for legal services to fail (Cooter 1998).

A final benefit of contingent fees is that they allow wealth-constrained plaintiffs to pursue lawsuits by letting them "borrow" the lawyer's services using the value of the suit as collateral. Standard credit markets fail in this case because lenders lack the knowledge or experience to properly price the loan (Posner 1998a, 624).

3.4.2 Contingent Fees and Settlement

We next consider the impact of contingent fees on the settlement of litigation (Miller 1987; Donahue 1991a). Recall from above that the condition for the plaintiff to settle is

$$S \geq P_p J - C_p. \tag{8.21}$$

Under a contingent fee contract, however, the plaintiff and lawyer will have conflicting incentives. Legally, the plaintiff controls the settlement decision, which implies that settlement will occur if $(1 - b)S \geq P_p(1 - b)J$, or if

$$S \geq P_p J.^{[18]} \tag{8.22}$$

Compared to (8.21), this shows that the plaintiff will opt for trial too often because she ignores the cost of trial borne by the lawyer.

In reality, lawyers exercise considerable control over the settlement decision. Under a contingent fee, the lawyer will prefer to settle if $bS \geq P_p bJ - C_p$, or if

$$S \geq P_p J - \frac{C_p}{b}. \tag{8.23}$$

Since $b < 1$, this implies that the lawyer will want to settle too often compared to (8.21). This is because the lawyer bears the full cost of trial but only expects to receive a fraction of the proceeds.

A numerical example illustrates the preceding analysis. Let $P_p J = \$50,000$, $C_p = \$10,000$, and $b = 1/3$. A combined plaintiff-lawyer will settle for any amount greater than the expected value of trial, which equals $\$50,000 - \$10,000 = \$40,000$. From the plaintiff's perspective, however, the minimum acceptable settlement offer is $\$50,000$, while the lawyer will settle for any amount greater than $50,000 - ($10,000 \times 3) = $20,000$. As this example shows, the extent of the conflict between the parties can be considerable.

3.4.3 Do Contingent Fees Promote Frivolous Suits?

A second criticism of contingent fees is that they encourage plaintiffs to pursue meritless claims—so-called frivolous suits (Miceli 1994a). The basis for this criticism is that plaintiffs ignore the cost of trial and therefore are willing to pursue claims with a negative expected value at trial (that is, claims for which $P_p J - C_p < 0$). What this criticism ignores is that lawyers will refuse to accept cases that do not promise a profit. In particular, given the contingency rate of b, lawyers will refuse to accept any cases for which $P_p b J - C_p < 0$, or

$$P_p J - \frac{C_p}{b} < 0. \tag{8.24}$$

This implies that lawyers will in fact *turn down* some cases for which $P_p J - C_p > 0$, which obviously implies that they will refuse any cases for which $P_p J - C_p < 0$. This suggests that, given the role of lawyers in screening cases, the general problem of frivolous suits may be overstated. We will argue in the next section, however, that such a conclusion would be premature.

3.5   Frivolous Suits

Frivolous suits are defined to be suits that have little or no chance of succeeding at trial.[19] That is, $P_p J$ is near zero (or at least less than the cost of trial). Assuming that plaintiffs (and their lawyers) are rational, the value of such suits therefore resides solely in their settlement value. But why would a defendant be willing to settle a case that has no value at trial?

The optimism model provides one answer (Cooter and Rubinfeld 1989, 1084). We showed above that if the parties split the surplus from settlement equally, then the equilibrium settlement amount under the American rule is given by the expression in (8.10). Now suppose the parties agree that the case has no merit, so that $P_p J = P_d J = 0$. The settlement amount reduces to

$$S = \frac{C_d - C_p}{2}. \tag{8.25}$$

Thus, the case will settle for a positive amount if the defendant has higher trial costs than the plaintiff.

In one sense, this is an appealing result because it says that defendants will settle meritless claims if they have more to lose at trial than the plaintiff does. What the model fails to account for, however, is that the plaintiff's threat to go to trial is not credible. To illustrate, suppose that the defendant offers nothing rather than the amount in (8.25). A rational plaintiff will drop the suit rather than proceed to trial where the case has a negative expected value. The key point is that the success of frivolous suits hinges on the credibility of the plaintiff's threat to go to trial.

Other models of settlement get around the credibility problem and thus make frivolous suits possible. Consider first the asymmetric information model (Bebchuk 1988; A. Katz 1990). Suppose there are two types of plaintiffs: those with a positive probability of victory, P, and those with a zero probability. Further, assume that $PJ - C_p > 0$, so plaintiffs with a positive probability will go to trial if no settlement is offered, while those with zero probability will drop the suit if no settlement is offered. Finally, assume that the defendant cannot observe the type of individual plaintiffs, though he knows that meritorious suits comprise a fraction a of all plaintiffs. What is the defendant's optimal strategy?

As we saw above, he has two options. First, he can make a positive offer of $S = PJ - C_p$, which both types will accept. Thus, plaintiffs with frivolous claims receive the same settlement amount as those possessing meritorious claims. The expected cost to the defendant of this pooling strategy is $PJ - C_p$. Alternatively, the defendant can offer nothing, causing plaintiffs with meritorious suits to go to trial and plaintiffs with frivolous suits to drop their claims. The expected cost of this separating offer is thus $a(PJ + C_d)$. The defendant will prefer the pooling strategy to the separating strategy if $PJ - C_p < a(PJ + C_d)$, or if

$$a > \frac{PJ - C_p}{PJ + C_d}. \tag{8.26}$$

Thus, if meritorious suits represent a large enough fraction of all suits, then it does not pay the defendant to separate out frivolous claims, and the latter succeed in obtaining a settlement.

As an example, let $P = .7$, $J = \$50,000$, and $C_p = C_d = \$10,000$. Based on (8.26), the defendant will offer a positive settlement of $25,000 if $a > .56$ and will offer nothing if $a < .56$.

Another model in which frivolous suits succeed involves sequential expenditure of costs by the plaintiff and defendant (Rosenberg and Shavell 1985). Suppose that the plaintiff files suit at cost f, at which time the defendant must incur an initial cost d to defend himself (for example, by retaining a lawyer). Otherwise, he will lose a default judgment of J. If the defendant spends d, the plaintiff must then decide whether to drop the suit or go to trial. A plaintiff with a frivolous suit will drop at this point since the expected value of trial is negative, whereas a plaintiff with a meritorious suit will proceed. Regardless of what type of defendant he faces, however, the defendant will prefer to settle at the time the case is filed for an amount $S < d$ rather than defend himself.

Anticipating this, plaintiffs will file frivolous suits as long as the expected settlement exceeds the filing cost. Thus, the equilibrium settlement amount in this model must satisfy the condition $f < S < d$, which has no relation to the merits of the plaintiff's case.

There are procedural rules aimed at deterring frivolous suits. For example, Rule 11 of the Federal Rules of Civil Procedure provides for monetary sanctions against plaintiffs whose suits are judged to be frivolous (Polinsky and Rubinfeld 1993). Another deterrent available to repeat defendants like insurance companies is to develop a reputation for taking cases to trial, even when this is not optimal in an individual case (Miceli 1993). This strategy turns on the credibility of the *defendant's* threat to go to trial, which can only be established as part of a larger pattern of behavior over a series of cases.

3.6 Court Delay*

A long-standing source of concern among observers of the legal process is the delay in disposing of cases. This concern became especially acute during the height of the "litigation explosion" in the 1970s and 1980s as court backlogs increased. A Rand study of civil cases in federal courts, however, showed that the backlog was almost entirely due to the increase in the filing rate, not to increased delay in termination rates (Dungworth and Pace 1990). As Figure 8.7 shows, the distribution of "time to termination" for civil cases remained stable over this period, suggesting that courts adjusted well to the increased strain.

It is nevertheless striking that 40 percent of cases take one year or more

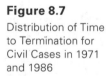

Figure 8.7

Distribution of Time to Termination for Civil Cases in 1971 and 1986

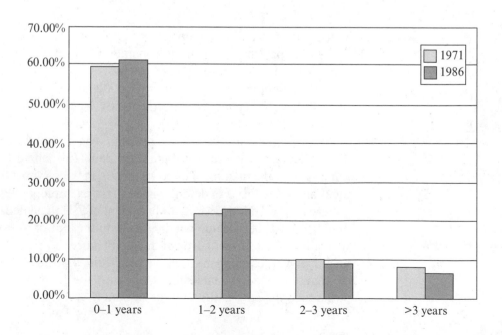

to be resolved. This obviously has implications for the costs of administering the system, but it also raises the oft-stated concern that "justice delayed is justice denied." The fact that better than 90 percent of suits settle suggests that these problems may be limited to the small fraction that go to trial, but Kessler (1996) found that court delay is a significant determinant of settlement delay. We suggest two reasons why this might be true.

First, in a theoretical analysis of the dynamics of pretrial negotiation, Spier (1992) showed that most settlements occur immediately, or just before trial (on the "courthouse steps"). The existence of this "deadline effect" suggests that as the time until trial increases, so will the average time until settlement.

A second explanation for the observed pattern of settlement is that defendants might use delay strategically to lower their costs (Miceli 1999b). For example, suppose plaintiffs differ in their valuation of time. Specifically, suppose that some discount future income at a rate of 5 percent, while others discount it at a rate of 10 percent. A case worth $10,000 at trial *in one year* thus has a present value of $9,524 = $10,000/1.05 for the first type of plaintiff, but only $9091 = $10,000/1.1 for the second type.

Now consider a defendant who is uncertain which type of plaintiff he is facing, though he believes each type is equally likely. One strategy is for him to offer $9,524, which both types will accept immediately. Under this pooling strategy, settlement occurs without delay and costs the defendant $9,524. He may be able to do better, however, by offering $9,091. Plaintiffs with the high discount rate will accept this amount immediately, but those with the lower rate will reject it, preferring to wait for trial. The defendant will therefore settle with them on the courthouse steps for $10,000.[20] The expected cost of this separating strategy, in present value terms, is

$$(.5)(\$9,091) + \frac{(.5)(\$10,000)}{(1 + r)},$$

where r is the defendant's discount rate. The defendant will prefer the strategy of delay if this cost is less than $9,524, which will be true as long as $r > .43\%$.[21]

This shows that if defendants have a sufficiently high discount rate, they will find it desirable to use settlement delay as a way of lowering their expected costs. In his study of the settlement process, Ross found evidence that defendants in fact behave in this way, especially when they are repeat players. One respondent expressed it this way: "In selected cases delay may well be a tool of considerable power, and on occasions it may well be used consciously to lower the settlement" (Ross 1970, 85).

3.7 Alternative Dispute Resolution

High litigation costs and lengthy court delays have increasingly prompted courts and legislatures to seek alternatives to the legal system for resolving disputes. In response, various methods of alternative dispute resolution, or ADR, have emerged.[22] The two most common are arbitration and mediation.

Arbitration involves a third party who, like a judge, oversees the resolution of a dispute. Unlike judges, however, arbitrators are chosen by the parties, usually because of some expertise in the issue in dispute. However, the arbitrator's decision is binding on the parties and will be enforced by courts. Most commonly, parties contract ahead of time to use arbitration as the method by which any future disputes will be resolved. For example, contract disputes in baseball are generally resolved by "final offer" arbitration, where an arbitrator chooses one of the final offers submitted by the parties.

Arbitration offers several advantages over court resolution. First, the expertise of the arbitrator presumably leads to more abbreviated fact-finding and a more accurate resolution of the dispute. Second, less formal procedural rules generally reduce the time and cost of completing the procedure. Finally, the binding nature of the arbitrator's decision eliminates the possibility of a lengthy appeal process. (Of course, this could have the drawback of allowing an errant decision to stand—see the discussion of appeals below.)

Although the full advantages of arbitration are realized when the parties can contractually commit to it beforehand, disputants with no prior relationship may still benefit from having a cheap alternative to trial once a dispute has arisen. On the downside, this type of ex post arbitration may actually lead to more cases being filed because, by lowering the cost of dispute resolution, it potentially increases the value of a suit. In addition, parties may resort to arbitration when they otherwise would have settled. The net effect on litigation costs is therefore ambiguous.

The other common form of ADR is mediation. Like arbitration, mediation involves the use of a third party to facilitate resolution of a dispute, but unlike arbitrators, mediators have no authority to impose a decision. Rather, their primary goal is to promote settlement. The above models of litigation therefore suggest that mediators will be most successful if they work to reduce divergent expectations about the outcome of trial or to eliminate asymmetries of information between the parties.

Available empirical evidence on ADR has not been particularly encouraging. For example, a Rand study of six pilot programs established by the Civil Justice Reform Act of 1990 found that use of ADR in federal courts had no statistically significant effect on (1) the time to resolution of disputes, (2) the number of lawyer hours worked, and (3) the fairness of outcomes (as assessed by lawyers) (Kakalik et al. 1996). These results, while preliminary, cast doubt on the ability of ADR to deliver on its promised benefits.

4   Evolution of the Law

One of the most compelling, and controversial, propositions in the economic analysis of law is that the common law—that body of law arising. from judicial decisions—has an inherent economic logic. In earlier chapters, we have illustrated this logic in the areas of torts, contracts, and property, but we have largely neglected the question of how it may have emerged. Is it because judges and litigants have an explicit preference for overturning inefficient rules and enacting efficient ones, or is the mechanism more subtle (if it exists at all)? In this section we begin to explore this question by examining the nature of legal change in light of the economic model of dispute resolution.

Initially, we focus solely on how the behavior of litigants (plaintiffs and defendants) affects the evolution of the law while ignoring the role of judges. The key here is how litigants' filing and settlement decisions determine which disputes end up at trial, since only cases that reach trial can result in legal change. In Section 5 we examine the role of judges in shaping the law.

4.1   Selection of Disputes for Trial

We saw above that only about 5 percent of lawsuits ever end up at trial, yet nearly everything we know about the common law is based on information from trials and appellate review of trial decisions. It is therefore important to ask whether disputes that end in trial are representative of the overall population of disputes, or whether there is a systematic difference (a selection bias) between cases that settle and those that go to trial. The question is a theoretical one whose answer depends on the underlying model of litigation (Baird, Gertner, and Picker 1994, 260–61).

Priest and Klein (1984) provided the first answer in the context of the optimism model.[23] They argued that plaintiffs and defendants assess the outcome of a trial by estimating the "quality" of the plaintiff's case relative to the legal standard that will be applied by the court. For example, in a tort case each party estimates how likely it is that the defendant will be found negligent. Because the parties make errors in their estimates, however, they will generally arrive at different assessments of the probability of plaintiff victory, and if both sides are optimistic, then the case will go to trial. (See condition (8.3) above.)

Recall that optimism requires the plaintiff to assess a high probability of victory and the defendant to assess a low probability of plaintiff victory. In other words, the parties must have divergent assessments. Priest and Klein argue that this will be most likely when the case is a close one—that is, when the actual quality of the plaintiff's case is close to the legal standard—because such cases are more likely to result in errors. This implies that cases that go to trial will be systematically different from cases that settle. In particular, they will be cases where the plaintiff's win rate is about 50 percent.

The asymmetric information model generates a different prediction regarding the selection of cases for trial.[24] As we saw above, if the plaintiff has private information about her probability of victory, then an uninformed defendant will offer a settlement amount that plaintiffs with a low probability of victory will accept, and plaintiffs with a high probability of victory will reject. Thus, trials should produce a relatively high probability of plaintiff victory. However, if the information asymmetry is reversed so that the defendant has private information—for example, he may know whether he was negligent—then the opposite conclusion will be reached. That is, the plaintiff will make an offer that negligent defendants (those likely to lose at trial) will accept and nonnegligent defendants (those likely to win at trial) will reject. In this case, trials should result in a low probability of plaintiff victory. Since the particular information structure can vary from case to case, the asymmetric information model leads to the prediction that any probability of plaintiff victory at trial is possible (Shavell 1996).

In view of these conclusions, it is not surprising that existing empirical evidence on the nature of the selection bias has not been conclusive. Since few doubt the existence of some bias, however, ongoing research involves more refined theoretical predictions and better empirical methods for identifying the precise nature of the bias.

4.2   Is the Common Law Efficient?

Richard Posner first advanced the proposition that the common law has an underlying economic logic, but he did not propose a clear reason for why this should be the case. Absent evidence that judges consciously promote efficiency, economists have sought to provide "invisible hand" explanations along the lines of Adam Smith's argument for the efficiency of the marketplace. As noted above, however, changes in legal rules can only occur as a result of trials, so any such explanation must account for the settlement-trial decisions of litigants.

Rubin (1977) and Priest (1977) proposed the first invisible-hand explanations for the efficiency of the common law based solely on the selection of cases for trial. (Judges are passive in their models in the sense that they decide cases reaching trial without regard to efficiency.) To see how these models work, suppose that common-law rules (precedents) are either *efficient* or *inefficient*. For example, consider a bilateral care accident model in which care by either the injurer or the victim will entirely eliminate the risk of an accident (so-called alternative care accidents). It is therefore efficient for only one party—the one with the lower costs—to take care. Thus, strict liability is the efficient rule if the injurer has lower costs of care, and no liability is the efficient rule if the victim has lower costs of care. For purposes of illustration, suppose that the prevailing rule is no liability, but the efficient rule is strict liability.

In order for the law to become efficient, accident victims must file suit and at least some cases must go to trial so that judges have the opportunity to replace the existing inefficient rule with an efficient one. Although trials are rare, we have seen that they will occur if the parties have sufficient disagreement over the expected outcome of trial, whether that disagreement is due to differing perceptions or asymmetric information.[25] Further, given disagreement, both the optimism and asymmetric information models predict that cases with higher stakes (that is, higher values of J) will be more likely to go to trial. (See conditions (8.3) and (8.6).) As a result, Priest (1977, 67) reasons:

> For the set of all legal disputes, the stakes will be greater for disputes arising under inefficient rules than under efficient rules. Inefficient assignments of liability by definition impose greater costs on the parties subject to them than efficient assignments. . . . It follows, therefore, that other factors held equal, litigation will be more likely for disputes arising under inefficient rules than for those arising under efficient rules.

This selective litigation result, together with the assumption that judges do not systematically favor inefficient rules over efficient rules, turns out to be sufficient for the common law to evolve toward efficiency. We prove this claim as follows.

Suppose that at a given point in time, the law consists of two rules, one that is efficient and one that is inefficient. Litigation then takes place over some fixed time period. Let a be the probability that the efficient rule will be litigated, and let b be the probability that the inefficient rule will be litigated. Finally, assume that judges decide cases in a random manner. That is, the judge in a given case will uphold the prevailing rule with probability 1/2, and overturn it with probability 1/2, regardless of whether the rule is efficient.[26] The question is what the law will look like at the end of this litigation process, assuming that no new rules are created.

Let N denote the expected number of efficient rules following litigation. (The number of inefficient rules must therefore be $2 - N$.) Given the above assumptions, we can write the expression for N as

$$N = (1 - a) + \frac{a}{2} + \frac{b}{2}. \tag{8.27}$$

The three terms in this expression represent the three possible sources of efficient rules. The first, $1 - a$, is the probability that the efficient rule is not litigated and so remains in place; the second, $a/2$, is the probability that the efficient rule is litigated and upheld; the third, $b/2$, is the probability that the inefficient rule is litigated and overturned. The overall number of rules has not changed, but litigation has caused the number of efficient rules to increase if $N > 1$. Using (8.27), we find that this condition reduces to

$$b > a, \tag{8.28}$$

which is just the assumption that inefficient rules are more likely to be litigated than are efficient rules.

The preceding example shows that selective litigation and judicial indifference to efficiency are sufficient conditions for the law to evolve toward efficiency. Note that this conclusion is independent of the number of rules of each type that we started with, or the probability that judges will overturn or uphold existing rules. It is therefore a very general result. It nevertheless needs to be qualified in several ways (Posner 1998a, 614).

First, if the costs of inefficient rules are dispersed, then individuals bearing those costs may not have sufficient incentive to file suit in an effort to overturn the rule. Similarly, if the costs of efficient rules are concentrated or if cost-bearers are well organized, then they may make a concerted effort to change the rule. Together, these effects counteract the tendency for inefficient rules to be litigated more frequently than efficient rules. Second, if adherence to precedent is an important judicial value, then selective litigation of inefficient laws may actually cause these laws to become more entrenched (Landes and Posner 1979, 262).

Finally, the above model ignores the possibility that efforts by litigants at trial may influence a judge's decision. For example, suppose that the probability of plaintiff victory depends positively on the plaintiff's effort and negatively on the defendant's effort (Goodman 1978). If the parties choose their efforts to maximize their returns, then the party with the higher stake in the case will choose greater effort and thus increase his or her chances of winning a favorable judgment. The implication for the law as a whole is that it will tend to evolve toward rules that favor parties with more at stake. If the parties' interests reflect social interests, then this will reinforce the tendency of the law toward efficiency. However, if private and social interests diverge, this will not necessarily be the case. For example, if manufacturers of dangerous products are more organized than are consumer groups, they will argue more vigorously for limited producer liability. This will tend to work against efficiency if strict liability is the efficient rule.

4.3   Empirical Evidence on Legal Change

The preceding model of legal change relies solely on the behavior of litigants. In particular, it relies on the assertion that litigant disagreement leads to trials, which result in new rules. Disagreement therefore causes change, which, if the theory is correct, propels the law toward efficiency. But what causes disagreement? One possibility is uncertainty in the law resulting from legal change. Thus, the causal direction is reversed and change causes disagreement (and hence greater litigation).

Priest (1987) and Cooter (1987b) test these competing hypotheses and find a statistical correlation between legal change and the litigation rate, but the evidence does not allow them to determine the direction of causation. This is consistent with the likely case that legal change and increased litigation operate according to a feedback relationship. Specifically, legal change leads to uncertainty and increased litigation, which then provides input for further legal change.

5   Judicial Decision Making and Legal Change

To this point we have done our best to avoid explicit examination of the role of judges in shaping the law. We have done this partly because of the appeal to economists of invisible-hand arguments that do not rely on the conscious choices of individual litigants or judges, and partly because economists do not yet have a good understanding of how judges behave. This is an important gap in the economic theory of law, however, because of the undeniable importance of judges in the common-law system. In this section we discuss some recent efforts economists have made to advance their understanding of the nature and impact of judicial decision making.

Existing models of judges have taken two approaches. One is to examine decision by precedent—that is, the practice of deciding a case by applying the ruling from previous, similar cases—without explicitly asking why judges follow the practice. The next section examines economic models of this sort. The second approach is to view judges as acting like any other economic agent to maximize utility. The key question here is what a judge's utility function looks like. We discuss various possibilities, along with their implications for the law, below.

5.1   Decision by Precedent

The body of common-law rules has largely arisen through the judicial practice of *stare decisis*, or decision by precedent. This means that judges reason by analogy to past cases rather than reexamining the issues of a particular type of case each time it comes before them. The obvious advantage of this strategy is that it economizes on decision costs; the disadvantage is that it may lead to errors if a given precedent is wrongly applied or if circumstances have changed since the last time this type of case arose. Decision by precedent and other "shortcuts," like rules of thumb or tossing a coin, reflect people's conscious efforts to respond to the limits of fully rational decision making. They do this by employing so-called second-order decisions—that is, "decisions about the appropriate strategies for reducing the problems associated with making a first-order decision" (Sunstein and Ullmann-Marglit 2000, 187). The following theory of precedent is based on this approach to decisionmaking.[27]

5.1.1   An Economic Model of Precedent

In a world of perfect information, judges would have unlimited discretion to decide each case based on its individual merits. In the real world, however, discretion can lead to high decision costs and, if judges are prone to errors, bad rules. Decision by precedent limits the costs associated with discretion, but may overly constrain the decision maker when the environment is changing rapidly and newly fashioned rules are desirable. The optimal choice between rules (precedent) and discretion minimizes the sum of the decision and error costs.

To illustrate, consider the choice between a *fully flexible* regime in which judges are free to choose the "best" rule to fit the circumstances of the case at hand, and an *inflexible* regime in which they must follow precedent. To keep things simple, suppose that the existing rule (or precedent), R, was efficient in the past, but there is some probability that the environment has changed, making a new rule, N, more efficient in the case at hand. To continue the example from above, suppose that the existing rule is no liability for producers of dangerous products, reflecting the fact that in the past, consumers could avoid accidents at lower cost. The increasing sophistication of products over time, however, may have made it cheaper to shift to strict producer liability.

In this setting, perfect judges will impose the new rule when the environment has changed, and retain the old rule when it has not. Judges who cannot perfectly determine when the environment has changed, however, may commit two types of errors: they may retain the old rule when the new one has become efficient (a type I error), and they may impose the new rule when the old one is still efficient (a type II error). Figure 8.8 shows the four possible outcomes along with their probabilities.

Figure 8.8

Outcomes Under a Fully Flexible Decision-Making Regime

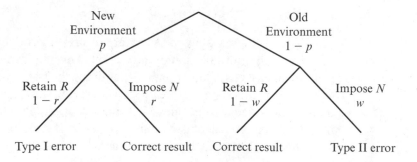

Figure 8.9

Outcomes Under
Decision by Precedent

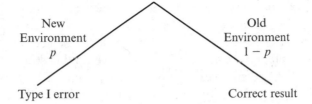

Suppose that p is the probability that the environment has changed, and $1 - p$ is the probability that it has remained the same. Also, let r be the conditional probability that a judge will correctly respond to a change in the environment by imposing the new rule N. Thus, $1 - r$ is the probability that he will incorrectly retain the old rule in this situation (a type I error). Similarly, let w be the probability that the judge will impose the new rule when the environment has not changed (a type II error). Thus, $1 - w$ is the probability that he will correctly retain the old rule in this situation.

Finally, let C_I and C_{II} be the social costs of type I and type II errors. In the context of the products liability example, C_I represents the excess of accident costs over the minimized level when consumers are inefficiently induced to take precaution, and C_{II} is the excess of accident costs over the minimized level when producers are inefficiently induced to take precaution. Combining these costs with the above probabilities yields the expected social cost associated with the fully flexible regime:

$$EC_F = p(1 - r)C_I + (1 - p)wC_{II}. \tag{8.29}$$

Now consider a regime in which judges are required to follow precedent. In this case, only two outcomes are possible: correct retention of R when the environment is the same, and incorrect retention of R when the environment has changed (a type I error). Figure 8.9 shows these outcomes. The expected social costs associated with this decision-making regime are

$$EC_P = pC_I. \tag{8.30}$$

Note that the probabilities of the two types of errors (r and w) are irrelevant here because the judge has no discretion over the rule. Only type I errors are possible for the same reason.

Decision by precedent results in lower expected error costs if $EC_P < EC_F$, or if

$$\frac{r}{w} < \frac{1 - p}{p} \ \cdots \ \frac{C_{II}}{C_I}. \tag{8.31}$$

According to this condition, the desirability of decision by precedent depends on three ratios. The first, r/w, reflects the *reliability* of a judge's ability to respond to environmental change. Precedent becomes more desirable as this ratio decreases because a judge is less likely to be able to enact the new rule only when the environment has changed. The second ratio, $(1 - p)/p$, reflects the *stability* of the environment. An increase in this ratio (that is, a decrease in p) favors precedent because the environment is less likely to change, resulting in a lower expected cost of retaining the old rule. Finally, precedent is less costly as the cost of type II errors increases relative to that of type I errors since precedent eliminates the possibility of type II errors.

EXERCISE 8.4

(a) Show that decision by precedent is never optimal when judges are perfectly reliable.
(b) Suppose that a rapidly changing environment has the simultaneous effect of reducing the reliability of judicial decision making. (That is, the ratios $(1 - p)/p$ and r/w are related.) Show that these combined effects have an ambiguous impact on the desirability of decision by precedent.

5.1.2   Precedents as a Stock of Knowledge

The preceding analysis viewed decision by precedent as an efficient response to imperfect decision making by judges. Another argument often made in favor of precedent is that it promotes *predictability* of the law. As Posner notes, the accumulation of precedents on a particular legal problem often acquires the force of a statute. When this happens, the body of precedents serves as "a stock of knowledge that yields services over many years to potential disputants in the form of information about legal obligations."[28]

We argued above, however, that the suitability of a particular precedent depreciates over time as the environment changes.[29] Rules that were once efficient eventually become inefficient. This in itself need not lead to less efficient behavior, however. Indeed, some have argued that stability of the common law is at least as important as its content because stability facilitates Coasian bargaining, which can lead to efficiency regardless of the prevailing legal rule (Rizzo 1987).

In most areas of the law, however, the content matters because transaction costs preclude bargaining around inefficient rules. Fortunately, the above models of the litigation process suggest that the law has restorative powers. As a precedent becomes less efficient (that is, as its informational value depreciates), parties will not be induced to minimize costs, so the litigation rate will increase because legal disputes will involve higher stakes. The result will be an increased production of legal precedents, which replenishes the stock of knowledge.

5.2   Procedural Responses to Legal Errors*

At this point, we digress a bit to examine procedural responses, other than limits on judicial discretion, to the problem of legal error. We examine two responses in this section: the standard of proof, and the appeals process.

5.2.1   The Standard of Proof

A trial represents a procedure for making a decision under uncertainty. In the adversarial system, two sides to a dispute present their best cases before the court, which then renders a decision in favor of one side or the other. The correct decision will rarely be clear-cut, however, for otherwise the parties would have settled before reaching trial. The best the court will be able to do is to assess a *probability* that each side's version of the facts is true. The standard of proof establishes a threshold that allows the court to translate this assessment into a decision.

To illustrate, suppose that the plaintiff in a tort case claims that the defendant was negligent, while the defendant claims he was not. After hearing the evidence from both sides, the court's assessment is that the defendant was in fact negligent with probability p. The court will therefore find the defendant negligent if p exceeds the legal standard of proof, In civil cases, the standard of proof is *preponderance of the evidence*, which means the court must believe that the plaintiff's claim is more probably true than the defendant's claim. That is, $\bar{p} = .5$.

How is this standard determined? From an economic perspective, it is set to minimize the expected cost of type I and type II errors.[30] In the negligence example, we define a type I error as a false finding of nonnegligence (a false acquittal), and a type II error as a false finding of negligence (a false conviction). Note that an increase in the standard of proof will increase the number of type I errors and reduce the number of type II errors. This is because a higher standard of proof will result in fewer convictions. Thus some negligent defendants who were correctly convicted under the lower standard are now acquitted. Similarly, some nonnegligent defendants who were incorrectly convicted under the lower standard are now acquitted. A reduction in the standard will have the reverse effect. The only way both types of errors can be simultaneously reduced is by gathering more evidence, which is costly, or by developing improved detection technologies, like DNA tests.

A preponderance of the evidence standard, because it sets $\bar{p}$ at .5, will result in roughly equal numbers of the two types of errors in civil cases. This implies that the costs of the two errors are comparable. (Otherwise, total costs could be lowered by adjusting the standard to reduce the frequency of the costlier error.) This seems to be a reasonable assumption given that civil cases ordinarily involve disputes over money, and there is no reason to believe that plaintiffs or defendants systematically place a higher value on a given dollar loss.[31]

The conclusion that the two types of errors impose roughly equal costs is probably *not* reasonable for criminal cases. False convictions (type II errors) almost certainly impose higher costs than false acquittals. This is true because criminal conviction often involves imprisonment, and even when it does not, there is a stigma attached to it that is not associated with liability in a civil case. For these reasons, the standard of proof in criminal cases is much higher—conviction requires proof beyond a reasonable doubt.

The high standard of proof for criminal cases does not necessarily imply, however, that guilty defendants frequently escape punishment. Criminal prosecutors, who represent the state, have vastly more resources to invest in seeking a conviction than do ordinary plaintiffs in civil cases. Thus, with some notable exceptions, the deck is heavily stacked against criminal defendants, so a large fraction end up pleading guilty, despite the high standard of proof.[32]

5.2.2   Appeals as a Means of Error Correction

The losing party in a lawsuit always has the option to appeal the decision to a higher court. The economic theory of appeals courts is that they serve to correct errors made by lower courts (Shavell 1995b). In this context, we ask two questions. First, is it always optimal to allow appeals as a means of error correction, given that this adds an extra layer of administrative costs? And second, why should litigants have the right to initiate appeals rather than letting the appeals court pick and choose the cases it wants to reexamine?[33]

To answer this question, consider a simple two-tiered court system in which cases are first adjudicated in a trial court, and losing litigants then have the option to bring an appeal, though doing so is costly. Assume that litigants can observe whether the trial court's decision was in error. This is crucial (and reasonable if litigants have private information that is difficult to verify) because it results in a filtering, or *separation*, of litigants at the appeals level. Specifically, litigants whose cases were decided in error are more likely to incur the costs of an appeal because they have a greater chance of winning. This separation is socially desirable because it limits the work of the appeals court to cases that are more likely to have been incorrectly decided. If the court were to decide which cases to hear, it would be less effective in achieving this separation because it lacks information that is available to litigants.

The preceding argument implies that appeals courts disproportionately hear cases that involve error. In the absence of appeals, those errors would not be corrected. Thus, appeals are socially desirable as a means of error correction if the gain from the possibility of reversal exceeds the additional cost of litigation. To illustrate, consider the following example (Shavell 1995b, 386). Suppose the cost of a legal error, if uncorrected, is $500,000, the cost of an appeal is $150,000, and the probability that the appeals court will reverse the error is 80 percent. The expected gain from the appeal is therefore $400,000 = (.8)($500,000), which exceeds the litigation costs of $150,000. Thus, the appeals process is efficient.

In addition to error correction, appeals courts serve a lawmaking function by enabling "uniform rules of law to be created and maintained" (Posner 1998a, 643). As noted above, there are external benefits associated with this function that arise from the information that appellate decisions convey to future disputants. (In this sense, decisions announced by appeals courts are like public goods.) Thus, one might suppose that litigants will bring too few appeals because they do not internalize the full benefits of error correction. But an offsetting effect is that as legal rules become less efficient, the litigation rate will increase, thus creating more opportunities for courts to correct errors.

5.3   What Do Judges Maximize?

We now turn to the question of what motivates judges in cases where they are not bound by precedent. The obvious starting point is to suppose that judges, like any other economic agents, maximize utility. But this just begs the question of what elements should be included in the judge's utility function. The problem is complicated by the fact that judges for the most part have secure tenure, and their income is not tied to their performance. (Even if it were, judicial performance is difficult to evaluate, which is also why election of judges, though sometimes employed, is not an effective way to achieve accountability.) All of this has led Richard Posner, a law and economics scholar and federal judge, to conclude, "It is the unique insulation of federal appellate judges from accountability that makes their behavior such a challenge to the economic analysis of law" (1995, 112).

Careful selection of judges is one way to ensure a minimum level of judicial quality, but it cannot assure that judges will work hard later.[34] Also, the political nature of the screening process often overwhelms considerations of judicial ability. So what can we say about the factors that actually affect a judge's decisions?

Some authors have suggested that reputation plays an important role in influencing judges' behavior.[35] In particular, they argue that judges derive utility from deciding cases in ways consistent with their personal preferences and from having future judges follow their decisions. At the same time, they receive disutility from having their decisions reversed. The practice of precedent plays an important dual role in this theory, both as the mechanism by which a judge's decision is perpetuated by other judges, and as protection against reversal. Thus, judges interested in establishing a reputation, as well as those seeking to avoid reversal (which may be the same judge at different times), will value the practice of precedent.

This theory implies that judges will be more inclined to depart from precedent (be "activist") as their disutility from following a precedent that they disagree with increases, as their aversion to reversal decreases, and as the probability that future judges will overturn them decreases. The latter result suggests that even judges who care little about being reversed will value precedent because, as Posner (1995, 121) notes, "by refusing to follow their predecessors' decisions and thus weakening the practice of decision according to precedent, they reduce the likelihood that their successors will follow their decisions." Even activist judges will therefore likely be sparing in their departures from precedent.

Empirical evidence on judicial self-interest is mixed. Higgins and Rubin (1980) found little evidence that the threat of reversal is an important constraint on judicial discretion, while Mark Cohen (1991) found that the desire for promotion is a significant factor. Clearly, further work is needed before we can definitively answer the question of what judges maximize.

5.3.1   Judicial Self-Interest and the Law

Is there any link between theories of judicial self-interest and the nature of the law? This is an important question about which economists until recently have had very little to say. Of particular interest is whether self-interested judges systematically affect the direction of legal change.

One possibility is that judges actively promote efficiency. For example, Posner (1995, 132) notes:

> Efficiency—not necessarily by that name—is an important social value and hence one internalized by most judges, and it may be the only social value that judges can promote effectively, given their limited remedial powers and the value of pluralism of our society. So it should be influential in judicial decision-making when judges are called upon to exercise the legislative function. The decision of a really new case establishes a precedent to guide future cases, and the rules of the judicial game require judges to follow precedent . . . rather than to decide each future case from the ground up. The subsequent cases may bear no visible imprint of economic thinking, yet they will be efficient decisions if the precedents that influence them . . . were based implicitly or explicitly on a desire

to enhance efficiency. Law can thus be efficient even if only a small minority of cases concern themselves with efficiency.

Another possibility, the one assumed in the invisible-hand arguments above, is that judicial self-interest is not inconsistent with efficiency. This will be true, for example, if judicial values like fairness and justice are equally likely to coincide with efficient and inefficient decisions. (In fact, Posner [1998a, 30] argues that one meaning of justice is efficiency.)

More realistically, however, judges, if unconstrained, will impart their own biases to the law. This will tend to have two detrimental effects. First, it will likely cause the law to veer systematically away from efficiency, and second, it will create instability in the law as judges with divergent preferences continue to overrule one another (Gennaioli and Shleifer 2007a,b). Two mitigating factors are precedent and selective litigation. Precedent acts as a stabilizing force, but it can only affect the *rate* of legal change, not its *direction*. Selective litigation, as we have seen, does help propel the law toward efficiency by disproportionately bringing inefficient laws before the court, but if the bias of judges is strong enough, it can overwhelm this effect.

Judicial activism is therefore a double-edged sword: while it allows judges to respond to changing circumstances by replacing inefficient precedents, it also permits them to impose their own biases on the law. The inescapable conclusion is that the direction of legal change will depend, at least in part, on the nature of judicial preferences.

5.3.2 The Optimal Level of Judicial Independence

The preceding discussion raises the normative question of how much independence judges should have. The advantage of an independent judiciary is that it insulates judges from political influence by other branches of government and lobbyists, but the disadvantage, as noted, is that it allows judges to impose their own biases on the law. This logic suggests that there is an optimal degree of judicial independence (Hansen 2004).

States vary in their degree of judicial independence as reflected by the ease with which judges can be replaced. For example, in some states judges are required to stand for re-election, in others they are appointed (and hence re-appointed) by the governor or legislature, and in still others they are subject only to "retention elections"—that is, they run unopposed and are either retained or removed. Hansen (2004) rates these methods as reflecting, respectively, an increasing degree of judicial independence. Using state-level data from 1950–1990 he shows that a more independent judiciary is associated with closer competition between political parties and greater differences in party platforms—in short, with a more competitive political climate. This makes sense since, in an uncertain political environment, legislatures would not want to allow the party in power to be able to exert undue influence on judges.

Berkowitz and Clay (2006) show that historical factors also affect the variation in judicial independence across states. Specifically, states that were settled by civil law countries (France, Spain, and Mexico), and states that were formerly in the Confederacy, tend to exhibit less independence of the judiciary. Further, the authors show that lesser independence translates into lower-quality courts (as measured by attorney ratings of court performance). This finding suggests that states with poorly performing courts might benefit from switching to less partisan methods for retaining judges.

5.3.3   Pragmatism and the Economic Approach to Law

We conclude this discussion of judicial decision making with a few words about legal philosophy. Law and economics is a relatively recent school of legal thought—one of many taught in law schools today—but it is closely related to an older school called *pragmatism*. Indeed, the most prominent contemporary adherent of pragmatism is Richard Posner, who is also one of the founders of the current law and economics movement. Posner (1995, 4) defines pragmatism as

> an approach that is practical and instrumental rather than essentialist—interested in what works and what is useful rather than what "really" is. It is therefore *forward looking*, valuing continuity with the past only so far as such continuity can help us cope with the problems of the present and of the future.

Pragmatists therefore do not relentlessly cling to past precedent (so-called black-letter law) when a better solution is at hand (though, as we have seen, following precedent can itself be a useful practice when judges are not good at finding better solutions). Nor do they look to logic as the proper basis for legal development, as though legal rules can be fashioned on the basis of an ideal case, in isolation from considerations of the specific aspects of the case at hand. Clearly, pragmatism and economics have much in common. More than one hundred years ago, Oliver Wendell Holmes, the most famous American judge and a pragmatist, examined logic and history as guides for legal reasoning. In dismissing both, he said:

> I look forward to a time when the part played by history in the explanation of dogma shall be very small, and instead of ingenious research we shall spend our energy on a study of the ends sought to be attained and the reasons for desiring them. As a step toward that ideal it seems to me that every lawyer ought to seek an understanding of economics. (1897, 474)

By now, the reader has hopefully been convinced that modern law and economics supplies the methodology by which Holmes's wish can be fulfilled, and that it has gone a long way toward doing so.

But Holmes's conception of the law went beyond this normative view of the role that economics *should* play in its development. In his classic treatise on the common law, he averred that there is an underlying tendency for functional rules to arise, despite the drag of history, by the continual reshaping of old precedents to fit current needs.[36] As an example, he argued that ancient forms of liability sprang from a primitive desire for vengeance (a point that we pursue in the next chapter), but they nevertheless continue to serve a purpose in modern society as a means of compensating victims and holding injurers responsible for their actions. This view, of course, is reminiscent of the theory that the law evolves toward efficiency without conscious direction.

6   Conclusion

Economic analysis of the litigation process is important for several reasons. First, by allowing us to understand the process by which parties resolve their disputes, it can suggest ways of lowering the cost of operating the legal system, an important policy goal. Toward this end, economists have developed sophisticated models of dispute resolution using the tools of game theory. Second, these models show that the set of cases that end up at trial is not a representative sample of the population of all legal disputes. Thus, researchers conducting empirical analysis of trial data must take account of this selection bias if they wish to draw inferences about the set of all disputes. Finally, litigation models tell us how the common law evolves according to the self-interested actions of litigants. The study of this evolutionary process has significant implications for the positive economic theory of law.

For the most part, economic models of litigation abstract from the role of judges in shaping the path of the law, both to maintain the notion of an invisible-hand process, and because good models of self-interested judges are lacking. There is, however, a growing literature on judicial decision making that has begun to shed some light on this question.

DISCUSSION QUESTIONS

1. Discovery rules compel litigants to disclose private information prior to trial. Can you explain why litigants may reveal information voluntarily, even when it is unfavorable to them, in the absence of compulsory disclosure?

2. A procedural means of lowering the cost of litigation is to "bifurcate" (separate) the issues of liability and damages into separate trials. This allows society to save the cost of a trial in cases where the defendant wins. Suggest why this may have the unwanted effect of increasing the litigation rate.

3. Suits that have no legal merit differ from those that have some merit but where the victim's damages are less than the cost of litigation. (The latter are sometimes referred to as negative expected value suits.) Given the existence of such suits, explain why class actions that bundle small meritorious cases serve an important economic function.

4. Describe the conditions that must be satisfied in order for the common law to evolve toward efficiency without the conscious help of judges or litigants. What factors work against this process?

5. If settlement is always cheaper than trial as a means of resolving disputes, why isn't it socially desirable for all cases to settle?

6. What does it mean to say that judges decide cases by precedent? Describe the costs and benefits of this method of judicial decision making.

7. Consider an individual accused of an assault. Suppose that, given the evidence against him, he is found innocent in a criminal trial. Does this necessarily imply that the victim of the assault has no chance of winning a tort suit for compensatory damages based on the same evidence? Explain.

8. How do you think the difference in the way judges and legislators are selected (judges are infrequently, if ever, subject to reelection) affects the way they fashion legal rules?

PROBLEMS

1. Suppose a plaintiff and defendant estimate the same probability of plaintiff victory at trial, P, but disagree about the amount that a victorious plaintiff will recover. The plaintiff estimates this amount to be J_p while the defendant estimates it to be J_d. Derive the conditions for settlement and trial. What must be true of J_p and J_d for a trial to occur?

2. Suppose settlement is costly. Specifically, let S_p and S_d be the costs of settlement for the plaintiff and defendant.

   (a) Derive the trial condition.
   (b) Suppose the plaintiff and defendant agree on both the probability of plaintiff victory and the expected recovery at trial. What is the trial condition in this case?

3. In the text we showed that if the plaintiff controls the settlement decision, a contingent fee results in a higher trial rate compared to a combined plaintiff-

lawyer (see Section 3.4.2, above). We assumed there, however, that the contingency rate, b, was the same whether the case settled or went to trial. Suppose instead that the rates differ. Specifically, let b_s be the rate for cases that settle, and b_t the rate for cases that go to trial.

(a) Write down the plaintiff's settlement condition.

  The lawyer's return from a case that settles is $b_s S - R$, where R is his pretrial cost, and his expected return from a case that goes to trial is $P_p b_t J - R - C_p$.

(b) Derive the values of b_s and b_t that result in zero expected profit for both types of cases.

(c) Use these values of b_s and b_t to show that the plaintiff's settlement condition under this "variable contingency contract" is identical to that of a combined plaintiff-lawyer.

4. Defendants who are frequent targets of lawsuits (repeat defendants) often hire full-time ("in-house") lawyers rather than hiring lawyers on an hourly basis as cases arise. The effect of a full-time lawyer is to lower the defendant's variable cost of taking a case to trial since the lawyer must be paid even if the case settles. In terms of the settlement model in the text, this implies that $C_d^f < C_d^h$, where C_d^f is the defendant's cost of trial with a full-time lawyer, and C_d^h is the corresponding cost with an hourly lawyer.

(a) Use the optimism model of settlement and trial to show that a defendant's use of a full-time lawyer makes settlement *less likely* (all else equal). Explain this result intuitively.

(b) Show that when settlement does occur, the equilibrium settlement amount will be lower with a full-time lawyer (assuming that the parties split the surplus from settlement evenly as in (8.10)).

5. Many states have enacted damage caps for tort suits, which have the effect of lowering the average stakes for such cases. What will be the likely effect of these caps on the settlement rate of tort suits?

6. An area of the law that is changing will tend to create greater uncertainty among litigants about the likely outcome of a trial. At the same time, it will increase the expected costs of trial. Describe the resulting effects on the settlement rate.

CHAPTER 9

THE ECONOMICS OF CRIME

Crime imposes a high cost on society, in terms of both the harm done to persons and property and the costs of preventing crime and punishing offenders. Anderson (1999) estimates the annual cost at more than $1 trillion, or over $4,000 per capita. It should therefore not be surprising that economists have much to say about the allocation of resources to law enforcement. It may surprise some, however, that economists have also developed models of criminal behavior, focusing specifically on how individual offenders respond to threatened punishments. Of course, these two efforts are linked, since one objective of criminal penalties (the primary one from an economic perspective) is to achieve an optimal level of deterrence.

Underlying the notion of deterrence is an implicit assumption that at least some criminals are rational calculators who decide whether to commit a crime just as they would make any other economic decision—by comparing the expected costs and benefits. Of course, some crimes are undoubtedly irrational—for example, crimes of passion or those committed by the mentally impaired—but so long as some criminals are rational, then the aggregate crime rate will be responsive to changes in the expected penalty, and it will make sense to talk about a goal of "optimal deterrence."

Since the pioneering work of Gary Becker (1968), the economics of crime has become a major field in law and economics. The purpose of this chapter is to provide an introduction to the field. We begin by asking why there is a separate category of harms called crimes that are treated differently from accidental harms. We propose several possible reasons but conclude that economics alone probably cannot provide a definitive answer. The remainder of the chapter reviews the economic model of crime as it has developed since

Becker. Topics include the choice between fines and imprisonment, the death penalty (does it deter crime?), plea bargaining, and the ongoing controversy over the link between guns and crime. We also examine primitive law enforcement institutions, as well as some constitutional issues such as free speech, the rule against self-incrimination, and privacy. Although these topics are far from exhaustive, they will give the reader a sense of the insights that economic theory can provide into the structure of the criminal justice system.

1   Distinguishing Crimes and Torts

Crimes and torts are both unlawful harms to persons or property, yet criminal law is structured very differently from tort law. Under tort law, victims must initiate legal action for recovery of monetary damages (private enforcement), whereas under criminal law, the state prosecutes offenders and often imprisons those convicted of serious crimes (public enforcement). Why does this difference exist? The remainder of this section proposes several possible explanations.

1.1   Crimes Are Intentional

The law imposes on members of society an obligation to refrain from inflicting harm on other individuals, backed by the threat of legal sanction. In the case of accidental harm, the sanction is generally limited to liability for compensatory damages, and only then if the injurer is at fault under negligence law. In order to be held criminally responsible, an injurer must also have acted with an intent to harm. That is, a criminal must have a mens rea, or a "guilty mind." This suggests that the law attaches greater gravity to harms that are *intentionally* caused, and thus wishes to call them by a different name (crimes) and impose a different sort of punishment.

But intent is merely one extreme on a continuum that includes negligence (inadvertant failure to take care) at its other extreme and recklessness (conscious disregard for risk) somewhere in between (Hart 1982, 137). The difference depends on the mental state of the injurer, which is unobservable to the court and hence not a good basis for making legal distinctions.[1] Besides, our analysis of intentional torts in Chapter 3 suggests that intent per se does not prevent tort law from internalizing the cost of intentional harms. It seems that we must look elsewhere for an economic basis of public enforcement.

1.2   Other Reasons for Public Enforcement

Several other reasons have been proposed for public prosecution of criminals, though most turn out to be related, directly or indirectly, to the presence of intent (D. Friedman 2000, ch. 18). First, if an injurer intentionally inflicts harm, he or she will generally take steps to cover up the act in order to evade responsibility. This could make it quite difficult for victims with limited resources to identify and bring suit against offenders. Public enforcement overcomes this problem by enlisting the resources of the state to apprehend the injurer and by appointing a public prosecutor to act as an agent of victims. There seems no reason, however, why this problem could not be solved by the market, for example by making damage claims transferable to private agents who would specialize in prosecution. Another solution to the problem of imperfect detection, suggested by our discussion of punitive damages in Chapter 3, is simply to inflate compensatory damages to reflect the probability of evasion, though recall that this has the offsetting effect of increasing litigation costs.[2]

A different argument for public enforcement, also based on the problem of imperfect detection, is that there are scale economies associated with the detection and apprehension of offenders. These scale economies arise from the high fixed costs associated with the establishment of a police force, which means that over some range, average costs are decreasing with the scale of operation. Thus, as in the case of a natural monopoly, it is efficient to allow a single provider of enforcement services within a given jurisdiction. It would be necessary to regulate the provider, however, to avoid the distortion due to monopoly. Thus, one solution is simply to organize the enforcement authority as a public enterprise, which is what we in fact observe.

A third argument for public prosecution of criminals is that acts we classify as crimes often impose "public harm" in addition to the harm suffered directly by victims. This public harm includes the fear of potential victims, but also the costs arising from "widespread social outrage and moral opprobrium" associated with certain acts (Adelstein 1979b, 239). An extreme example is the so-called victimless crime (like prostitution), the social costs of which are entirely of this public sort.

The problem that public harm creates for a system of private enforcement is that individual victims may have an inadequate incentive to pursue and prosecute offenders. The reason is that the dispersed nature of the harm may not make it worthwhile for any one victim to incur the necessary cost. Recall that we made a similar argument for the use of government regulation as a substitute for private legal action as a way of restricting certain risky activities.[3] The analog here is government (public) prosecution of offenders whose actions impose substantial public harm.

A final problem with private enforcement, also related to detection costs, was pointed out by Landes and Posner (1975). Consider a system in which the state sets fines for various offenses and delegates enforcement to private firms. The first firm to apprehend an offender and demonstrate his guilt would then be entitled to retain the fine revenue. In other words, enforcement would be based on a sort of competitive bounty system (Becker and Stigler 1974). Would this system achieve the efficient level of enforcement? Landes and Posner argued that it would not.

To understand their argument, note that optimal deterrence of crime is achieved by appropriately setting the *expected fine*, given by the product pf, where p is the probability of apprehension and f is the actual fine on conviction. (See the discussion of optimal punishment schemes below.) The problem with the bounty system is that once f is set by the state, p is determined by competition among private enforcers, which will not generally produce the correct value.[4] Only public control of both the fine and the enforcement level will guarantee that the optimal combination is achieved.

1.3   Examples of Private Enforcement

Despite the above arguments in favor of public prosecution of certain injurers, there are historical examples of societies that have relied, in whole or in part, on private enforcement of criminal law. (In addition, private enforcement efforts continue to be used as a supplement to public enforcement, as discussed in Section 2.9 below.) The examples help illustrate some of the advantages of public enforcement but also that other solutions are possible.

The first example we consider is tenth-century Iceland, which instituted a purely private system of law enforcement.[5] In this society, if an individual committed a criminal offense, it was the victim's responsibility to file suit for damages. The accused party had no obligation to show up and defend himself, and there was no police force to compel him to do so. However, if he was convicted and failed to pay the fine, the victim could go to court again and have him declared an outlaw, in which case anyone could kill him with impunity.

Above, we pointed out several potential problems with private enforcement that public enforcement solves, but the Icelandic system also had responses to these problems. For example, victims incapable of bringing suit could transfer their claims to those better able to prosecute them, and defendants who could not afford to pay the court's judgment could face temporary servitude as a way of paying off the debt. Finally, the detection problem was dealt with by making concealment itself a criminal offense.

The Icelandic system survived for more than three centuries, suggesting that public enforcement is not the only workable approach to criminal law. Its ultimate demise was due to increasing violence, which perhaps is the inevitable result of a system based purely on private enforcement.

The second example of private enforcement is England in the early eighteenth century, which had criminal law as we know it, but no police or public prosecutors to enforce it. Instead, private citizens (usually, but not exclusively, the victim) were responsible for prosecuting crimes. This suggests that there must have been a serious underenforcement problem because, unlike a purely private system, the victim-plaintiff could not collect damages. So why would he bother to prosecute?

David Friedman (2000, 267–68) suggests three possible reasons. First, the defendant was often willing to settle out of court to avoid a worse penalty. Second, victims susceptible to repeat offenses (like business owners) benefited from establishing a reputation for prosecuting offenders. Finally, people formed "prosecution societies" that would pool their resources and pursue anyone who committed an offense against a member. These societies performed a function similar to that of modern police forces in that they exploited scale economies in enforcement (as noted above), though one advantage of the public version is that it could be organized at the efficient scale.

1.4   Property Rules, Liability Rules, and Criminal Sanctions

We conclude this discussion with an explanation for a separate criminal category that is based, not on technological differences between public and private enforcement, but on the function of criminal sanctions in maintaining an efficient transaction structure.[6] Recall from Section 2.4 of Chapter 6 that the transaction structure is the legal framework that is jointly concerned with the *assignment* of rights and the rules for *protecting* those rights. The two rules we focused on were property rules and liability rules. Under property-rule protection, recall, a right-holder can refuse any unacceptable offer to acquire the right, whereas under a liability rule, he or she cannot refuse an offer so long as the acquirer is willing to pay an amount of compensation set by the court.

To see what all this has to do with criminal law, consider a thief who steals someone else's property. When the thief is caught, why not simply make him pay the cost of the item stolen as a fine? If he values the item more than the owner, he will gladly pay the fine, but if not, he will return it. In this way, the item properly ends up with the party who values it most, as in a competitive market. An obvious problem with the market analogy, however, is that detection of the thief is not certain. But, as we noted above, this can be dealt with by simply inflating the fine to reflect the likelihood of apprehension. Assuming that this probability can be measured accurately, the resulting expected fine will induce potential thieves to commit only "efficient thefts."

The real problem with this argument, however, is that it permits individuals to violate the transaction structure. In particular, it allows individuals to *convert property rules into liability rules* by allowing them to take another's property and pay compensation afterward. The reason this is not desirable is that when transaction costs are low, market exchange under property rules is the preferred method for arranging transactions because it guarantees a mutual benefit. In contrast, forced exchange under liability rules can result in inefficient transfers if compensation is set too low.

If this argument makes sense in the case of theft of property, then it is all the more persuasive when bodily injury is involved. Indeed, our discussion of inalienability rules in Chapter 6 (Section 2.2.4) revealed that we are reluctant to contemplate the sale of one's "bodily integrity," or other fundamental rights (like freedom of speech or religion), under any circumstances and so wish to deter such transactions altogether (Calabresi and Melamed 1972). The role of criminal law in this context is to add a penalty on top of compensatory damages (a "kicker") as a way of discouraging these unwanted violations of property and inalienability rules (specifically, their transformation into liability rules). The penalty may take the form of an additional fine or imprisonment—in either case it is a form of punishment for an *illegitimate* transaction, as opposed to compensation under a liability rule, which is ex post payment for a *legitimate* transaction (Cooter 1984).

The preceding argument is very attractive to those who seek a unified economic approach to law because it plausibly explains criminal law within the same framework that we used in Chapter 6 to link the civil law areas of torts, contracts, and property. At its base is a coherent view of the role of the legal system in facilitating economic exchange by channeling transactions through the market when that is feasible and by providing an alternative transaction structure when it is not. At the same time, this argument will (understandably) be unpersuasive to many (and offensive to a few) because it views criminal punishment as nothing more than a system of prices, thereby trivializing the moral content of the law. As Coleman (1988, 165) notes, "A purely economic theory of crime can only impoverish, not enrich, our understanding of the nature of crime." Most economists would probably agree.

2   The Economic Model of Crime

Although eighteenth-century writers like Cesare Beccaria and Jeremy Bentham discussed economic theories of law enforcement, the first sophisticated economic analysis did not appear until Gary Becker published his classic article in 1968. Since then, there has been a tremendous amount of scholarship expanding on Becker's basic insights.[7]

The basic economic model of crime is developed in two stages. The first concerns the decision of individual offenders to commit a crime. In making this decision, offenders compare the gain from committing the act to the expected punishment, which they take as given. Aggregating across all offenders yields the "supply of offenses" function, which policymakers then use in the second stage to determine the socially optimal punishment scheme. In the standard economic model, this involves choosing the probability of apprehension and the punishment on conviction (a fine and/or imprisonment) to maximize a social welfare function that depends on (1) the cost of apprehension, (2) the benefit of the crime to the offender less the cost to victims, and (3) in the case of prison, the cost of punishment. In the following sections we develop this model formally and then consider extensions.

2.1   The Offender's Decision to Commit a Crime and the Supply of Offenses

Economists do not claim that all criminals act as rational, cost-benefit calculators, but the notion of deterrence requires that at least some do. The assumption certainly seems plausible for so-called white-collar crimes like insider trading or embezzlement, whose primary objective is monetary gain, but less so for violent crimes like rape and murder that are often driven by emotion or mental illness. Obviously, economics has nothing to say about the decision making of these latter individuals, so our analysis focuses on the former.

Suppose that an individual contemplates committing an illegal act that will yield a gain of g dollars. (The gain need not be explicitly monetary, but we assume that individuals can assign a monetary value to utility gains.) The cost of committing the act is the expected punishment, which equals the probability of apprehension, p, times the actual punishment, which may consist of a fine, f, a term of imprisonment, t, or both.[8] If c is the dollar cost of prison to the offender per unit of time, then the expected punishment is $p(f + ct)$. (Of course, $t = 0$ if punishment is only a fine, and $f = 0$ if it is only prison.) The offender will commit the act if the gain exceeds the expected cost, or if

$$g > p(f + ct). \tag{9.1}$$

Now suppose that potential offenders vary in the gain that they would receive from the contemplated act. In particular, suppose that g varies across the population of offenders, ranging from zero up to a maximum of $\overline{g}$. Then all individuals for whom condition (9.1) holds will commit the crime, while those for whom it does not hold will be deterred from committing it.

Figure 9.1 depicts this choice graphically. The 45° line shows the gain from committing the crime, and the horizontal line shows the expected punishment. Using the figure, we can define the supply of offenses, $S(g^*)$, to be the number of individuals with g greater than the threshold g^*, where $g^* = p(f + ct)$. It follows that an increase in p, f, or t will reduce the number of offenses by increasing the expected punishment.[9] This would be shown in the graph by an upward shift in the punishment line, causing an increase in the threshold point g^* and a reduction in the number of individuals for whom condition (9.1) holds.

Figure 9.1

Supply of Offenses

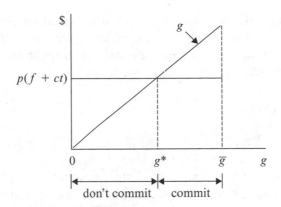

2.2   Optimal Punishment

We now turn to the problem facing the enforcement authority regarding the choice of the policy variables p, f, and t. In order to do this, we need to specify the components of the social objective function. As noted above, in the standard economic model of crime these consist of the cost of apprehension, the gain to offenders less the harm to victims, and punishment costs (if any). The first and third of these elements are not controversial, because they reflect direct costs of enforcement, but the second is because it counts the gain to offenders along with the harm to victims as part of social welfare. This has been standard practice in economic models of crime since Becker, but it deserves some comment (Lewin and Trumbull 1990).

George Stigler (1970, 527) was the first to question the practice when he asked, "What evidence is there that society sets a positive value upon the utility derived from murder, rape, or arson? In fact, the society had branded the utility from such activities as illicit." But the issue is not so simple since some illicit acts can yield benefits to the offender that most would consider a valid part of social welfare, as when a lost hiker breaks into a cabin for food and shelter, or a man exceeds the speed limit to get his pregnant wife to the hospital.

The question of which benefits to include and which not to include is a difficult ethical problem that economists are not well equipped to solve. Further, David Friedman has argued that once we start sorting criminals "into the deserving and the undeserving," we make the mistake of "assuming our conclusions" about how criminals should be treated rather than deriving them as results (D. Friedman 2000, 230). To avoid this problem, we adopt the standard practice of including all offenders' benefits in social welfare, while noting that exclusion of those benefits would simply have the effect of increasing the desired level of deterrence (Polinsky and Shavell 2000, 48).

Now that we have specified social welfare, we can derive the optimal punishment scheme. To simplify the analysis, we do this in steps. We begin by treating expenditures on detection, and hence the probability of apprehension, p, as fixed since many of the key insights can be obtained in this simple setting. We first consider fines alone (that is, we set $t = 0$) and then fines and imprisonment together. Later, we allow the enforcement authority to choose p along with the type and magnitude of punishment.

2.2.1   The Optimal Fine

In the case where punishment is limited to a fine, we set $t = 0$ and condition (9.1) reduces to $g > pf$. Since we are assuming that p is fixed at some predetermined level, the only remaining choice variable for the punishment authority is the magnitude of the fine. We assume (for now) that it is costless to impose and collect fines, so the magnitude of f has no direct effect on social welfare.[10] It can therefore be chosen freely to achieve the optimal level of crime.

In order to determine this level, we must first define the harm suffered by victims of crime. Let h measure the dollar value of this harm per crime committed.[11] Efficiency therefore dictates that only those crimes should be committed for which $g > h$, that is, for which the gain to the offender exceeds the harm to the victim. Note that if $\bar{g}$, the gain to the offender who attaches the highest value to the crime, exceeds h, then some crimes are "efficient" because there exist some offenders for whom $g > h$. However, if $\bar{g} < h$, then no offender values the crime more than the harm it imposes, so complete deterrence is efficient (more on this in the next section). Which situation is relevant depends on the distribution of gains to offenders relative to the size of the harm.

It turns out, however, that the enforcement authority does not need to know anything about the distribution of benefits in order to achieve the efficient solution; it only needs to know the victim's harm. In particular, if it sets the expected fine equal to the harm, or $pf = h$, then only those offenders whose gain exceeds the harm will commit the crime, which is exactly the efficient solution. This implies that the optimal fine is given by

$$f^* = \frac{h}{p}.\tag{9.2}$$

According to this formula, convicted offenders should pay a fine in excess of the harm they impose, where the multiplier, $1/p$, reflects imperfect detection (given $p < 1$). The logic is therefore identical to that used to justify punitive damages in torts when injurers sometimes escape liability.[12]

2.2.2   Gain Versus Harm-Based Fines

The optimal fine in the previous section is "harm-based" in that it sets the fine at a multiple of the victim's harm; the amount of the offender's gain is irrelevant to the calculation. Setting the fine in this way will always give offenders the correct incentives, but there is a circumstance in which a "gain-based" fine will also work. That circumstance is when it is optimal to deter all crimes (Hylton 2005).

Recall from above that complete deterrence is optimal when the offender with the highest gain from the crime receives less benefit than the harm suffered by the victim, or when $\bar{g} < h$. Suppose that when this is true, the enforcement authority sets the fine equal to

$$f_g^* = \frac{g}{p}, \tag{9.3}$$

which is identical to (9.2) except that h is replaced by g, the offender's gain. In other words, offenders, if apprehended, must disgorge their profits plus some additional amount to reflect imperfect detection. Faced with this fine, offenders will commit crimes if and only if $g > pf_g^*$, which, given (9.3), implies that they expect no net benefits. Assuming that when indifferent all offenders are deterred, we conclude that the gain-based fine achieves the efficient outcome (that is, no crime).

A harm-based fine will work equally well in this situation, so why might a gain-based fine be used? One reason is that in some cases, the gain to the offender will be easier to measure than the harm to victims.[13] An example is insider trading, where it is surely easier to observe the profit earned by the insider than to try to measure the loss in market efficiency that resulted from his or her actions.

EXERCISE 9.1

Consider a crime that, if committed, would impose a cost of $100 on the victim. Suppose that there are two potential offenders, one who gains $40 from the crime and one who gains $80. Assume that the probability of apprehension is fixed at .5.

(a) Is it efficient for either of the offenders to commit the crime?
(b) Suppose the fine is set equal to the actual harm (that is, $f = \$100$). Will either of the offenders commit the crime?
(c) Calculate the optimal harm-based fine and show that it achieves the efficient outcome.
(d) Calculate the optimal benefit-based fine for each offender and show that they also achieve the efficient outcome. (Assume that when indifferent, offenders do not commit crimes.)

Figure 9.2

The Optimal Fine
When Offender's
Wealth Is Limited

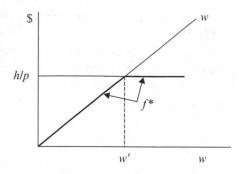

2.2.3   Fines and Imprisonment

To this point we have implicitly assumed that offenders have sufficient wealth to pay whatever fine is implied by the optimal policy. In many cases this will not be true, leading to a potential judgment-proof problem if fines are the only form of punishment.[14] This provides the economic justification for using imprisonment to achieve additional deterrence. Prison differs from fines, however, in that it is costly to impose. Thus, adding a prison term (or increasing its length) not only imposes a cost on the offender but also a cost on society. This implies that *it is optimal to use fines up to the maximum wealth of the offender before prison is used* (Polinsky and Shavell 1984).

   More formally, if w is the wealth of the offender, then the optimal fine can be specified as follows:

$$f^* = \begin{array}{l} h/p, \ \ \text{if } h/p \leq w \\ w, \ \ \ \ \text{if } h/p > w. \end{array} \tag{9.4}$$

Thus, the fine is set at h/p (according to (9.2)) if the offender's wealth permits, but if h/p exceeds his wealth, then the fine is set as high as possible. As an example, let $h = \$1{,}000$ and $p = .5$. The optimal fine is thus \$2,000 or the offender's wealth, whichever is larger. Figure 9.2 shows this graphically.

   When the offender's wealth causes the fine to be less than h/p (that is, for $w < w'$ in Figure 9.2), the fact that prison is costly to impose means that it may or may not be optimal to use it as a way of achieving additional deterrence. Prison will only be desirable if the marginal benefit from greater deterrence exceeds the marginal cost to society of imposing the additional sanction. This will be most likely for offenders with the least wealth since the degree of underdeterrence is largest for them. (We expand on this point in section 2.2.6, below.) The following exercise asks you to calculate the optimal combination of a fine and prison term, assuming that prison is socially desirable.

EXERCISE 9.2

Suppose it has been determined that optimal deterrence involves setting the dollar cost of the expected punishment to offenders (fine plus prison) equal to $4,000. (That is, offenders who gain less than $4,000 from the crime should be deterred from committing it.) Let the probability of apprehension equal .5, the offender's wealth equal $2,000, and the cost to the offender per month in prison equal $500. Use the formula in (9.1) to calculate the optimal fine and prison term in months.

2.2.4 Prison, Probation, and Parole

Imprisonment is not the only form of nonmonetary sanction that can be imposed on offenders. As Table 9.1 shows, of all adults under correctional supervision in the United States in 2004, more than two-thirds were not in prison but were on some form of supervised release—either parole (early release from prison) or probation (release in lieu of prison). An important social benefit of supervised release is that it substantially reduces the cost of punishment compared to prison. As an example, Table 9.2 compares the average cost of various forms of supervision in North Carolina in 2001–2002.

Although release reduces the cost of punishment to society, it also likely reduces the cost of punishment to offenders, thereby lessening its value as a

TABLE **9.1** Adults in Prison or Jail, on Probation, or on Parole, 2004

	Number	Percent of total
Prison or jail	2,135,901	30.3
Parole	765,355	10.9
Probation	4,151,125	58.9

SOURCE: Statistical Abstract of the U.S. *(2007, table 335).*

TABLE **9.2** Average Yearly Cost of Supervision, North Carolina, 2001–2002

Prison	$22,787
Community supervision (parole and probation)	668
Intensive supervision	4,187
Electronic house arrest	2,891

SOURCE: *North Carolina Department of Corrections (www.doc.state.nc.us/DOP/cost/cost2002.htm).*

deterrent. Moreover, offenders on supervised release are capable of committing further crimes. Despite these drawbacks, probation and parole, if properly used, can be important components in the overall arsenal of criminal punishments (Miceli 1994b).

For example, probation is an effective sanction for first-time offenders who are unlikely to commit further crimes and who suffer a high cost from the stigma of criminal conviction alone.[15] It would not be cost-effective to imprison such individuals because the marginal cost of punishment is high while the marginal gain in deterrence is virtually nil. So why impose *any* punishment on such individuals beyond a fine? One reason is that a limited period of probation gives the justice system a low-cost way of correcting errors in assessing the threat posed by a given offender. If an offender commits a crime or violates the rules of his probation, he can be imprisoned without the need to go through a full-blown trial.

The primary benefit of parole, beyond the direct cost savings, is that it gives prisoners an incentive to behave well, thereby reducing the cost of monitoring them. As a result, policies aimed at reducing or eliminating the possibility of parole (like "three strikes and you're out") may have the detrimental effect of creating more unruly prisoners.[16] It is therefore an empirical question whether the increased deterrence from these harsher punishments more than offsets the higher punishment costs.

2.2.5 The Probability of Apprehension Is Variable

The analysis to this point has treated the probability of apprehension as fixed, but policymakers also have control over this variable by their choice of a level of expenditure on enforcement (primarily police). We first consider the optimal choice of p when fines alone are used, and then when prison may also be used.

Fines Only.   We showed above that when a fine alone is used to punish criminals, optimal deterrence is achieved by setting the expected fine, pf, equal to the victim's harm, h. When p was fixed, this led to an optimal fine of h/p. The outcome is different when p is variable. Note first that as long as the expected fine, pf, remains constant, the level of crime (deterrence) is unaffected.[17] Thus, for any desired level of deterrence (that is, for any choice of the product pf), the problem for the enforcement authority is to choose the combination of p and f that minimizes the sum of enforcement and punishment costs. But since there is no social cost of imposing a fine while apprehension is costly, *the optimal fine should be set as high as possible (implying that the probability of apprehension should be set as low as possible).*

Figure 9.3 shows this result graphically. The negatively sloped curve is an "iso-deterrence line" because it shows those combinations of p and f that hold

Figure 9.3

Optimal Fine and Probability of Apprehension for a Given Level of Deterrence

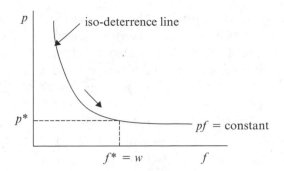

the product pf (and hence the level of deterrence) constant. (The curve is thus a rectangular hyperbola.) Since it is costly to increase p but not f, enforcement costs are lowered for any given level of deterrence by moving down the curve, that is, by lowering p and raising f, as shown by the arrow. The optimal strategy thus involves setting the fine as high as possible (equal to the offender's wealth, or $f^* = w$), and then setting the probability of apprehension (p^*) at the corresponding point on the chosen iso-deterrence line.

The conclusion that a low probability of apprehension coupled with a high fine is an optimal enforcement strategy originated with Becker and is one of the central insights of the economic model of crime. Below, we consider several reasons why it seems not to be employed in practice.

The next step in formulating the optimal enforcement strategy is to determine which iso-deterrence line is optimal. Generally, the level of deterrence should be increased (that is, the crime rate should be reduced) to the point where the marginal reduction in net social harm equals the marginal increase in enforcement costs.[18] No simple formula exists for the resulting value of p^*, but it is possible to prove that at the optimum, $p^*f^* = p^*w < h$—that is, *the expected fine is less than the social harm from the crime.* As a result, there is some "underdeterrence" in the sense that some offenders will commit crimes for which their private gain (g) exceeds the social cost.[19]

To see why some underdeterrence is desirable, suppose that we initially set $pf^* = h$ (as was optimal when p was fixed). If we now lower p slightly, we save enforcement costs, but some additional crimes are committed (remember, we cannot offset the decrease in p by raising f because it is already set at w). However, the social loss from these crimes is slight because $g = pf^* = h$ for the marginal offender, so $h - g = 0$. Thus, there is a net social gain from lowering p, proving that $p^*f^* = h$ could not have been optimal.[20] Eventually, however, the additional crimes do impose a net loss as the marginal offender's gain falls below h. The optimal p occurs at the point where this marginal loss equals the marginal savings in enforcement costs.

Fines and Imprisonment.   When the fine, prison term, and probability of apprehension are all variable, it continues to be desirable to first set the fine equal to the offender's wealth. The choice between the two remaining variables then depends on their relative effects on social welfare and is best illustrated by means of an example. Suppose that the optimal level of deterrence involves setting the expected punishment equal to $4,000.[21] Also, suppose that the cost to the offender per month in prison is $500, and let the offender's wealth be $2,000.

Optimal enforcement involves first setting the fine equal to the offender's wealth, $2,000, and then using condition (9.1) to write an equation for optimal deterrence as a function of p and t:

$$p[\$2,000 + (\$500)t] = \$4,000. \tag{9.5}$$

If we initially set $p = .5$, then the optimal prison term is 12 months (see Exercise 9.2). Note that the *expected* prison term, pt, is thus $(.5)(12) = 6$ months. Now suppose we reduce the probability of apprehension to .4, which results in a savings of, say, $1,000. It follows from (9.5) that, in order to maintain optimal deterrence, we need to increase the prison term to 16 months, which raises the expected prison term to $(.4)(16) = 6.4$ months. Since we are holding the level of deterrence fixed in this example, the effect on social welfare of lowering p depends on whether the savings in enforcement costs is enough to offset the increase in punishment costs from having to increase the expected prison term from 6 to 6.4 months.[22] For example, if the social cost of imprisonment is $2,000 per month, then the extra cost is $(.4)(\$2,000) = \$800$, which is less than the hypothesized savings of $1,000 from lowering p. Thus, there is a net gain from raising t in this example.[23]

2.2.6   Why Are Fines Not Equal to Offenders' Wealth?

The prescription in the preceding sections that it is efficient to use fines up to the limit of offenders' wealth, both to save on enforcement costs and avoid the use of prison, seems to be inconsistent with practice. In this sense, economic theory does not explain actual criminal punishments. In this section we examine possible reasons for why fines are not set as high as possible. Not surprisingly, several reflect values besides efficiency that are fundamental to the criminal justice system.

1. Fines Are Not Costless to Impose.   We have been assuming that there is no social cost of imposing fines or varying their magnitude, but there are several reasons why this might not be the case in practice. The first set of reasons is based on the argument that it is not generally costless to collect fines (Levitt 1997). This might be true, first, because offenders have private information about their wealth and simply refuse to pay, claiming bankruptcy. Second, a large portion of offenders' wealth might take the form of physical assets that would be costly to confiscate and sell.

Even if offenders have little financial wealth, they still might have substantial human capital that could theoretically generate a stream of future income that the government could expropriate over time as a fine. This too would be very costly to collect, however, since there is no way to compel an individual to work hard enough to generate the desired income. Penal slavery could yield some revenue, but probably not enough to cover the costs (D. Friedman 2000, 237). As a result of these costs, optimal punishment will often involve jail time for those unable (or unwilling) to pay the prescribed fine.

A second type of enforcement cost associated with collecting fines is that increases in their magnitude may elicit greater avoidance efforts by offenders (for example, as fines for speeding increase, people are more likely to install radar detectors) (Malik 1990). To illustrate, suppose $p(x)$ is the probability of apprehension as a function of an offender's investment in avoidance, x. If the fine is f, the offender will choose x to minimize

$$x + p(x)f. \tag{9.6}$$

Since the marginal benefit of avoidance is the reduction in the expected fine, $p(x)f$, the optimal x will be increasing in the actual fine.[24] As a result, there will be a social cost of raising the level of the fine, both in the form of increased avoidance expenditures by offenders (which are socially wasteful) and increased public costs of apprehension.

2. False Convictions Are Costly.   Another social cost of raising fines is associated with the possibility of wrongful punishment of innocent defendants. As we argued in Chapter 8, uncertainties in the judicial determination of guilt result in two types of errors, false acquittals (type I errors) and false convictions (type II errors). We further suggested that the high standard of proof for criminal convictions reflects the high cost of type II errors relative to type I errors, but even this and other procedural safeguards cannot completely eliminate erroneous convictions. Thus, since the social loss from a wrongful punishment is likely to be increasing in the severity of punishment, the optimal fine will tend to be lower when the cost of such errors enters into social welfare (Harris 1970; Miceli 1991b).

Of course, the cost of erroneous punishment is even higher for false imprisonment, so this argument does not explain why prison would be *substituted* for fines. (In fact, it suggests that the reverse should be done.) Prison might be preferred over fines, however, if incapacitation of dangerous offenders is one goal of criminal punishment. (See Section 2.4 below.)

3. Punishments Should Be Proportional to Offenses.   Perhaps the most important factor limiting the magnitude of fines, or any other criminal penalty, is the widely held view that the punishment should fit the crime. For example, Adelstein (1981, 7), in describing the Anglo-American system of criminal justice, observes, "Over hundreds of years, ours has been a legal order of retributive punishment tempered by the norm of proportionality, one that seeks to exact an eye, but only that, for an eye." Of course, the concept of proportionality is far older, dating back to Roman law, the Old Testament, and the Koran.[25]

It should be clear from our earlier discussion of optimally deterring fines, however, that proportional punishments will underdeter. The simple reason is imperfect detection. If detection were certain, then proportional fines would also achieve optimal deterrence. As equation (9.2) implies, if $p = 1$, $f^* = h$—the optimal fine equals the harm done. (Note that this is the usual assumption for civil liability in torts, where compensation and deterrence are mutually consistent.) However, if $p < 1$, proportional fines will be too low and the resulting crime rate too high.

It is worth noting that the conflict between proportional and optimally deterring fines is closely related to the aversion to wrongful punishment. To see why, note that the use of a multiplier to achieve optimal deterrence implies that a given offender is punished not only for his own crime *but also for the crimes of those who avoided detection.* As an example, suppose that three crimes are committed causing harm of $1,000 per crime, but only one offender is apprehended. The optimally deterring fine should therefore be $3,000, which imposes the harm of all three victims on the single offender, even though he personally only caused harm of $1,000. The one offender is therefore "burdened with the sins of others."[26] Before the fact, however, each offender faces an *expected fine* of $1,000 (assuming equal probabilities of apprehension), which achieves optimal deterrence by setting the expected punishment equal to the social harm.

Probably the most important institutional factor enforcing the proportionality norm is the sequential nature of the criminal process, coupled with the discretion of judges and juries. To see why, note that optimal deterrence is essentially a *forward-looking* theory of punishment in that it aims at preventing future crimes. It is therefore most appealing before any crime has occurred and criminals are faceless individuals. In contrast, proportionality (or retribution) is a *backward-looking* theory that focuses on the particulars of a given crime after it has been committed. At this stage in the criminal process, the offender is a real person, and there is evidence that judges and juries are resistant to the imposition of overly stiff sentences relative to the specific harm that the particular offender imposed.[27]

If this is true, the only way to achieve optimal deterrence is to remove judicial discretion from sentencing. Recent legislative efforts at mandatory sentencing (for example, the "three-strikes" rule) thus reflect the interplay between forward- and backward-looking approaches to criminal punishment. But stiffer mandatory penalties may simply cause jurors to increase the standard of evidence before they vote to convict (Andreoni 1991). An extreme example of this strategy is so-called jury nullification, where juries refuse to convict defendants, despite the evidence, to avoid imposing what they perceive to be unjust punishments. In the end, it may simply be that the economic strategy of increasing fines and lowering enforcement efforts to save costs is in fundamental conflict with the criminal process as it is currently structured.

4. The Rich and Poor Should Receive Equal Treatment.   The fact that optimal fines should be set equal to offenders' wealth implies that the rich and poor will be treated differently. In particular, the rich will pay higher fines, while the poor will be more likely to face prison time. This policy has led many to ask whether it is acceptable to allow the rich to "buy" their way out of prison. Those who believe in equal treatment say no, implying that fines should not be limited by the wealth of individual offenders but by the wealth of the *poorest* offender.

Setting the same fine and/or prison term for the rich and poor (given that they have committed the same offense) will likely have offsetting effects on deterrence, however. On the one hand, it will probably take a higher fine to discourage a rich person from committing a wrongful act like speeding because the act is worth more to him. On the other hand, it will take a shorter prison term because the rich person's time is worth more (D. Friedman 2000, 232–34). A further complication is that rich defendants will be able to afford better lawyers, thus lowering the probability that they will face any punishment at all (Lott 1987).

5. Risk Aversion.   To this point we have assumed that offenders are risk neutral in the sense that they decide whether or not to commit a crime by comparing the gain from the offense to the expected punishment. If offenders are risk averse, however, then the uncertainty of punishment itself imposes a cost on the offender. Thus, if we count the offender's utility as part of social welfare, optimal fines will not generally be maximal because offenders suffer disutility as the fine is raised and the probability of apprehension is lowered. In effect, it becomes socially costly to raise fines (Polinsky and Shavell 1979).

In contrast, Becker (1968, 178) argues that offenders tend to be those who prefer risk because of "the widespread generalization that [they] are more deterred by the probability of conviction than by the punishment when convicted." This, of course, reverses the policy implications of the preceding paragraph. In any case, because the risk preference of offenders is unobservable, it is not a good basis for formulating optimal penalties.

6. Marginal Deterrence.   A final reason for not setting fines maximally is to preserve "marginal deterrence."[28] Consider, for example, an individual who contemplates embezzling from his company. If the fine for embezzlement is set at the offender's entire wealth, then what prevents him from committing the additional offense of framing a coworker? The fine for the first offense is already maximal, and the second offense has the added benefit of lowering his probability of apprehension. Marginal deterrence generally requires that fines (or other forms of punishment) rise with the severity of the offense in order to discourage commission of additional, or more serious, crimes. But this obviously implies that fines cannot be maximal except for the most severe offenses.

EXERCISE 9.3

Consider fines for speeding. Assume that speeders can drive at either 75 mph or 90 mph (the speed limit is 65 mph), and that the probability of being caught at either speed is .01. Also, assume that the maximum possible fine is $10,000, which is set for driving at 90.

(a) Suppose an individual has already decided to speed. Calculate the fine for driving at 75 that will discourage her from increasing her speed to 90 unless her gain from doing so is $50 or more.

(b) Show that the same degree of marginal deterrence can be achieved by setting the fine at $10,000 for driving at either speed but pulling over those driving at 90 more frequently.

2.3 Repeat Offenders

Federal sentencing guidelines and recent three-strikes legislation provide for more severe punishment of repeat offenders, and intuition suggests that this is an appropriate policy, but it is surprisingly difficult to provide an economic basis for it. If punishment reflects the social harm from an act, then it is efficient for an offender to commit the act if his gain exceeds the harm. The fact that he is a repeat offender is immaterial. In this context, setting harsher punishments for repeat offenders would overdeter—it would be analogous to charging higher prices for repeat customers in ordinary markets.[29]

In a more general setting, however, there are several economic justifications for punishing repeat offenders more harshly. First, the fact that an offender is apprehended multiple times suggests that the risk of type II error (false punishment) is low (it is unlikely that an innocent person would be apprehended more than once), and hence the cost of a punishment is less. Second, individuals who commit multiple crimes signal to society that they are more dangerous and hence need to face harsher punishments to be deterred.[30] Third, offenders might become more proficient at avoiding detection as they commit more crimes (a "learning by doing" effect). For example, equation (9.2) implies that the optimal fine is inversely proportional to the probability of detection. Thus, the optimal fine will rise for repeat offenses as this probability decreases.[31]

A final reason for imposing harsher punishments on repeat offenders is due to the stigma associated with criminal conviction, which may lessen a convict's ability to find legal employment. To illustrate, recall that the net gain from committing a crime is given by $g - pf$ (assuming punishment by a fine), and let w be the income that someone without a criminal record can earn in legal employment. If individuals must choose between crime and legal employment, then only those for whom $g - pf \leq w$ will choose legal employment. Thus, the minimally deterring fine for a first-time offender is given by

$$f_d = \frac{g - w}{p}.$$
(9.7)

Now suppose that a convicted offender can earn at most $w - s$ in legal employment, where s represents the stigma associated with a criminal record. (For example, this may reflect the extra cost employers expect to bear from hiring such a person.) If the expected gain from committing crimes is the same for first-time and repeat offenders, then the repeat offender will choose legal employment over crime if $g - pf \leq w - s$. The minimally deterring fine is now

$$f_d^r = \frac{g - w + s}{p},$$
(9.8)

which is clearly larger than the expression in (9.7).

Intuitively, because the repeat offender faces inferior employment opportunities compared to the first-timer, he will continue his life of crime unless the expected punishment increases correspondingly. Of course, it is possible to do this by raising p as well as (or instead of) f, and indeed, known repeat offenders are generally pursued with more vigor. In many cases, however, a offender's past record (if any) will not be known until he is caught, leaving harsher punishment as the only way to achieve the desired level of deterrence.

2.4 Incapacitation

We noted in the previous section that one reason for punishing repeat offenders more harshly is that, by committing multiple criminal acts, they reveal themselves as being more dangerous to society. Higher threatened punishments may deter individuals from committing further acts, but for those individuals who cannot be deterred, longer prison terms also serve the goal of incapacitation. Incapacitation is socially desirable to the extent that it protects society from dangerous offenders by holding them in prison, where they presumably can do less harm. The optimal length of imprisonment in this context depends on a comparison of the marginal savings in harm each period compared to the marginal cost of imprisonment. Generally, this will result in eventual release given that the propensity of an individual to commit harmful acts tends to decline with age (Shavell 2004, 532).

2.5   Empirical Evidence on the Economic Model of Crime

A growing area in the economic analysis of crime is empirical analysis of various implications of the economic model (Sykes 2002). In this section, we review some of the recent findings, especially those regarding the rational criminal hypothesis, which is a central assumption of the model. (We leave to the next section discussion of empirical evidence on the deterrent effect of capital punishment.)

The model of rational criminal behavior requires, most fundamentally, that potential offenders recognize and respond to changes in expected sanctions. A recent study by Anderson (2002), however, casts doubt on the validity of this assumption. Based on a survey of 278 male inmates, he found that 76 percent of convicts either did not know what the punishment would be if they were convicted, or did not think about it. This fraction rose to 89 percent for the most violent offenders. Further, those who did consider the possibility of punishment seemed to have underestimated the probability. Finally, a high proportion of offenders claimed that no threat of punishment would have deterred them from committing their crimes. These results suggest that a policy of increasing punishments is unlikely to have a significant effect on the crime rate.

Several studies nevertheless find an inverse relationship between punishments and crime. (For example, see the survey by Eide (1994).) One problem plaguing such studies, however, is that longer prison sentences may reduce crime as a result of incapacitation (fewer criminals are on the loose) rather than deterrence. To isolate the deterrence effect, Kessler and Levitt (1999) looked for changes in the crime rate immediately after enactment of "sentence enhancement" laws—laws that increase the punishment for certain crimes. If the rate of such crimes drops, then the effect must be pure deterrence because the extended prison term would not yet have been applied to any convicts (hence, there can be no incapacitation effect). Using data from California in 1982, they did find a decrease in the rate of targeted crimes, but no change for those crimes not covered by the new laws. This provides strong support for the deterrence hypothesis.

Recently enacted three-strikes laws in several states similarly provide an opportunity to test the deterrence hypothesis. Three-strikes laws impose increased penalties for repeat offenders, and "maximal" penalties (life in prison) for third-time offenders. In a cross-state study, Marvell and Moody (2001) found that such laws actually increased the homicide rate by up to

30 percent in the long run. While this result seems contrary to the rational criminal model, recall that the issue of "marginal deterrence" implies that criminals facing the maximal penalty for a crime have no incentive to avoid committing further crimes (for example, murdering witnesses) in an effort to avoid apprehension. Thus, the findings of this study are in fact consistent with rational offender behavior.

Shepherd (2002), however, suggested that Marvell and Moody's results are flawed for several reasons. Most important, the passage of three-strikes laws may have been a response by states to the increased murder rate rather than a cause of it. (This is referred to as a *simultaneity bias*.) After correcting for this and other problems, Shepherd found that the passage of a three-strikes law in California reduced the rate of "strikeable" offenses, not only by two-time losers facing maximal punishment, but also by first-time offenders, though there is some evidence that offenders substituted away from strikeable crimes toward those not covered by the law. (Note that this itself is evidence of rational criminal behavior.)

Not all empirical studies of crime have focused on the impact of expected punishments. For example, below we consider the effect of economic conditions on the crime rate (Section 4.1), and the relationship between guns and crime (Section 4.2). Other studies have examined such issues as the impact of the race of police officers on arrest rates—so-called racial profiling (Donahue and Levitt 2001b), the apparent inverse relationship between abortion rates and crime rates over the past decade (Donahue and Levitt 2001a), and the question of why crime rates are higher in cities (Glaeser and Sacerdote 1999).

2.6   The Death Penalty

The death penalty is obviously the most severe, and also the most controversial, form of punishment that can be imposed on a convicted offender. But while most western democracies have abolished capital punishment, in recent decades it has experienced something of a revival in the United States (see Table 9.3).

Economic theory can provide little by way of insights regarding the ethical and moral dimensions of the death penalty. We therefore restrict attention here to two issues: whether the death penalty deters crime, and constitutional challenges to the death penalty.[32]

2.6.1   Economics of the Death Penalty

The earliest economic studies of the deterrent effects of the death penalty were done by Isaac Ehrlich in the 1970s (Ehrlich 1975, 1977). Based on Becker's model, Ehrlich hypothesized that an increase in the use of the death

TABLE **9.3** **Prisoners Executed in the United States, 1930–2004**

Period	Number executed	Yearly average
1930–1939	1,667	166.7
1940–1949	1,284	128.4
1950–1959	717	71.7
1960–1967	191	23.9
1968–1976	0	0
1977–1989	120	9.2
1990–2000	563	46.9
2001–2004	261	65.3

SOURCE: Statistical Abstract of the U.S., *various years.*

penalty should reduce the murder rate, holding all other factors of the criminal justice system constant. He tested this theory with U.S. data both over time (from 1935 to 1969) and across states (for the years 1940 and 1950). In general, his results supported the predictions of the deterrence model. In particular, he found that one additional execution per year reduced the number of murders by between seven and eight. (He also found that the murder rate was decreasing in both the probability of arrest and the probability of conviction.)

Given the controversial nature of Ehrlich's conclusions, it is not surprising that there has been considerable criticism both of his theoretical underpinnings and methodology. More recent studies, however, have continued to find a deterrent effect.[33] Avio (1998, 204) sums up the state of this debate as follows: "The overall impression one gets from reviewing Ehrlich's two papers and the controversy they generated is that the evidence favouring the deterrence hypothesis is not quite so strong as some enthuse and not quite so weak as others aver." Further studies are clearly warranted. But even if it can be established that the death penalty does deter crime, the cost of wrongful punishment (type II errors) looms much larger for execution than for imprisonment or fines. Thus, even those who accept the goal of deterrence may still oppose the death penalty, or at least favor severe limits in its use.

In addition to error costs, there are high costs of actually imposing the death penalty. This is true for several reasons (Cooter and Ulen 1988, 566–67). First, the cost of death penalty trials will generally be higher than ordinary trials because there is so much more at stake than in non–death penalty cases. In addition, death penalty cases are often bifurcated into a guilt phase and a penalty phase, thus lengthening the process. Second, the appeals process, which is generally mandatory in death penalty cases to ensure the utmost protection of the convict's rights, is lengthy and expensive. Finally, the cost of housing death row inmates is higher than for other inmates because there is no harsher sanction that can be threatened to prevent them from being unruly or committing crimes while in prison. (In other words, the sanction is maximal so marginal deterrence is impossible.)

2.6.2 Constitutional Issues

The death penalty has been the subject of constitutional challenges on a variety of grounds (Adelstein 1979a). In 1972, after steady declines in the use of capital punishment during the twentieth century (see Table 9.3), the Supreme Court declared it unconstitutional by a narrow 5–4 vote. Two justices cited the Eighth Amendment's prohibition on "cruel and unusual punishment," while the other three in the majority focused on the Fourteenth Amendment's requirement of "equal protection."[34] The crux of their argument was the fact that legislatures had failed to provide sufficient guidance to courts on the use of the death penalty, which had the practical effect of disproportionately condemning poor and minority (especially black) defendants.

State legislatures responded to the court's directive by establishing procedures aimed at eliminating the "capricious" use of the death penalty. It was a difficult challenge to meet because it required a careful balance between establishing clear ex ante standards for the imposition of the death penalty while maintaining sufficient discretion ex post to allow courts to tailor penalties to individual defendants. The new procedures were quickly tested in the courts and upheld in a series of Supreme Court cases in 1976. One such case, for example, validated the use of separate guilt and penalty phases (bifurcated trials), and introduced the use of so-called mitigating and aggravating factors into the penalty phase.[35]

The debate about the relative costs and benefits of the death penalty will undoubtedly continue. Economics can inform this debate, but the outcome will ultimately depend on considerations outside the scope of economic analysis.

2.7 Judicial Discretion in Sentencing

Historically, judges have had considerable discretion in determining criminal sentences under so-called indeterminate sentencing, but federal sentencing guidelines enacted in 1987 greatly curtailed the discretion of judges. The guidelines, which mirrored reforms enacted by many states in the 1970s and early 1980s, imposed much tighter limits on the discretion of judges. Under the guidelines, sentences are dictated by a table that lists the seriousness of the offense on one axis, and the offender's criminal history on the other. Average sentences are increasing in both the seriousness of the crime and the offender's record; other factors are not supposed to be taken into account.

What was the motivation for this reform? Politically, the guidelines were supported by a coalition of liberals and conservatives who found common ground in the need to limit judicial discretion in sentencing. Liberals believed that reduced discretion would result in fairer punishments by removing unwarranted discrepancies in sentences that reflected the judge's own preferences rather than the observable facts of the case, while conservatives felt that the guidelines were necessary to eliminate lax penalties, thereby enhancing deterrence (Shepherd 2007). Can economic theory shed light on these seemingly conflicting objectives of sentencing reform?

In terms of fairness, the goal of reform was to eliminate differences in sentences for offenders who committed the same crime and had similar records. This reflects the concept of horizontal equity, which says that individuals who are alike in all relevant respects should be treated alike. The problem with this notion of fairness is that it depends on how one defines "relevant respects"; that is, what factors justify differences in criminal sentences and what factors do not? The objection to indeterminate sentencing apparently was that it left this question entirely in the hands of judges. The actual structure of the guidelines implies that Congress intended sentences to vary based only on the seriousness of an offender's crime and his criminal history.

As for deterrence, economic theory suggests that the guidelines will have conflicting effects. To the extent that they impose stiffer average sentences, the guidelines should reduce crime, but the greater predictability of sentences may raise or lower the crime rate, depending on the risk preferences of criminals. If criminals are risk loving, then more predictable sentences will further increase deterrence because risk-loving individuals actually get utility from the riskiness of the act. Conversely, if criminals are risk averse, greater predictability will actually reduce deterrence.

Several empirical studies have sought to measure the impact of sentencing guidelines on both fairness and deterrence. Regarding fairness, Anderson et al. (1999) looked at criminal cases decided between 1981 and 1993 and found that inter-judge differences in sentences (i.e., differences attributed solely to the identity of the judge) declined after enactment of the guidelines. In contract, LaCasse and Payne (1999), looking at cases between 1981 and 1995, found that sentence variation attributable to judges actually *increased* following the guidelines. Regarding deterrence, Shepherd (2007) found that at the state level, the guidelines have been associated with an increase in the crime rate. Using data from 1960 to 2000, she found that violent crimes increased by 8% and property crimes increased by 7%, holding all other factors fixed. In light of the evidence, it appears that the sentencing guidelines have not lived up to the promises of their advocates.

2.8 The Bail System*

Defendants charged with a crime generally face a long delay before trial. This raises the question of what to do with them between apprehension and trial. The presumption of innocence suggests that they should remain free, but the risk that they might flee and possibly commit further crimes argues for detention. The practical solution to this trade-off is the bail system, which sets an amount of money that a defendant must post as a bond in order to be released pending trial. An economic model of the bail system views the level of bail as being set to maximize the gains minus the costs of pretrial release (Landes 1973).

To illustrate, suppose that the number of defendants released on bail is equal to $n(b)$, which is decreasing in the level of bail, b. The function $n(b)$ in effect describes a demand for pretrial release, and the bail level is the price of release. The gains from release are the savings in detention costs per defendant, d, and the private gain to each defendant, g, which consists of the direct benefits of freedom, any income he can earn, and the benefit from being able to assist in his defense. The total gains from release are thus $n(b)(g + d)$.

The costs of release arise if the defendant jumps bail. Suppose this is expected to occur with probability $p(b)$, which is decreasing in b. If a defendant jumps, he imposes two costs: the potential harm from additional crimes he may commit, h, and the cost of reapprehension, c. Total expected costs from release are thus $n(b)p(b)(h + c)$. The court's problem is to set the level of bail to maximize benefits minus costs, or

$$n(b)(g + d) - n(b)p(b)(h + c). \tag{9.9}$$

The trade-off is reflected by the fact that as b is increased, benefits decrease because fewer defendants can make bail, but costs also decrease because fewer defendants jump bail (both because the number on release declines and fewer of them jump). The optimal bail, b^*, occurs at the point where the marginal reduction in benefits equals the marginal reduction in costs.

In general, the optimal bail will be individual-specific, primarily because defendants will differ in both the expected harm they may impose while on release, and the likelihood that they will jump bail (holding b fixed). Consistent with actual practice, the model implies that a higher bail will be set for those more likely to commit harm, and those more likely to flee for any given bail level.

One criticism of the bail system is that it gives yet another advantage to wealthy defendants, who can more easily obtain release. This problem is partially offset by the existence of bail bondsmen, who, in return for a fee, post bail for those unable to pay it themselves. One suspects, however, that defendants are somewhat more likely to flee when someone else has posted bail (due to moral hazard), despite the best efforts of bail bondsmen to protect their investment.

Another criticism of the bail system is that minority defendants face higher bail than do white defendants, holding all other factors constant. Ayres and

Waldfogel (1994) provide some evidence for this charge based on observed differences in bail bond rates for minority and white defendants. They argue that if the market for bail bondsmen is competitive, then the bail bond rate—defined to be the ratio of the fee charged by the bondsman to the bail amount—should be approximately equal to the defendant's flight risk.[36] Thus, defendants with equal flight risks (as assessed by the bail bondsman) should face the same bail bond rate. In fact, Ayres and Waldfogel (1994, 993) found that minority defendants faced a lower rate than did comparable white defendants, implying that "judges in setting bail demanded lower probabilities of flight from minority defendants." In other words, judges attributed a higher flight risk to minority defendants than was justified by the available evidence.

2.9. Private Protection*

To this point we have focused exclusively on public expenditures aimed at preventing crime, but private individuals invest in a variety of self-protection measures as well, including alarm systems, dead bolts, and private security guards.[37] Beyond these dollar costs, individuals may change their behavior to avoid situations and locations involving a high risk of crime. All told, the total cost of private protection is substantial.

From an economic perspective, expenditures on private protection against crime closely resemble victim precaution against accidents.[38] To illustrate, write the harm from a crime as $h(y)$, which is decreasing in the victim's expenditure on self-protection, y. For example, h might be her dollar losses from burglary while y is the cost of an alarm system. Suppose q is the probability that a burglar will target an individual's house. Then the victim will choose y to minimize

$$y + qh(y). \tag{9.10}$$

She will therefore invest in self-protection until the last dollar spent yields a reduction of one dollar in expected losses.

It is worth noting that in solving this problem, the victim acts as if her spending on y reduces her losses from a given crime, $h(y)$, but has no effect on the *likelihood* of a crime, q. This reflects two assumptions: (1) the efforts of individual victims are not observable to offenders before they decide whom to victimize; and (2) the number of potential victims is so large that no one victim expects her efforts to affect the overall crime rate.[39]

It is the case, however, that in equilibrium, the *collective* efforts of victims *will* affect the crime rate. To see why, suppose that the aggregate effect of victim protection is to impose a cost, $c(y)$, on offenders that is increasing in y. For example, an alarm system makes it harder to burglarize a car or house.

Given this cost, the net gain from an offense is now $g - c(y)$, and the condition for an offender to commit the act (assuming punishment by fines) is

$$g - c(y) \geq pf. \tag{9.11}$$

Since increases in y lower the left-hand side, greater self-protection by victims reduces the crime rate; that is, q is decreasing in y. It follows that if victims were able to act in concert, they would invest in more self-protection than is individually optimal because they would internalize the effect of their collective efforts on the aggregate crime rate.[40]

3 Plea Bargaining

Plea bargaining in criminal cases is analogous to settlement in civil cases, and it occurs nearly as frequently. As Table 9.4 shows, in 1992 the percentage of criminal convictions in U.S. district courts obtained by means of a guilty plea ranged from 70 to 95 percent, depending on the crime. But unlike settlements of civil cases that are generally encouraged, negotiated guilty pleas have been the source of considerable controversy, the chief concern being that innocent defendants might be induced to plead guilty when faced with an uncertain outcome at trial. At the same time, practical considerations suggest that some guilty pleas are needed to conserve on limited judicial resources. In its evaluation of the practice of plea bargaining, the Supreme Court has emphasized just this trade-off (Adelstein 1998).

TABLE **9.4** **Criminal Convictions, Guilty Pleas, and Percentage Receiving Prison, by Offense, U.S. District Courts, 1992**

	Convictions	Guilty pleas	% by plea	% Receiving prison
Total	48,392	42,339	87.5	64.2
Homicide	157	109	69.4	91.2[a]
Robbery	1,496	1,339	89.5	97.5
Assault	427	358	83.8	67.2
Burglary	122	114	93.4	96.7
Larceny-theft	3,177	2,994	94.2	34.1
Embezzlement-fraud	9,149	8,509	93.0	48.7
Auto theft	258	245	95.0	69.4
Forgery	1,262	1,193	94.5	51.0
Sex offenses	346	282	81.5	79.2
Drugs	17,200	14,347	83.4	87.4
Misc. offenses	14,798	12,849	86.8	50.1

SOURCE: Statistical Abstract of the U.S. *(1993, 206, table 333).*
[a] Includes prison and other forms of punishment.

For example, in *Santobello v. New York* (404 U.S. 257, 1971), the court conceded the necessity of the practice, arguing, "When properly administered, it is to be encouraged. If every criminal charge were subjected to a full-scale trial, the States and Federal government would need to multiply many times the number of judges and court facilities." The court emphasized, however, that cost considerations could not overshadow the primary goals of the criminal justice system, namely, to impose prompt punishment on the guilty and avoid punishing the innocent. In *Brady v. United States* (397 U.S. 742, 1970), however, the court noted that plea bargaining may actually promote the goal of punishment: "The more promptly imposed punishment after an admission of guilt may more effectively attain the objective of punishment."

The sticking point, therefore, is the risk that the reduced sentence typically offered as part of a plea bargain might induce innocent defendants to plead guilty. As the *Brady* court noted, "We would have serious doubts about this case if the encouragement of guilty pleas by offers of leniency substantially increased the likelihood that defendants, advised by competent counsel, would falsely condemn themselves." This echoes the argument above that the criminal justice system places considerable importance on the avoidance of type II errors. The court nevertheless satisfied itself that the risk was not great, or at least that it was worth bearing in view of the offsetting advantages of plea bargaining.

3.1   Economic Models of Plea Bargaining

Economic models of plea bargaining have largely focused on the outcome of bargaining between prosecutors and defendants prior to trial. The first model, developed by Landes (1971), illustrated the fundamental similarity of plea bargaining and settlement of civil cases, while later models have incorporated broader social concerns (like those addressed by the Supreme Court) not present in private legal disputes. We consider these models in turn.

Landes viewed the prosecutor as maximizing the sum of expected punishments imposed on defendants subject to a budget constraint.[41] One justification for this objective on social grounds is that it promotes maximal deterrence of crime, but it is perhaps more descriptive of the self-interest of prosecutors seeking to maximize their reputations and/or probabilities of reelection. Whatever the justification, this objective suggests that the benefits of plea bargaining to the prosecutor are twofold: to obtain a conviction, and to save the costs of a trial. In pursuit of these goals, prosecutors are generally willing to offer defendants a "sentence discount" in exchange for a guilty plea.

Landes's model is virtually identical to the optimism model of settlement and trial developed in the previous chapter and has similar implications (see

Section 2.1 in Chapter 8.) Specifically, trials can only occur as a result of mutual optimism (that is, each party must assess a high probability of winning at trial), and given optimism, trials are more likely the greater are the "stakes" of the case. Landes offered some empirical evidence in support of this latter prediction by using state and federal court data to show that cases are more likely to go to trial in courts where average sentences tend to be higher.

The data in Table 9.4 also offer some evidence on this point. In addition to the number of convictions for each crime, the table shows the fraction of defendants receiving prison time (or, in the case of homicide, execution) rather than probation or a fine. If prison or execution represent the most severe form of punishment, then the model predicts a negative correlation between the percentage of convicts receiving these punishments and the percentage pleading guilty. The correlation coefficient for the two variables, a statistical measure of correlation, is $-.448$, suggesting a moderate degree of negative correlation.[42] Although this is far from a rigorous test in that it does not control for the multitude of factors that affect plea bargaining rates and criminal sentences, it is consistent with the predictions of the model.

The Landes model focused on the conservation of judicial resources as the primary justification for plea bargaining, but under certain conditions, the practice can also be used by prosecutors to promote the other goals articulated by the court—namely, appropriately punishing the guilty and sparing the innocent (Grossman and Katz 1983). To illustrate, suppose that the probability of conviction at trial for truly guilty defendants is uniformly higher than it is for innocent defendants; that is, $P_G > P_I$. Further, assume that both prosecutors and defendants estimate these probabilities equally (in contrast to the Landes model). The expected cost of trial is therefore higher for guilty as compared to innocent defendants:

$$P_G S + C_d > P_I S + C_d,\tag{9.12}$$

where S is the sanction, and C_d is the defendant's cost of trial. Faced with this situation, the prosecutor can pursue one of three strategies: (1) go to trial with both types of defendants; (2) make a plea offer S_o such that only the guilty will accept (that is, set S_o such that $P_G S + C_d > S_o > P_I S + C_d$); or (3) make a plea offer that both types will accept (that is, set $S_o < P_I S + C_d$). Note that options (1) and (3) are "pooling" strategies because the prosecutor does not attempt to distinguish between innocent and guilty defendants prior to trial. In contrast, option (2) is a "separating" strategy because it induces guilty defendants to identify themselves at the plea bargaining stage.

It should be clear that option (1) can never be socially optimal. This is true because the prosecutor can impose the same overall cost on guilty defendants, while saving trial costs, by making the highest plea offer that the guilty will accept (that is, by offering $S_o = P_G S + C_d$).[43] And since innocent defendants

Figure 9.4

Distributions of
the Probability of
Conviction for Innocent
and Guilty Defendants

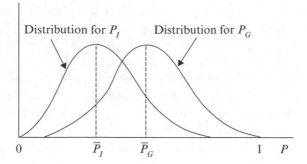

go to trial either way, there is no effect on the cost of wrongful punishments. The choice is therefore between options (2) and (3). It turns out that either may be optimal depending on the magnitudes of two offsetting effects. Option (2) has the advantage of imposing a higher cost on guilty defendants, but option (3) involves a lower cost of wrongful punishment because innocent defendants, by pleading guilty, receive a lesser penalty than their expected cost of trial (that is, $S_o < P_I S + C_d$ in option (3)). Option (3) also saves the cost of trials with innocent defendants. Generally speaking, the separating plea bargain (option (2)) will be preferred as the fraction of innocent defendants, and the cost of wrongful punishments (type II errors), become smaller.

The reader may have noticed the following feature of the separating option: that trials only involve innocent defendants, which implies that all convictions at trial are erroneous![44] This, of course, is an artifact of the assumption that $P_G > P_I$, which says that *all* guilty defendants have a higher probability of conviction than *all* innocent defendants. In reality, uncertainties in evidence gathering will cause the probability of conviction to vary across both types of defendants. This situation is illustrated in Figure 9.4, which shows the frequency distribution of conviction probabilities for innocent and guilty defendants. Although the distribution for guilty defendants is shifted to the right, implying a higher *average* probability of conviction (that is, $\bar{P}_G > \bar{P}_I$), any given innocent defendant could face a high probability of conviction and any given guilty defendant could face a low probability of conviction.

In this more realistic setting, the outcome of bargaining between the prosecutor and defendant can result in innocent defendants pleading guilty and guilty defendants going to trial (Reinganum 1988), although it remains true that, on average, guilty defendants will be more likely to accept a given plea bargain.

3.2   Plea Bargaining and Deterrence

Our discussion of plea bargaining to this point has focused on the outcome of bargaining between the prosecutor and defendant after a crime has been committed. But given the prominent role of the practice in determining criminal penalties, it is important to consider its impact on deterrence. To do this, we need to step back and ask how plea bargaining affects the expected penalties facing potential offenders.

The economic model of deterrence that we developed earlier in this chapter treated the "punishment authority" as a single entity that could credibly commit to a particular penalty structure before any crimes have occurred. Such a structure is quite conducive to the economic model of deterrence, but in reality, punishments are determined sequentially by various decision makers whose objectives may differ. In simplest terms, punishments are determined in a two-stage process. The first involves legislative establishment of punishment guidelines for various crimes before they are committed. It is at this stage that considerations of deterrence most likely dominate. Once a crime has been committed and a suspect apprehended, however, the task of imposing actual punishments falls to the judicial process. As we have seen, plea bargaining plays a paramount role at this stage, and the goals of the prosecutor often trump those of the legislature. This raises the question of whether the practice of plea bargaining promotes or counteracts the pursuit of deterrence.[45]

Our discussion of the objectives of prosecutors in the previous section (based on mandates issued by the Supreme Court) suggests that they will resist overly harsh punishments, both to minimize the cost of wrongfully punishing the innocent, and to maintain proportionality between punishments and crimes for the guilty. As we suggested above, these ex post objectives represent important obstacles to the pursuit of high-penalty, low-probability enforcement schemes associated with the economic model. In this context, the discretion given to prosecutors in the United States (like that given to judges) can be viewed as an institutional mechanism designed to maintain a balance between the ex ante goal of deterrence and the ex post goal of proportionality.

3.3   A Comparative Perspective

Despite its prevalence in the United States, plea bargaining is not an essential component of a criminal justice system, as illustrated by the inquisitorial systems of continental Europe, where it is, in principle, forbidden (Adelstein 1998). In particular, prosecutors are bound by the rule of "compulsory prosecution," which requires them to try all cases on the maximum charge supported by the evidence. Since trials cannot be avoided by guilty pleas, the system has responded to the scarcity of judicial resources by simplifying trials and weakening some procedural protections of defendants' rights (Langbein 1979). In this section, we offer some speculative comments on how economic theory might explain these vastly different institutional responses to the common problems facing any criminal justice system—namely, how best to punish criminals in a world of scarce resources and imperfect adjudication (Adelstein and Miceli 2001).

The question of interest may be simply stated as follows: When will a regime of compulsory prosecution better promote the goals of the criminal justice system than one with unlimited plea bargaining? The answer depends on the particular social values that the system embodies. Consider first the aversion to punishing the innocent. Given the reality that conviction depends on evidence against a defendant rather than his or her actual guilt (see Figure 9.4), plea bargaining actually becomes more desirable as the cost of punishing the innocent rises. This is true for the simple reason that an innocent defendant against whom the evidence is strong may face a far lesser punishment by pleading guilty than by facing the uncertain prospect of trial. As Frank Easterbrook (1983, 320), himself a federal judge, has argued, there is "no reason to prevent [an innocent] defendant from striking a deal that seems advantageous. If there is injustice here, the source is not the plea bargain. It is, rather, that innocent people may be found guilty at trial."

Conversely, if a system places a high value on punishing the guilty, then compulsory prosecution is the preferred route, precisely because it does not allow the truly guilty to use plea bargaining as a way of mitigating their punishment. Taken together, these conclusions imply "that plea bargaining is more likely to evolve in systems that emphasize the protection of innocent defendants, and systems that stress punishing the guilty are more likely to be able to sustain a regime of compulsory prosecution" (Adelstein and Miceli 2001, 60). If correct, this suggests that the American system places relatively more weight on protecting the innocent, while European systems place more weight on punishing the guilty.

But even these values must sometimes bend to the constraints of limited resources, and European systems, while remaining committed to the goal of compulsory prosecution, have had to develop ways of circumventing costly trials. Thus, most have created categories of lesser offenses that are disposed of without trial in what amount to thinly veiled plea bargains (Langbein 1979). As Adelstein (1998, 50) notes, the European and American systems, despite divergent values, "may be converging in a desire for streamlined trials and effective procedures, where appropriate, to avoid them."

4 Topics

In this final section we examine several topics in the economics of crime, including the relationship between the crime rate and the business cycle, the effect of gun control laws on crime, and primitive law roots of modern criminal law. We conclude by discussing several constitutional issues as they relate to the economics of crime.

4.1 Crime and the Business Cycle*

The model of rational criminals suggests that the crimes committed for the primary purpose of monetary gain should be sensitive to general economic conditions. As the economy worsens and legal employment opportunities decline, criminal activity should become more attractive as a source of income. This leads to the prediction that the crime rate should be countercyclical—that is, the crime rate should fall as unemployment declines.

To see this formally, recall that the net expected gain from committing a crime is given by $g - pf$ (assuming punishment by a fine), which varies across offenders depending on the gain, g (reflecting different criminal opportunities), while legal employment promises an expected return of w, which will fluctuate according to the general conditions of the economy. Assuming, as above, that individuals must choose between crime and legal employment, those for whom $g - pf > w$ will become criminals and those for whom $g - pf < w$ will choose legal employment.[46] This is shown graphically in Figure 9.5, which is a modified version of Figure 9.1. (In Figure 9.1, we implicitly assumed that $w = 0$.)

According to the graph, when income from legal employment is w, individuals with $g > g^*$ choose to become criminals. However, when income falls to, say, w' as a result of an increase in the unemployment rate, individuals with $g > g'$ become criminals, and the crime rate rises.[47] The question is whether the evidence on crime rates over the business cycle supports this prediction.

Figure 9.6 offers some evidence by graphing the unemployment rate and the rate of property crimes (those most likely to be motivated by economic

Figure 9.5

Impact of
Unemployment
on the Crime Rate

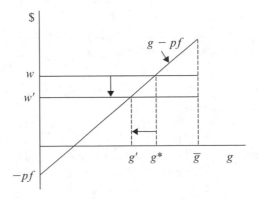

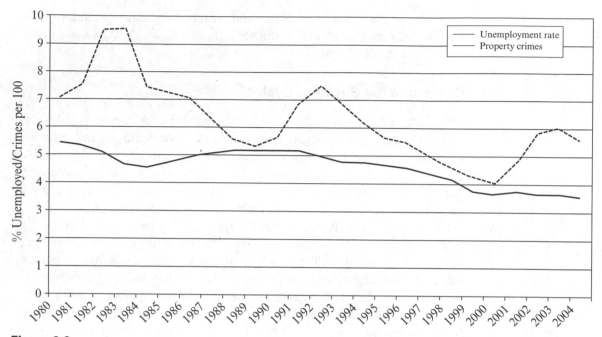

Figure 9.6
Unemployment and Property Crime Rates, 1980–2004

gain) from 1980 to 2004. While there appears to be a positive relationship (as predicted) during the 1990s as both rates declined, there is no clear correlation prior to or after that. Of course, this does not control for the multiple factors affecting the two variables.

Two recent studies provide more rigorous evidence on the relationship between unemployment and crime during the period 1949 to 1997.[48] Both studies find clear evidence that the unemployment rate is a significant positive determinant of the overall rate of property crimes. In particular, they find that a drop of 1 percent in the unemployment rate results in a decrease in the property crime rate of between 1.6 and 5 percent. In contrast, there is little if any evidence of an impact of unemployment on violent crimes. This is consistent with the argument that property crimes like burglary and larceny are economically motivated, whereas violent crimes like murder and rape are not.[49]

4.2   Gun Laws and Crime

Undoubtedly one of the most controversial policy questions when it comes to crime is gun control. The debate is often a heated one, pitting gun control advocates on one side against supporters of the Second Amendment right to bear arms on the other. As with any inherently dangerous product, the issue from an economic perspective is how to balance the legitimate uses of the product (sport, protection) against its hazards. Although an ideal gun control policy would reduce the latter without infringing on the former, realistic regulations would most likely have a disproportionate effect on law-abiding citizens since criminals would find ways to circumvent the law or substitute other dangerous weapons for guns. The overall effect of gun laws is therefore an empirical question that can only be answered by examining the data. This is where economic theory can influence the debate.

Tests of the effect of gun laws on crime can be done in two ways.[50] The first is to look at cross-sectional data from various cities or states to see if differences in gun laws at a given point in time result in different crime rates. The second is to look at the crime rate in a given city or state before and after a given law has been enacted. Both types of studies, however, are subject to certain biases that might distort the results. For example, in cross-sectional studies, suppose that areas where crime rates are lowest to begin with are also the most likely to enact tough gun laws. Then, even if these laws have no effect on deterrence, a snapshot of crime rates may lead one to falsely conclude that the laws reduce crime.

This problem can be overcome by tracking the impact of a change in the law over time, but time series studies have limitations as well. For example, focusing on a single jurisdiction may not allow one to isolate the effect of changes in the law if other variables affecting the crime rate also change. The ideal study therefore uses both time series and cross-sectional data—referred to as panel data—to examine the impact of gun laws over time while simultaneously controlling for other variables affecting the crime rate.

The most extensive such study to date (and also the most controversial) has been done by the economist John Lott (1998).[51] Lott used data from all 3,054 counties in the United States for the period 1977–92 to examine the effect of concealed-handgun laws—laws that allow licensed citizens to carry concealed handguns—on the crime rate. Theory predicts that such laws should lower the crime rate by raising the cost of committing crimes, and Lott's evidence seems to support this prediction. For example, Table 9.5 shows that the rates of violent and property crimes in 1992 were lowest in states where concealed handguns were issued to all qualified applicants (nondiscretionary laws); next lowest in states where they were issued on a discretionary basis (according to "compelling need"); and highest where they were prohibited.

Of course, these results are subject to the "snapshot" bias note above, but rigorous statistical analysis over the full sample period largely confirmed the conclusions. Specifically, concealed-handgun laws reduced the rate of violent crime, though possibly at the expense of an increase in the rate of property

TABLE **9.5**   **Effect of Concealed-Handgun Laws on Crime Rates, 1992**

	Crimes per 100,000 of population		
	Nondiscretionary handgun laws	Discretionary handgun laws	Concealed handguns prohibited
Violent crimes	378.8	653.1	715.9
Property crimes	3,786.3	4,666.3	4,725.5

SOURCE: *Lott (1998, 46, table 3.2).*

crimes (in contrast to what Table 9.5 shows), where the criminal is less apt to have direct contact with his victim. Further, more permissive gun laws did not significantly raise the number of accidental gun deaths or suicides, a major concern of opponents. Finally, Lott's results provided evidence for other aspects of the economic model of crime, for example, that higher arrest and conviction rates deter crime.

Lott's conclusions have not gone unchallenged, however. For example, Mocan and Tekin (2006) found that the availability of guns in the home increased the propensity for juveniles to commit crime, but did not reduce the chances of victimization. Ayres and Donahue (1999, 466) summarize the various criticisms that have been leveled against Lott's study, on both theoretical and methodological grounds. Many raise legitimate concerns, prompting the authors to conclude that, given the gravity of the issue, "it is probably wiser to push for more study than for more laws."

4.3   Primitive Law Enforcement

We noted above that retribution—the concept of proportionality of punishments to harms—is an important characteristic of the Anglo-American criminal justice system. And while it is a concept that we normally associate with modern attitudes about appropriate punishment, it actually had its origins in primitive notions of retaliation and vengeance.[52] Although we tend to view such impulses as irrational, they may well have served an important function in societies that lacked formal law enforcement institutions.

In modern societies, the government has a monopoly on criminal punishment, but in primitive societies with no public law enforcement, that responsibility fell to private individuals. The basic mechanism by which punishment was exacted was retaliation by the victim or his kinship group. It seems hard to view this practice as rational, however, since the risks to the victim and his kin, and the high probability that a feud would erupt, surely must have exceeded any perceived benefit. But sometimes, the mere perception of irrationality can prove beneficial. To illustrate, suppose that a potential offender knows that the intended victim and his kin have

> an unshakable *policy* of retaliation that is not reexamined or changed each time he suffers some aggression. Knowledge that a victim will retaliate when attacked without making a fresh cost-benefit analysis will discourage aggression more effectively than knowledge that the victim will respond "rationally" to each act of aggression by weighing the costs and benefits of retaliation as they then appear. (Posner 1983, 210)

The policy of "mutually assured destruction" between the United States and Soviet Union during the cold war similarly relied on each side's commitment to retaliate after a first strike, even though such an action would have been irrational after the fact (Schell 1982, 196–208).

Modern societies solve the commitment problem by establishing a public policy to apprehend and punish offenders. In this setting, the notion of retribution, though originally grounded in the impulse for revenge, actually serves as a *limit* on the severity of punishment according to the norm of proportionality, and, as we have seen, impedes the use of high-severity, low-probability punishment schemes as prescribed by economic theory.

Another noteworthy attribute of primitive law enforcement is that retaliation was not limited to the offender, but also extended to his kinship group. Like notions of revenge, this practice seems objectionable to modern sensibilities because it severs the link between guilt and responsibility. Again, however, this can be interpreted as an efficient response to the absence of public enforcement because it gives kinsmen an incentive to police themselves before the commission of harmful acts, and also to turn over offenders after the fact. Moreover, this reliance on "group responsibility" to save on enforcement costs is not without its modern counterparts, ranging from the imposition of sanctions on college fraternities for pranks committed by their members, to military operations against countries harboring terrorists.[53]

4.4 Some Constitutional Issues

An extensive survey of the relatively new field of constitutional law and economics is well beyond the scope of this book (see Cooter 2000), but it is worth examining some issues as they relate to criminal law. We have already examined constitutional aspects of the death penalty and plea bargaining; here we examine free speech, the rule against self-incrimination, and the right of privacy.

4.4.1 Free Speech

Economists view restrictions on speech in the same way that they view regulations of ordinary markets: Will the proposed restriction increase the efficiency of the "market for ideas"?[54] This view may seem contrary to the First

Amendment's guarantee of free speech, but this protection, as interpreted by courts, is not absolute, suggesting that a balancing of costs and benefits may be a useful way to think about the limits of free speech. For example, in the case of *Schenk v. United States* (249 U.S. 47, 1919), the Supreme Court upheld the conviction of a man for spreading antiwar propaganda because it created a "clear and present danger" to the war effort. In the case, Justice Holmes, writing for the majority, used the now famous example that the Constitution does not protect one's right to falsely shout fire in a crowded theater.

This decision suggests that the benefits of speech must be weighed against the expected harm. The benefits come from the communication of ideas. As we saw in our discussion of intellectual property in Chapter 6, ideas have the characteristics of public goods in the sense that they can be simultaneously consumed by many people without diminishing their value. Thus, efficiency dictates that they should be disseminated broadly. But speakers cannot easily capture the value of their ideas, so they will tend to undersupply them to the "market." This argues against restrictions on speech, which would only exacerbate the problem of undersupply.

But not all speech is purely beneficial; some can be harmful (falsely shouting fire) or offensive (hate speech or pornography). This tends to work in the direction of regulating speech for the same reason that it is efficient to regulate markets with negative externalities like pollution. An efficient test for regulation of speech balances the benefits of regulation (prevention of harm) against the cost (suppression of ideas). Formally, a restriction on speech is efficient if and only if

$$B < pH + O, \tag{9.13}$$

where B is the benefit of the targeted speech, H is the harm that will occur with probability p, and O is the offensiveness (Posner 2001, 67). (O is not multiplied by p because it is assumed to occur as soon as the offensive speech is uttered.)

This condition, which represents a formalization of the Supreme Court's "clear and present danger" standard (and resembles the Hand test for negligence), can be used to examine the desirability of restricting certain kinds of speech. Political speech has the highest degree of constitutional protection because wide dissemination of competing ideas about government is essential to the maintenance of a vigorous democracy. In terms of condition (9.13), B is very high. This is not to say that the costs of political speech are zero—it can incite violence or be offensive, but the presumption is that on balance, the costs of restricting political speech far outweigh the benefits.

An extreme example of this is flag burning (Rasmusen 1998a). In 1989, the Supreme Court invalidated a Texas statute criminalizing flag burning.[55]

Opponents of such laws argue that desecration sends an important political message, and hence is entitled to the highest degree of protection. Advocates of laws against flag burning counter that, so long as other forms of speech are unrestricted, the *idea* underlying the act can often be communicated nearly as effectively but in less offensive ways. This suggests that the benefits of flag burning (relative to other forms of political expression) may be small compared to the costs, which explains why laws against flag burning are more likely to be acceptable compared to restrictions on ordinary political speech.

Statutory limits on campaign contributions similarly raise the question of whether constitutional protections extend to the *manner* of communicating an idea, as opposed to its content. It is clear that wealthier individuals have greater access to various means of influencing public opinion, but at what point does that justify regulations aimed at leveling the playing field? The effects are offsetting—on the one hand, a spending limit will reduce the overall amount of speech, but on the other, it will decrease the weight given to wealthy interests. Again, economic theory suggests that it is a close call.

Finally, consider laws against libelous speech, which allow a plaintiff to recover damages suffered as a result of false and defamatory assertions. In general, a statement about an individual is efficient if the social benefits (the probability the statement is true times the value if true) exceed the costs (the probability the statement is false times the cost if false). Imposing liability for false statements makes sense because it forces the speaker to internalize the expected harm of his statement. But if the target of the speech is a public figure like a politician or entertainer, the speaker may not be able to internalize the full benefits. In this case, strict liability overly deters such speech. Consistent with this logic, courts tend to be less willing to allow recovery of damages for libel against public figures. (For example, a public figure needs to prove malice on the part of the speaker while a private figure does not.) (Cooter 2000, 326 27.)

4.4.2 The Rule Against Self-Incrimination

Although we have seen that a high percentage of criminal defendants plead guilty in return for a reduced sentence, the Fifth Amendment gives them the right to refuse to testify against themselves. Some have criticized this protection on the grounds that it primarily protects the guilty. An economic analysis shows, however, that in some circumstances, the right to silence can actually benefit innocent defendants by making their denials of guilt more believable (Seidmann and Stein 2000).

To see why, suppose that a right to silence were not available. What this means is that juries would be entitled to draw an inference of guilt from silence since truly innocent defendants would presumably always be willing to assert their innocence. Knowing this, guilty defendants have a strong incentive to assert their innocence as well since, although they may be discovered in a lie, they are still better off attempting to mimic the behavior of the truly innocent to avoid the negative inference. This "pooling equilibrium," however, adversely affects the innocent because it reduces the believability of all defendants' testimony. (In effect, the behavior of guilty defendants imposes a negative externality on innocent defendants.)

In contrast, the right to silence allows guilty defendants to refuse to make possibly incriminating statements without creating a presumption of guilt. In so doing, they separate themselves from innocent defendants (who have no incentive to remain silent), thus increasing the believability of the latter's denials of guilt.

A simple model helps to clarify this argument. Suppose a defendant has been apprehended, and, based on the evidence against him, faces a probability of conviction equal to p. Let a be the probability that the defendant is innocent and $1 - a$ the probability that he is guilty. As noted, innocent defendants will always have an incentive to testify in an effort to refute the evidence, but guilty defendants may or may not testify, depending on how the court is allowed to interpret their silence.

Suppose first that there is no right to silence, so the court can infer guilt from silence. In this case, all guilty defendants will testify because, although they may implicate themselves, they will be seen as guilty with certainty if they remain silent. As a result, however, the court can make no inferences about the guilt or innocence of a defendant by his mere act of testifying. Specifically, the conditional probability that the defendant is innocent, given that he testified, is equal to the prior probability of innocence, a.

Now suppose that defendants have the right to remain silent, which means that the court *cannot* draw an inference of guilt from their refusal to testify. Innocent defendants will continue to testify, but some guilty defendants will now refuse to do so because they are more likely to incriminate themselves than to be found guilty on the evidence. Let $g < 1$ be the probability that guilty defendants will testify based on these considerations. In this case, the conditional probability that the defendant is innocent, given that he testifies, is

$$\Pr(\text{innocent} \mid \text{testify}) = \frac{a}{a + (1 - a)g}. \tag{9.14}$$

It should be easy to see that, so long as $g < 1$, this expression is greater than a. It follows that the court can give greater credence to the defendant's testimony than in the case where the right to silence was not available. (In the extreme case where $g = 0$, (9.14) equals one, or testimony is a sure sign of innocence.) This helps innocent defendants by making their denials of guilt more believable.

Consider the following example as an illustration. Suppose that 10 percent of defendants are innocent ($a = .1$), and, when they have a right to silence, 15 percent of guilty defendants choose to testify ($g = .15$). The expression in (9.14) equals approximately .43. Thus, the right to silence has resulted in a fourfold increase in the probability of innocence, conditional on testifying.

4.4.3   The Right of Privacy

The notion of privacy touches on many areas of the law, most controversially, a woman's right to an abortion, which is based on the constitutional right to privacy.[56] In this section, however, we limit discussion to two areas of criminal law that involve privacy: namely, the constitutional prohibition of unreasonable searches and seizures, and the law of blackmail. The economic factor that ties these two issues together is the "social interest in preserving deservedly good reputations *and* in preserving deservedly bad reputations from concealment" (Posner 1998b, 104). (It should therefore be apparent that the right of privacy also underlies laws against libelous and defamatory speech as discussed above.)

Searches and Seizures.   The Fourth Amendment protects people from unreasonable searches and seizures in connection with criminal investigations. The use of a reasonableness standard, however, suggests that some searches should be allowed and others prohibited based on a balancing of costs and benefits (Posner 1998a, ch. 28).

To illustrate, suppose a person is suspected of committing a crime, but he cannot be convicted without evidence. The expected benefit of a search is the product of P, the probability that sufficient evidence will be found to obtain a conviction, and B, the social benefit of the conviction. The cost of the search, C, is the cost of the invasion of the suspect's privacy, a large part of which may be the loss in reputation of an innocent person from the cloud of suspicion that falls on any individual who is a target of a criminal investigation. Based on these factors, a search is reasonable if

$$C < PB. \tag{9.15}$$

The law enforces this standard in two ways. The first is the requirement that the police must obtain a warrant prior to initiating a search. This gives an impartial judge the opportunity to evaluate the inequality in (9.15). The second remedy is the "exclusionary rule," which disallows the use of evidence that was acquired by an unconstitutional search. The object of the rule, of course, is to deter such searches, but some have argued that it results in overdeterrence while conferring a benefit on guilty defendants.

An alternative to the exclusionary rule is tort liability for unreasonable searches. Advocates argue that this is a superior remedy because it sets a "price" for illegally acquired evidence that the police will only pay "when the evidentiary benefits exceeded the costs to the victim of the search" (Posner 2001, 398). As a result, the efficient amount of evidence will be obtained. This solution, however, abstracts from the agency problem of how the police department would impose the incentive effects of tort liability on individual officers who may be judgment proof. It also suffers from the possibility that juries may be reluctant to award damages to defendants who turn out to be guilty.

Blackmail.   The paradigmatic case of blackmail occurs when someone acquires compromising or embarrassing information about another person (for example, infidelity to a spouse) and then withholds that information in return for a monetary payment. On first glance, the criminality of blackmail seems puzzling to an economist because it makes illegal a transaction that apparently produces a mutual benefit to the two parties. On further consideration, however, it is clear that there is a market failure involved.

To see why, consider a proposed "transaction" between two parties, a buyer B and a seller S. (They could be potential marriage partners.) Based on the information she has, B believes that the "good" she is acquiring is of high quality and is worth V_H, when in fact, S knows it is of low quality and only worth $V_L < V_H$. (For example, S is a philanderer.) Now suppose that a third party, T, learns of the true quality of the good. T can profit from this information in one of two ways: by selling it to B so that she can break the contract with S (or renegotiate it), or by charging S to withhold it. In both cases, the price would be $V_H - V_L$, so T should be indifferent between the two transactions.

Note, however, that a sale of the information to B presents some difficulties. Before making the payment, B would naturally request to see evidence that the good is of low quality, but once she has seen the evidence, she may claim she already knew it and refuse to pay. Thus, T may have difficulty in appropriating the value of the information in a transaction with B. Such a problem does not exist in the transaction with S, however, because S already knows the true quality of the good he is selling and wants the information withheld. For this reason, T will likely favor the transaction with S.[57]

But why is the transaction between T and S illegal? Consider the problem from the perspective of efficiency. The original transaction between B and S involves asymmetric information about the quality of a good being traded, which is a potential source of market failure. Increasing the amount of information available to uninformed parties—as would occur if T sells his information to B—therefore enhances efficiency by allowing goods to be priced at the correct level. In contrast, transactions that prevent the revelation of information (like that between T and S) impede efficiency. Since traders may prefer the latter transaction for reasons noted above, it is necessary to criminalize it in order to encourage transactions in which information is revealed. This same logic explains why it is perfectly legal for third parties to gather information about product quality and sell it to consumers (for example, in magazines like *Consumer Reports*), but illegal for them to charge companies for agreeing to withhold the same information.

5   Conclusion

This chapter surveyed the economic model of criminal law. We began by suggesting several reasons why criminal law (public enforcement) may be preferred to tort law (private enforcement) for the prevention of certain kinds of harmful activities. Our conclusions, while suggestive, revealed that a fully satisfactory theory of the distinction between crimes and torts remains lacking.

We then turned to the economic model of crime, which is based on the assumption that criminals are (for the most part) rational calculators who weigh the costs and benefits before committing illegal acts. Given this "rational offender" model, we derived optimal punishment schemes based on the goal of deterrence. Actual punishments, however, tend to deviate from those prescribed by the theory in at least three ways: fines are not maximal, punishments are not scaled to reflect imperfect apprehension, and imprisonment is overused. These deviations offer important insights into the range of values beyond efficiency that are embodied in the criminal justice system.

In addition to deriving optimal punishment schemes, we used economic theory to shed light on various policy issues related to criminal justice, such as the desirability of the death penalty, gun laws, and the practice of plea bargaining. Finally, we used economic analysis to gain insight into some constitutional issues that touch on criminal law, including the right of free speech, the right against self-incrimination, and the right of privacy. Throughout the chapter, we highlighted empirical tests of the economic model of crime, as this constitutes one of the fastest-growing areas of research in law and economics.

DISCUSSION QUESTIONS

1. Explain the sense in which criminal penalties are "prices" designed to elicit the "efficient" level of crime.

2. Should unsuccessful attempts to commit a crime be punished? If so, why?

3. Police often use undercover agents to induce individuals to commit crimes (deal drugs, solicit prostitution) and then arrest them. In some such cases, however, a defendant can avoid prosecution by claiming entrapment. Can you give an economic argument for when the defense of entrapment should be allowed?

4. Conspiracies to commit a crime are ordinarily punished more severely than if a single person committed the same crime. Why does this make economic sense?

5. Suppose an individual commits a crime while employed by another. Under what conditions will optimal deterrence be achieved by a policy of sanctioning the employer rather than (or in addition to) the employee?

6. Why might deterrence be enhanced by awarding a share of criminal fines to enforcers? What problems might such a compensation scheme create?

PROBLEMS

1. Suppose the following information has been gathered on the enforcement of a speed limit on a particular highway over a holiday weekend:

Expenditure on enforcement	Probability of apprehension (p)	Expected fine (pf)	No. of speeders
$ 1,000	.1	$ 0	1,000
10,000	.5	50	500
100,000	.9	100	100
		1,000	5

(a) Suppose the goal is to limit the number of speeders to 500. What actual fine, f, and what probability of apprehension, p, minimizes the cost of achieving this goal?

(b) Suppose the actual fine for speeding is statutorily capped at $100. What now is the minimum expenditure on enforcement that achieves the goal of 500 speeders?

2. Suppose that a drug dealer can earn $1,000 from selling drugs illegally and that the probability of apprehension is .25.

(a) Show that a penalty requiring drug dealers to surrender their profits in the event of conviction will fail to deter them.

(b) What is the lowest fine that will just deter the drug dealer?

3. A potential offender contemplates committing burglary in one of two neighborhoods. If caught, he faces a fine of $5,000 regardless of where he commits

the crime. (Assume he can afford to pay it.) However, the gain from committing the crime, g, and the probability of apprehension, p, differ by neighborhood as follows:

	g	p
Neighborhood 1	$1,000	.1
Neighborhood 2	$2,000	.25

(a) What is the net expected return from crime in each of the two neighborhoods?

(b) Suppose the criminal can work legally for $700, or commit a crime in one of the neighborhoods. What is his optimal strategy?

(c) What is the lowest fine that would just deter the criminal from committing any crimes?

4. Suppose that optimal deterrence of a particular crime requires setting the expected punishment equal to $2,000. Assume that the probability of apprehension is fixed at .2.

(a) Suppose an offender has wealth of $5,000 and incurs a cost of $1,000 per month spent in prison. What combination of a fine and prison term achieves optimal deterrence at the lowest cost?

(b) What combination of a fine and prison term is optimal for an offender with wealth of $7,000? (Assume he incurs the same monthly cost of imprisonment.)

(c) Suppose considerations of fairness dictate that the prison term of offenders who commit the same crime must be the same. What fine and prison term must be imposed on the two offenders to maintain optimal deterrence? Explain the sense in which this policy reflects a trade-off between fairness and efficiency.

5. Suppose a prosecutor expects to convict a defendant with probability .5, and that the sentence on conviction is ten years in prison. Assume the prosecutor values prison time at $1,000 per year (its value as a deterrent of crime), and incurs a cost of trial equal to $2,000.

(a) What is the minimum prison sentence the prosecutor will offer as part of a plea bargain if her objective is to maximize the expected value of the sentence imposed, less the cost of trial (if any)?

(b) Suppose the defendant believes his chances of being convicted are .30, his cost of prison time is $5,000 per year, and his cost of a trial is $1,000. Will he accept the plea bargain in (a)?

6. Suppose a crime has been committed and a suspect apprehended. The prosecutor estimates that the probability of conviction is .3 for innocent defendants and .4 for guilty defendants. Suppose that the legislated punishment on con-

viction at trial imposes a dollar cost of $1,000 on both types of defendants, and the cost of a trial is $50 for both.

(a) For each of the following plea offers, state whether each type of defendant will accept or reject the offer:

(i) $300

(ii) $400

(iii) $500

(b) Which offer (or offers) results in different treatments of innocent and guilty defendants? Is it possible to make an offer that is acceptable to an innocent defendant but would be rejected by a guilty defendant? Explain.

10

THE ECONOMICS OF ANTITRUST LAW

This chapter examines the economic justification for antitrust laws, or that body of statutes and judicial rulings whose objective is to prevent anticompetitive business practices. Economists have long contributed to this area of law, leading many to label it as the "old" law and economics (as opposed to the "new" law and economics, which refers to the economic study of areas of law not explicitly concerned with markets—that is, the subject of the previous nine chapters of this book). Antitrust nevertheless remains a vigorous subfield of law and economics. This is true because, unlike many areas of law studied by economists, there is little doubt that economic theory has much to contribute to our understanding of the efficient operation of markets.

Of course, the starting point for any investigation of market regulation must be the Invisible Hand Theorem, which says that competitive markets, if left unregulated, will achieve an efficient allocation of resources. While this may suggest a laissez-faire attitude toward regulation, the conditions for perfect competition are rarely if ever met in practice. Thus, when significant departures from competition exist, whether through the efforts of a single firm, or a group of firms acting in concert, to exercise monopoly power, the resulting misallocation of resources may justify government intervention. This is the economic rationale for antitrust law.

The literature on antitrust is vast, so this chapter only offers an overview of some of the key issues, with an emphasis on the insights economic theory can offer. We begin with a review of the economics of perfect competition, which provides a benchmark for measuring the efficiency losses due to monopoly. We then turn to the role of the law in promoting competition.

1 Perfect Competition Versus Monopoly

A monopoly is defined to be a market that is served by a single seller. The problem of monopoly, and the economic justification for legal intervention to prevent it, is that monopolistic firms set a price and output level that are inefficient, resulting in a loss of welfare. The nature of this loss is best seen in relation to a perfectly competitive market, which, because it allocates resources efficiently, maximizes social welfare.

1.1 Competitive Markets and Welfare

The defining characteristic of a competitive market is the large number of firms, which makes it impossible for any one firm to affect the market price. For this reason, we say that firms are "price takers." Figure 10.1 illustrates the determination of equilibrium price and quantity in a competitive market. The left panel shows the market output and price, which is determined by the intersection of the supply and demand curves. At this point, the amount of the good that consumers want to buy at the market price exactly equals the aggregate amount that producers supply to the market. The right panel of Figure 10.1 shows the corresponding output of an individual firm, q^*, which occurs where the equilibrium price of the good (the firm's marginal revenue), equals its marginal cost, or where $P^* = MC$.[1]

The outcome depicted in Figure 10.1 represents a competitive equilibrium in the sense that neither consumers nor producers have an incentive to change

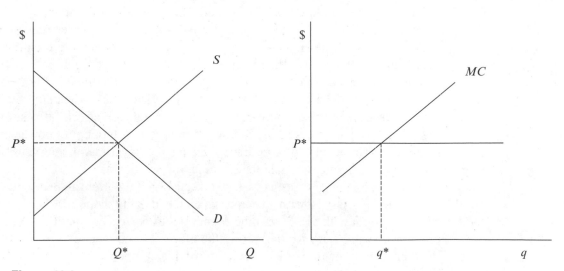

Figure 10.1
Market and Individual Firm Output and Price in a Competitive Market

their behavior given the established price. Individual firms are supplying the quantities that maximize their profits, and the aggregate amount supplied is just enough to satisfy the demands of consumers at that price. Further, this outcome is efficient in that the cost of producing the last unit of output just equals the value of that unit to the marginal consumer. Another way to say this is that all mutually beneficial trades between consumers and producers are made.

A dollar measure of the resulting gains from trade is shown in the left panel of Figure 10.1 by the area between the demand and supply curves, up to the equilibrium level of output, Q^*. The portion of this area below the demand curve and above the price is called the *consumer surplus*, which is defined to be the net gains from trade enjoyed by consumers. Similarly, the area above the supply curve and below the price is called the *producer surplus*, which is defined to be the net gains from trade enjoyed by producers.[2] It is a fundamental result of economic theory—referred to as the Invisible Hand Theorem—that competitive markets maximize the sum of consumer and producer surplus. This is why the competitive market provides the benchmark for evaluating the welfare loss associated with monopoly.

1.2 Monopoly

Monopolistic firms seek to maximize profit, just like competitive firms, but because they control the entire market, their output and pricing decisions are different. The monopolist, like the competitor, produces output at the point where marginal revenue equals marginal cost, but marginal revenue for the monopolist is not the same as for a competitor. Recall that for a competitive firm that takes price as given, marginal revenue equals price because every unit is sold for the same price. But for a monopolist who faces the market demand curve, marginal revenue is less than price. This is true because the market demand curve is downward sloping, which means that in order to sell an additional unit of the good, the monopolist must lower the price for that unit, as well as for all previous units. (This assumes that the monopolist cannot charge different prices to different consumers, a practice called price discrimination.)

To illustrate, suppose the monopolist can sell ten units of a good for $50, yielding total revenue of $500. In order to sell eleven units, however, it must lower the price, say to $48, yielding total revenue of $528. The marginal revenue from the eleventh unit is thus $28, which is less than the price. Marginal revenue is actually made up of two components: the gain of $48 from selling the last unit, minus the loss of $20 from having to sell the original ten units for $2 less. Together, these amounts yield the net gain of $28.

Figure 10.2 illustrates the demand (*D*) and marginal revenue (*MR*) curves

Figure 10.2

Output and Price
under a Monopoly
with Constant
Marginal Costs

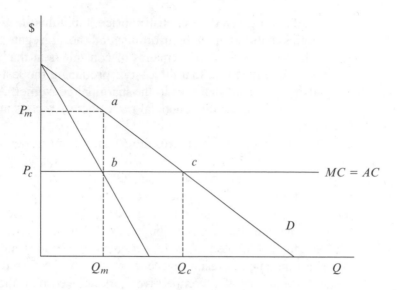

for the monopolist. It also shows the profit-maximizing output and price for the case where the monopolist has a constant marginal (= average) cost ($MC = AC$). Output, Q_m, is determined by the intersection of the marginal revenue and marginal cost curves, while price, P_m, is determined by locating the point on the demand curve corresponding to optimal output. This represents the highest price consumers would pay for that level of output. The resulting producer surplus for the monopolist is given by the area of the rectangle P_mabP_c.

For comparison, the graph shows the outcome that would result if the industry were organized competitively but had the same demand and cost conditions. In this case, output (Q_c) and price (P_c) would be determined by the intersection of the demand and marginal cost curves, resulting in greater output and a lower price compared to the monopoly outcome. The welfare loss associated with monopoly is due to the restriction in output from Q_c to Q_m, which deprives society of the gains from trade associated with those foregone units. This loss can be quantified in Figure 10.2 as the triangle *abc*, which represents the loss in consumer surplus compared to the competitive case.[3] In addition to this *deadweight loss*, consumers suffer a loss of the area P_mabP_c, which represents a *transfer* of consumer surplus to profit. Preventing or minimizing these losses from monopoly is an important economic rationale for antitrust law.

1.3 Cartels

A monopoly outcome does not require existence of a single firm; it can also arise if multiple firms successfully collude to set the market price and quantity. Antitrust law is therefore also concerned with prevention of this sort of price fixing, or any other practices seen as significantly impeding the attainment of a competitive outcome. Economic theory shows, however, that, despite the potential gains from such agreements, collusive behavior is quite difficult to sustain.

To illustrate, consider two firms who share a particular market. Suppose initially that they collude to set the monopoly price and output, yielding aggregate profits of $16, which they share equally. As shown above, sustaining the monopoly outcome requires each firm to set a price above its marginal cost. But note that this creates a situation where each firm, acting on its own, has an incentive to lower its price slightly, thereby capturing a larger share of the market and increasing its profits (though aggregate profits must fall). For purposes of the example, suppose that the cheater captures the entire market by this action, earning a profit of $12, while the other firm gets nothing. However, if both firms cheat they again split the market, yielding each of them $6 in profit.

Table 10.1 summarizes these returns, assuming that each firm has only two strategies: "cheat" or "comply." To determine the equilibrium outcome of this interaction, consider the optimal behavior of firm one. Since it does not know what strategy firm two will follow, we begin by deriving its optimal reaction for each of firm two's options. First, if firm two cheats (the top row of Table 10.1), it is best for firm one also to cheat because it earns $6 versus zero. Alternatively, if firm two complies (the bottom row of Table 10.1), it is again best for firm one to cheat because it earns $12 versus $8. Since it is better for firm one to cheat regardless of firm two's choice, we say that cheating is a *dominant strategy* for firm one. It should be clear that the same logic applies to firm two's optimal behavior, implying that the unique equilibrium is for both firms to cheat.[4] This outcome is an equilibrium because neither firm wishes to change its behavior given the behavior of the other firm.

The preceding analysis reveals the inherent instability of cartel agreements, suggesting that antitrust law need not be terribly concerned with preventing price fixing. This conclusion would be premature, however, because it relies on a simple model that ignores various enforcement strategies by which firms

TABLE **10.1** **Payoffs for the Cartel Example**

		Firm 1	
		Cheat	Comply
Firm 2	Cheat	$6 each	$0 for Firm 1 $12 for Firm 2
	Comply	$0 for Firm 2 $12 for Firm 1	$8 each

may succeed in sustaining collusive agreements. For example, collusion will become more likely as firms recognize that they are playing a long term, or "repeated," game with one another, which implies that cheating will involve a larger cost than is reflected by the "one shot" game described above. In this setting, deviation from the collusive strategy by a firm (for example, by undercutting the cartel price) can be met by a lengthy period during which the cheating firm is denied a share of the cartel profits. The longer is the perceived time horizon, the larger is the cost from cheating, and hence, the more effective this sort of punishment can be for maintaining collusion.[5]

2 Antitrust Law

The first major anti-monopoly act passed by Congress was the Sherman Act (1890), which prohibited "Every contract, combination in the form of trust or otherwise, or conspiracy, in the restraint of trade or commerce" (Section 1), and also made it illegal to "monopolize, or attempt to monopolize, or combine or conspire with any person or persons, to monopolize any part of the trade or commerce among the several States, or with foreign nations . . ." (Section 2). Penalties for violating these provisions included both criminal and civil sanctions, as discussed further below.

The Sherman Act was criticized, however, as lacking specificity as to what exactly constituted an actionable restraint of trade, as well as for failing to provide for certain practices that "did not present an existing condition of monopoly, but were likely to create unacceptable levels of market power" (Gilbert and Williamson 1998, 82–83). In response Congress passed the Clayton Act (1914), which made illegal a specific set of acts that were deemed to be anticompetitive. These included *price discrimination* (the practice of charging different prices to different consumers for the same good), *tie-in sales* and *exclusive dealing* arrangements (agreements that limit a buyer's options), and *mergers* that tend to result in monopoly (Hylton 2003, 30). The Clayton Act nevertheless remained vague in that the preceding practices were deemed to be illegal only to the extent that they "substantially" lessened competition.

The Federal Trade Commission (FTC) was also created in 1914 to enforce the antitrust laws. In addition, the FTC was empowered "to prosecute . . . anticompetitive practices that the Sherman or Clayton Acts may be unable to punish, due to the difficulty of meeting proof requirements under those statutes" (Hylton 2003, 40). After nearly a hundred years, however, courts and policymakers continue to wrestle with the exact meaning of the antitrust statutes and how they should be enforced. One reason for this is political, reflecting different attitudes on the part of courts and policymakers regarding the proper role of the government in the economy, but another is simply the practical difficulty of distinguishing truly monopolistic behavior from benign business practices that in some cases may enhance efficiency in the presence of other market imperfections (as discussed further in Section 4 below).

2.1　Enforcement and Remedies

Enforcement of antitrust laws occurs through a number of channels, both public and private. In addition to the FTC, the antitrust division of the Justice Department can enforce the Sherman and Clayton Acts, by means of either civil or criminal prosecution. The Clayton Act can also be enforced by any persons or businesses seeking damages caused by conduct in violation of the antitrust laws. Successful plaintiffs are entitled to recover treble damages (three times the amount of damages incurred), plus the cost of the suit and reasonable attorneys' fees. (See the further discussion of optimal fines below.) Finally, state attorneys general can bring suit on behalf of the citizens of their states under the Clayton Act (Hylton 2003, 47–49).

2.2　The Per Se Rule Versus the Rule of Reason

Despite this array of mechanisms, enforcement of antitrust laws is not easy, owing to the vague language of the various statutes. It has therefore fallen to the courts to clarify the nature of prohibited acts. Early on, for example, the U.S. Supreme Court ruled that the Sherman Act did not prohibit all restraints of trade, only those that were deemed to be "unreasonable." The resulting *rule of reason* test is based on a "balancing of the likely competitive harm from a restraint of trade against its likely pro-competitive benefits" (Gilbert and Williamson 1998, 83).

The first case establishing this idea was *Standard Oil Co. v. United States* (221 U.S. 1, 1911). Prior to coming under antitrust scrutiny by the government, Standard Oil of New Jersey had controlled at least 80 percent of the refining capacity in the United States. The Supreme Court ruled, however, that the existence of this monopoly power was not itself a violation of the Sherman Act; the company must also have used that power abusively or unreasonably. In the end, the Court found that Standard Oil had in fact done so, and hence ordered the company broken into multiple independent companies.

The rule of reason test consists of two components: first, the court must identify a *conduct* in violation of the Sherman Act, and second, it must find an *intent to monopolize*, usually inferred from the absence of an efficiency justification for the conduct in question (Hylton 2003, 187). This standard is in contrast to the so-called *per se* rule, which prohibits a particular conduct or business practice irrespective of its actual impact on competitiveness.

The Court affirmed the rule of reason test in *United States v. U.S. Steel Corp.* (251 U.S. 417, 1920) when it held that U.S. Steel had not violated the Sherman Act despite its large market share. In arriving at this ruling, the Court re-iterated the proposition that the "law does not make mere size an offense." The Court concluded, based on the second prong of the reasonableness test from *Standard Oil*, "that U.S. Steel's growth came through superior efficiency rather than competition-stifling tactics" (Hylton 2003, 188).

The reader may have noticed that the relationship between the rule of reason and the per se rule is analogous to that between negligence and strict liability in tort law. (See Section 2.1.3 of Chapter 2.) While the former involves a balancing of the costs and benefits of a particular practice (similar to the Hand test), the latter finds the practice unlawful if meets the statutory definition of a prohibited practice. As we have previously argued, the optimal choice between these two approaches to legal rule making depends on which minimizes the expected costs of legal error plus administrative costs. Generally, we would expect that the per se rule will result in a greater risk of legal error because of its inflexibility, while the rule of reason will involve significantly higher administrative costs because of the greater amount of judicial fact-finding needed to implement it (Hylton 2003, ch. 6). (Recall that we made a similar argument about the higher cost of administering negligence compared to strict liability.) The choice between the two rules therefore depends on a comparison of the resulting costs.

Still, the rule of reason is not immune to error, principally because it places a high burden on the court to evaluate the market effects of various business practices. As an illustration, in *U.S. v. Aluminum Co. of America (Alcoa)* (148 F.2d 416, 1945), Judge Learned Hand (of the Hand rule) ordered the break-up of Alcoa because the company controlled 90 percent of the aluminum market, despite the fact that this monopoly power apparently had not translated into excess profits for the company. Judge Hand nevertheless argued that Alcoa's monopoly position was illegal because the company had acquired it by expanding its capacity to block entry rather than to meet demand. But, as Hylton (2003, 191) observes, "Most of the entry-blocking actions Judge Hand described could also serve as examples of superior skill, foresight, and industry", in short, as legitimate economic reasons to expand. Note that the presumption that certain acts are deemed anticompetitive effectively transforms the rule of reason into a per se rule, much as the tort doctrine of *res ipsa loquitur* transforms a negligence rule into strict liability. (See Section 3.3.3 in Chapter 2.)

2.3 Optimal Fines

Given a guilty verdict in an antitrust suit, what is the optimal magnitude of the fine?[6] If the goal is to deter socially harmful practices, then our analysis of tort law in Chapter 2 suggests that the defendant should face a fine equal to the external harm suffered by victims—in this case, consumers. (Theoretically, the fine could also be used to compensate consumers, but this would be nearly impossible to carry out in practice.)

Considering first the situation of costless enforcement (that is, violators are caught with certainty and litigation is costless), the optimal fine is simply equal to the sum of the deadweight loss from monopoly, plus the transfer of consumer surplus to producer surplus. Return to Figure 10.2 and recall that the deadweight loss, denoted D, is given by the area of the triangle abc, while the monopoly transfer, denoted T, is given by the area of the rectangle $P_m abP_c$. The optimal fine is thus

$$f = D + T. \tag{10.1}$$

We noted above, however, that enforcement of antitrust laws is not easy, both because of the cost of detecting and proving a violation (which makes it uncertain that a violator will be penalized), and because litigation is costly. To capture the uncertainty of punishment, let p be the probability that a violator will be detected and convicted, and let C be the plaintiff's cost of bringing the suit. In this case, the optimal fine becomes

$$f = (D + T)/p + C, \tag{10.2}$$

where the multiplier $1/p$ corrects for the uncertainty of conviction, and the addition of C forces the defendant to internalize the plaintiff's legal costs. Note that the formula in (10.2) reflects the economic justification for punitive damages in Chapter 2 (Section 3.5), as well as the optimal criminal fine in Chapter 9 (Section 2.2.1).

As noted, private parties are allowed to sue for compensation under antitrust laws—indeed, the bulk of antitrust suits come from private parties as opposed to the government. Recall that under the Clayton Act, winners of such suits can collect treble damages plus the costs of bringing to suit. How does this rule comport with the optimal fine derived in (10.2)? Suppose initially that the court sets damages equal to the total harm, $D + T$, implying that $f = 3(D + T) + C$. Comparison of this expression with (10.2) implies that the two are equivalent if and only if $p = 1/3$, or if the probability of conviction is exactly one-third. It follows that treble damages underdeters if $p < 1/3$ and overdeters if $p > 1/3$.

More realistically, only the transfer, T, will be compensable because the court will not be able to measure D. In this case, the treble damages rule implies a fine of $f = 3T + C$. Equating this with (10.2) yields

$$3T = (D + T)/p. \tag{10.3}$$

For purposes of evaluating this condition, we consider the case of a straight-line demand curve and constant marginal costs, as shown in Figure 10.2. It is easy to show that under these assumptions, $D = T/2$. That is, the magnitude of the deadweight loss is exactly equal to one-half of the transfer.[7] Substituting this into (10.3) yields the result that $p = 1/2$; that is, the treble damages rule is optimal if and only if $p = 1/2$. (It therefore underdeters if $p < 1/2$ and overdeters if $p > 1/2$.)

Absent information about the value of p in actual antitrust cases, it is impossible to say whether either version of the treble damage rule approximates the optimal fine. It is noteworthy that the law nevertheless operates as if it were correcting for the underdetection problem.

EXERCISE 10.1

Suppose that the inverse demand curve for a particular good is given by $P = \$60 - Q$, marginal revenue is $MR = \$60 - 2Q$, and marginal cost is constant at $MC = \$10$.

(a) Derive the monopolist's profit-maximizing price and output.
(b) Calculate the resulting profit and deadweight loss.
(c) What is the optimal fine in the case of costless and certain enforcement?
(d) What is the optimal fine if the probability of detection is .25 and the cost of a suit is $100? How does this compare to the fine under a treble damages rule when damages are set at $D + T$? What about the case where damages are limited to T?

3   The "New" Antitrust Law and Economics

The goal of antitrust law—promoting competition—is simple in theory but complex in practice. Under the traditional view, any departure from the standard competitive model, for example, in the form of a "nonstandard" or "unfamiliar" business practice, was viewed with skepticism. However, a more recent perspective, often associated with the Chicago School, has been open to seeking efficiency justifications for many practices that were previously seen as promoting monopoly. This section reviews some of the insights of this "new" view.[8]

3.1   Contestable Markets

A traditional test of monopoly power is to measure the market share of firms in an industry. The greater is the market share of an individual firm, the more market power it is presumed to have. Markets in which one or a few firms have substantial market shares are said to be highly concentrated, and hence are targets for antitrust enforcement. However, Baumol, Panzar, and Willig (1982) have pointed out that high market concentration is a necessary, but not a sufficient, condition for monopoly. If there is free entry and exit, they argue, new firms will enter if the incumbent firm (or firms) attempts to set prices above the competitive level. For this reason, firms in highly concentrated industries will nevertheless have an incentive to behave competitively in order to deter entry of potential competitors. Markets that have this characteristic are called "contestable markets." While this argument does not imply that concentrated markets should never be regulated, it does show that high concentration per se does not necessarily imply anticompetitive behavior.

3.2 Transaction Cost Economics

Transaction cost economics is based on the idea, first proposed by Coase (1937), that firms arise to coordinate economic transactions when markets become too costly. This perspective, which has been elaborated on by Williamson (1968, 1985), has significant implications for antitrust law, especially as regards the interpretation of long-term contracts and mergers.

Long-Term Contracts.   Traditional antitrust law viewed the firm as a production function and assumed that market failures could be identified by comparing market outcomes to the competitive ideal. In this view, any nonstandard business practice was seen as an effort to acquire monopoly power. Long-term contracts that seem to limit the options of contractors provide an example. The potential efficiency gains from such contracts, however, can be illustrated by recalling the discussion of the reserve clause in major league baseball from Chapter 5 (Section 3.3). Although the reserve clause was traditionally viewed as evidence of the collusive behavior of owners aimed at preventing players from negotiating with other teams,[9] we argued that there is also an efficiency justification for the restriction based on the incentive it creates for owners to make long-term investments in player development, given the transferability of the resulting human capital once a player is trained. It is one of the key insights of transaction cost economics that long-term contracts can actually enhance efficiency by promoting such investments.

Vertical Mergers.   Vertical mergers (that is, mergers between firms at different levels in the production process) raise antitrust concerns because they can potentially deter entry of rivals, or put them at a disadvantage by raising their costs. For example, a manufacturer may merge with retailers ("forward" integration) in order to gain a monopoly of desirable sales locations, or merge with suppliers ("backward" integration) in order to restrict a competitor's access to a key input (Hylton 2003, 335).

From the perspective of transaction cost economics, however, vertical mergers often serve the same function as long-term contracts. Specifically, two firms engaged in an ongoing contractual relationship may find it cheaper to organize their transactions within a single firm rather than by means of market exchange when the market becomes too costly.[10] As an illustration, recall the case of the contract between the ice company and the brewery from Chapter 4.[11] The contract called for the ice company to supply ice to the brewery during the summer to prevent spoilage of its beer. However, a dispute arose when the ice company demanded a price increase when an unexpectedly warm winter caused a short supply of ice. The cost of resolving disputes of this sort in court represents one of the costs of transacting via the market. Thus, in relationships where such disputes are expected to be common or costly (due to the presence of transaction-specific investments), it may be cheaper for the companies to merge. The point is that vertical mergers are not necessarily aimed at increasing market power; in many cases they may actually enhance efficiency by lowering transaction costs, with the savings often passed on to consumers.

Horizontal Mergers.   Horizontal mergers, or mergers between competing firms, represent a somewhat greater threat to competition compared to vertical mergers because they do increase the concentration of the market. However, as in the case of vertical mergers, there may be an offsetting efficiency gain if the merged firm is more efficient due to economies of scale.[12]

To illustrate the trade-off, consider a market that is initially served by two competitive firms that then merge to create a monopoly. Suppose the merger causes the average cost of the consolidated firm to be lower than it was for the two firms operating separately. The situation is illustrated in Figure 10.3, where AC_0 is the average cost for the individual firms, and AC_1 is the average cost for the merged firm. (For simplicity, we continue to assume a constant AC, so that $AC = MC$.) Since the firms were assumed to be competitive before the merger, they each set $P_c = AC_0$, but after the merger, the single firm exercises monopoly power and sets $P_m > AC_1$ as shown. In terms of welfare, the impact of the merger consists of a gain, given by the area of the rectangle $P_c bde$, all of which is realized as profit for the firm, and a deadweight loss, given by the area of the triangle *abc*. The net effect depends on the relative magnitudes of these offsetting effects, the lesson being that horizontal mergers are not necessarily bad things from an efficiency perspective.

In terms of enforcement policy, the discussion in this section has suggested that applying a per se rule of prohibiting mergers, whether vertical or horizontal, is not supported by economic theory. Rather, a reasonableness test should be used by courts that permits defenses based on the efficiency gains (if any) from a proposed merger. As noted above, however, implementation of

Figure 10.3

Welfare Trade-off from a Cost-Reducing Horizontal Merger

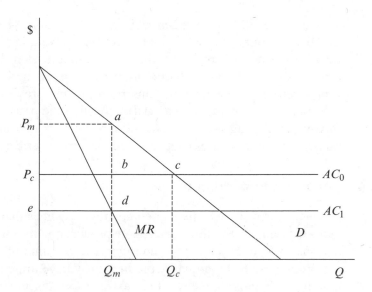

such a test is costly in practice because it places a high informational burden on the court to sort out the offsetting gains and losses.

3.3 Network Effects

Another issue that complicates the enforcement of antitrust law is the existence of so-called network effects in certain industries. A network effect exists when the value to a consumer of a particular product depends in part on how many other consumers purchase that same or complementary products. This effect is most commonly associated with high-tech industries where, for example, the more people who adopt a particular computer operating or video-recording system, the more useful that system is to consumers because they can more easily interact with other users. The downside is that such effects can be a barrier to entry of competing systems, even when those systems may be superior to the dominant one.

The recent antitrust case brought by the Justice Department against Microsoft illustrates the offsetting antitrust implications of network effects. Although there initially were competing operating systems for PCs, the Windows system eventually became dominant in the market. But, according to the Justice Department, Microsoft acted illegally when it used its resulting market power to bundle its operating system with a web browser, constituting a "so-called" tie-in sale of the two products. As noted above, tie-in sales are specifically prohibited by the Clayton Act. However, as in the case of mergers, tie-ins can enhance efficiency as well as reduce it, for example, by economizing on consumers' search costs, lowering production costs (due to economies of scope), or serving as a quality-assuring device (as detailed in the next section.)

In the case of Microsoft (*United States v. Microsoft*, 84 F.Supp.2d 9, 1999), the district court ruled that on net, consumers were harmed by Microsoft's bundling of its web browser with its operating system because competing browsers were effectively barred from entering the market. There has, however, been much debate about this ruling (some provisions of which were subsequently overturned on appeal), reflecting the practical difficulty courts face in untangling the offsetting welfare impacts of various marketing arrangements in industries characterized by network effects.

3.4   Imperfect Information

The benchmark case of perfect competition assumes that all market participants have complete information about product quality. Often, however, product quality is unobservable to consumers at the time of purchase, in which case producers of high-quality products may have difficulty charging prices that are high enough to cover their extra costs. Absent some means of credibly distinguishing their products, high-quality producers may therefore be forced to exit the market, leaving mostly low-quality products (the so-called lemons problem).[13] Economists have studied several methods by which firms seek to convey information about product quality. It turns out that some of these methods have also been challenged as anticompetitive. Some examples follow.

Tying.   As noted above, the practice of tie-in sales has been outlawed as anticompetitive. Most commonly, it has been seen as a barrier to entry of competing products, as was alleged in the Microsoft case, but in addition it has been posited as a device for facilitating price discrimination. For example, the manufacturer of a copying machine may require purchasers of the machine to grant the manufacturer exclusive rights to provide maintenance of the machine. Such a tie-in promotes price discrimination because high-volume users will generally require more maintenance than low-volume users, thus resulting in their paying a higher overall cost for the combined product-service package.

An alternative argument, however, suggests that tying can also serve as a quality-assuring device in markets with uninformed buyers. For example, *IBM v. United States* (293 U.S. 131, 1936) concerned a practice whereby IBM leased its machines to customers on the condition that they also purchase IBM punch cards. While the court held that such a practice violated the Clayton Act, IBM argued that it was aimed at protecting the company's goodwill, a legitimate economic purpose. Another example of the efficient use of tying is a franchise arrangement that requires individually owned outlets to buy their products exclusively from the franchisor. While such an arrangement may exclude competing suppliers, it also prevents individual outlets from profiting on the franchisor's reputation by purchasing lower-quality products from other suppliers and still selling them under the brand name. The difficult question for courts confronting these scenarios is whether a given tying arrangement is efficiency enhancing (as the defendant usually claims), or is a device for exploiting monopoly power (Hylton 2003, ch. 14).

Quality-Assuring Price.   Another way a producer can maintain a reputation for providing high-quality products is to charge a price above production costs so as to generate a stream of profits that will be lost if consumers detect any reduction in quality. In effect, the lost future profits represent a potential penalty to the firm from cheating on its implied promise (Klein and Leffler 1981). Formally, the mechanism is the same as that which prevents cheating by members of a cartel in a repeated-game setting, as described in Section 2.3 above. In practice, firms will often use the resulting profit to invest in advertising of the brand name, the value of which would be forfeited if the firm did not live up to its reputation for high quality. (This mechanism therefore requires that consumers will "eventually" detect low quality.) The point, however, is that the observation of price above marginal *production* costs in this case is not a sign that the firm is engaging in anticompetitive behavior.

Resale Price Maintenance.   Resale price maintenance is an arrangement between a supplier of a good and a dealer that prevents the dealer from selling the product for less than some minimum price. On its face, this practice (sometime referred to as vertical price fixing) seems blatantly anticompetitive. It has been argued, for example, that it allows the supplier to facilitate a cartel agreement among dealers. Early on, the Supreme Court therefore ruled that resale price maintenance was a violation of antitrust law (see *Dr. Miles Medical Co. v. John D. Park & Sons Co.*, 220 U.S. 373, 1911)

There nevertheless exists a possible efficiency justification for the practice. Suppose purchasers of a particular product value special presale services provided by the dealer, for example, advice on use. This is often the case for certain high-tech products like computers and cell phones. Since it is difficult for the manufacturer to monitor this service, some dealers would have an incentive to avoid providing it, allowing them to lower their prices (discount dealers). The problem this creates, however, is that consumers could seek the advice from the high-price (full-service) dealers, but then buy the product from the discount dealers, a situation that clearly could not persist as high-price dealers would be driven out of the market. By setting a minimum price, the manufacturer can assure that at least some dealers exist who would be willing to provide the advice.[14] Again, this argument suggests that resale price maintenance should not be viewed as a per se violation of antitrust law.

Occupational Licensing.   A final response to uninformed consumers is the requirement, sometimes imposed by the government, that providers of certain services must attain a minimum level of training in order to obtain a license to practice. Licensing requirements exist for a number of professions, including law, medicine, and real estate brokerage. The efficiency rationale for licensing is to prevent entry of low-quality providers, thus avoiding the lemons problem (Leland 1979), but an offsetting cost is that entry is limited, which potentially allows licensees to earn excess (monopoly) profits. Such profits may serve an important purpose, however. Because certain occupations require practitioners to make large up-front investments in education, as in the case of medicine, it is only the promise of this future stream of profits as a return on that investment that induces them to make it. The logic is similar to that which justifies patents, which are, after all, government-created monopolies. (See Section 4.3.1 of Chapter 6.)

4   Natural Monopoly

Some industries have the characteristic that average production costs are minimized when a single firm serves the entire market. Such an industry is referred to as a natural monopoly.[15] Electricity generation is a classic example. (We also argued in Chapter 9, Section 1.2, that law enforcement has the characteristics of natural monopoly.) The underlying reason for natural monopoly is technological: either production involves very high fixed costs, or it exhibits significant economies of scale, both of which cause average costs to decline throughout the relevant range of production. Figure 10.4 shows the average and marginal cost curves for such an industry. Note that the marginal cost curve is everywhere below the average cost curve, which must be true when average costs are falling.

From a policy perspective, the problem raised by natural monopoly is how to allow society to benefit from the cost savings available from single-firm production without permitting the firm to exploit its monopoly power. One approach is simply to do nothing. This might be appropriate in cases where the deadweight loss from monopoly pricing is not expected to be large, as when fairly close substitutes are available. However, when the deadweight loss is expected to be substantial, some form of regulation may be necessary. We consider two approaches: price regulation and government ownership (public enterprise).

Figure 10.4

Price Regulation of a
Natural Monopoly

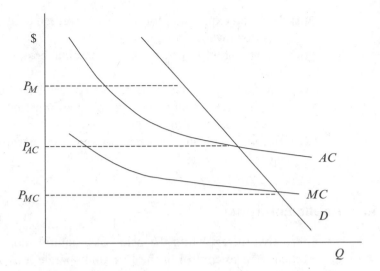

4.1 Price Regulation

Ideally, the price charged by a natural monopoly should be set so as to replicate the efficient (competitive) outcome. Recall that this occurs where price
equals marginal cost. The problem with this solution, however, is that the
resulting price, given by P_{MC} in Figure 10.4, is below average costs. Thus,
the firm suffers a loss. Three responses are possible. First, the price could
simply be adjusted so that revenues exactly equal costs. This involves raising
the price to P_{AC} in Figure 10.4, or the point where the demand curve intersects
the average cost curve. While this solution solves the problem of insufficient
revenue, it results in an inefficient level of output (because $P_{AC} > MC$) and
therefore involves a welfare loss (though less than under monopoly pricing).

A second possibility is to restore the efficient unit price, P_{MC}, but then have
the government pay the firm a subsidy to cover its loss. This approach, however, requires taxation, which may cause distortions elsewhere in the economy. A final possibility is to charge customers a "two-part price" consisting
of a fixed fee that does not depend on the quantity of the good purchased (and
hence does not affect the marginal consumption decision), coupled with a per-
unit fee equal to the marginal cost. The fixed component would then be set at
the firm's loss, divided by the number of consumers, so that the aggregate fee
just covers the loss. Such pricing schemes are often used by public utilities.

EXERCISE 10.2

Return to the example in Exercise 10.1 where demand was $P = \$60 - Q$,
marginal revenue was $MR = \$60 - 2Q$, and marginal cost was $MC = \$10$. Now add fixed costs of $F = \$400$.

(a) Write an expression for the firm's average total cost and verify that it is downward sloping.

(b) Show that when price is set at marginal cost, the firm operates at a loss.

(c) Derive the price and output under average cost pricing. (*Hint:* This will involve solving a quadratic equation with two roots for Q. Use the larger of the two.)

(d) Compare the outcomes under monopoly, marginal cost, and average cost pricing.

4.2 Public Enterprise

An alternative to regulating the price of a natural monopoly is simply for government to take control of the firm and operate it as a public enterprise. The U.S. Postal Service is the obvious example. Public enterprise solves the problem of monitoring regulated firms, but it brings with it the organizational costs of operating a business. In addition, because public enterprises often are not aimed at maximizing profit, but rather at covering costs (or some other objective), it is unlikely that they will operate as efficiently as private firms.

In the end, the various ways of dealing with natural monopoly—doing nothing, regulating price, or organizing it as a public enterprise—all involve some sort of inefficiency. Thus, as usual, the best choice involves a comparison of the respective costs.

5   Conclusion

This chapter has provided an overview of the economics of antitrust law. While economic theory provides a solid justification for the regulation of monopolistic markets, recent scholarship suggests that many practices once thought to be anticompetitive may also have efficiency-enhancing justifications. The result is that there is no clear-cut standard for determining when government intervention is welfare improving. This places a heavy burden on courts seeking to implement antitrust statutes, and fosters disagreement among policymakers, often along political rather than economic lines, regarding the appropriate role of the government in the economy.

DISCUSSION QUESTIONS

1. Describe the source of the inefficiency associated with monopoly.

2. Fast food outlets located on limited-access highways have a monopoly compared to their counterparts located in busy commercial areas, which explains why they can charge higher prices. Explain why that probably does not translate into monopoly profits for the highway outlets. Who do you think gets the resulting profits?

3. One response to monopoly is to break the monopolist into several smaller firms that will compete with one another. Why would this not be a good solution for a natural monopoly?

4. Explain why a polluting industry may be more efficiently organized as a monopoly than as a competitive industry.

PROBLEMS

1. The elasticity of demand is defined to be $e = |\Delta Q/\Delta P|(P/Q)$, where $\Delta Q/\Delta P$ is the slope of the demand curve. (The use of the absolute value in the formula is to make e positive, given the negative slope.) It is possible to show that marginal revenue can be written as $MR = P[1 - (1/e)]$. Use the fact that $MR = MC$ at the monopolist's optimum to derive a formula relating $P - MC$, the divergence of price from marginal cost, to e. Use the formula to show that the monopolist's market power (as measured by this divergence) decreases as e increases (i.e., as the demand curve becomes more elastic). Provide an intuitive explanation for this result.

2. Consider an industry in which two identical firms share the market. Each firm chooses between "high" and "low" output. The resulting profits are as follows: if both firms choose low output, they receive $16 each; if both choose high output, they receive $12 each; and if one chooses high and the other low, they receive $20 and $4, respectively. What is the equilibrium choice of each firm, assuming that they cannot make binding promises to each other? What choices maximize the joint profits of the firms? If they are different, explain why.

3. Let the demand curve for a certain industry be given by $P = 100 - Q$, and suppose initially that there are two firms serving the market, each with constant $MC = AC = 40$.

   (a) Assume that the two firms acting independently behave competitively by setting $P = MC$. What is the equilibrium price and total output of the industry?

   (b) Now suppose the two firms merge to form a monopoly, resulting in a cost savings due to economies of scale. Specifically, suppose that the AC

curve shifts down to 30. (It continues to be true that $AC = MC$.) Given that the marginal revenue for the monopolist is $MR = 100 - 2Q$, calculate the profit-maximizing price and output.

(c) Calculate the cost savings due to the merger over the monopolist's range of output. Also calculate the deadweight loss resulting from the reduced output compared to the pre-merger case. Compare the two and determine whether society is better off or worse off as a result of the merger.

4. Consider a competitive industry that the government taxes in order to raise revenue (e.g., the sale of alcoholic beverages). Show graphically that the amount of revenue generated by a per-unit tax on the industry can in principle be duplicated by reorganizing it as a state-run monopoly and using the profits as government revenue.

EXERCISE 1.1   Starting from a herd size of three, note that, since the annual cost of fencing is $9, the marginal cost of adding the fourth steer is now $3 (the cost of the fence minus the $6 in damages from three steers), which is less than the marginal benefit of $3.50. Thus, it is efficient to add the fourth steer. Clearly, the rancher, if liable for crop damage, will increase his herd to four and erect a fence to minimize his costs. Now suppose the rancher is not liable. In this case, starting from a herd size of three, the farmer will only offer $3 to prevent the rancher from adding the fourth steer. But since the rancher values the fourth steer at $3.50, he will refuse the deal. Thus, the rancher will again increase his herd to four, and the farmer will fence his land at a cost of $9 rather than bear the damage of $10.

EXERCISE 2.1   (a) The cost of hiring an attendant for 24 hours is $94, while the marginal benefit is the reduction in expected accident costs, or $(.25) \times (\$400) = \$100$. Since $94 < $100, the defendant would be found negligent for failure to post an attendant.

(b) The cost of hiring an attendant during the day is $50, and the reduction in expected accident costs is $(.25 - .10) \times (\$400) = \$60$. Since $50 < $60, the defendant would again be found negligent for failing to post an attendant during the day.

(c) The plaintiff's claim in this case is that the defendant should be found negligent for failing to post an attendant for 24 hours rather than only during the day. The marginal cost of hiring an attendant for the additional time is $94 - $50 = $44, while the marginal reduction in expected damages is $(.10) \times (\$400) = \$40$. Since $44 > $40, the barge owner would *not* be found negligent for failing to post an attendant for the additional hours.

(d) Total expected accident costs, $B + PL$, for each of the three options are given as follows:

No attendant:	$\$0 + (.25) \times (\$400) = \$100$
Attendant during the day:	$\$50 + (.10) \times (\$400) = \$90$
Attendant for 24 hours:	$\$94 + (0) \times (\$400) = \$94$

Costs are therefore minimized when an attendant is only posted during the day. Parts (a)–(c) showed that the marginal Hand rule produces the cost-minimizing result when the three options are compared in a pairwise manner. Specifically, we saw that it is cheaper to hire an attendant for 24 hours rather than not at all, but hiring an attendant only for the day is cheaper still.

EXERCISE 2.2

In order to prove that (x^*, y^*) is a Nash equilibrium, we need to show that if the injurer expects the victim to choose y^*, the best thing for him to do is to choose x^*, and vice versa. Thus, suppose first that the injurer expects the victim to choose y^*. Under the definition of pure comparative negligence, s, the injurer's share of damages, equals one if the injurer chooses $x < x^*$, and zero if he chooses $x \geq x^*$. His decision is thus identical to that under simple negligence; that is, he chooses $x = x^*$ to avoid liability. Now suppose that the victim expects the injurer to choose x^*. In that case, she bears the full damages ($s = 0$), so she will choose y to minimize $y + p(x^*, y)D(x^*, y)$, which causes her to choose y^*. Again, the outcome is identical to that under simple negligence. Note that in this equilibrium, there is no sharing of damages; the victim bears the full amount.

EXERCISE 2.3

(a) The injurer will face liability in one out of three cases. Thus, $\alpha = 1/3$, which yields a punitive multiplier of $(2/3)/(1/3) = 2$.

(b) Compensatory damages equal the victim's actual losses of $500,000. Using the formula in (2.11) and the result in (a), we obtain punitive damages of $(2)(\$500,000) = \$1,000,000$. The injurer therefore faces overall liability of $1,500,000.

EXERCISE 3.1

First consider no liability ($s = 0$). In this case, the consumer's demand, net of expected damages, is $20 - q - (.01)(1,000) = 10 - q$. Equating this to marginal costs of $5 and solving for q yields $q^{**} = 5$. The price in this case is $P_0 = c = 5$.

Now consider strict liability ($s = 1$). Demand is simply $20 - q$, but marginal costs are $5 + (.01)(1,000) = 15$. Equating demand and marginal costs and solving for q again yields $q^{**} = 5$. In this case, price is given by $P_1 = c + pD = 15$.

EXERCISE 3.2

(a) When consumers overestimate the risk of an accident to be .012, demand is given by $20 - q - (.012)(1,000) = 8 - q$. Equating this to marginal cost of 5 and solving for q yields $q = 3$.

(b) When consumers underestimate the risk to be .008, demand is given by $20 - q - (.008)(1,000) = 12 - q$. Equating this to 5 and solving yields $q = 7$.

EXERCISE 4.1

(a) The information that the land has a mineral deposit is socially valuable because it increases the value of the land from $10,000 to $500,000.

(b) The information in this case was discovered casually. The buyer did not set out to discover if the land had mineral deposits. Rather, he discovered it accidentally while preparing the land for development.

(c) Because the information was discovered casually, the court's decision to invalidate the contract will probably not reduce the rate of discovery of mineral deposits. One might argue, however, that it will reduce the rate of land development slightly if the value of development includes a small premium for the possibility that mineral deposits will be accidentally discovered.

(d) The answers to (b) and (c) will change. The information in this new scenario was acquired deliberately rather than casually. Thus, the court's decision to invalidate the contract will almost certainly affect the discovery of mineral deposits because it will discourage buyers from investing resources to identify potential locations.

EXERCISE 5.1

(a) Expectation damages $= V - P = \$100,000 - \$75,000 = \$25,000$
Reliance damages $= R = \$5,000$.

(b) It is efficient to breach over the range where $C > V$. In this example, the builder should therefore breach if $C > \$100,000$.

(c) Recall that the builder will actually breach if $C > P + D$. Thus, under expectation damages, he will breach if $C > \$75,000 + \$25,000$, or if $C > \$100,000$, which is the efficient range. Under reliance damages, the builder will breach if $C > \$75,000 + \$5,000$, or if $C > \$80,000$, which results in too much breach. Finally, under zero damages, the builder will breach if $C > \$75,000$, which again results in too much breach.

EXERCISE 5.2

Assuming that the price is payable on performance, the builder will offer an amount less than $50,000 (his loss from performance) to rescind the contract, and the buyer will accept an amount greater than $25,000 (his net gain from performance). Thus, a mutually acceptable buyout price exists, and performance will not occur.

EXERCISE 6.1

In this case, the efficient outcome is for the rancher to fence in his herd at a cost of $100 rather than to allow them to stray, causing damage of $120.

(a) Under a property rule, the parties resolve the externality by bargaining. In this case, the rancher will pay the farmer up to $100 to let his cattle stray (that is, to avoid fencing in the herd), and the farmer will accept an amount greater than $120. Since the rancher's maximum offer is less than the farmer's lowest acceptable price, no transaction will occur. Thus, the farmer will obtain an injunction requiring the rancher to fence his land and the rancher will do so.

(b) Under a liability rule with damages set at $120 (the farmer's actual losses), the rancher will again find it cheaper to fence his land at a cost of $100 rather than letting his cattle stray and paying damages.

(c) In this case, the rancher would prefer to let his cattle stray and pay the $80 in damages. This outcome is inefficient but it is not the final outcome if the parties can bargain. The farmer will pay up to $40, his uncompensated damages, to induce the rancher to fence in his herd; and the rancher will accept any amount above $20, the difference between the cost of fencing ($100) and the court-imposed damages ($80). Since the farmer is willing to offer more than the rancher's lowest acceptable price, they will strike a deal to erect the fence.

EXERCISE 6.2   In this case, the maximum amount Atlantic will pay to remove the injunction is $1 million, the difference between the value of the plant in the residential area and its next best location. It is still efficient for the plant to locate in the residential area, but the bargaining range is now much smaller: between $183,000 and $1 million. The difference between this situation and the actual *Boomer* case is that here, Atlantic has an alternative site that is nearly as valuable as the proposed residential site, so its bargaining position relative to the residents is much stronger.

EXERCISE 6.3   In this example, the cost of the fence exceeds the damage caused by the straying cattle, so it is efficient to let the cattle stray. The resulting net wealth is $200 + $200 − $120 − $280. This outcome is achieved in each of the four cases as follows:

I. The rancher has the right to let his cattle stray protected by a property rule. The farmer can only stop straying cattle by paying the rancher to erect a fence, but since this would cost at least $140, he prefers to suffer the crop damage. The returns to the two parties are

    Farmer: $200 − $120 = $ 80
    Rancher: $200
    Aggregate: $280

II. The farmer has the right to be free from damage protected by a property rule. In this case, the rancher can build a fence at a cost of $140, or purchase the right to let his cattle stray, which the farmer will sell for some amount greater than $120. Assuming they split the surplus evenly, the rancher buys the right for $130. The returns are

    Farmer: $200 − $120 + $130 = $210
    Rancher: $200 − $130 = $ 70
    Aggregate: $280

III. The rancher has the right protected by a liability rule. The farmer can therefore buy the rancher a fence for $140 or suffer the crop damage of $120. He chooses the latter, yielding returns to the parties of

    Farmer: $200 − $120 = $ 80
    Rancher: $200
    Aggregate: $280

IV. The farmer has the right to be free from crop damage protected by a liability rule. The rancher can therefore buy a fence for $140 or pay damages of $120. He chooses the latter, yielding

Farmer:	$200
Rancher:	$200 − $120 = $ 80
Aggregate:	$280

As in the example in the text, the outcome is efficient in all four cases, and the distribution of wealth varies depending on the initial assignment of rights.

EXERCISE 7.1 In this case, the enhanced value of the film is the result of a legal activity. Further, the film is valuable both as an historic record, and as evidence for forensic analysis, of the crime. Thus, to encourage creation of such records, the creator (or his heirs) should be given the full market value of the film. This is in contrast to socially undesirable or harmful acts, which should be discouraged by requiring offenders or their heirs to surrender the gains.

EXERCISE 7.2 Let $\overline{C}$ be any fixed amount of compensation. From (7.5) the landowner's problem is to choose x to

$$\text{maximize} \quad p\overline{C} + (1 - p)V(x) - x.$$

Since $\overline{C}$ is independent of x, the term $p\overline{C}$ has no effect on the maximum point of the objective function; it only affects the height. Thus, the value of x that maximizes the objective function for any choice of $\overline{C}$ is the same value that maximizes $(1 - p)V(x) - x$, which by definition is the efficient value, x^*.

EXERCISE 7.3 (a) The sale price under a rule of zero compensation equals

$$(.9)(\$10,000) + (.1)(\$100,000) = \$19,000,$$

reflecting a 90 percent chance of a regulation (in which case the land is worth $10,000) and a 10 percent chance of no regulation (in which case it is worth $100,000). Since the land was worth $100,000 before the threat of a regulation arose, the loss to the initial owner is $100,000 − $19,000 = $81,000.

(b) Full compensation would be $100,000 − $10,000 = $90,000.

(c) The sale price of the land under a rule of full compensation equals

$$(.9)(\$10,000 + \$90,000) + (.1)(\$100,000) = \$100,000.$$

In this case, the owner suffers no loss.

EXERCISE 8.1 The injurer (defendant) calculates his expected judgment to be $(.4)(\$50,000) = \$20,000$. Thus, his total expected cost of trial is $20,000 + $10,000 = $30,000, which is the maximum amount he will offer in a settlement. As for the victim (plaintiff), she expects to recover $(.9)(\$50,000) = \$45,000$ at trial. Thus, the minimum amount she will accept to settle is $\$45,000 - \$10,000 = \$35,000$. Since this amount is larger than the defendant's maximum offer, a settlement is not possible.

EXERCISE 8.2

(a) Substituting the numerical values into (8.9) shows that $\$9 < \$10.5$. Thus, it is socially desirable for victims to file suit. It is also privately desirable since $\$210 > \$200$.

(b) It continues to be socially desirable to file suit since (8.9) implies $\$9 < \$9.5$. However, it is no longer privately desirable since $\$190 < \$200$.

(c) Suits are no longer socially desirable for either value of D since (8.9) implies $\$9 > \$4.2$ when $D = \$210$, and $\$9 > \$3.8$ when $D = \$190$. The change in p_n, however, has no effect on the private decision of plaintiffs, who will file when $D = \$210$, and will not file when $D = \$190$. These examples show that there is no necessary relationship between the private and social desirability of lawsuits in a costly legal system.

EXERCISE 8.3

(a) First, for the plaintiff:

$$P_p J - C_p = (.7)(\$1,000) - \$200 = \$500 \quad \text{(American rule)}$$
$$P_p J - (1 - P_p)(C_p + C_d) = (.7)(\$1,000) - (.3)(\$400) = \$580$$
$$\text{(English rule)}$$

Now for the defendant:

$$P_d J + C_d = (.4)(\$1,000) + \$200 = \$600 \quad \text{(American rule)}$$
$$P_d(J + C_p + C_d) = (.4)(\$1,000 + \$400) = \$560 \quad \text{(English rule)}$$

The defendant's cost of trial is thus larger than the plaintiff's value of trial under the American rule ($\$600 > \$500$), but not under the English rule ($\$560 < \$580$). Thus, a settlement is feasible under the former but not under the latter.

(b) The English rule raises the plaintiff's expected value of trial from $\$500$ to $\$580$. If $P_p = .45$, however, a switch to the English rule lowers the plaintiff's expected value from $\$250$ to $\$230$. The reason for the different effects is that

$$.7 > \frac{C_d}{C_p + C_d} > .45$$

given $C_d/(C_p + C_d) = .5$. Thus, as shown in Figure 8.4, the English rule raises the value of the high-probability suit and lowers the value of the low-probability suit.

EXERCISE 8.4

(a) When judges are perfectly reliable, the probabilities of the two types of errors are zero. That is, $r = 1$ and $w = 0$. Thus, the ratio r/w approaches infinity, in which case condition (8.31) can never hold.

(b) A changing environment implies that p is large and that the ratio $(1 - p)/p$ is small. At the same time, less reliability by judges implies that the ratio r/w is also small. The overall impact on the condition in (8.31) is therefore ambiguous (holding C_{II}/C_I fixed).

EXERCISE 9.1

(a) It is not efficient for either offender to commit the crime because neither receives a benefit greater than the harm of $100.

(b) Given that the probability of apprehension is .5, the *expected fine* in this case is equal to $(.5)(\$100) = \$50$. Thus, the offender who receives a gain of $40 will be deterred, but the offender who receives a gain of $80 will not be. The outcome is thus inefficient because it does not achieve complete deterrence.

(c) The optimal harm-based fine, f^*, is equal to $h/p = \$100/.5 = \$200$. The expected fine in this case is thus $pf^* = \$100$, which will deter both offenders.

(d) The optimal benefit-based fine is g/p, which equals $\$40/.5 = \$80$ for the first offender, and $\$80/.5 = \$160$ for the second offender. The corresponding expected fines are thus $(.5)(\$80) = \$40$ and $(.5)(\$160) = \$80$, which are just sufficient to deter both offenders.

EXERCISE 9.2

Optimal deterrence requires that offenders must face an expected punishment equal to $4,000. Thus, from (9.1) we have

$$g^* = p(f + ct) = \$4,000.$$

Setting $p = .5$, we obtain $f + ct = \$8,000$. Since $8,000 exceeds the offender's wealth, the fine should equal that wealth. Thus, substituting $f = \$2,000$ into the equation implies that $ct = \$6,000$. Finally, setting $c = \$500$ and solving yields $t = 12$ months. The optimal punishment scheme for an offender with wealth of $2,000 therefore involves a fine of $2,000 and 12 months in prison.

EXERCISE 9.3

(a) The expected fine for driving at 90 mph is $(.01)(\$10,000) = \$100$. In order to achieve the desired level of marginal deterrence, the expected fine for driving 75 mph must be less than this amount by $50, the efficient threshold for driving at the higher speed. Thus,

$$\$100 - (.01)(f_{75}) = \$50.$$

Solving yields $f_{75} = \$50/.01 = \$5,000$.

(b) Marginal deterrence can also be achieved by adjusting the probability of apprehension rather than the fine. Thus, set the fine for both offenses at $10,000 and assume that the probability of apprehension for driving at 75 continues to be .01. As in part (a), the expected fines must differ by $50, so the optimal probability of apprehension for driving at 90 solves

$$(p_{90})(\$10,000) - (.01)(\$10,000) = \$50.$$

Solving yields $p_{90} = .015$.

EXERCISE 10.1   (a) Set $MR = MC$ and solve for Q to obtain $Q_m = 25$. Then substitute this value back into the inverse demand function to obtain $P_m = \$35$.

(b) The resulting profit for the monopolist is given by $(\$35 - \$10)25 = \$625$. The deadweight loss is equal to half of this amount, or $312.50.

(c) The optimal fine when enforcement is certain and costless is simply the sum of the profit and the deadweight loss, or $937.50.

(d) The optimal fine in this case is given by $(D + T)/p + C = (\$937.50)/.25 + \$100 = \$3,850$. Under treble damages with damages set at $D + T$, the fine is $3(D + T) + C = \$2,912.50$, which is less than the optimal fine. Thus, there is underdeterrence (as there must be since $p = .25 < 1/3$). In the case where damages are limited to T, the fine under treble damages is $3T + C = \$1,975$, which is also less than the optimal fine, and again there is underdeterrence (as there must be since $.25 < 1/2$).

EXERCISE 10.2   (a) In this case, $AC = MC + F/Q = \$10 + \$400/Q$. Clearly, this is decreasing in Q.

(b) Equating the inverse demand function with marginal cost (i.e., setting $P = MC$) yields $Q^* = 50$ and $P^* = \$10$. The resulting profit for the firm is $(P^* - AC)Q^* = -F = -\$400$.

(c) To obtain output under average cost pricing, equate the inverse demand function with the expression for average costs derived in part (a) to obtain $\$60 - Q = \$10 + \$400/Q$. Then multiply through by Q and rearrange to obtain the quadratic equation $Q^2 - 50Q + 400 = 0$. This factors to $(Q - 40)(Q - 10) = 0$, which has two roots, 40 and 10. The relevant output is the larger of the two because it minimizes the deadweight loss while yielding zero profit. Finally, substituting $Q_{AC} = 40$ into the demand function yields $P_{AC} = \$20$.

(d) The monopolist's optimal output and price are unaffected by fixed costs. Thus, as in Exercise 10.1, we proceed by first equating MR and MC to obtain $Q_m = 25$, and then substituting the result into the demand function to obtain $P_m = \$35$. (The profit for the monopolist in this case is $\$625 - \$400 = \$225$.) Finally, comparing the outcomes under the various cases, we have $P_{MC} = \$10$, $P_{AC} = \$20$, and $P_m = \$35$ for the prices, and $Q_{MC} = 50$, $Q_{AC} = 40$, and $Q_m = 25$ for the output levels.

REFERENCE
MATTER

CHAPTER 1

1. Holmes (1897). We will encounter Holmes throughout the book.

2. The foremost proponent of this view is Posner (2003).

3. The determination of how these goods and services are produced from the available resources is based on the productive efficiency of the economy. Here, we focus on exchange efficiency, taking the level of goods and services as given.

4. This assumes that people are not motivated by envy, which might cause some to object to changes that benefit others even if they themselves are not hurt.

5. See Coleman (1982) for a comparison of the Pareto and Kaldor-Hicks concepts of efficiency.

6. See chapter 3 of Posner (2001) for an examination of cost-benefit analysis as a means of evaluating social policy.

7. Coase (1960). Many date the origin of modern law and economics to the publication of this article, which is undoubtedly the most cited in the law and economics literature.

8. The answers to in-chapter problems are contained in the back of the book.

9. This conclusion is closely related to the Second Fundamental Theorem of welfare economics.

10. Few laws are voted on directly by the people, which makes the United States a representative democracy, or a republic, rather than a true democracy.

11. Economists have also studied the process of lawmaking by legislatures as part of the field of public choice (the classic reference is Buchanan and Tullock [1962]), and they have also begun to develop an economic theory of constitutional law (Cooter 2000). We will encounter some aspects of constitutional law in Chapters 7 and 9.

12. 159 F.2d 169 (2d Cir. 1947). This citation shows how lawyers refer to cases in law reporters. The first number, 159, refers to the volume of the reporter; F.2d refers to the series of the reporter—in this case, it is the Federal Reporter, second series; the second number, 169, is the first page of the written opinion; and the information in parenthesis is the court (here, the Second Circuit) and year in which the case was decided.

13. This argument is presented and evaluated in Chapter 8.

14. This discussion is based on Mermin (1982, 58–60 and 166–69).

15. There is also one each in Puerto Rico, the Virgin Islands, the Northern Mariana Islands, and Guam.

CHAPTER 2
1. See *Anderson v. Minneapolis, St. Paul & Sault Ste. Marie Railway Co.*, 146 Minn. 430, 179 N.W. 45 (1920).

2. Judge Andrews disagreed in his dissent, arguing that care is owed to any victims who are injured, not just those to whom harm was reasonably foreseeable.

3. The basic accident model was first developed by Brown (1973) and elaborated on by Cooter (1985), Landes and Posner (1987), and Shavell (1987).

4. See Leong (1989) and Arlen (1990).

5. In the more general case where the injurer suffers damages as well, the injurer will take some care, but less than the efficient level.

6. Formally, the victim chooses y to minimize $y + p(0, y)D(0, y)$, which yields $y^*(0)$. That is, the victim chooses optimal care *given the expectation that the injurer will choose zero care*. Depending on the accident technology, this will generally differ from $y^*(x^*)$, the victim's optimal care, given that the injurer is also taking optimal care. In the most common case where x and y are substitutes, $y^*(0) > y^*(x^*)$, the case of compensating precaution. The same will be true of the injurer's care under strict liability.

7. Some economists have proposed "de-coupled" liability rules that allow a difference between what the injurer pays and what the victim receives (Polinsky and Che 1991).

8. B is defined to be the slope of the x curve in Figure 2.1, and PL is defined to be the slope of the $p(x)D(x)$ curve.

9. Keeton et al. (1984, 175), quoting in part from the Restatement (Second) of Torts.

10. This discussion is based on Landes and Posner (1987, ch. 5).

11. The condition for injurers to choose to violate the due standard in this way is $c_j x_j^* + p(x_j^*)D(x_j^*) < c_j x^*$.

12. This problem is examined in Wittman (1981), Shavell (1983), and Grady (1988). For a technical analysis, see Miceli (1997, 58–69).

13. Note that this was not a problem in the simultaneous care model because the victim presumed that the injurer would take efficient care. Thus, even if the injurer in fact failed to do so, the victim would have taken efficient care based on her presumption.

14. See Keeton et al. (1984) §67 on the various forms of comparative negligence. On the efficiency of pure comparative negligence, see Landes and Posner (1987, ch. 3) and Shavell (1987, ch. 2).

15. Regarding uncertainty about legal standards, see the discussion in Section 3.9 below.

16. The case is discussed in Kahan (1989). The first discussion of the impact of cause-in-fact on the operation of the negligence rule was by Grady (1983).

17. Formally, the injurer's minimization problem under negligence with cause-in-fact is to choose x to

$$\text{minimize} \quad \begin{cases} x, & \text{if } x \geq x^* \\ x + p(x)D(x) - p(x^*)D(x^*), & \text{if } x < x^*, \end{cases}$$

where $p(x^*)D(x^*)$ is expected damages at the efficient level of care. Since $p(x^*)D(x^*)$ is a constant, it does not affect the solution to the above problem. Thus, the injurer chooses efficient care.

18. The idea of "untaken precautions" is discussed in Grady (1989). Also see Miceli (1996a).

19. The reason for the "bias" in the Hand test is the diminishing marginal benefit of care coupled with the constant or increasing marginal cost. Thus, as the plaintiff chooses larger untaken precautions, PL gets closer to B.

20. See *Summers v. Tice*, 33 Cal.2d 80, 199 P.2d 1 (1948).

21. Note that this is another illustration of the above assertion that proximate cause and negligence are redundant tests.

22. See *Sindell v. Abbott Laboratories*, 163 Cal.Rptr. 132, 607 P.2d 924 (1980).

23. We discuss products liability in detail in Chapter 3.

24. The analysis in this section is based on Shavell (1980c).

25. In other words, the accident technology displays constant returns to scale with respect to activity levels.

26. The reason that negligence rules can induce efficient bilateral incentives for care but not for activity levels is that courts set a due standard for care but not for activity levels. The usual argument is that the information costs of developing a "Hand test" for activity levels is too high. For example, courts would have to determine the efficient number of miles for a motorist to drive, or the efficient output of a dangerous product. See the discussion of this point by Gilles (1992).

27. For example, in *City of Newport v. Fact Concerts, Inc.*, 454 U.S. 247 (1981), the court said that "punitive damages . . . are . . . intended to punish the tortfeasor whose wrongful action was intentional or malicious, and to deter him and others from similar extreme conduct."

28. The discussion in this section is based on Polinsky and Shavell (1998). Also see Cooter (1989).

29. We discuss the impact of litigation costs on incentives for injurer care in more detail in Section 3.8 below.

30. See Landes and Posner (1987, 302–7), Shanley (1991), and Eisenberg et al. (1997).

31. The critical value of α can be calculated as follows. Let x_α be the level of care that minimizes costs in (2.10), where $x_\alpha < x^*$ for $\alpha < 1$. The injurer will choose due care if $x^* < x_\alpha + p(x_\alpha)\alpha D(x_\alpha)$, or if $\alpha > (x^* - x_\alpha)/p(x_\alpha)D(x_\alpha)$.

32. See, for example, Shavell (1987, ch. 8).

33. We also examine the social value of suits, which hinges on the trade-off between litigation costs and incentives. See Section 2.3 in Chapter 8.

34. The discussion is based on Landes and Posner (1987, ch. 6).

35. To illustrate, suppose the probability of harm from sale of a single chainsaw is p. Thus, the probability of no accident after one chainsaw is sold is $1 - p$, but after n are sold, the probability of no accident is $(1 - p)^n$. The probability of at least one accident after n are sold is therefore $1 - (1 - p)^n$. For example, if $p = .01$, then after 500 chainsaws are sold, the probability of at least one accident is .993.

36. We have also seen that underdetection can occur for reasons other than intent to conceal harm, which is why punitive damages may be called for in some cases of accidental harm.

37. The discussion in this section is based on Viscusi (1998).

CHAPTER 3

1. See Viscusi (1991), who notes that while much of the increase in the 1980s was attributable to asbestos cases, nonasbestos products liability suits increased as well. We discuss asbestos litigation in Section 3.3 below.

2. This section is based on Epstein (1980). Also see Landes and Posner (1987, ch. 10).

3. See *Winterbottom v. Wright*, 10 M&W 109, 152 Eng.Rep. 402 (Exch. 1842).

4. For simplicity, we ignore cases where there are intermediate parties such as wholesalers. That the analysis could be extended to such cases should be apparent.

5. This section is largely based on Landes and Posner (1985).

6. The assumption of constant marginal costs of production implies that the size of individual firms is indeterminate.

7. For purposes of this discussion, we assume that the manufacturer and the seller are the same party.

8. See the discussion in Landes and Posner (1987, 131–39) and Epstein (1992).

9. We note one exception to this rule below in Section 2.2.

10. Viscusi (1988) offers evidence on risk-adjusted wages.

11. But see Beard (1990).

12. See *Summers v. Tice*, 33 Cal.2d 80, 199 P.2d 1 (1948).

13. See Landes and Posner (1987, ch. 7) and Shavell (1987, ch. 7).

14. Another problem associated with a long latency period is that the risk of bankruptcy increases.

15. See Miceli and Segerson (2005) for a formal analysis of a tort for risk. Although such a rule may increase incentives for injurer care, it also increases litigation costs and may result in bankruptcy of the injurer.

16. Much of this section is based on Menell (1991).

17. See *Borel v. Fibreboard, et al.*, 493 F.2d 1076 (5th Cir. 1973).

18. See *Metro-North Commuter Railroad v. Buckley*, 521 U.S. 424 (1997).

19. Fenn, Gray, and Rickman (2007) find evidence that the threat of liability induces greater use of certain costly diagnostic tests by British hospitals, but their results cannot determine whether this represents efficient or excessive care.

CHAPTER 4

1. This illustration is based on the case of *Hamer v. Sidway*, 124 N.Y. 538, 27 N.E. 256 (Court of Appeals of New York, 1891).

2. We will see, however, that under the doctrine of "unconscionability," courts do sometimes invalidate contracts based solely on the appearance of unfairness of the terms. See Section 3.4 below.

3. In the days before refrigerators, ice companies cut blocks of ice from ponds during the winter and stored them in barns, insulated by sawdust or hay, for use during the summer.

4. See Kronman (1978), Smith and Smith (1990), Rasmusen and Ayres (1993), and Shavell (1994).

5. In affecting the distribution of gains from the contract, the court's decision determines the allocation of risk from the uncertainty over the cow's type. In the case of enforcement, the buyer bears the risk, whereas in the case of nonenforcement, the seller bears the risk. See Posner (1998a, 114).

6. This distinction is made by Kronman, who notes that "the term 'deliberately acquired information' means information whose acquisition entails costs which would not have been incurred but for the likelihood, however great, that the information in question would actually be produced." Kronman further notes that the costs of acquisition include "not only direct search costs . . . but the costs of developing an initial expertise as well" (Kronman 1978, 13). The latter cost is apropos of the cow example.

7. See, for example, *Obde v. Schlemeyer*, 56 Wash.2d 449, 353 P.2d 672 (1960). The law against blackmail has a similar interpretation. See Section 4.4.3 of Chapter 9.

8. This asymmetry is pointed out by Shavell (1994).

CHAPTER 5

1. These examples and much of the material on breach and reliance are based on Shavell (1980b) and Rogerson (1984).

2. More generally, the investment may be partially salvageable without affecting the basic conclusions. See Shavell (1980b).

3. Cooter (1985) first pointed out this analogy.

4. This requires that $C_H > V(R) > C_L$, where V is evaluated at the efficient level of reliance to be derived below.

5. But see the discussion of commercial impracticability in Section 1.4.2 below.

6. *Hadley v. Baxendale*, 9 Ex. 341, 156 Eng.Rep. 145 (1854).

7. See Craswell (1989, 377). Rose-Ackerman (1989) examines a similar rule in the context of bilateral torts.

8. Bebchuk and Shavell (1991) emphasize this aspect of the *Hadley v. Baxendale* rule.

9. For example, the Uniform Commercial Code (Section 2-175) limits liability to damages that "could not reasonably be prevented," and the Restatement (Second) of Contracts (Section 35) says that "a party cannot recover damages for loss that could have been avoided by reasonable efforts."

10. It turns out that the duty to mitigate damages is not always present in real estate leases. See Section 4.1.2 in Chapter 6.

11. See Posner and Rosenfield (1977), Goldberg (1988), and White (1988).

12. Bebchuk and Png (1999) refer to this as a model of "inadvertant breach." Also see Cooter (1985) and Bebchuk and Shavell (1991).

13. This example is taken from Posner and Rosenfield (1977).

14. Recall our earlier discussion (in Chapter 3) of market versus self-insurance in the context of products liability.

15. This example is also taken from Posner and Rosenfield (1977).

16. Interestingly, medieval farmers apparently did diversify their land holdings geographically as a form of insurance against crop variability. See McCloskey (1976).

17. This section is based on Sykes (1990). Also see Miceli (1997, 104–6).

18. Since $\$5,000 = (1/3)(\$7,000) + (2/3)(\$4,000)$, the contractor apparently expects to encounter difficult jobs one-third of the time. This assumes a competitive industry where contractors earn zero profits.

19. See, for example, Ulen (1984) and Friedmann (1989). For more formal analysis, see Rogerson (1984).

20. See Muris (1983). We return to the notion of subjective value in connection with various aspects of property law in the next chapter.

21. In some cases, courts award *restitution damages* to discourage this sort of "unfair" breach. Restitution damages is defined to be an amount of money that leaves the promisor indifferent between breach and performance (in contrast to expectation damages, which leaves the promisee indifferent). In the present case, the amount of restitution damages would be $15,000, the difference between B2's offer and the original price, as compared to the $10,000 expectation damages.

22. This section is based on Rea (1998).

23. If the mill learned its actual costs after the contract was made but before breach, then

it would have been efficient for it to communicate this information to the transport company.

24. See, for example, Aghion and Bolton (1987) and Posner (1998a, 142–45).

25. Another view, not examined here, is that warranties optimally share the risk of product failure.

26. The assumption of perfect competition is not necessary for the results.

27. See Section 1.2.2 in Chapter 3.

28. To be specific, let $q(x, y)$ be the probability of product failure, where y is consumer care. Consumers will therefore choose y to maximize $V - q(x, y)(1 - w)K - P - y$, taking P as given. Thus, they will tend to underinvest in care for any $w > 0$. Generally, setting w between zero and one (partial coverage) will induce some care by both producers and consumers.

29. Thus, $r = 1 - q$, where q is the probability of product failure.

30. On this problem, see Goldberg (1976), Klein, Crawford, and Alchian (1978), and Williamson (1983).

31. VMP is the increment in firm revenue from hiring an additional worker. Formally, it is given by the product of the worker's marginal product and the output price (assuming a competitive output market).

32. Note that this is still more than it would earn by letting the worker go and replacing him with an unskilled worker, which would yield a profit of $100 - $100 - $125 = -$125$. By retaining the worker, the firm at least gains the $100 difference between the worker's VMP to the firm and the transferable portion.

33. See Telser (1980). Williamson (1983) refers to self-enforcement as "private ordering," as opposed to "court ordering."

34. On the incentive effects of an increasing wage structure, see Becker and Stigler (1974) and Lazear (1979).

35. See Rottenberg (1956) and Miceli (2004). In Chapter 6, we examine a different aspect of the reserve system.

36. On the general problem of enforcing rules on oneself, see Schelling (1985).

37. This is in contrast to "horizontal mergers" between competing firms. See Section 3.2 in Chapter 10.

38. This is the basis for the transaction-cost theory of the firm, which originated with Coase (1937).

CHAPTER 6

1. The discussion in this section is based on Demsetz (1967). Also see Barzel (1989) and D. Friedman (2000, ch. 10).

2. The landlord, however, may retain the right (or duty) to enter the property under some circumstances. See Section 4.1 below.

3. See Wiggins and Libecap (1985), who discuss the difficulties firms face in arriving at an efficient contractual solution to this problem.

4. Of course, this interpretation ignores the cost associated with destruction of Native American property regimes.

5. This discussion is based on Lueck (1995). Also see Epstein (1979).

6. See Mortensen (1982). We will encounter these problems again in our discussion of patents in Section 5.1 below.

7. A similar distinction applies to wildlife. In a famous American case, the rule of capture was invoked to award ownership of a fox to the hunter who actually killed it rather than the hunter who had first seen and pursued it. See *Pierson v. Post*, 3 Cal.R. 175, 2 Am.Dec. 264 (Sup. Ct. of N.Y. 1805). Also see Dharmapala and Pitchford (2002).

8. We return to the choice between private and public enforcement in our discussion of optimal law enforcement in Chapter 9.

9. The result would be the same if the farmer could exclude straying cattle altogether. See the discussion of trespass and nuisance law in Section 2.2.3 below.

10. The Coase Theorem can be stated in a number of ways. See, for example, Coleman (1982).

11. See L. Friedman (1985, 300–301), citing Horwitz (1977). Also see Grady (1988).

12. See Section 1.2.1 in Chapter 3.

13. *New York Times*, May 13, 2002, Section A, p. 1.

14. Rottenberg (1956) was the first to make this argument (ironically, prior to publication of the Coase article). Also see Demsetz (1967).

15. Drahozal (1986) provides similar evidence.

16. Sanchez and Nugent (2000) conduct a similar analysis using data from Kansas in 1875, where some counties had "fence laws" requiring farmers to fence out straying animals, while others had "herd laws" requiring owners of animals to keep them in herds.

17. More recent analyses of enforcement rules are by Polinsky (1980a) and Kaplow and Shavell (1996).

18. The discussion in this section is based on Landes and Posner (1987, 41–44) and Merrill (1985b, 1998).

19. In some cases, this right is limited. See the discussion of adverse possession below. Also, as we will discuss in the next chapter, the landowner does not have the right to exclude the government from taking land under eminent domain.

20. See Section 1 in Chapter 3 and Section 3.2 in Chapter 5.

21. We examine the holdout problem in more detail in Chapter 7, Section 2.1.1.

22. See Goldberg (1985) and Landes and Posner (1987, 45).

23. See Klevorick (1985) and Coleman (1988, ch. 2).

24. This ensures that both have enough wealth either to purchase the right or pay liability. This precludes the possibility of a judgment-proof problem (see Section 3.6 in Chapter 2).

25. See Merrill (1998, 618) and Section 3 in the next chapter.

26. The model is based on Miceli, Sirmans, and Kieyah (2001).

27. In the graph, we assume that $p(0) = p_0 > 0$, which implies that if the owner devotes no resources to security, he still retains title with some probability.

28. This result is derived using calculus by taking the derivative of the expression $p(c)V - c$ with respect to c and setting the result equal to zero. Rearranging yields the equation $p'(c) = 1/V$, where $p'(c)$ is the slope of the $p(c)$ function.

29. For more general discussion, see Shavell (2004, 38–45) and Baird and Jackson (1984).

30. On the problem of optimal title search, see Baker et al. (2002).

31. See Bostick (1987), Shick and Plotkin (1978), and Janczyk (1977).

32. Recall that the notion of subjective value for breach of contract arose in the context of the *Peevyhouse* case, which concerned the promisees' valuation of land.

33. Cited in Merrill (1985a, 1131). Also see Holmes (1897, 477).

34. See Shick and Plotkin (1978) for a history of land registration in the United States.

35. A more conservative estimate puts the value of the embedded capital at $3.6 trillion (Woodruff 2001), still a considerable amount.

36. The focus in this section will be on leases of land, but the arguments generalize to any durable asset. See, for example, Flath (1980).

37. See Cribbet (1975, ch. 4) and M. Friedman (1990, ch. 1).

38. The leading case is *Javins v. First Nat'l Realty Corp.*, 428 F.2d 1071 (1970). Also see Rabin (1984).

39. See Section 1.3 in Chapter 5.

40. See Cribbet (1975, 209–11) and Posner (1998a, 83).

41. In some cases, the law even recognizes improvements in property as waste (so-called meliorating waste).

42. Note that this argument is similar to the justification for limited product warranties in contract law. In effect, limited warranties share liability between the consumer and producer, thereby providing each with an incentive to take care. See Section 3.2 in Chapter 5.

43. Ellickson (1993, 1327). Also see Demsetz (1967), Field (1989), and Ostrom (1990).

44. We discuss the issue of boundary disputes in the context of adverse possession in the next chapter.

45. Public goods differ in the degree of scale economies, which explains why some are provided by the federal government, while others are provided by state or local governments.

46. For book-length surveys of the law and economics of intellectual property, see Blair and Cotter (2005) and Landes and Posner (2003).

47. The patent thus serves a similar function to the reserve clause in baseball regarding the incentive for teams to invest in training of players. See Section 3.3 in Chapter 5.

48. For a straight-line demand curve, the marginal revenue curve always has the same intercept and twice the slope as the demand curve.

49. See Nordhaus (1969, ch. 5) for a derivation of the optimal patent life. Miceli and Sirmans (2005) provide a general discussion of time-limited property rights.

50. See, for example, Loury (1979) and Mortensen (1982). This is an example of the more general problem of "rent seeking" (Tullock 1967).

51. See Mortensen (1982) on the ability of a particular reward system to prevent races to innovate.

52. See *A&M Records v. Napster*, 284 F.3d 1091 (9th Cir. 2002).

CHAPTER 7

1. See the companion articles by Epstein (1986) and Ellickson (1986). Also see Miceli and Sirmans (1995a) and Merrill (1985a).

2. See Section 3.10 in Chapter 2.

3. The data were obtained from Leiter (1999). Some states have shorter statute lengths if an adverse possessor has "color of title," which is a document or other evidence that appears to (but does not actually) convey title.

4. We assume that the improver captures the full surplus from any trade.

5. See Merrill (1986, 88–89). Also see the discussion in Chapter 9 (Section 1.4) of criminal sanctions as "kickers" aimed at preventing this sort of violation of the "transaction structure."

6. This is contrary to the so-called Maine rule, which holds that intentional encroachment is actually necessary for a claim to ripen into title. See Miceli and Sirmans (1995a) for a discussion.

7. See Stake (1998) for an economic perspective on inheritance law in general.

8. See the discussion of public goods in Cornes and Sandler (1986).

9. See L. Cohen (1991) and Posner (1998a, 62). For a formal analysis of the holdout problem in the context of private land assembly, see Strange (1995).

10. Ulen (1992) also advocates limiting the use of eminent domain to this case.

11. Richard Epstein (1985, ch. 18) argues that taxation is itself a form of taking because of its coercive nature. We pursue this point below in the context of defining just compensation.

12. See Fischel (1996), who examines the military draft as a form of taking.

13. See, for example, Fischel (1995b, 72) and L. Friedman (1985, 182).

14. The difficulty of this issue is illustrated by a pair of cases decided by the Michigan Supreme Court. In *Poletown v. City of Detroit* (304 N.W.2d 455, 410 Mich. 616, 1981), the Court allowed the city of Detroit to condemn an entire ethnic neighbor-

hood in order to clear the way for a new General Motors plant. As in *Kelo*, the Court justified its decision based on the promised jobs and increased tax base (the ends approach) rather than the likely holdout problem (the means approach). Interestingly, the same court reversed itself in 2004 in the case of *Wayne v. Hathcock* (684 N.W.2d 765, 471 Mich. 445), arguing that its earlier ruling in *Poletown* was contrary to the fundamental protection of property rights afforded by the Constitution.

15. See Section 2 in Chapter 5.

16. Note that this conclusion is consistent with Corollary 2 to the Coase Theorem (see Section 2.2.2 in Chapter 6).

17. See the discussion of land title systems (Section 3.2 in Chapter 6) and specific performance as a remedy for breach of contract (Section 2 in Chapter 5).

18. See Adelstein (1974).

19. See *Porter v. United States*, 473 F.2d 1329 (5th Cir. 1973).

20. Formally, B affects the intercept of the objective function but not its slope or maximum point.

21. Others include Fischel and Shapiro (1989), Hermalin (1995), and Nosal (2001).

22. See Section 1.2 in Chapter 5.

23. As provided, for example, by Fischel's "normal behavior" standard. See Fischel (1995b, 351–55).

24. Fischel and Shapiro (1988) offer a useful interpretation of Michelman's criterion in light of recent scholarship.

25. See the fascinating discussion of this case in Fischel (1995b, ch. 1).

26. See Fischel (1995b, 352). The standard is based on Ellickson (1973). Also see Wittman (1984).

27. It is probably more restrictive, though, since prohibited uses under the normal behavior standard (for example, businesses in residential areas) are not necessarily nuisances.

28. More generally, the government will overregulate whenever compensation is less than full. In the model, however, we consider only zero and full compensation.

29. Keeton et al. (1984, 630). Also see Section 2.2.3 in Chapter 6.

30. *Keystone Bituminous Coal Assn. v. DeBenedictus* (1987). The quote is from *Block v. Hirsh*, 256 U.S. 135 (1921).

31. See Fischel (1995b, 48), who observes that "by the 1960s [when the Subsidence Act was passed], general growth in personal incomes had driven up the demand for housing and a pleasant environment. Technological changes over the same period had reduced concern over the extraction of coal, because many substitutes for it had developed."

32. See Fischel and Shapiro (1988, 287–89) and Epstein (1985, 151–58).

33. See Shavell (1984), on which the following analysis is based.

CHAPTER 8

1. See, for example, Olson (1991) and Howard (1994).

2. In truth, there is probably a feedback effect. More litigation increases the demand for lawyers, but more lawyers also likely increase the rate of litigation.

3. See Shavell (1993b) for an analysis of disputes in which plaintiffs seek nonmonetary judgments.

4. The model was first developed by Landes (1971) and J. Gould (1973). Also see Shavell (1982b), Cooter and Rubinfeld (1989), and Baird, Gertner, and Picker (1994).

5. It is not essential that the parties agree on J. See problem number 1 at the end of this chapter.

6. See Bebchuk (1984) and Nalebuff (1987). Baird, Gertner, and Picker (1994, ch. 8) compare the optimism and asymmetric information models.

7. To see this, note that the defendant's expected cost from the strategy of taking both types of plaintiffs to trial is $\bar{P}J + C_d$, which can be written $a(P_h J + C_d) + (1-a)(P_l J + C_d)$. Subtracting the expression in (8.5) from this expression leaves $(1-a)(C_p + C_d)$, which is positive. Thus, the separating strategy is always cheaper.

8. See Shavell (1996) and Miceli (1998).

9. This is especially true in the case of frivolous suits, where plaintiffs' only hope of a positive recovery is by settling. See Section 3.5 below.

10. See Shavell (1989) and Baird, Gertner, and Picker (1994, ch. 8).

11. On differences between the legal systems in the two countries, see Posner (1996).

12. It is interesting to note that, once this selection effect was taken into account, the probability of a case actually settling increased under the English rule. Apparently, cases that were not dropped were disproportionately likely to settle.

13. See Miller (1986) and Chung (1996). Spier (1994) examines this question in the context of the asymmetric information model.

14. Thus, in contrast to the English rule under which losers pay, the contingent fee is a sort of "winner pays" rule.

15. There is a substantial literature on contingent fees. For surveys, see Rubinfeld and Scotchmer (1998) and Gravelle (1998).

16. In the graph, we assume a diminishing marginal benefit and increasing marginal cost of effort.

17. But see Danzon (1983), who argues that if lawyers compete for clients based on the percentage rate, b, rather than treating it as fixed, they will choose optimal effort.

18. This assumes that the percentage rate b is the same whether the case settles or goes to trial. Some lawyers, however, charge a lower rate for settlements. (See problem number 3 at the end of this chapter.)

19. For a survey of the literature on frivolous suits, see Rasmusen (1998b).

20. Note that delay is crucial for this strategy since if high-rate plaintiffs expected the

defendant to offer $9,524 immediately to any plaintiffs rejecting the lower offer (thereby revealing themselves to be low-rate plaintiffs), then the high-rate plaintiffs would reject it too.

21. If $r > .10$, the defendant will actually prefer delaying settlement with both types until the eve of trial. We have assumed in this analysis that the defendant incurs no cost of carrying the trial.

22. See Mnookin (1998) for a survey, and Shavell (1995a) for a formal economic analysis of ADR.

23. There has since developed a fairly large literature. For a recent study, see Hersch (2006). For a fuller survey, see Waldfogel (1998).

24. See Hylton (1993), Baird, Gertner, and Picker (1994, 260–61), and Shavell (1996).

25. In Rubin's (1977) model, trials occur not because of disagreement but because one or both of the litigants have a long-term interest in the legal rule. In this respect, Rubin's model is less general than Priest's (1977).

26. For example, suppose judges decide cases based on criteria like justice or fairness that are neutral regarding efficiency.

27. The analysis here is based on Heiner (1986). Also see Blume and Rubinfeld (1982), Kornhauser (1989), and Macey (1989).

28. Posner (1998a, 587). Also see Macey (1989).

29. In fact, Landes and Posner (1976) actually estimate the rate of depreciation by using citations to a particular decision as a measure of its precedential value.

30. See Posner (1998a, 602–5) and Miceli (1990).

31. There is an asymmetry in the sense that a losing plaintiff foregoes income, while a losing defendant suffers an out-of-pocket loss.

32. We pursue this point in more detail in Section 3 of Chapter 9.

33. Only the highest appeals court has discretion over the cases it will hear.

34. See Greenberg and Haley (1986), who argue that low salaries will cause only those individuals who value the act of judging rather than monetary gains to become judges.

35. See, for example, Higgins and Rubin (1980), Cooter (1983), and Miceli and Cosgel (1994).

36. See Holmes (1881), especially Lecture 1. For an analogy in biological evolution, see S. J. Gould (2002, ch. 11).

CHAPTER 9   1. For example, L. Katz (1987, ch. 3) examines the problems associated with the use of mens rea as a basis for assigning criminal responsibility.

2. See Section 3.5 in Chapter 2.

3. See Section 4 in Chapter 7.

4. Specifically, Landes and Posner (1975) show that competition will lead to overinvestment in enforcement, a form of rent seeking. Also see Polinsky (1980b).

5. This example and the next are taken from D. Friedman (2000, ch. 17).

6. See Calabresi and Melamed (1972), Klevorick (1985), and Coleman (1988, chs. 2 and 6).

7. See the survey by Polinsky and Shavell (2000), on which much of the following is based.

8. Actually, p is a composite of the probability of apprehension and conviction.

9. The exact amount of the decrease will depend on the "density" of offenders at each value of g over the range of offenders.

10. This is true because the cost to criminals of paying the fine is exactly offset by the revenue received by the government.

11. As in our discussion of tort law, we assume that, when necessary, dollar values can be attached to bodily harms (see Section 3.12 in Chapter 2).

12. See Section 3.5 in Chapter 2.

13. Polinsky and Shavell (1994) argue, however, that measurement error will generally favor harm-based penalties.

14. See Section 3.6 in Chapter 2.

15. On the role of stigma, or shame, in deterring crime, see Rasmusen (1996) and Kahan and Posner (1999).

16. The incentive effects of parole are therefore similar to the idea of marginal deterrence. See Section 2.2.6 below.

17. This assumes that criminals are risk neutral. The conclusion is different if they are either risk averse or risk loving. See Section 2.2.6 below.

18. The problem is analogous to a firm that minimizes input costs for any level of output and then chooses output to maximize profits. Here, p and f correspond to the firm's inputs, and the crime rate corresponds to its output.

19. This is true because, given (9.1), the marginal offender has $g = p^*f^* < h$.

20. This result was first demonstrated by Polinsky and Shavell (1984).

21. At the optimum, $4,000 will be less than the harm caused by the crime for reasons noted in the previous section.

22. In general, it would not be optimal to hold deterrence fixed as we adjust p and t, but the general point is not affected by this assumption. The social cost of imprisonment includes the cost to the offender ($500 in this example) plus the cost to society of housing and feeding him.

23. Note that one factor favoring an increase in t is that it is discounted by p since only those offenders who are actually apprehended are imprisoned.

24. Note the similarity of this problem to that of the injurer choosing an optimal level of precaution.

25. See Posner (1980, 71). We discuss the idea of retribution as retaliation or revenge below (see Section 4.3).

26. Wittman (1974, 217). Note that this form of punishment violates the principle of "horizontal equity," which says that like individuals should be treated alike.

27. See, for example, Dawson (1969, 201), Wittman (1974, 233–34), and Mermin (1982, 54) for anecdotal evidence. For empirical evidence for and against proportional punishments, see Snyder (1990) and Waldfogel (1993).

28. Stigler (1970) apparently was the first to use the phrase "marginal deterrence." Also see Posner (1998a, 245), Polinsky and Shavell (2000, 63–64), and Friedman (2000, 235).

29. See Posner (1998a, 250–52), Polinsky and Shavell (2000, 66–67), and Shavell (2004, 528–30).

30. On this point, see Chu, Hu, and Huang (2000) and Polinsky and Rubinfeld (1991).

31. To illustrate, suppose the probability of apprehension for first-time offenders is .10, and the harm from the offense is $500. The optimal fine is thus $500/.10 = $5,000. But suppose that repeat offenders are only caught with probability .05. Optimal deterrence therefore implies that they should face a fine of $500/.05 = $10,000.

32. For recent surveys of the economics of the death penalty, see Avio (1998) and Cooter and Ulen (1988).

33. See, for example, Dezhbakhsh, Rubin, and Shepherd (2003) and Shepherd (2004). In contrast, see Katz, Levitt, and Shustorovich (2003), who find little deterrent effect of the execution rate. Instead, they find that the quality of prison life has a significant effect. See Donahue and Wolfers (2005) for a general critique of the deterrence studies.

34. See *Furman v. Georgia*, 408 U.S. 238 (1972).

35. See *Gregg v. Georgia*, 428 U.S. 153 (1976).

36. For example, let F = the bondsman's fee. The bondsman's expected profit is thus $F - pb$, where p and b are defined as above. In a competitive market, expected profit equals zero, which implies that $F/b = p$.

37. For economic models of private protection against crime, see Shavell (1991) and Hylton (1996).

38. The fact that crime victims are not compensated for their harm actually gives them an incentive to undertake such precaution. The situation is similar to a rule of no liability in torts (see Chapter 2). Victims can, however, often file a separate claim for compensation under tort law.

39. See Shavell (1991) for a model in which victim efforts are observable.

40. Shavell (1991) was the first to point out this result. It does not necessarily follow, however, that collective choice of y is more efficient than individual choice. The point

is a subtle one and depends on whether offenders' gains (including the cost $c(y)$) are counted as part of social welfare. If they are counted (as we assumed above), then individual choice of y by victims is not optimal (assuming that the fine is set optimally at $f = h/p$). The reason is that victims acting collectively ignore the impact of y on the net gains to offenders and instead choose y to minimize their aggregate harm. In contrast, if offenders' gains are not counted in social welfare, then collective choice of y by victims is optimal.

41. Also see Forst and Brosi (1977).
42. A correlation coefficient of -1 implies perfect negative correlation, whereas a coefficient of zero implies no correlation.
43. We assume that when indifferent between a plea bargain and a trial, defendants opt for the plea bargain in order to avoid the uncertainty of trial.
44. It would therefore seem to follow that prosecutors should drop the cases against all defendants who turn down the plea offer under option 2. If such a strategy were anticipated, however, then guilty defendants would also turn down the plea offer and the equilibrium would break down.
45. See Miceli (1996b), on which this section is based, and Reinganum (1993). The impact of settlement on deterrence in civil litigation is examined by Polinsky and Rubinfeld (1988).
46. For a more general model in which individuals can divide their time between legal and illegal activities, see Raphael and Winter-Ebmer (2001).
47. This assumes no offsetting changes in the expected punishment of criminals.
48. See Cook and Zarkin (1985), whose results cover the period 1949 to 1979, and Raphael and Winter-Ebmer (2001), whose results cover the period 1971 to 1997.
49. The evidence on robbery, classified as a violent crime but also possibly motivated by economic gain, is mixed.
50. See Lott (1998, ch. 2) and Cook and Leitzel (1998).
51. Also see Lott and Mustard (1997).
52. See Posner (1983, chs. 7 and 8), on which this discussion is based. Also see Holmes (1881, 6), who says that "it is commonly known that early forms of legal procedure were grounded in vengeance."
53. It is also related to forms of vicarious liability like respondeat superior, as discussed in Section 2.1 of Chapter 3. See Miceli and Segerson (2007) for a formal analysis of group punishment.
54. For general discussions, see Spitzer (1998), Cooter (2000, ch. 13), and Posner (2001, ch. 2).
55. See *Texas v. Johnson*, 491 U.S. 397 (1989).
56. For an overview of privacy and the law, see Posner (1998b). Also see Scheppele (1988). The constitutional right to abortion was famously established in *Roe v. Wade*,

410 U.S. 113 (1973). Also see Posner (1983, ch. 11). The word "privacy," however, appears nowhere in the Constitution.

57. The transaction between T and S, however, presents other problems, such as "What makes T's threat to reveal the information if S does not pay credible?" and, "What prevents the blackmailer from repeating his threat multiple times?" On the former point, the blackmailer in the Sherlock Holmes story, "The Adventure of Charles Augustus Milverton," explains why it is profitable to carry out such a threat: "An exposure would profit me indirectly to a considerable extent. I have eight or ten similar cases maturing. If it was circulated among them that I had made a severe example of the Lady Eva, I should find all of them much more open to reason. You see my point?" (Doyle 1986). For economic analyses of this aspect of blackmail, see Shavell (1993a) and Posner (1998b, 107).

CHAPTER 10   1. We do not distinguish here between the short and long run, the difference being that in the short run, firms may earn an economic profit (i.e., price may exceed average cost), whereas in the long run, entry of firms will drive economic profits to zero (i.e., price must equal long-run average cost).

2. Producers' surplus is related to profit but differs from it by the amount of firms' fixed costs. Specifically, producers' surplus equals profit before fixed costs are subtracted.

3. There is no loss in producer surplus in the case of constant marginal costs.

4. Readers may have noticed that the structure of this game is that of a prisoner's dilemma (Poundstone 1992), which economists have used to explain a variety of social and economic situations in which cooperation fails despite the existence of joint gains.

5. See the discussion in Dick (1998). Also see Telser (1980) for a more general discussion of this type of self-enforcing agreement.

6. This section is based on Hylton (2003, pp. 43–47).

7. To prove this, note that for a straight-line demand curve, the marginal revenue curve always has the same intercept as the demand curve and twice the slope. Thus, in Figure 10.2, $Q_c = 2Q_m$, or, equivalently, $Q_c - Q_m = Q_m$. Now, recall that the area of the transfer, T, is $(P_m - P_c)Q_m$, while the area of the deadweight loss, D, is $(P_m - P_c)(Q_c - Q_m)/2$. It follows immediately that $D = T/2$ as claimed.

8. This view is exemplified by Gilbert and Williamson (1998).

9. Owners avoided scrutiny by antitrust laws based on the Supreme Court's ruling in *Federal Baseball Club of Baltimore, Inc. v. National League of Professional Baseball Clubs*, 259 U.S. 200 (1922), which held that baseball was exempt from antitrust enforcement because it was a "public exhibition" rather than a form of interstate commerce.

10. This view of firms began with Coase (1937) and was elaborated on by many others, principally Williamson (1985).

11. The case was *Goebel v. Linn* (47 Mich. 489, 11 N.W. 284, 1882), as discussed in Section 3.2 of Chapter 4.

12. See Hylton (2003, 315–17), citing Williamson (1968).

13. This is also referred to as an adverse selection problem. See Akerlof (1970).

14. See Hylton (2003, 252–62). Also see Blair, Fesmire, and Romano (2000).

15. This section is based on Viscusi, Harrington, and Vernon (2005, ch. 11).

WORKS CITED

Adelstein, Richard. 1998. Plea Bargaining: A Comparative Approach. In *The New Palgrave Dictionary of Economics and the Law*, ed. P. Newman. New York: Stockton Press.

———. 1981. Institutional Function and Evolution in the Criminal Process. *Northwestern University Law Review* 76: 1–99.

———. 1979a. Informational Paradox and the Pricing of Crime: Capital Sentencing Standards in Economic Perspective. *Journal of Criminal Law and Criminology* 70: 281–98.

———. 1979b. The Moral Costs of Crime: Prices, Information, and Organization. In *The Costs of Crime*, ed. C. Gray. Beverly Hills, Calif.: Sage Publications.

———. 1974. Just Compensation and the Assassin's Bequest: A Utilitarian Approach. *University of Pennsylvania Law Review* 122: 1012–32.

Adelstein, Richard, and Thomas Miceli. 2001. Toward a Comparative Economics of Plea Bargaining. *European Journal of Law and Economics* 11: 47–67.

Adelstein, Richard, and Steven Peretz. 1985. The Competition of Technologies in Markets for Ideas: Copyright and Fair Use in Evolutionary Perspective. *International Review of Law and Economics* 5: 209–38.

Aghion, Philippe, and Patrick Bolton. 1987. Contracts as Barriers to Entry. *American Economic Review* 77: 388–410.

Aivazian, Varouj, Michael Trebilcock, and Michael Penny. 1984. The Law of Contract Modifications: The Uncertain Quest for a Benchmark of Enforceability. *Osgoode Hall Law Journal* 22: 173–212.

Akerlof, George. 1970. The Market for 'Lemons': Quality Uncertainty and the Market Mechanism. *Quarterly Journal of Economics* 84: 488–500.

Allen, Douglas. 1998. Cropshare Contracts. In *The New Palgrave Dictionary of Economics and the Law*, ed. P. Newman. New York: Stockton Press.

———. 1991. Homesteading and Property Rights; or, "How the West Was Really Won." *Journal of Law and Economics* 34: 1–23.

Allen, Douglas, and Dean Lueck. 1995. Risk Preferences and the Economics of Contracts. *American Economic Review* 85: 447–51.

Alston, Lee, Gary Libecap, and Robert Schneider. 1996. The Determinants and Impact of Property Rights: Land Title on the Brazilian Frontier. *Journal of Law, Economics & Organization* 12: 25–61.

Anderson, David. 2002. The Deterrence Hypothesis and Picking Pockets at the Pickpocket's Hanging. *American Law and Economics Review* 4: 295–313.

———. 1999. The Aggregate Burden of Crime. *Journal of Law and Economics* 42: 611–42.

Anderson, James, Jeffrey Kling, and Kate Smith. 1999. Measuring Interjudge Sentencing Disparity: Before and After the Federal Sentencing Guidelines. *Journal of Law and Economics* 42: 271–307.

Andreoni, James. 1991. Reasonable Doubt and the Optimal Magnitude of Fines. *Rand Journal of Economics* 22: 385–95.

Arlen, Jennifer. 1990. Re-examining Liability Rules When Injurers as Well as Victims Suffer Losses. *International Review of Law and Economics* 10: 233–39.

Avio, Kenneth. 1998. Capital Punishment. In *The New Palgrave Dictionary of Economics and the Law*, ed. P. Newman. New York: Stockton Press.

Ayres, Ian, and John Donahue. 1999. Nondiscretionary Concealed Weapons Laws: A Case Study of Statistics, Standards of Proof, and Public Policy. *American Law and Economics Review* 1: 436–70.

Ayres, Ian, and Joel Waldfogel. 1994. A Market Test for Race Discrimination in Bail Setting. *Stanford Law Review* 46: 987–1047.

Babcock, Linda, and George Loewenstein. 2000. Explaining Bargaining Impasse: The Role of Self-Serving Biases. In *Behavioral Law and Economics*, ed. Cass Sunstein. Cambridge: Cambridge University Press.

Bailey, Martin. 1992. Approximate Optimality of Aboriginal Property Rights. *Journal of Legal Studies* 35: 183–98.

Baird, Douglas, Robert Gertner, and Randal Picker. 1994. *Game Theory and the Law.* Cambridge, Mass.: Harvard University Press.

Baird, Douglas, and Thomas Jackson. 1984. Information, Uncertainty, and the Transfer of Property. *Journal of Legal Studies* 13: 299–320.

Baker, Matthew, and Thomas Miceli. 2005. Land Inheritance Rules: Theory and Cross-Cultural Analysis. *Journal of Economic Behavior and Organization* 56: 77–102.

———. 2000. Statutes of Limitations for Accident Cases: Theory and Evidence. *Research in Law and Economics* 19: 47–67.

Baker, Matthew, Thomas Miceli, C. F. Sirmans, and Geoffrey Turnbull. 2002. Optimal Title Search. *Journal of Legal Studies* 31: 139–58.

———. 2001. Property Rights by Squatting: Land Ownership Risk and Adverse Possession Statutes. *Land Economics* 77: 360–70.

Barzel, Yoram. 1989. *Economic Analysis of Property Rights.* Cambridge: Cambridge University Press.

Baumol, William, John Panzar, and Robert Willig. 1982. *Contestable Markets and the Theory of Industrial Structure*. San Diego: Harcourt Brace Jovanovich.

Beard, T. Randolph. 1990. Bankruptcy and Care Choice. *Rand Journal of Economics* 21: 626–34.

Bebchuk, Lucian. 1988. Suing Solely to Extract a Settlement Offer. *Journal of Legal Studies* 17: 437–50.

———. 1984. Litigation and Settlement Under Imperfect Information. *Rand Journal of Economics* 15: 404–15.

Bebchuk, Lucian, and I. P. L. Png. 1999. Damage Measures for Inadvertant Breach of Contract. *International Review of Law and Economics* 19: 319–31.

Bebchuk, Lucian, and Steven Shavell. 1991. Information and the Scope of Liability for Breach of Contract: The Rule of *Hadley v. Baxendale*. *Journal of Law, Economics & Organization* 7: 284–312.

Becker, Gary. 1968. Crime and Punishment: An Economic Approach. *Journal of Political Economy* 76: 169–217.

Becker, Gary, and George Stigler. 1974. Law Enforcement, Malfeasance, and Compensation of Enforcers. *Journal of Legal Studies* 3: 1–18.

Berkowitz, Daniel, and Karen Clay. 2006. The Effect of Judicial Independence on Courts: Evidence from the American States. *Journal of Legal Studies* 35: 399–440.

Besley, Timothy. 1995. Property Rights and Investment Incentives: Theory and Evidence from Ghana. *Journal of Political Economy* 103: 903–37.

Blair, Roger, and Thomas Cotter. 2005. *Intellectual Property*. Cambridge: Cambridge University Press.

Blair, Roger, James Fesmire, and Richard Romano. 2000. Applying the Rule of Reason to Maximum Resale Price Fixing: *Albrecht* Overruled." In *Industrial Organization: Advances in Applied Microeconomics*, Vol. 9, ed. Michael R. Baye. New York: JAI Press.

Blume, Lawrence, and Daniel Rubinfeld. 1984. Compensation for Takings: An Economic Analysis. *California Law Review* 73: 569–628.

———. 1982. The Dynamics of the Legal Process. *Journal of Legal Studies* 11: 405–19.

Blume, Lawrence, Daniel Rubinfeld, and Perry Shapiro. 1984. The Taking of Land: When Should Compensation Be Paid? *Quarterly Journal of Economics* 99: 71–92.

Bostick, C. Dent. 1987. Land Title Registration: An English Solution to an American Problem. *Indiana Law Journal* 63: 55–111.

Brooks, Richard. 2002. Liability and Organizational Choice. *Journal of Law and Economics* 45: 91–125.

Brown, John. 1973. Toward an Economic Theory of Liability. *Journal of Legal Studies* 2: 323–49.

Buchanan, James. 1983. Rent Seeking, Noncompensated Transfers, and Laws of Succession. *Journal of Law and Economics* 26: 71–85.

Buchanan, James, and Gordon Tullock. 1962. *The Calculus of Consent: Logical Foundations of Constitutional Democracy.* Ann Arbor: University of Michigan Press.

Calabresi, Guido, and A. Douglas Melamed. 1972. Property Rules, Liability Rules, and Inalienability: One View of the Cathedral. *Harvard Law Review* 85: 1089–1128.

Casad, Robert. 1968. The Mistaken Improver—A Comparative Study. *Hastings Law Journal* 19: 1039–70.

Cheung, Steven. 1969. *The Theory of Share Tenancy.* Chicago: University of Chicago Press.

Chu, C.Y. Cyrus, Sheng-cheng Hu, and Ting-yuan Huang. 2000. Punishing Repeat Offenders More Severely. *International Review of Law and Economics* 20: 127–40.

Chung, Tai-Yeong. 1996. Settlement of Litigation Under Rule 68: An Economic Analysis. *Journal of Legal Studies* 25: 261–86.

Coase, Ronald. 1960. The Problem of Social Cost. *Journal of Law and Economics* 3: 1–44.

———. 1937. The Nature of the Firm. *Economica* 4: 386–405.

Cohen, Lloyd. 1991. Holdouts and Free Riders. *Journal of Legal Studies* 20: 351–62.

Cohen, Mark. 1991. Explaining Judicial Behavior, or What's Constitutional About the Sentencing Commission? *Journal of Law, Economics & Organization* 7: 183–99.

Coleman, Jules. 1988. *Markets, Morals, and the Law.* Cambridge: Cambridge University Press.

———. 1982. The Economic Analysis of Law. In *NOMOS XXIV: Ethics, Economics, and the Law*, ed. J. Roland Pennock and John Chapman. New York: New York University Press.

Colwell, Peter, and Henry Munneke. 1999. Land Prices and Land Assembly in the CBD. *Journal of Real Estate Finance and Economics* 18: 163–80.

Cook, Philip, and James Leitzel. 1998. Gun Control. In *The New Palgrave Dictionary of Economics and the Law*, ed. P. Newman. New York: Stockton Press.

Cook, Philip, and Gary Zarkin. 1985. Crime and the Business Cycle. *Journal of Legal Studies* 14: 115–28.

Cooper, Russell, and Thomas Ross. 1985. Product Warranties and Double Moral Hazard. *Rand Journal of Economics* 16: 103–33.

Cooter, Robert. 2000. *The Strategic Constitution.* Princeton, N.J.: Princeton University Press.

———. 1998. Liability Rights as Contingent Claims. In *The New Palgrave Dictionary of Economics and the Law*, ed. P. Newman. New York: Stockton Press.

———. 1989. Punitive Damages for Deterrence: When and How Much? *Alabama Law Review* 40: 1143–96.

———. 1987a. Torts as the Union of Liberty and Efficiency: An Essay on Causation. *Chicago-Kent Law Review* 73: 1–51.

———. 1987b. Why Litigants Disagree: A Comment on George Priest's "Measuring Legal Change." *Journal of Law, Economics & Organization* 3: 227–34.

———. 1985. Unity in Tort, Contract, and Property: The Model of Precaution. *California Law Review* 73: 1–51.

———. 1984. Prices and Sanctions. *Columbia Law Review* 84: 1523–60.

———. 1983. The Objectives of Private and Public Judges. *Public Choice* 41: 107–32.

Cooter, Robert, Stephen Marks, and Robert Mnookin. 1982. Bargaining in the Shadow of the Law: A Testable Model of Strategic Behavior. *Journal of Legal Studies* 11: 225 51.

Cooter, Robert, and Daniel Rubinfeld. 1994. An Economic Model of Legal Discovery. *Journal of Legal Studies* 23: 435–63.

———. 1989. An Economic Analysis of Legal Disputes and Their Resolution. *Journal of Economic Literature* 27: 1067–97.

Cooter, Robert, and Thomas Ulen. 1988. *Law and Economics.* Glenview, Ill.: Scott, Foresman and Co.

———. 1986. An Economic Case for Comparative Negligence. *New York University Law Review* 61: 1067–1110.

Cornes, Richard, and Todd Sandler. 1986. *The Theory of Externalities, Public Goods, and Club Goods.* Cambridge: Cambridge University Press.

Cosgel, Metin, Thomas Miceli, and John Murray. 1997. Organization and Distributional Equality in a Network of Communes: The Shakers. *American Journal of Economics and Sociology* 56: 129–44.

Coursey, Don, and Linda Stanley. 1988. Pretrial Bargaining Behavior Within the Shadow of the Law: Theory and Experimental Evidence. *International Review of Law and Economics* 8: 161 79.

Craswell, Richard. 1989. Performance, Reliance, and One-sided Information. *Journal of Legal Studies* 18: 365–401.

Craswell, Richard, and Alan Schwartz, eds. 1994. *Foundations of Contract Law.* New York: Oxford University Press.

Cribbet, John. 1975. *Principles of the Law of Property.* 2d ed. Mineola, N.Y.: The Foundation Press.

Curran, Christopher. 1992. The Spread of the Comparative Negligence Rule. *International Review of Law and Economics* 12: 317–32.

Danzon, Patricia. 1998. Medical Malpractice. In *The New Palgrave Dictionary of Economics and the Law*, ed. P. Newman. New York: Stockton Press.

———. 1991. Liability for Medical Malpractice. *Journal of Economic Perspectives* 5: 51–69.

————. 1983. Contingent Fees for Personal Injury Litigation. *Bell Journal of Economics* 14: 213–24.

Dawson, Robert. 1969. *Sentencing: The Decision as to Type, Length, and Conditions of Sentence.* Boston: Little, Brown.

Demsetz, Harold. 1972. When Does the Rule of Liability Matter? *Journal of Legal Studies* 1: 13–28.

————. 1967. Toward a Theory of Property Rights. *American Economic Review* 57: 347–59.

De Soto, Hernando. 2000. *The Mystery of Capital.* New York: Basic Books.

Dewees, Donald. 1998. Occupational Disease and the Tort System: The Case of Asbestos. In *The New Palgrave Dictionary of Economics and the Law*, ed. P. Newman. New York: Stockton Press.

Dezhbakhsh, Hashem, Paul Rubin, and Joanna Shepherd. 2003. Does Capital Punishment Have a Deterrent Effect? New Evidence from Postmoratorium Panel Data. *American Law and Economics Review* 5: 344–76.

Dharmapala, Dhammika, and Rohan Pitchford. 2002. An Economic Analysis of "Riding to Hounds": *Pierson v. Post* Revisited. *Journal of Law, Economics & Organization* 18: 39–66.

Dick, Andrew. 1998. Cartels and Tacit Collusion. In *The New Palgrave Dictionary of Economics and the Law*, ed. P. Newman. New York: Stockton Press.

Dickinson, Kelvin. 1985. Mistaken Improvers of Real Estate. *North Carolina Law Review* 64: 37–75.

Donahue, John. 1991a. The Effects of Fee Shifting on the Settlement Rate: Theoretical Observations on Costs, Conflicts, and Contingency Fees. *Law and Contemporary Problems* 54: 195–222.

————. 1991b. Opting for the British Rule, or If Posner and Shavell Can't Remember the Coase Theorem, Who Will? *Harvard Law Review* 104: 1093–1119.

Donahue, John, and Steven Levitt. 2001a. The Impact of Legalized Abortion on Crime. *Quarterly Journal of Economics* 116: 379–420.

————. 2001b. The Impact of Race on Policing and Arrests. *Journal of Law and Economics* 44: 367–94.

Donahue, John, and J. Wolfers. 2005. Uses and Abuses of Empirical Evidence in the Death Penalty Debate. *Stanford Law Review* 58: 791–846.

Doyle, Sir Arthur Conan. 1986. *Sherlock Holmes: The Complete Novels and Stories.* 2 vols. New York: Bantam Books.

Drahozal, Christopher. 1986. The Impact of Free Agency on the Distribution of Playing Talent in Major League Baseball. *Journal of Economics and Business* 38: 113–22.

Dungworth, Terence, and Nicholas Pace. 1990. *Statistical Overview of Civil Litigation in the Federal Courts,* R-3885-ICJ. Santa Monica, Calif.: Rand Corp.

Easterbrook, Frank. 1983. Criminal Procedure as a Market System. *Journal of Legal Studies* 12: 289–332.

Ehrlich, Isaac. 1977. Capital Punishment and Deterrence: Some Further Thoughts and Additional Evidence. *Journal of Political Economy* 85: 741–88.

———. 1975. The Deterrent Effect of Capital Punishment: A Question of Life and Death. *American Economic Review* 65: 397–417.

Ehrlich, Isaac, and Richard Posner. 1974. An Economic Analysis of Legal Rulemaking. *Journal of Legal Studies* 3: 257–86.

Eide, Erling (in cooperation with J. Aasness and T. Skjerpen). 1994. *Economics of Crime: Deterrence and the Rational Offender.* North-Holland: Amsterdam.

Eisenberg, Theodore, John Goerdt, Brian Ostrom, David Rottman, and Martin T. Wells. 1997. The Predictability of Punitive Damages. *Journal of Legal Studies* 26: 623–61.

Ellickson, Robert. 1993. Property in Land. *Yale Law Journal* 102: 1315–1400.

———. 1991. *Order Without Law: How Neighbors Settle Disputes.* Cambridge, Mass.: Harvard University Press.

———. 1986. Adverse Possession and Perpetuities Law: Two Dents in the Libertarian Model of Property Rights. *Washington University Law Quarterly* 64: 723–37.

———. 1973. Alternatives to Zoning: Covenants, Nuisance Rules, and Fines as Land Use Controls. *University of Chicago Law Review* 40: 681–782.

Epstein, Richard. 1992. The Path to *The T. J. Hooper*: The Theory and History of Custom in the Law of Torts. *Journal of Legal Studies* 21: 1–38.

———. 1986. Past and Future: The Temporal Dimension in the Law of Property. *Washington University Law Quarterly* 64: 667–722.

———. 1985. *Takings: Private Property and the Power of Eminent Domain.* Cambridge, Mass.: Harvard University Press.

———. 1980. *Modern Products Liability Law.* Westport, Conn.: Quorum Books.

———. 1979. Possession as the Root of Title. *Georgia Law Review* 85: 970–90.

———. 1975. Unconscionability: A Critical Reappraisal. *Journal of Law and Economics* 18: 293–315.

Eswaran, Mukesh, and Ashok Kotwol. 1985. A Theory of Contractual Structure. *American Economic Review* 75: 162–77.

Fenn, Paul, Alastair Gray, and Neil Rickman. 2007. Liability, Insurance and Medical Practice. *Journal of Health Economics*, forthcoming.

Field, Barry. 1989. The Evolution of Property Rights. *Kyklos* 42: 319–45.

Fischel, William. 1996. The Political Economy of Just Compensation: Lessons from the Military Draft for the Takings Issue. *Harvard Journal of Law and Public Policy* 20: 23–63.

———. 1995a. The Offer/Ask Disparity and Just Compensation for Takings: A Constitutional Choice Perspective. *International Review of Law and Economics* 15: 187–203.

———. 1995b. *Regulatory Takings: Law, Economics, and Politics.* Cambridge, Mass.: Harvard University Press.

———. 1985. *The Economics of Zoning Laws: A Property Rights Approach to American Land Use Controls.* Baltimore, Md.: Johns Hopkins University Press.

Fischel, William, and Perry Shapiro. 1989. A Constitutional Choice Model of Compensation for Takings. *International Review of Law and Economics* 9: 115–28.

———. 1988. Takings, Insurance, and Michelman: Comments on Economic Interpretations of "Just Compensation" Law. *Journal of Legal Studies* 17: 269–93.

Flath, David. 1980. The Economics of Short-Term Leasing. *Economic Inquiry* 18: 247–59.

Forst, Brian, and Kathleen Brosi. 1977. A Theoretical and Empirical Analysis of the Prosecutor. *Journal of Legal Studies* 6: 177–91.

Friedman, David. 2000. *Law's Order: What Economics Has to Do with the Law and Why It Matters.* Princeton, N.J.: Princeton University Press.

Friedman, Lawrence. 1986. A Search for Seizure: *Pennsylvania Coal Co. v. Mahon* in Context. *Law and History Review* 4: 1–22.

———. 1985. *A History of American Law.* 2d ed. New York: Touchstone.

Friedman, Milton. 1990. *Friedman on Leases.* 3d ed. New York: Practicing Law Institute.

Friedmann, Daniel. 1989. The Efficient Breach Fallacy. *Journal of Legal Studies* 18: 1–24.

Gallini, Nancy. 1992. Patent Protection and Costly Imitation. *Rand Journal of Economics* 23: 52–63.

Gennaioli, Nicola, and Andrei Shleifer. 2007a. Overruling and the Instability of Law. *Journal of Comparative Economics* 35: 309–28.

———. 2007b. The Evolution of Common Law. *Journal of Political Economy* 115: 43–68.

Gerard, David. 2001. Transaction Costs and the Value of Mining Claims. *Land Economics* 77: 371–84.

Gilbert, Richard, and Oliver Williamson. 1998. Antitrust Policy. In *The New Palgrave Dictionary of Economics and the Law*, ed. P. Newman. New York: Stockton Press.

Gilles, Stephen. 1992. Rule-Based Negligence and the Regulation of Activity Levels. *Journal of Legal Studies* 21: 319–63.

Glaeser, Edward, and Bruce Sacerdote. 1999. Why Is There More Crime in Cities? *Journal of Political Economy* 107: S225–58.

Goetz, Charles, and Robert Scott. 1983. The Mitigation Principle: Toward a General Theory of Contractual Obligation. *Virginia Law Review* 69: 967–1025.

Goldberg, Victor. 1988. Impossibility and Related Excuses. *Journal of Institutional and Theoretical Economics* 144: 100–116.

———. 1985. Relational Exchange, Contract Law, and the *Boomer* Problem. *Journal of Institutional and Theoretical Economics* 141: 570–75.

———. 1976. Regulation and Administered Contracts. *Bell Journal of Economics* 7: 426–48.

Goodman, John. 1978. An Economic Analysis of the Evolution of the Common Law. *Journal of Legal Studies* 7: 393–406.

Gordon, Wendy. 1982. Fair Use as Market Failure: A Structural and Economic Analysis of the *Betamax* Case and Its Predecessors. *Columbia Law Review* 82: 1600–1657.

Gould, John. 1973. The Economics of Legal Conflicts. *Journal of Legal Studies* 2: 279–300.

Gould, Stephen Jay. 2002. *The Structure of Evolutionary Theory.* Cambridge, Mass.: Belknap Press of Harvard University Press.

Grady, Mark. 1989. Untaken Precautions. *Journal of Legal Studies* 18: 139–56.

———. 1988. Common Law Control of Strategic Behavior: Railroad Sparks and the Farmer. *Journal of Legal Studies* 17: 15–42.

———. 1983. A New Positive Economic Theory of Negligence. *Yale Law Journal* 92: 799–829.

Gravelle, Hugh. 1998. Conditional Fees in Britain. In *The New Palgrave Dictionary of Law and Economics*, ed. P. Newman. New York: Stockton Press.

Greenberg, Paul, and James Haley. 1986. The Role of the Compensation Structure in Enhancing Judicial Quality. *Journal of Legal Studies* 15: 417–26.

Grossman, Gene, and Michael Katz. 1983. Plea Bargaining and Social Welfare. *American Economic Review* 73: 749–57.

Hansen, F. Andrew. 2004. Is There a Political Optimal Level of Judicial Independence? *American Economic Review* 94: 712–29.

Hardin, Garrett. 1968. The Tragedy of the Commons. *Science* 162: 1243–48.

Harris, John. 1970. On the Economics of Law and Order. *Journal of Political Economy* 78: 165–74.

Hart, H. L. A. 1982. *Punishment and Responsibility: Essays in the Philosophy of Law.* Oxford: Clarendon Press.

———. 1961. *The Concept of Law.* London: Oxford University Press.

Hause, John. 1989. Indemnity, Settlement, and Litigation, or I'll Be Suing You. *Journal of Legal Studies* 18: 157–79.

Heiner, Ronald. 1986. Imperfect Decisions and the Law: On the Evolution of Legal Precedent. *Journal of Legal Studies* 15: 227–61.

Heller, Michael. 1998. The Tragedy of the Anti-Commons: Property in Transition from Marx to Markets. *Harvard Law Review* 111: 621–88.

Helmholz, R. H. 1983. Adverse Possession and Subjective Intent. *Washington University Law Quarterly* 61: 331–58.

Henderson, Vernon, and Yannis Ioannides. 1983. A Model of Housing Tenure Choice. *American Economic Review* 73: 98–113.

Hensler, Deborah, et al. 1991. *Compensation for Accidental Injuries in the United States,* R-3999–HHS/ICJ. Santa Monica, Calif.: Rand Corp.

Hermalin, Benjamin. 1995. An Economic Analysis of Takings. *Journal of Law, Economics & Organization* 11: 64–86.

Hersch, Joni. 2006. Demand for a Jury Trial and the Selection of Cases for Trial. *Journal of Legal Studies* 35: 119–42.

Higgins, Richard, and Paul Rubin. 1980. Judicial Discretion. *Journal of Legal Studies* 9: 129–38.

Hirshleifer, Jack. 1971. The Private and Social Value of Information and the Reward to Inventive Activity. *American Economic Review* 61: 561–74.

Hoffman, Elizabeth, and Matthew Spitzer. 1982. The Coase Theorem: Some Experimental Tests. *Journal of Law and Economics* 25: 73–98.

Holmes, Oliver Wendell. 1897. The Path of the Law. *Harvard Law Review* 10: 61–478.

———. 1881. *The Common Law.* Boston: Little, Brown.

Horwitz, Morton. 1977. *The Transformation of American Law, 1780–1860.* Cambridge, Mass.: Harvard University Press.

Howard, Philip. 1994. *The Death of Common Sense.* New York: Random House.

Hughes, James, and Edward Snyder. 1995. Litigation and Settlement Under the English and American Rules: Theory and Evidence. *Journal of Law and Economics* 38: 225–50.

Hylton, Keith. 2005. The Theory of Criminal Penalties and the Economics of Criminal Law. *Review of Law and Economics* 1: 175–201.

———. 2003. *Antitrust Law: Economic Theory and Common Law Evolution.* Cambridge: Cambridge University Press.

———. 1996. Optimal Law Enforcement and Victim Precaution. *Rand Journal of Economics* 27: 197–206.

———. 1993. Asymmetric Information and the Selection of Disputes for Litigation. *Journal of Legal Studies* 22: 187–210.

———. 1990. The Influence of Litigation Costs on Deterrence Under Strict Liability and Under Negligence. *International Review of Law and Economics* 10: 161–71.

Janczyk, Joseph. 1977. An Economic Analysis of the Land Title Systems for Transferring Real Property. *Journal of Legal Studies* 6: 213–33.

Johnson, D. Bruce. 1986. The Formation and Protection of Property Rights Among the Southern Kwakiutl Indians. *Journal of Legal Studies* 15: 41–67.

Jolls, Christine. 2000. Behavioral Economic Analysis of Redistributive Legal Rules. In *Behavioral Law and Economics*, ed. Cass Sunstein. Cambridge: Cambridge University Press.

Kahan, Dan, and Eric Posner. 1999. Shaming White Collar Criminals: A Proposal for the Reform of the Federal Sentencing Guidelines. *Journal of Law and Economics* 42: 365–91.

Kahan, Marcel. 1989. Causation and Incentives to Take Care Under the Negligence Rule. *Journal of Legal Studies* 18: 427–47.

Kahneman, Daniel, Jack Knetsch, and Richard Thaler. 2000. Experimental Tests of the Endowment Effect and the Coase Theorem. In *Behavioral Law and Economics*, ed. Cass Sunstein. Cambridge: Cambridge University Press.

Kakalik, J. S., et al. 1996. *An Evaluation of Mediation and Early Neutral Evaluation Under the Civil Justice Reform Act,* MR-803-ICJ. Santa Monica, Calif.: Rand Corp.

Kakalik, J. S., and R. L. Ross. 1983. *Cost of the Civil Justice System: Court Expenditures for Various Types of Civil Cases,* R-2985-ICJ. Santa Monica, Calif.: Rand Corp.

Kaplow, Louis, and Steven Shavell. 2002. *Fairness Versus Welfare.* Cambridge, Mass.: Harvard University Press.

———. 1996. Property Rules Versus Liability Rules. *Harvard Law Review* 109: 713–90.

Katz, Avery. 1990. The Effect of Frivolous Litigation on the Settlement of Legal Disputes. *International Review of Law and Economics* 10: 3–27.

Katz, Lawrence, Steven Levitt, and Ellen Shustorovich. 2003. Prison Conditions, Capital Punishment, and Deterrence. *American Law and Economics Review* 5: 318–43.

Katz, Leo. 1987. *Bad Acts and Guilty Minds: Conundrums of the Criminal Law.* Chicago: University of Chicago Press.

Keeton, W. Page, Dan Dobbs, Robert Keeton, and David Owen. 1984. *Prosser and Keeton on Torts.* 5th ed. St. Paul, Minn.: West Publishing Co.

Kelly, Daniel. 2006. The "Public Use" Requirement in Eminent Domain Law: A Rationale Based on Secret Purchases and Private Influence. *Cornell Law Review* 92: 1–65.

Kessler, Daniel. 1996. Institutional Causes of Delay in the Settlement of Legal Disputes. *Journal of Law, Economics & Organization* 12: 432–60.

Kessler, Daniel, and Steven Levitt. 1999. Using Sentence Enhancements to Distinguish Between Deterrence and Incapacitation. *Journal of Law and Economics* 42: 343–64.

Kitch, Edmund. 1977. The Nature and Function of the Patent System. *Journal of Law and Economics* 20: 265–90.

Klein, Benjamin, Robert Crawford, and Armen Alchian. 1978. Vertical Integration, Appropriable Rents and the Competitive Contracting Process. *Journal of Law and Economics* 21: 297–326.

Klein, Benjamin, and Keith Leffler. 1981. The Role of Market Forces in Assuring Contractual Performance. *Journal of Political Economy* 84: 615–41.

Klein, Benjamin, Andres Lerner, and Kevin Murphy. 2002. The Economics of Copyright "Fair Use" in a Networked World. *American Economic Review, Papers and Proceedings* 92: 205–8.

Klemperer, Paul. 1990. How Broad Should the Scope of Patent Protection Be? *Rand Journal of Economics* 21: 113–30.

Klevorick, Alvin. 1985. On the Economic Theory of Crime. In *NOMOS XXVII: Criminal Justice*, ed. J. Roland Pennock and John Chapman. New York: New York University Press.

Knetsch, Jack, and Thomas Borcherding. 1979. Expropriation of Private Property and the Basis for Compensation. *University of Toronto Law Journal* 29: 237–52.

Komesar, Neil. 1994. *Imperfect Alternatives: Choosing Institutions in Law, Economics, and Public Policy.* Chicago: University of Chicago Press.

Kornhauser, Lewis. 1989. An Economic Perspective on Stare Decisis. *Chicago-Kent Law Review* 65: 63–113.

Kronman, Anthony. 1978. Mistake, Disclosure, Information, and the Law of Contracts. *Journal of Legal Studies* 7: 1–34.

Kull, Andrew. 1992. Unilateral Mistake: The Baseball Card Case. *Washington University Law Quarterly* 70: 57–84.

LaCasse, Chantale, and A. Abigail Payne. 1999. Federal Sentencing Guidelines and Mandatory Minimum Sentences: Do Defendants Bargain in the Shadow of the Judge? *Journal of Law and Economics* 42: 245–69.

Landes, William. 1973. The Bail System: An Economic Approach. *Journal of Legal Studies* 2: 79–105.

———. 1971. An Economic Analysis of the Courts. *Journal of Law and Economics* 14: 61–107.

Landes, William, and Richard Posner. 2003. *The Economic Structure of Intellectual Property Law.* Cambridge: Belknap Press of Harvard University Press.

———. 1989. An Economic Analysis of Copyright Law. *Journal of Legal Studies* 18: 325–63.

———. 1987. *The Economic Structure of Tort Law.* Cambridge, Mass.: Harvard University Press.

———. 1985. A Positive Economic Theory of Products Liability. *Journal of Legal Studies* 14: 535–67.

———. 1979. Adjudication as a Private Good. *Journal of Legal Studies* 8: 235–84.

———. 1976. Legal Precedent: A Theoretical and Empirical Analysis. *Journal of Law and Economics* 19: 249–307.

———. 1975. The Private Enforcement of Law. *Journal of Legal Studies* 4: 1–46.

Langbein, John. 1979. Land Without Plea Bargaining: How the Germans Do It. *Michigan Law Review* 78: 204–25.

Lazear, Edward. 1979. Why Is There Mandatory Retirement? *Journal of Political Economy* 87: 1261–84.

Leiter, Richard. 1999. *National Survey of State Laws.* 3d ed. Detroit, Mich.: Gale Research.

Leland, Hayne. 1979. Quacks, Lemons, and Licensing: A Theory of Minimum Quality Standards. *Journal of Political Economy* 87: 1328–46.

Leong, Avon. 1989. Liability Rules When Injurers as Well as Victims Suffer Losses. *International Review of Law and Economics* 9: 105–11.

Levitt, Steven. 1997. Incentive Compatibility Constraints as an Explanation for the Use of Prison Sentences Instead of Fines. *International Review of Law and Economics* 17: 179–92.

Lewin, Jeff, and William Trumbull. 1990. The Social Value of Crime? *International Review of Law and Economics* 10: 271–84.

Lott, John. 1998. *More Guns, Less Crime.* Chicago: University of Chicago Press.

———. 1987. Should the Wealthy Be Able to "Buy Justice"? *Journal of Political Economy* 95: 1307–16.

Lott, John, and David Mustard. 1997. Crime, Deterrence, and Right-to-Carry Concealed Handguns. *Journal of Legal Studies* 26: 1–68.

Loury, Glenn. 1979. Market Structure and Innovation. *Quarterly Journal of Economics* 93: 395–410.

Lueck, Dean. 1995. The Rule of First Possession and the Design of the Law. *Journal of Law and Economics* 38: 393–436.

———. 1989. The Economic Nature of Wildlife Law. *Journal of Legal Studies* 18: 291–323.

Lueck, Dean, and Jeffrey Michael. 2003. Preemptive Habitat Destruction Under the Endangered Species Act. *Journal of Law and Economics* 46: 27–61.

Macauley, Stewart. 1963. Non-Contractual Relations in Business: A Preliminary Study. *American Sociological Review* 28: 55–61.

Macey, Jonathan. 1989. Internal and External Costs and Benefits of Stare Decisis. *Chicago-Kent Law Review* 65: 91–113.

Malik, Arun. 1990. Avoidance, Screening and Optimum Enforcement. *Rand Journal of Economics* 21: 341–53.

Manning, Richard. 1997. Products Liability and Prescription Drug Prices in Canada and the United States. *Journal of Law and Economics* 40: 203–43.

———. 1994. Changing Rules in Tort Law and the Market for Childhood Vaccines. *Journal of Law and Economics* 37: 247–75.

Marvell, Thomas, and Carlisle Moody. 2001. The Lethal Effects of Three-Strike Laws. *Journal of Legal Studies* 30: 89–106.

McCloskey, Donald. 1976. English Open Fields as Behavior Towards Risk. *Research in Economic History* 1: 124–70.

Menell, Peter. 1991. The Limitations of Legal Institutions for Addressing Environmental Risks. *Journal of Economic Perspectives* 5: 93–113.

Mercuro, Nicholas, and Steven Medema. 1997. *Economics and the Law: From Posner to Post-Modernism.* Princeton, N.J.: Princeton University Press.

Mermin, Samuel. 1982. *Law and the Legal System: An Introduction.* 2d ed. Boston: Little, Brown.

Merrill, Thomas. 1998. Trespass and Nuisance. In *The New Palgrave Dictionary of Law and Economics,* ed. P. Newman. New York: Stockton Press.

———. 1986. The Economics of Public Use. *Cornell Law Review* 72: 61–116.

———. 1985a. Property Rules, Liability Rules, and Adverse Possession. *Northwestern University Law Review* 79: 1122–54.

———. 1985b. Trespass, Nuisance, and the Cost of Determining Property Rights. *Journal of Legal Studies* 14: 13–48.

Miceli, Thomas. 2004. A Principal-Agent Model of Contracting in Major League Baseball. *Journal of Sports Economics* 5: 213–20.

———. 2000. Deterrence, Litigation Costs, and the Statute of Limitations for Tort Suits. *International Review of Law and Economics* 20: 383–94.

———. 1999a. Property. In *The Elgar Companion to Law and Economics*, ed. J. Backhaus. Cheltenham, U.K.: Edward Elgar.

———. 1999b. Settlement Delay as a Sorting Device. *International Review of Law and Economics* 19: 265–74.

———. 1998. Settlement Strategies. *Journal of Legal Studies* 27: 473–81.

———. 1997. *Economics of the Law: Torts, Contracts, Property, Litigation.* New York: Oxford University Press.

———. 1996a. Cause-in-Fact, Proximate Cause, and the Hand Rule: Extending Grady's Positive Economic Theory of Negligence. *International Review of Law and Economics* 16: 473–82.

———. 1996b. Plea Bargaining and Deterrence: An Institutional Approach. *European Journal of Law and Economics* 3: 249–64.

———. 1994a. Do Contingent Fees Promote Excessive Litigation? *Journal of Legal Studies* 23: 211–24.

———. 1994b. Prison and Parole: Minimizing the Cost of Non-Monetary Sanctions as Deterrents. *Research in Law and Economics* 16: 197–211.

———. 1993. Optimal Deterrence of Nuisance Suits by Repeat Defendants. *International Review of Law and Economics* 13: 135–44.

———. 1991a. Compensation for the Taking of Land Under Eminent Domain. *Journal of Institutional and Theoretical Economics* 147: 354–63.

———. 1991b. Optimal Criminal Procedure: Fairness and Deterrence. *International Review of Law and Economics* 11: 3–10.

———. 1990. Optimal Prosecution of Defendants Whose Guilt Is Uncertain. *Journal of Law, Economics & Organization* 6: 189–201.

Miceli, Thomas, and Richard Adelstein. 2006. An Economic Model of Fair Use. *Information Economics and Policy* 18: 359–73.

Miceli, Thomas, and Metin Cosgel. 1994. Reputation and Judicial Decision-making. *Journal of Economic Behavior and Organization* 23: 31–51.

Miceli, Thomas, and Joseph Kieyah. 2003. The Economics of Land Title Reform. *Journal of Comparative Economics* 31: 246–56.

Miceli, Thomas, Henry Munneke, C. F. Sirmans, and Geoffrey Turnbull. 2002. Title Systems and Land Values. *Journal of Law and Economics* 45: 565–82.

Miceli, Thomas, and Kathleen Segerson. 2007. Punishing the Innocent Along with the Guilty: The Economics of Individual Versus Group Punishment. *Journal of Legal Studies* 36: 81–106.

———. 2005. Do Exposure Suits Produce a Race to File? An Economic Analysis of a Tort for Risk. *Rand Journal of Economics* 36: 613–27.

———. 1996. *Compensation for Regulatory Takings: An Economic Analysis with Applications.* Greenwich, Conn.: JAI Press.

———. 1994. Regulatory Takings: When Should Compensation Be Paid? *Journal of Legal Studies* 23: 749–76.

Miceli, Thomas, and C. F. Sirmans. 2005. Time-Limited Property Rights and Investment Incentives. *Journal of Real Estate Finance and Economics* 31: 405–12.

———. 2000. Partition of Real Estate; or, Breaking Up Is (Not) Hard to Do. *Journal of Legal Studies* 29: 783–96.

———. 1999. The Mistaken Improver Problem. *Journal of Urban Economics* 45: 143–55.

———. 1995a. An Economic Theory of Adverse Possession. *International Review of Law and Economics* 15: 161–73.

———. 1995b. The Economics of Land Transfer and Title Insurance. *Journal of Real Estate Finance and Economics* 10: 81–88.

Miceli, Thomas, C. F. Sirmans, and Joseph Kieyah. 2001. The Demand for Land Title Registration: Theory with Evidence from Kenya. *American Law and Economics Review* 3: 275–87.

Miceli, Thomas, C. F. Sirmans, and Geoffrey Turnbull. 2001. The Property-Contract Boundary: An Economic Analysis of Leases. *American Law and Economics Review* 3: 165–85.

Michelman, Frank. 1967. Property, Utility, and Fairness: Comments on the Ethical Foundations of "Just Compensation" Law. *Harvard Law Review* 80: 1165–1258.

Miller, Geoffrey. 1987. Some Agency Problems in Settlement. *Journal of Legal Studies* 16: 189–215.

———. 1986. An Economic Analysis of Rule 68. *Journal of Legal Studies* 15: 93–125.

Mnookin, Robert. 1998. Alternative Dispute Resolution. In *The New Palgrave Dictionary of Economics and the Law*, ed. P. Newman. New York: Stockton Press.

Mocan, H. Naci, and Erdal Tekin. 2006. Guns and Juvenile Crime. *Journal of Law and Economics* 49: 507–31.

Mortensen, Dale. 1982. Property Rights and Efficiency in Mating, Racing, and Related Games. *American Economic Review* 72: 968–79.

Munch, Patricia. 1976. An Economic Analysis of Eminent Domain. *Journal of Political Economy* 84: 473–97.

Muris, Timothy. 1983. The Cost of Completion or Diminution of Market Value: The Relevance of Subjective Value. *Journal of Legal Studies* 12: 379–400.

Nalebuff, Barry. 1987. Credible Pretrial Negotiation. *Rand Journal of Economics* 18: 198–210.

Netter, Jeffry, Philip Hersch, and William Manson. 1986. An Economic Analysis of Adverse Possession Statutes. *International Review of Law and Economics* 6: 217–27.

Nordhaus, William. 1969. *Invention, Growth, and Welfare: A Theoretical Treatment of Technological Change.* Cambridge, Mass.: MIT Press.

Nosal, Ed. 2001. The Taking of Land: Market Value Compensation Should Be Paid. *Journal of Public Economics* 82: 431–43.

Nozick, Robert. 1974. *Anarchy, State, and Utopia.* New York: Basic Books.

Olson, Walter. 1991. *The Litigation Explosion.* New York: Penguin Books.

Ordover, Janusz. 1978. Costly Litigation in the Model of Single Activity Accidents. *Journal of Legal Studies* 7: 243–61.

Ostrom, Elinor. 1990. *Governing the Commons: The Evolution of Institutions for Collective Action.* New York: Cambridge University Press.

Png, I. P. L. 1986. Optimal Subsidies and Damages in the Presence of Legal Error. *International Review of Law and Economics* 6: 101–5.

Polinsky, A. Mitchell. 1983. Risk Sharing Through Breach of Contract Remedies. *Journal of Legal Studies* 12: 427–44.

———. 1980a. On the Choice Between Property Rules and Liability Rules. *Economic Inquiry* 18: 233–46.

———. 1980b. Private Versus Public Enforcement of Fines. *Journal of Legal Studies* 9: 105–27.

Polinsky, A. Mitchell, and Y. K. Che. 1991. Decoupling Liability: Optimal Incentives for Care and Litigation. *Rand Journal of Economics* 22: 562–70.

Polinsky, A. Mitchell, and William Rogerson. 1983. Products Liability, Consumer Misperceptions, and Market Power. *Bell Journal of Economics* 14: 581–89.

Polinsky, A. Mitchell, and Daniel Rubinfeld. 1993. Sanctioning Frivolous Suits: An Economic Analysis. *Georgetown Law Review* 82: 397–435.

———. 1991. A Model of Optimal Fines for Repeat Offenders. *Journal of Public Economics* 46: 291–306.

———. 1988. The Deterrent Effects of Settlements and Trials. *International Review of Law and Economics* 8: 109–16.

Polinsky, A. Mitchell, and Steven Shavell. 2000. The Economic Theory of Public Enforcement of Law. *Journal of Economic Literature* 38: 45–76.

———. 1998. Punitive Damages: An Economic Analysis. *Harvard Law Review* 111: 869–962.

———. 1994. Should Liability Be Based on the Harm to the Victim or the Gain to the Injurer? *Journal of Law, Economics & Organization* 10: 427–37.

———. 1984. The Optimal Use of Fines and Imprisonment. *Journal of Public Economics* 24: 89–99.

———. 1979. The Optimal Tradeoff Between the Probability and Magnitude of Fines. *American Economic Review* 69: 880–91.

Posner, Richard. 2003. *Economic Analysis of Law.* 6th ed. New York: Aspen Law & Business.

———. 2001. *Frontiers of Legal Theory.* Cambridge, Mass.: Harvard University Press.

————. 1998a. *Economic Analysis of Law.* 5th ed. New York: Aspen Law & Business.

————. 1998b. Privacy. In *The New Palgrave Dictionary of Economics and the Law*, ed. P. Newman. New York: Stockton Press.

————. 1996. *Law and Legal Theory in the UK and USA.* Oxford: Oxford University Press.

————. 1995. *Overcoming Law.* Cambridge, Mass.: Harvard University Press.

————. 1983. *The Economics of Justice.* Cambridge, Mass.: Harvard University Press.

————. 1980. Retribution and Related Concepts of Punishment. *Journal of Legal Studies* 9: 71–92.

————. 1977. Gratuitous Promises in the Law. *Journal of Legal Studies* 6: 411–26.

Posner, Richard, and Andrew Rosenfield. 1977. Impossibility and Related Doctrines in Contract Law: An Economic Analysis. *Journal of Legal Studies* 6: 83–118.

Poundstone, William. 1992. *Prisoner's Dilemma: John von Neumann, Game Theory, and the Puzzle of the Bomb.* New York: Doubleday.

Priest, George. 1988. Products Liability Law and the Accident Rate. In *Liability: Perspectives and Policy,* ed. R. Litan and C. Winston. Washington, D.C.: The Brookings Institution.

————. 1987. Measuring Legal Change. *Journal of Law, Economics & Organization* 3: 193–225.

————. 1977. The Common Law Process and the Selection of Efficient Rules. *Journal of Legal Studies* 6: 65–82.

Priest, George, and Benjamin Klein. 1984. The Selection of Disputes for Litigation. *Journal of Legal Studies* 13: 1–55.

Quirk, James, and Rodney Fort. 1992. *Pay Dirt: The Business of Professional Team Sports.* Princeton, N.J.: Princeton University Press.

Rabin, Edward. 1984. The Revolution in Residential Landlord-Tenant Law: Causes and Consequences. *Cornell Law Review* 69: 517–84.

Raphael, Steven, and Rudolf Winter-Ebmer. 2001. Identifying the Effect of Unemployment on Crime. *Journal of Law and Economics* 44: 259–83.

Rasmusen, Eric. 1998a. The Economics of Desecration: Flag Burning and Related Activities. *Journal of Legal Studies* 27: 245–69.

————. 1998b. Nuisance Suits. In *The New Palgrave Dictionary of Economics and the Law*, ed. P. Newman. New York: Stockton Press.

————. 1996. Stigma and Self-fulfilling Expectations of Criminality. *Journal of Law and Economics* 39: 519–43.

Rasmusen, Eric, and Ian Ayres. 1993. Mutual and Unilateral Mistake in Contract Law. *Journal of Legal Studies* 22: 309–43.

Rea, Samuel. 1998. Penalty Doctrine in Contract Law. In *The New Palgrave Dictionary of Law and Economics*, ed. P. Newman. New York: Stockton Press.

————. 1987. The Economics of Comparative Negligence. *International Review of Law and Economics* 7: 149–62.

————. 1984. Efficiency Implications of Penalties and Liquidated Damages. *Journal of Legal Studies* 13: 147–67.

Reinganum, Jennifer. 1993. The Law Enforcement Process and Criminal Choice. *International Review of Law and Economics* 13: 115–34.

————. 1988. Plea Bargaining and Prosecutorial Discretion. *American Economic Review* 78: 713–28.

Ringleb, Al, and Steven Wiggins. 1990. Liability and Large-Scale, Long-Term Hazards. *Journal of Political Economy* 98: 574–95.

Rizzo, Mario. 1987. Rules Versus Cost-Benefit Analysis in the Common Law. In *Economic Liberties and the Judiciary*, ed. J. Dorn and H. Manne. Fairfax, Va.: George Mason University Press.

Robinson, Glen. 1985. Probabilistic Causation and Compensation for Tortious Risk. *Journal of Legal Studies* 14: 779–98.

Rogerson, William. 1984. Efficient Reliance and Damage Measures for Breach of Contract. *Rand Journal of Economics* 15: 39–53.

Rose-Ackerman, Susan. 1989. Dams, Dikes, and Vicious Hogs: Entitlement and Efficiency in Tort Law. *Journal of Legal Studies* 18: 25–50.

Rosen, Sherwin. 1992. The Market for Lawyers. *Journal of Law and Economics* 35: 215–46.

Rosenberg, David, and Steven Shavell. 1985. A Model in Which Suits Are Brought for Their Nuisance Value. *International Review of Law and Economics* 5: 3–13.

Ross, H. Laurence. 1970. *Settled Out of Court: The Social Process of Insurance Claims Adjustments.* Chicago: Aldine Publishing Co.

Rottenberg, Simon. 1956. The Baseball Players' Labor Market. *Journal of Political Economy* 64: 242–58.

Rubin, Paul. 2001. The State of Nature and the Evolution of Political Preferences. *American Law and Economics Review* 3: 50–81.

————. 1977. Why Is the Common Law Efficient? *Journal of Legal Studies* 6: 51–63.

Rubinfeld, Daniel. 1987. The Efficiency of Comparative Negligence. *Journal of Legal Studies* 16: 375–94.

Rubinfeld, Daniel, and Suzanne Scotchmer. 1998. Contingent Fees. In *The New Palgrave Dictionary of Economics and the Law*, ed. P. Newman. New York: Stockton Press.

Sanchez, Nicolas, and Jeffrey Nugent. 2000. Fence Laws Versus Herd Laws: A Nineteenth-Century Kansas Paradox. *Land Economics* 76: 518–33.

Schell, Jonathan. 1982. *The Fate of the Earth.* New York: Alfred A. Knopf.

Schelling, Thomas. 1985. Enforcing Rules on Oneself. *Journal of Law, Economics and Organization* 1: 357–74.

Scheppele, Kim. 1988. *Legal Secrets: Equality and Efficiency in the Common Law.* Chicago: University of Chicago Press.

Schmalensee, Richard, Paul Joskow, A. Denny Ellerman, Juan Pablo Montero, and Elizabeth Bailey. 1998. An Interim Evaluation of Sulphur Dioxide Emissions Trading. *Journal of Economic Perspectives* 12: 53–68.

Segerson, Kathleen. 1997. Legal Liability as an Environmental Policy Tool: Some Implications for Land Markets. *Journal of Real Estate Finance and Economics* 15: 143–59.

———. 1993. Liability Transfers: An Economic Assessment of Buyer and Lender Liability. *Journal of Environmental Economics and Management* 25: S46–63.

Seidmann, Daniel, and Alex Stein. 2000. The Right to Silence Helps the Innocent: A Game-Theoretic Analysis of the Fifth Amendment Privilege. *Harvard Law Review* 114: 430–510.

Shanley, Michael. 1991. The Distribution of Post-Trial Jury Awards. *Journal of Legal Studies* 20: 463–81.

Shavell, Steven. 2004. *Foundations of Economic Analysis of Law.* Cambridge: Belknap Press of Harvard University Press.

———. 1996. Any Frequency of Plaintiff Victory Is Possible. *Journal of Legal Studies* 25: 493–501.

——— 1995a. Alternative Dispute Resolution: An Economic Analysis. *Journal of Legal Studies* 24: 1–28.

———. 1995b. The Appeals Process as a Means of Error Correction. *Journal of Legal Studies* 24: 379–426.

———. 1994. Acquisition and Disclosure of Information Prior to Sale. *Rand Journal of Economics* 25: 20–36.

———. 1993a. An Economic Analysis of Threats and Their Illegality: Blackmail, Extortion, and Robbery. *University of Pennsylvania Law Review* 141: 1877–1903.

——— 1993b. Suit Versus Settlement When Parties Seek Non-Monetary Judgments. *Journal of Legal Studies* 22: 1–13.

———. 1991. Individual Precautions to Prevent Theft: Private Versus Socially Optimal Behavior. *International Review of Law and Economics* 11: 123–32.

———. 1989. Sharing Information Prior to Settlement or Litigation. *Rand Journal of Economics* 20: 183–95.

———. 1987. *Economic Analysis of Accident Law.* Cambridge, Mass.: Harvard University Press.

———. 1986. The Judgment Proof Problem. *International Review of Law and Economics* 6: 45–58.

———. 1985. Uncertainty over Causation and the Determination of Civil Liability. *Journal of Law and Economics* 28: 587–609.

———. 1984. A Model of the Optimal Use of Liability and Safety Regulation. *Rand Journal of Economics* 15: 271–80.

———. 1983. Torts in Which Victim and Injurer Act Sequentially. *Journal of Law and Economics* 26: 589–612.

———. 1982a. The Social Versus Private Incentive to Bring Suit in a Costly Legal System. *Journal of Legal Studies* 11: 333–39.

———. 1982b. Suit, Settlement, and Trial: A Theoretical Analysis Under Alternative Methods for the Allocation of Legal Costs. *Journal of Legal Studies* 11: 55–81.

———. 1980a. An Analysis of Causation and the Scope of Liability in the Law of Torts. *Journal of Legal Studies* 9: 463–516.

———. 1980b. Damage Measures for Breach of Contract. *Bell Journal of Economics* 11: 466–90.

———. 1980c. Strict Liability Versus Negligence. *Journal of Legal Studies* 9: 1–25.

———. 1979. On Moral Hazard and Insurance. *Quarterly Journal of Economics* 93: 541–62.

Shavell, Steven, and Tanguy Van Ypersele. 2001. Rewards Versus Intellectual Property Rights. *Journal of Law and Economics* 44: 525–47.

Shepherd, Joanna. 2007. *Blakely*'s Silver Lining: Sentencing Guidelines, Judicial Discretion, and Crime. *Hastings Law Journal* 58: 533–89.

———. 2004. Murders of Passion, Execution Delays, and the Deterrence of Capital Punishment. *Journal of Legal Studies* 33: 283–321.

———. 2002. Fear of the First Strike: The Full Deterrence Effect of California's Two- and Three-Strikes Legislation. *Journal of Legal Studies* 31: 159–201.

Shick, Blair, and Irving Plotkin. 1978. *Torrens in the United States: A Legal and Economic History of American Land-Registration Systems.* Lexington, Mass.: Lexington Books.

Smith, Janet, and Richard Smith. 1990. Contract Law, Mutual Mistake, and Incentives to Produce and Disclose Information. *Journal of Legal Studies* 19: 467–88.

Snyder, Edward. 1990. The Effect of Higher Criminal Penalties on Antitrust Enforcement. *Journal of Law and Economics* 33: 439–62.

Snyder, Edward, and James Hughes. 1990. The English Rule for Allocating Legal Costs: Evidence Confronts Theory. *Journal of Law, Economics & Organization* 6: 345–80.

Spence, A. Michael. 1977. Consumer Misperceptions, Product Failure and Producer Liability. *Review of Economic Studies* 44: 561–72.

Spier, Kathryn. 1994. Pretrial Bargaining and the Design of Fee-Shifting Rules. *Rand Journal of Economics* 25: 197–214.

———. 1992. The Dynamics of Pretrial Negotiation. *Review of Economics Studies* 59: 93–108.

Spitzer, Matthew. 1998. Freedom of Expression. In *The New Palgrave Dictionary of Economics and the Law*, ed. P. Newman. New York: Stockton Press.

Stake, Jeffrey. 1998. Inheritance Law. In *The New Palgrave Dictionary of Economics and the Law*, ed. P. Newman. New York: Stockton Press.

Stigler, George. 1970. The Optimum Enforcement of Laws. *Journal of Political Economy* 78: 526–36.

Stiglitz, Joseph. 1974. Incentives and Risk Sharing in Sharecropping. *Review of Economic Studies* 79: 578–95.

Strange, William. 1995. Information, Holdouts, and Land Assembly. *Journal of Urban Economics* 38: 317–32.

Sunstein, Cass, ed. 2000. *Behavioral Law and Economics*. Cambridge: Cambridge University Press.

Sunstein, Cass, Daniel Kahneman, and David Schkade. 2000. Assessing Punitive Damages (with Notes on Cognition and Valuation in Law). In *Behavioral Law and Economics*, ed. Cass Sunstein. Cambridge: Cambridge University Press.

Sunstein, Cass, and Edna Ullmann-Marglit. 2000. Second-Order Decisions. In *Behavioral Law and Economics*, ed. Cass Sunstein. Cambridge: Cambridge University Press.

Sykes, Alan. 2002. New Directions in Law and Economics. *The American Economist* 46: 10–21.

———. 1990. The Doctrine of Commercial Impracticability in a Second-Best World. *Journal of Legal Studies* 19: 43–94.

Telser, Lester. 1980. A Theory of Self-Enforcing Agreements. *Journal of Business* 53: 27–44.

Tietenberg, Thomas. 1985. *Emissions Trading: An Exercise in Reforming Pollution Policy*. Washington, D.C.: Resources for the Future.

Tullock, Gordon. 1967. The Welfare Costs of Tariffs, Monopolies, and Theft. *Western Economic Journal* 5: 224–32.

Ulen, Thomas. 1992. The Public Use of Private Property: A Dual Constraint Theory of Efficient Government Takings. In *Taking Property and Just Compensation: Law and Economics Perspectives of the Takings Issue*, ed. N. Mercuro. Boston: Kluwer Academic Publishers.

———. 1984. The Efficiency of Specific Performance: Toward a Unified Theory of Contract Remedies. *Michigan Law Review* 83: 341–403.

Umbeck, John. 1981. *A Theory of Property Rights with Application to the California Gold Rush*. Ames: Iowa State University Press.

Viscusi, W. Kip. 1998. Valuing Life and Risks to Life. In *The New Palgrave Dictionary of Economics and the Law*, ed. P. Newman. New York: Stockton Press.

———. 1991. *Reforming Products Liability*. Cambridge, Mass.: Harvard University Press.

———. 1988. Liability for Occupational Accidents and Illnesses. In *Liability: Perspectives and Policy*, ed. R. Litan and C. Winston. Washington, D.C.: The Brookings Institution.

————. 1986. The Impact of Occupational Safety and Health Regulation, 1973–1983. *Rand Journal of Economics* 17: 567–80.

Viscusi, W. Kip, Joseph Harrington, and John Vernon. 2005. *Economics of Regulation and Antitrust,* 4th ed. Cambridge, Mass.: MIT Press.

Waldfogel, Joel. 1998. Selection of Cases for Trial. In *The New Palgrave Dictionary of Law and Economics*, ed. P. Newman. New York: Stockton Press.

————. 1993. Criminal Sentences as Endogenous Taxes: Are They "Just" or "Efficient"? *Journal of Law and Economics* 36: 139–51.

White, Michelle. 2006. Asbestos Litigation: Procedural Innovations and Forum Shopping. *Journal of Legal Studies* 35: 365–98.

————. 1989. An Empirical Test of the Comparative and Contributory Negligence Rules in Accident Law. *Rand Journal of Economics* 20: 308–30.

————. 1988. Contract Breach and Contract Discharge Due to Impossibility: A Unified Theory. *Journal of Legal Studies* 17: 353–76.

Wiggins, Steven, and Gary Libecap. 1985. Oil Field Unitization: Contractual Failure in the Presence of Imperfect Information. *American Economics Review* 75: 368–85.

Williamson, Oliver. 1985. *The Economic Institutions of Capitalism.* New York: Free Press.

————. 1983. Credible Commitments: Using Hostages to Support Exchange. *American Economic Review* 73: 519–40.

————. 1968. Economies as an Antitrust Defense: The Welfare Tradeoffs. *American Economic Review* 58: 18–36.

Wittman, Donald. 1984. Liability for Harm or Restitution for Benefit? *Journal of Legal Studies* 13: 57–80.

————. 1981. Optimal Pricing of Sequential Inputs: Last Clear Chance, Mitigation of Damages, and Related Doctrines in the Law. *Journal of Legal Studies* 10: 65–91.

————. 1980. First Come, First Served: An Economic Analysis of "Coming to the Nuisance." *Journal of Legal Studies* 9: 557–68.

————. 1974. Punishment as Retribution. *Theory and Decision* 4: 209–37.

Woodruff, Christopher. 2001. Review of de Soto's *The Mystery of Capital. Journal of Economic Literature* 39: 1215–23.

Wright, Brian. 1983. The Economics of Invention Incentives: Patents, Prizes, and Research Contracts. *American Economic Review* 83: 691–707.

INDEX